IRELAND'S WOMEN

WRITINGS PAST AND PRESENT

SELECTED BY
KATIE DONOVAN, A. NORMAN JEFFARES
AND BRENDAN KENNELLY

GILL & MACMILLAN

Published in Ireland in 1994 by
Gill & Macmillan
Goldenbridge
Dublin 8
with associated companies throughout the world.

Reprinted 1994

This book is published with the assistance of the Arts Council/
An Chomhairle Ealaíon, Ireland.

ISBN 0–7171–2202–6

This collection first published in Great Britain in 1994 by
Kyle Cathie Limited
7–8 Hatherley Street, London SW1P 2QT

Typeset by York House Typographic Ltd
Printed and bound in Great Britain
by Cox & Wyman Ltd, Reading, Berkshire

This book is dedicated to
Mary Robinson,
President of Ireland

CONTENTS

3: LOVE

5: THE BIT O' STRANGE

6: MONEY AND POWER

Introductions by the editors

Katie Donovan

The aim of this anthology is straightforward: to celebrate women in Irish writing. Women's lives, from the earliest times right up to the present day, are at the centre of this book. Poems, stories, novels, plays, letters, diaries, folktales, articles, travel books, academic essays – extracts from all these and more have been put together to form a kaleidoscopic picture of Irish women through the centuries.

Irish women have been written about from the inside and from the outside and they have not always been portrayed in a complimentary way. Our selection is intended to give the reader a taste of the varied spectrum, from the courtly praise of men to swinish male chauvinism; from women's declarations of outrage against church and state to their celebrations of childbirth and motherhood.

Inevitably there are omissions. In our enthusiasm, we compiled far more excellent material than we could possibly ever use, and a difficult process of sifting and selecting ensued. Our opinions were not always in harmony, but we were all keen to make a good representation of women writers in each section, without excluding male writers who have made woman a central subject in their work, such as Synge and Joyce. As for writing by women, the pickings tend to be thin up until the last twenty years or so. In that time, Irish women have produced an impressive volume of writing, particularly in the genres of poetry and fiction.

We have included the more established of these women, such as Edna O'Brien, Jennifer Johnston, and Eavan Boland. And we have attempted to show the range of the younger women writers who are in the process of gaining widespread recognition, such as Paula Meehan, Anne Enright and Mary O'Donnell; as well as a smattering of those who are on their way.

The format of the anthology was devised as a method of disciplining our choices according to themes which we felt were germane to Irish women's lives. Each topic is intended to go beyond its most superficial meaning to deeper permutations. In Section 6, for example, which is entitled 'Money and Power', we felt it was important to include material on women and madness. For example Dr Elizabeth Malcolm's essay shows that a sudden loss of income had a devastating effect on the mental equilibrium of young and untrained middle-class women in the last century.

Similarly in Section 11, entitled 'Talk', we have Swift's hilarious *Dialogue III: The Ladies at Their Tea*, while in stark contrast, there is also Ailbhe Smyth's essay on how women's 'right to bodily integrity' was 'caught in a web of male-generated words' during the notorious X case in 1992.

By juxtaposing certain extracts in deliberate ways, we have sought to create vivid contrasts, such as that, for example, between the childhood experiences of Daisy Fingall and Bernadette Devlin. Other extracts, placed alongside each other, create ironic dialogues.

It is our wish to stimulate, divert and entertain the reader with a selection of the material on Irish women which has given us the most satisfaction. The spread is by no means modest. We have cast the net wide for the sake of variety, without trying to claim that we have caught all the bright and wonderful specimens that exist, and which are increasing in number even as I write. There is room for a second anthology – indeed, a third – but for now we must content ourselves with the limits of this one, and hope that you enjoy reading it as much as we enjoyed putting it together.

A. NORMAN JEFFARES

We have chosen over 300 items for this book. They deal with women in Ireland from Queen Maeve to President Mary Robinson. Some are written by women, some by men: we have chosen them for various reasons. First, we have enjoyed reading them and wish to share that pleasure with our readers. Second, we have found them illuminating in their illustration of the multiple roles women have played over the centuries in Ireland. Though they will probably arouse differing reactions among readers (as they have among the three of us who have chosen them) we think that the overall picture they give is itself extremely varied, for the book generally presents the views and behaviour, the actions and reactions of many individual Irish women, whether real or imagined – in short it selects crucial aspects of these lives in public or private situations as seen by the women or by those who have given them literary life.

We have left the texts to speak for themselves, supplying some details about their authors at the back. We have not arranged the book chronologically; none the less patterns emerge. The women of the heroic tales, for instance, can be considered personages in their own right, rulers, wives, lovers, servants, whatever they may be. The same can be said of the individual women who emerge in the early Christian monastic periods. With the arrival of the Normans, chivalric elements entered into the love poetry. The disruption of Gaelic civilization after the Flight of the Earls and the eventual disappearance of the powerful poets created a vacuum: an oral culture was hardly replaced on a national scale by writings in English and particularly not by any about women. Women do, however, appear as vital characters in those witty Restoration comedies written by Irishmen for the London stage. (Yet Farquhar, for all his sense of fun in *The Beaux Stratagem*, was advanced in his serious treatment of the case for divorce.) The succeeding heroines of sentimental comedy made popular by Steele, a Wexford man, were quickly counterbalanced by the livelier creations of Goldsmith and Sheridan in the eighteenth century, notably in *She Stoops to Conquer* and *The School for Scandal*.

The effect of the popular movements of the nineteenth century which turned attention to Irish history and mythology – at first through the work of pioneers such as Charlotte Brooke, carried on by Lady Morgan and Thomas Moore and later extended by the writers of *The Nation* – as well as the programme of the National Schools which increased knowledge of English as a language – was to spread frequently romanticized concepts of women. But it was the consequences of the famine of the mid-century and the emigration that followed it that need to be considered as a turning point. Life that had been lived exuberantly in Ireland (something well brought out in those novels such as Carleton's, which emphasize the effects of whiskey and the easily cultivated and, up to then, apparently reliable potato crop) now became more precious; the effects of the new Jansenism and the temperance campaign were to hasten the spread of a restrictive puritanism which became a feature of life in the twentieth century Irish Free State and still continues to fight in what now seems a rearguard action.

Some of the recently written items included in this anthology demonstrate the forthright views of contemporary Irish women on their present position in the state and their attitudes to matters of public concern – such as sexual relations, contraception, abortion and divorce – which have become openly controversial. What is particularly impressive is the sheer volume of fine – and arresting – poetry being written in many genres by contemporary Irish women: it has been most difficult to select from its wealth while keeping within the overall limits of this wide-ranging book. Indeed in the course of choosing the extracts we have assembled enough material to fill several anthologies with what we consider excellent, lively, provocative, innovative and thoughtful writing. This book, then, is the result of our first selection from the rich treasury of writing by and about Irish women.

BRENDAN KENNELLY

The history, or herstory, of Irish women is rather like that of the Irish language – much talked about but little heard. Of recent years, however, Irish women have been discovering, or re-discovering, their own voices, with beneficial consequences for the life and literature of the island. Although these women are still victims of men's language – the clever, often unconscious tyrannies and urbane manipulations effectively implanted in its uses – they are now creating their own language, a proper vehicle for their feelings and ideas, spoken with passion and conviction from their own perspective, jolting many Irish men into the recognition that the world and everything in it, including its languages, do not belong solely to them.

A person is trapped in his or her language in ways he or she may not even begin to suspect let alone understand enough to wish to question. That said, however, I'm going to have a bash at saying what I have to say about these women.

The ancient mythology of Ireland features many powerful, aggressive women who take the sexual initiative, run the show and dictate the fun. These are strong pagan women and, thanks be to God, there's a fair amount of paganism left in many Irish women still. The spirit of Maeve and Deirdre never died out completely. It was that spirit which helped many Irish women to survive onslaught after onslaught of turgid, humourless, self-important 'morality' ('I cannot forgive your mortal sin until you conceive again') emanating from Maynooth and other places. Quite a few of them did *not* survive the pious tyranny of that kind of thinking (see Austin Clarke's poem *The Redemptorist*); and great numbers of them went along approvingly with their own subjugation, cooperating with it since it was 'the right thing to do', Father Murphy said so and how could that man be wrong?

Quite a lot of women, however, retained and guarded, albeit privately, their own ways of thinking and feeling alive in their own hearts and minds. That tough genius for survival is typical of many women in Irish literature. My own deepening belief is that women are, in fact, stronger than men; but it is a different *kind* of strength. It is less obvious, less showy, more allied to apparent fragility, more threatened with being overcome even as it is often more aware of the reasons for that possibility. This strength of women is more concerned with endurance than with exhibitionism. It is longer lasting, it is marked by grit, shrewdness, calmness, patience, watchfulness and, very frequently but not inevitably, by a smile that seems to emanate quietly from the remote corners of a woman's being. There is very little cocky self-importance in this strength though it has its own peaceful and fierce egotism. This strength of women may often go unnoticed but it is constant, deep and real as the sea. One of its most fascinating aspects is that some men choose, or unconsciously compel themselves, to interpret it as weakness; it is not *like* men's strength; how, in God's name, therefore can it be strong? The word 'strength' means something different to most men than it does to women. If this is so, then the literature written by men, so often preoccupied with notions of strength and power and therefore, inevitably, with weakness and failings or inadequacies that add up to powerlessness, is not quite the same thing in a woman's ears as it is in a man's. There's a gulf here. Do we admit this fact? If we do, do we wish to bridge that gulf? How shall we bridge it? Is it possible to do so successfully?

It is. How? By listening. Listening to women's voices in the literature they write. Listening to women's voices in literature written by men, interesting, at least, as another kind of failure. If we listen, we shall hear crucial differences, interesting, illuminating differences.

Can a man really imagine what it is to be a woman? Is Molly Bloom credible? Did Joyce 'get her'? Is her language convincing? What Sligo woman of Crazy Jane's vintage would say 'excrement' rather than 'shit'? Are we getting Yeats's struggling inhibitions or Crazy Jane's genuine freedom? Or a fascinating mixture of both? Does the man define the woman he is trying to imagine into being? Or does the imagined woman define the limitations of the imagining man?

Part of the value of this anthology is that readers may compare men's attempts to express their visions and versions of women with women's efforts to express theirs. To what extent is a male writer an outsider in this enterprise? And if he is an outsider, does this necessarily mean that he is always at a disadvantage in his writing? May not such a disadvantage be turned to acute, imaginative advantage?

How do modern Irish women feel about their 'cultural heritage', whatever that is? A revealing aspect of this anthology is the way it captures a wide range of responses to both past and present. The articulate consciousness of many Irish women is re-interpreting the past and deeply influencing the present. There's a freshness in these deliberate acts of re-interpretation, as well as a note of passionate understanding which help to give this anthology its special character: it is many-voiced, dramatic, questioning, daring, deliberately structured, experimental and exciting. It has a quality of sustained and challenging otherness, of deep difference which will serve to interrogate and enlighten the reader. Irish men often cope with the 'problem' of women by treating them almost as if they didn't exist. For some Irish men, the non-existence of women would be the ultimate convenience. The two most effective ways for a man to arrive at this way of treating women is to adore them or ignore them; either put women on pedestals or keep them well obscured in the background. In this anthology, women are in the foreground, exploring and expressing themselves and the world in which they live.

There is much anger and compassion in this book, there is horror and injustice, a lot of humour, bitterness and sympathy, and an unfailing sense of drama. This is not simply the other side of the rich coin of Irish writing; it *is* Irish writing at its most penetrating and most open. By being open in itself, it opens up the entire literature in a ruthless and revealing way. It lets in a lot of startling light where an unchallenged darkness had threatened to prevail.

1

Bodies

MOY MCCRORY

Katie-Ellen Takes on the World

Hot with sudden anger, I said, 'Leave me alone.'

But I meant completely alone, not with this volcano waiting to explode inside me. Why couldn't they do something? They, and I, were useless. And as I realized this, saw how helpless were our gestures against this terrifying life that took me up to throw me down gasping, I heard the gas hissing and felt the strength of another movement which flooded into me and took me after it. I knew then that I would go on; despair was no match for it.

Voices came softly out of the shadows, coaxing, cooing, urging me onwards, supportive voices as the tide swept me up and crashed me down again.

'Don't push.'

I thought I had misheard.

'Don't push.'

There was no mistaking its cool authority.

Everything tensed around me. I fought against the next urge and sickness swept over me. I resisted the awful pain. How long could I hold out?

I wanted to tell them what I was enduring, tell them that it was impossible, tell them that I must push, but I had no method of speech left. Nausea had robbed me, and all I sent out were moans and growls, pathetic as any animal in pain.

I struggled until the hurt dragged itself off, but I knew it lurked in the brightening room, waiting to kick.

'I can't do that again,' I told the midwife.

'You won't have to. You can push next time. You're ready.'

When the pain came back, I moved into it gladly. I moved it away and out. I felt relief and almost pleasure.

'One more!' the midwife said.

I made another effort and felt something drag, something hard. Bob's voice shot across the room.

'The head! The head's out!' and there was stillness in which none of us breathed.

As soon as I had the urge to push again, I did so, and felt at once the slippery, wet rush of my baby as she came into the world to lie warmly along my inner thigh. The nurse scooped her up and laid her on my breast.

I reached out and touched her carefully, stroking and exploring this new person who bellowed with healthy lungs, breathing on her own in the strange atmosphere, ruddy and drunk on oxygen. I stroked her downy back, with its soft whorls of hair, and rubbed her ears with their little tufts.

'In a few days that will be gone,' the nurse told me.

'We won't wash her face until the tear ducts open. Those marks will wear off.'

My daughter wore proudly on her crown, the blood streaks she had been baptized in.

I looked around me and noticed for the first time that the room was full of people. Some were crying.

'This is Katie-Ellen,' I said, introducing her.

Her mouth opened and her tiny fingers made gentle pawing movements. I whispered to her that she had taken on the world and as I held her fiercely to me, I felt her small strong life vibrate.

JAMES JOYCE

from *Ulysses* – *'Penelope'*

itll be a change the Lord knows to have an intelligent person to talk to about yourself not always listening to him and Billy Prescotts ad and Keyess ad and Tom the Devils ad then if anything goes wrong in their business we have to suffer Im sure hes very distinguished Id like to meet a man like that God not those other ruck besides hes young those fine young men I could see down in

Margate strand bathingplace from the side of the rock standing up in the sun naked like a God or something and then plunging into the sea with them why arent all men like that thered be some consolation for a woman like that lovely little statue he bought I could look at him all day long curly head and his shoulders his finger up for you to listen theres real beauty and poetry for you I often felt I wanted to kiss him all over also his lovely young cock there so simple I wouldnt mind taking him in my mouth if nobody was looking as if it was asking you to suck it so clean and white he looks with his boyish face I would too in ½ a minute even if some of it went down what its only like gruel or the dew theres no danger besides hed be so clean compared with those pigs of men I suppose never dream of washing it from 1 years end to the other the most of them only thats what gives the women the moustaches Im sure itll be grand if I can only get in with a handsome young poet at my age Ill throw them the 1st thing in the morning till I see if the wishcard comes out or Ill try pairing the lady herself and see if he comes out Ill read and study all I can find or learn a bit off by heart if I knew who he likes so he wont think me stupid if he thinks all women are the same and I can teach him the other part Ill make him feel all over him till he half faints under me then hell write about me lover and mistress publicly too with our 2 photographs in all the papers when he becomes famous O but then what am I going to do about him though

Nuala Ní Dhomhnaill

Blodewedd

Translated by John Montague

At the least touch of your fingertips
I break into blossom,
my whole chemical composition
transformed.
I sprawl like a grassy meadow
fragrant in the sun;
at the brush of your palm, all my herbs
and spices spill open

frond by frond, lured to unfold
and exhale in the heat;
wild strawberries rife, and pimpernels
flagrant and scarlet, blushing
down their stems.
To mow that rushy bottom;
no problem.

All winter I waited silently
for your appeal.
I withered within, dead to all,
curled away, and deaf as clay,
all my life forces ebbing slowly
till now I come to, at your touch,
revived as from a deathly swoon.

Your sun lightens my sky
and a wind lifts, like God's angel,
to move the waters,
every inch of me quivers
before your presence,
goose-pimples I get as you glide
over me, and every hair
stands on end.

Hours later I linger
in the ladies toilet,
a sweet scent wafting
from all my pores,
proof positive, if a sign
were needed, that at the least
touch of your fingertips
I break into blossom.

PATRICIA McCARTHY

Abortion

Feet up in stirrups I lie,
a queer jockey mounted
on distress, counting the minutes
racing to your rejection.

Although the going is good,
I fall at every fence,
my smile at the doctor a way
of weeping over the jackpot

for which I can't compete
but, kept, would have had
to be given away. I wish
he wouldn't banter like that.

I'm not his accomplice.
This morning started wrong,
my threshold of pain already
too low to tolerate injustice

to you. I should have donned black
instead of multi-colours,
reverently coping. Courses
unfinished before practised me

little for this. The nurse
hangs on me the weights
of her euphemisms as I wonder
what victory might have been.

A broken bone, I pretend.
With hands stupidly cupped
for you in Moses' baskets,
it's just as well I can't hear

the rocking horses bolting
from their rainbow-runners
into the grins of bookies
as the final post bends

in two. Crouching low,
still, over your loss,
I land all wrong on the stretcher
where, without substance enough

here even to die,
backstreet courtesies
cover you dark as turf,
as the choice I didn't have.

To substitute, regrets shy
onto the pad between my legs,
stakes lost, and I'm lonelier
than an empty grandstand.

Julie O'Callaghan

Content and Tasteful

Here I am in my kitchen.
I look content and tasteful.
When my darling grandchildren
visit their grandma, I give them
windmill cookies — the ones with chunks
of nuts that come wrapped
in the orange cellophane package
with scenes of old Holland.
In this oven I cook up a storm.
Ya gotta garnish your recipes.
Cut out pictures from magazines
like *McCall's* or *Family Circle*
and always make your dishes
look like in the photographs.
I keep a few tricks up my sleeve
in these cabinets only I don't tell them
to anybody except my daughter
in Sarasota Florida who's trying
to get to a man's heart
through his stomach.
That's the only exception.
Do you get the aroma of my
Devil's Food Cake baking?
Ladies, don't waste your time
with most of these new appliances.
Get your basics, keep 'em clean, buy fresh,
and I guarantee you your mouth
will be watering and your girdle
will be killing you.

Jonathan Swift

The Lady's Dressing-Room

Five Hours, (and who can do it less in?)
By haughty *Cælia* spent in Dressing;
The Goddess from her Chamber issues,
Array'd in Lace, Brocade and Tissues:
Strephon, who found the Room was void,
And *Betty* otherwise employ'd,
Stole in, and took a strict Survey
Of all the Litter, as it lay:
Whereof to make the Matter clear,
An *Inventory* follows here.

And first, a dirty Smock appear'd,
Beneath the Arm-pits well besmear'd;
Strephon, the Rogue, display'd it wide,
And turn'd it round on ev'ry Side:
In such a Case, few Words are best,
And *Strephon* bids us guess the rest;
But swears how damnably the Men lye,
In calling *Cælia* sweet and cleanly.

Now listen, while he next produces
The various Combs for various Uses;
Fill'd up with Dirt so closely fixt,
No Brush cou'd force a Way betwixt;
A Paste of Composition rare,
Sweat, Dandriff, Powder, Lead and Hair,
A Forehead-Cloath with Oil upon't,
To smooth the Wrinkles on her Front:
Here, Alum Flour to stop the Steams,
Exhal'd from sour unsav'ry Streams;
There, Night-Gloves made of *Tripsey*'s Hide,
Bequeath'd by *Tripsey* when she dy'd;

With Puppy-Water, Beauty's Help,
Distill'd from *Tripsey*'s darling Whelp,
Here Gally-pots and Vials plac'd,
Some fill'd with Washes, some with Paste;
Some with Pomatums, Paints, and Slops,
And Ointments good for scabby Chops,
Hard by, a filthy Bason stands,
Foul'd with the scow'ring of her Hands;
The Bason takes whatever comes,
The Scrapings from her Teeth and Gums,
A nasty Compound of all Hues,
For here she spits, and here she spues . . .

Why, *Strephon*, will you tell the rest?
And must you needs describe the Chest?
That careless Wench! No Creature warn her,
To move it out from yonder Corner,
But leave it standing full in Sight,
For you to exercise your Spight!
In vain the Workman shew'd his Wit,
With Rings and Hinges counterfeit,
To make it seem in this Disguise,
A Cabinet to vulgar Eyes;
Which *Strephon* ventur'd to look in,
Resolv'd to go thro' *thick and thin*,
He lifts the Lid: There need no more,
He smelt it all the Time before.

As, from within *Pandora*'s Box,
When *Epimetheus* op'd the Locks,
A sudden universal Crew
Of human Evils upward flew;
He still was comforted to find,
That *Hope* at last remain'd behind.

So, *Strephon*, lifting up the Lid,
To view what in the Chest was hid,
The Vapours flew out from the Vent;
But *Strephon*, cautious, never meant
The Bottom of the *Pan* to grope,
And foul his Hands in search of *Hope*.

O! ne'er may such a vile Machine
Be once in *Cælia*'s Chamber seen!
O! may she better learn to keep
Those *Secrets of the hoary Deep*!

As Mutton-Cutlets, *Prime of Meat*,
Which, tho' with Art you salt and beat,
As Laws of Cookery require,
And roast them at the clearest Fire;
If from *adown* the hopeful Chops,
The Fat upon a Cinder drops,
To stinking Smoak it turns the Flame,
Pois'ning the Flesh from whence it came,
And up exhales a greazy Stench,
For which you curse the careless Wench:
So, Things which must not be exprest,
When *plumpt* into the reeking Chest,
Send up an excremental Smell,
To taint the Parts from whence they fell:
The Petticoats and Gown perfume,
And waft a Stink round ev'ry Room.

Thus finishing his grand Survey,
The Swain disgusted slunk away,
Repeating in his am'rous Fits,
Oh! *Cælia*, *Cælia*, *Cælia*, sh –

But *Vengeance*, Goddess, never sleeping,
Soon punish'd *Strephon* for his peeping.
His foul Imagination links
Each Dame he sees with all her Stinks;
And, if unsavoury Odours fly,
Conceives a Lady standing by.
All Women his Description fits,
And both Ideas jump like Wits,
By vicious Fancy coupled fast,
And still appearing in *Contrast*.

I pity wretched *Strephon*, blind
To all the Charms of Woman-kind.
Should I the *Queen of Love* refuse,
Because she rose from stinking Ooze?
To him that looks behind the Scene,
Statira's but some pocky Quean.

When *Cælia* all her Glory shows,
If *Strephon* would but stop his Nose,
Who now so impiously blasphemes
Her Ointments, Daubs, and Paints, and Creams;
Her Washes, Slops, and ev'ry Clout,
With which he makes so foul a Rout;
He soon would learn to think like me,
And bless his ravish'd Eyes to see,
Such Order from Confusion sprung,
Such gaudy *Tulips* rais'd from *Dung*.

BRIAN MOORE

from *The Lonely Passion of Judith Hearne*

Her angular face smiled softly at its glassy image. Her gaze, deceiving, transforming her to her imaginings, changed the contour of her sallow-skinned face, skilfully refashioning her long pointed nose on which a small chilly tear had gathered. Her dark eyes, eyes which skittered constantly in imagined fright, became wide, soft, luminous. Her frame, plain as a cheap clothes-rack, filled now with soft curves, developing a delicate line to the bosom.

She watched the glass, a plain woman, changing all to the delightful illusion of beauty. There was still time: for her ugliness was destined to bloom late, hidden first by the unformed gawkiness of youth, budding to plainness in young womanhood and now flowering to slow maturity in her early forties, it still awaited the subtle garishness which only decay could bring to fruition: a garishness which, when arrived at, would preclude all efforts at the mirror game.

So she played. Woman, she saw her womanish glass image. Pulled her thick hair sideways, framing her imagined face with tresses. Gipsy, she thought fondly, like a gipsy girl on a chocolate box.

But the little clock chittering through the seconds said eight-fifteen and O, what silly thoughts she was having. Gipsy indeed! She rose, sweeping her hair up, the hairpins in her mouth coming out one by one and up, up to disappear in her crowning glory. There (pat) much better. A little more (pat) so. Good. Now, what to wear? A touch of crimson, my special *cachet*. But which? Reds are so fickle. Still, red is my colour. Vermilion. Yes. The black dress with the vermilion touch at collar and cuffs. Besides, it hasn't been crushed by the moving.

She opened the wardrobe, breaking the unity of its imagined face. Her dressing-gown fell like a dismantled tent at her feet as she shrugged her angular body into the tight waist seams of the dress. Then, her garnets and the small ruby on her right hand. She rummaged in the jewel box, deciding that the pink and white cameo would be a little too much. But she wore her watch, the little gold wristlet watch that Aunt D'Arcy had given her on her twenty-first birthday. It didn't really work well any more. The movement was wearing out. But it was a good watch, and very becoming. And goodness knows, she thought, first impressions are often last impressions, as old Herr Rauh used to say.

Then back to the dressing-table to tidy the strands of hair which her dress had ruffled. A teeny touch of rouge, well rubbed in, a dab of powder and a good sharp biting of her lips to make the colour come out. There, much better. She smiled fondly at her fondly smiling image, her nervous dark eyes searching the searching glass. Satisfied, she nodded to the nodding, satisfied face. Yes. On to breakfast.

ÁINE NÍ GHLINN

Cuair

Curves

(translated by A. MacP.)

Ó ghoid máinlia
a banúlacht uaithi
bíonn sí de shíor
ag stánadh
ar éirí na gréine
ar chomhchruinneas na gcnoc.

Since the surgeon stole
her womanliness
she stares
unceasingly
at the rising sun
the rounded hills.

Ar pháipéar déanann
stuanna ciorcail
ceann i ndiaidh a chéile
Ó fágadh coilm sceana
mar a mbíodh a brollach
tá sí ciaptha ag cuair.

Draws on paper
arcs, circles,
one after the other.
Since knife-scars mark
where her breast had been
curves torment her.

Tadhg Dall O'Huiginn

A Vision

(Sixteenth Century)

Art thou the woman who was here last night with me in a vision? uncertain about thee as I am, thou bright form, my mind is bewildered.

If thou be not she who came before, O slender figure, gentle and soft of hand, and dainty of step, thou art exactly similar.

Thy glowing cheek, thy blue eye – never were there formed from the four-fold element two more similar in form, O yellow, curly, plaited locks.

Thy white teeth, thy crimson lips which make sufficing lullaby, brown brows of the hue of the sloe, and all that lies between them.

Throat like the blossom of the lily, long, slender hands; supple, plump flesh, of the hue of the waves, dulling the whiteness of the river's foam.

Small, smooth, white breasts rising above a lovely, shining slope; gentle expanses, with borders most fair and delightful, they are to be likened to fairy knolls.

On the ends of thy luxuriant tresses are flocks not unusual in winter, which have been bathed in pure gold; a most wondrous flock.

I am worthy of trust, thou art in no danger, tell me was it thou who came before to the land of *Fál* to trouble me, thou shining white-toothed, modest-faced lady?

Or art thou she who came afore-time to visit the Round Table, thou head of smooth, fair, bright locks, to wondrous King Arthur?

AUSTIN CLARKE

The Redemptorist

'How many children have you?' asked
The big Redemptorist.
   'Six, Father.'
    'The last,
When was it born?'
   'Ten months ago,'
'I cannot absolve your mortal sin
Until you conceive again. Go home,
Obey your husband.'
  She whimpered:
   'But
The doctor warned me . . . '
   Shutter became
Her coffin lid. She twisted her thin hands
And left the box.
    The missioner,
Red-bearded saint, had brought hell's flame
To frighten women on retreat:
Sent on his spiritual errand,
It rolled along the village street
Until Rathfarnham was housing smoke
That sooted the Jesuits in their Castle.
'No pregnancy. You'll die the next time,'
The Doctor had said.
    Her tiredness obeyed

That Saturday night: her husband's weight
Digging her grave. So in nine months, she
Sank in great agony on a Monday.
Her children wept in the Orphanage,
Huddled together in the annexe,
While, proud of the Black Cross on his badge,
The Liguorian, at Adam and Eve's,
Ascended the pulpit, sulphering his sleeves
And setting fire to the holy text.

GEORGE EGERTON

from *Rosa Amorosa*

Do you know what I did? Don't scold me. I simply undressed and
went for a swim in the river; there is a kind of drawbridge, so that
it can be pulled back once a year to establish the farmer's right of
private way; and he takes a penny a year from the labourers who
make a short cut across it to their work. I swung in by the chains
and startled the rats and sent an otter; I never believed there was
one although a 'spraint' of some kind marked the grass along the
bank, but there he was, sure enough. It was glorious; the water
was warmish and like silk. I tried to sit on the moon, but it slid
away on a ripple of gurgling laughter as the water rocked. The
water mint emitted fragrance as I crushed it. Pan would have loved
to lurk on such a night, even in England. Poor old Goat God, his
reed pipe nowadays has a note of music-hall melody, he has
deteriorated as most else. The long green washes of reeds caught in
my toes and slid over my shoulders; the buoyancy and snap of salt
water with its clear freshness was missing; yet none the less, it was
a delicious moonlight water frolic.

   As I ran across the meadow to my garments my own shadow was
startling by its unfamiliarity. I dried with my cambric petticoat

and started for a walk, with my shawl over my head, up the lane. It is frightful, when you think of it, that we are never alone enough to go naked. I have often thought that if by some sudden, subtle, painless combustion every shred of wool, cotton, or silk in the world were to be consumed, that on people's bodies as well as off, so that the whole world of men and women would suddenly stand in nudity, the moral effect would be colossal. All false shame would die a summary death, and the exigencies of continuing the ordinary duties of life would compel people to cast all consideration of it aside. The common idea of beauty would be entirely revolutionised; the human face would lose its undue prominence and become a mere detail in a whole; straight, clean limbs and a beautiful form be the only thing admirable; disease and bodily blemishes the one right cause for shame, and, as a result, concealment.

NELL McCAFFERTY

It is my belief that Armagh is a feminist issue

There is menstrual blood on the walls of Armagh Prison in Northern Ireland. The 32 women on dirt strike there have not washed their bodies since February 8th 1980; they use their cells as toilets; for over 200 days now they have lived amid their own excreta, urine and blood.

The windows and spy holes are boarded up. Flies and slugs grow fat as they grow thin. They eat and sleep and sit in this dim, electrically-lit filth, without reading materials or radio or television. They are allowed out for one hour per day, hopefully to stand in the rain. The consequences for these women, under these conditions, will be, at the least, urinary, pelvic and skin infections. At worst, they face sterility, and possible death.

They are guarded by male warders presided over by a male
governor, and attended by a male doctor. Relations between the
women and these men have never been very good. In an ordinary
medical atmosphere, in, for example, a Dublin hospital, women
who have depended on men for advice, consultation and treatment
have often had grounds for complaint.

In the present situation of confrontation and hostility that exists
in Armagh jail, it would be fair to assume that the relationship
between the women prisoners and the men charged with responsibility for them is not such as to allay anxiety about the bodily
health of the women.

What business, if any, is it of ours?

The choices facing feminists on the matter of Armagh jail are
clear cut. We can ignore these women or we can express concern
about them. Since the suffering of women anywhere, whether self-
inflicted or not, cannot be ignored by feminists, then we have a
clear responsibility to respond. The issue then is the nature of our
response.

We can condemn the dirt strike of these women and call on
them to desist. We can deplore the consequences to these women
of the dirt strike and urge that action be taken to resolve the
problem. Or we can support them.

It is my belief that Armagh is a feminist issue that demands our
support. I believe that the 32 women there have been denied one
of the fundamental rights of women, the right to bodily integrity,
and I suggest that an objective examination of the events that gave
rise to the dirt strike will support this contention.

On February 7th, there occurred, by common admission, a
confrontation in Armagh jail between 32 Republican women on
the one hand, and on the other, upwards of 40 male warders, 30
female warders and an unspecified number of men engaged in
work within the prison. The confrontation occurred shortly after
noon, in the dining section, where the women prisoners were
partaking of an unusually attractive meal of chicken followed by
apple pie.

The women were informed by the prison governor that their
cells would be searched while they remained in the dining area.

The authorities were looking for the black berets and skirts which the women occasionally wore in the exercise yard, when conducting a political parade in commemoration or celebration of some Republican happening on the outside.

The wearing of this makeshift uniform was a symbolic rejection of the criminal status which the authorities had imposed on them, and a palpable projection of the women's own self-image as political prisoners. The arguments for and against political status are well rehearsed to the initiated.

The position of Britain is, briefly, that those who commit offences against the State are criminals. The position of Republicans is, briefly, that having been charged with scheduled or political offences, in consequence of which they are denied the right to trial by jury and must appear before a special Diplock court, they are by definition political prisoners. In support of their case, Republicans point to the existence of political prisoners within Northern Ireland jails who were sentenced before March 1st 1976. The British case for criminalisation is arbitrary, resting on the decision to abolish political status after that date.

In February of this year, the British authorities were preparing to take an even more arbitrary step. Legislation was about to be enacted which would deny retrospective political status to those who were now facing conviction for acts committed before March 1976. To that end, it was presumably necessary to remove even the physical vestiges of imaginary political status. The statutory right of women prisoners in Northern Ireland to wear their own clothes was changed to an obligation to wear civilian clothes that were not of a certain colour or cut – no black berets or skirts allowed.

As a result of the confrontation in Armagh on February 7th, the women prisoners, many of whom suffered physical injury, were locked in their cells for 24 hours. Bodily integrity was denied them as they were refused access to toilets or a washing facility during this time. For those 24 hours the women, some of them menstruating, were not allowed to wash and were forced to use chamber pots for all bodily functions.

The chamber pots overflowed. The outrageous humiliation was complete . . . The dimensions of their suffering, both mentally and physically, which can only be guessed at, make one cringe.

COUNTESS OF BLESSINGTON

from *Journal of a Lady of Fashion*

Monday – Awoke with a headache, the certain effect of being bored all the evening before by the never-dying strain at the Countess of Leyden's. Nothing ever was half so tiresome as musical parties: no one gives them except those who can exhibit themselves, and fancy they excel. If you speak, during the performance of one of their endless pieces, they look cross and affronted: except that all the world of fashion are there, I never would go to another; for, positively, it is ten times more fatiguing than staying at home. To be compelled to look charmed, and to applaud, when you are half-dead from suppressing yawns, and to see half-a-dozen very tolerable men, with whom one could have had a very pleasant chat, except for the stupid music, is really too bad. Let me see, what have I done this day? Oh! I remember everything went wrong, as it always does when I have a headache. Flounce, more than usually stupid, tortured my hair; and I flushed my face by scolding her. I wish people could scold without getting red, for it disfigures one for the whole day; and the consciousness of this always makes me more angry, as I think it doubly provoking in Flounce to discompose me, when she must know it spoils my looks.

Dressing from twelve to three. Madame Tornure sent me a most unbecoming cap: mem. I shall leave her off when I have paid her bill. Heigh-ho! when will that be? Tormented by duns, jewellers, mercers, milliners: I think they always fix on Mondays for dunning: I suppose it is because they know one is sure to be horribly vapored after a Sunday-evening's party, and they like to increase one's miseries.

Máighréad Medbh

Coming Out

my hands began it
and now I love it
my cunt is swelling
thinking of it
thinking of a tongue on it

a warm ache between my legs
my hands begin
stroke up my breasts
my breasts are steaming
nipples standing staring
my hands are drawing the world
from the mound of my head
to the round of my small toe
feel my legs
the inside thigh beginning
to blush then shining
then my stomach a mass of tingle
I touch my clit it sings
a touch is a step inside
I am queen and land
where east meets west
my hands unclose a passage north to south
my face is full upon me
all of me my face
all become a globe
the full of my spread legs
and between them
the centre is thickening
the lips are pursing out
I am speeding up
my hands are driving

my cunt is driving
I am zooming to my inner space
only one direction
I am in there
it is blowing out
ballooning out
quickly quickly
my self steering
my self steered
all a flow
all a rush
a tidal wave
wet on my fingers
heat running in my thighs
in my tail
my tail is spinning shaking swishing
I am the world
I am spinning
taking space
making whirlwinds out of space
I am space
I am spilling in
I am spilling out
I am coming
streaming steaming
coming out

Pierce Ferriter

Lay Your Arms Aside

(Seventeenth Century)

Version by Eiléan Ní Chuilleanáin

Gentlest of women, put your weapons by,
Unless you want to ruin all mankind;
Leave the assault or I must make reply,
Proclaiming that you are murderously inclined.
Put by your armour, lay your darts to rest,
Hide your soft hair and all its devious ways:
To see it lie in coils upon your breast
Poisons all hope and mercilessly slays.

Protest you never murdered in your life;
You lie: your hand's smooth touch, your well-shaped knee
Destroy as easily as axe or knife.
Your breasts like new spring flowers, your naked side
– I cry for aid to heaven – conceal from me;
Let shame for the destruction you have made
Hide your bright eyes, your shining teeth, away;
If all our sighs and trembling and dismay
Can touch your heart or satisfy your pride,
Gentlest of women, lay your arms aside.

'LISA'

from *Lisa: The Story of an Irish Drug Addict*

She had only got the H an hour before we came on her, and she was in such a state that she was totally incapable of shooting it into a vein. She had been popping valium by the bottle. We carried her into her pad. In between the ramblings, she kept begging us to cook up the H for her and shoot it into her ourselves. So we got the powder onto a spoon, mixed it with water and heated it up. Two of us held her down and kept her arm steady, while another found a vein for the needle. But then she started to jerk, and gasp, and turn a ghastly colour. Then she went unconscious. We had given her too big a dose by accident. So we called an ambulance. One of my friends was giving her mouth-to-mouth resuscitation. At last the ambulance came and they took her away to hospital. We weren't allowed to come with her. But we did manage to get in touch with her family. She was in the intensive care unit for three days, in a coma. When she came out of the coma, they moved her to Jervis Street. Later, she moved on to Coolemine, stayed for (I think) four months and then split. Back onto the street. Back shooting smack. And a year and a half later she was found by her brother in her bedroom, dead . . .

One day, I swallowed a packet of darning needles, a box of nails, and some open safety pins. Part of me desperately wanted to die, part of me wanted help. One of the darning needles got stuck in my throat. So I rang my doctor. That was the part of me that wanted help. I was rushed into hospital in the middle of the night. They brought me down to the theatre at three o'clock in the morning. Part of the needle was nearly perforating the wall of my gullet, and although I don't understand the medical jargon the doctors used after the operation when they explained how the needle was lodged, I know they had quite a job getting it out. I want to thank the staff of that hospital, who were so kind and understanding and anxious to help. I started facing up honestly to reality and myself again, just in a small way – but it was a start.

Then, when I was back in my flat, the strain I was under got worse and became totally unbearable again, and my mind felt as if it had been blown open. I don't know if I had been going through a breakdown, but anyway, at 2 a.m. one night my head exploded and I got the carving knife and smashed a glass and slashed and slashed and slashed into my arms, then flung away the knife and the piece of glass and ran to the phone and rang the Samaritans screaming for help. Two volunteers came over at once and brought me in to Jervis Street. The doctors there stitched me up, but because I had lost so much blood, they refused to let me go home again with the two volunteers, who had stayed on waiting for me. I was determined to get back to my flat, but gave in finally because I was feeling so awful.

Two weekends later, back in the flat, I overdosed. I didn't know I was going to overdose. The thought was certainly not in my mind. I remember getting on a bus, early on the Saturday. Then I remember waking up, undressed – just in my nightdress – on the floor of my living-room in the flat, surrounded by empty medicine bottles. Four empty bottles, all of different kinds of tablets, different types of tranquillisers. These tabs can only be got on scripts, but I had no prescription. It was three o'clock in the afternoon – Monday afternoon. That frightened me – oh, I can't express *how* it frightened me.

JOHN BANVILLE

from *The Newton Letter*

Of all the mental photographs I have of her I choose one. A summer night, one of those white nights of July. We had been drinking, she got up to pee. The lavatory was not working, as so often, and she had brought in from the garage, to join her other treasures, an ornate china vessel which she quaintly called the jolly-pot. I watched her squat there in the gloaming, her elbows on her knees, one hand in her hair, her eyes closed, playing a tinkling chamber music. Still without opening her eyes she came stumbling back to bed, and kneeling kissed me, mumbling in my ear. Then she lay down again, her hair everywhere, and sighed and fell asleep, grinding her teeth faintly. It's not much of a picture, is it? But she's *in* it, ineradicably, and I treasure it.

Susan McKay

from *Report on the Kilkenny Incest Case* 9.5.93

Alison had friends, and they knew her father was violent. She thinks at least one of them 'had a fair idea' about the sexual violence, but she did not break her father's injunction to keep it secret. 'When you are living in total fear like that, you just don't tell,' she said.

Alison's father was not just violent to his family. 'Anything I ever cared for he killed,' said Alison. 'He went for my puppy with a slash hook, and he strangled my canaries. One I had, she was a real old pet. She used to stick her tongue out. After he killed her, he told me she had sung for him while he had his hands round her throat.'

In 1981, when Alison was 15, her periods stopped. When she found she couldn't zip up her jeans, she told her mother, who 'didn't seem exactly surprised'. She brought the girl to a doctor, who said she had wind. A second doctor told her she was three months pregnant. She did not reveal who the father was. 'I suppose I was stupid enough to think my mother could sort this out, make it go away,' she said.

Alison was confused. She wanted to die, and drank washing up liquid to poison herself. Then she thought about the baby, and made herself throw up. Her father continued to rape her until about a week before she went into labour. Her mother took her to the hospital where she had a natural birth. She refused pain relief. 'It was agony,' she said. 'I think I had to get 28 stitches. But it was worth it to have Ben.' She laughed. 'Actually, it was bliss being in hospital. There was no one there to hurt me, and I had the baby. It was peaceful.' She said her father came to visit and joked about throwing the baby out of the window to see if he would bounce.

Because she was a single parent, Alison was interviewed by a social worker. 'I told her there were a few problems in the house. I told her about the beatings. I told her my father had raped me, though I didn't say how often – I just wanted to see could she get me out of it. Mammy was there listening and she agreed with what I was saying. She said that yes, it was pure hell.'

'The social worker said that it was a family matter and she couldn't get involved.' Because Alison was 16 by this time, the health board would have been unable to initiate care proceedings. They went home.

'My mother just sort of totally gave in then. She just let herself go. She really lost interest in herself,' said Alison. 'From that time, my father started to treat me as if I was his wife.' Within a week of childbirth, he raped her again. 'He really clamped down on me. He took me everywhere with him, me and the baby. If I talked to anyone, he called me a whore and I got beaten.'

She had hiding places around the farm that she'd run to, but there was no reliable way of avoiding the violence. Once when he saw that she had not pumped up the wheels of her bike, he threw a hammer at her head. 'He'd go out, get drunk, come home. You didn't have to do anything. You didn't have to start an argument. I tried staying quiet – I got beaten for that. I tried saying what he wanted to hear. I got beaten for that. So, in the end, I just gave up. You were going to get beaten and you might get sexually attacked as well.'

EDNA O'BRIEN

from *Night*

My next Romeo after Dr Flaggler was a Finn. Had the air of a chieftain. Turned fish eyes into fish bait, and the flesh itself into a luscious stew. Had ideals, wanted to introduce market gardening to those who lived in the Archipelago, wanted those lonely creatures to grow lettuces and fennel and strawberries. Very carnal. Always roscid and rosy for him. It is a wonder where the nectars of woman lurk at slack times, the mateless eras. No sleeping at all, only a doze before the fresh violations, and the Finn murmuring his sea shanties. He said the sea is not dark at all because he had gone down, there were flowers down there, a different breed, brain and branch coral, figures like dolomites, fauna golden and bewitching plus spitfires and xiphios and playing fish. Beautiful his attentions, his assaults. Jade gate, Jade gate, Jade gate. He had a bit of Chinese lore. But in everything else he was a Viking, a sailing man, a sea man, a dark winding eel. His favourite animal the boar. Liked it all ways, somersaults, a maiden's closed purse, the old podicum sursum, the romp, the wrangling brandlebuttock. Saw women and girls as related to water, sedges, pools, whirls, creatures that invited him in. He'd have gone with old Scylla across the Styx, he'd have gone anywhere then. He carried a little torch in the back of vehicles, to be able to have a close look at me at any moment, my lips, the brown of my eyes, my teeth. We were to motor all over the world, or rather be motored, and have blinds fitted to the windows so that at any moment we could couch down and with his hands that were capable as butter pats, he could smack me into any shape or crenellation. Malleable I was. In the quiet after, I used to snuggle down, hearing about the islands and the fishermen, the kind of boats they rowed, their take of herrings, the spirits they drank and the dragons and sea-serpents that they feared . . .

The Finn followed me to the land where the King has piles. Gala days, carnival, kissing and joking and kipping between meals, the Finn expanding, more than one man, a clan of men, an Eisteddfod, one of the ancients, in things and finikins, surrounding the bones of the house, ambushing, words soft, blasphemous, loud, incantatory; balls sacheting, breeches down, buttons, cracked leather buttons rolling all over the floor, the Finn making grunting sounds, the execrations and then the little bits of slop, the same words as in an autograph book – love and violets and always and ever and now; the Finn drawing the drapes, donning a nightshift like Old King Cole, feeling the bedcovers, climbing, saying Heigh ho and the sea shanties. A kind of embargo, the billow, the bruises, the bites, tossed, and turned, inside out, raucous, dulcet, a pandemonium, rumps rearing, slathering, words, wet words, tongues, coals, baskets of fire, and devil's pokers going through.

MARY MORRISSY

from *Possibilities*

At forty-one, Grace Davey's biggest fear was that she would dry up. When she rose in the morning she would be relieved and delighted to find her loins pleasingly damp. The milky secretion of mid-cycle was a cause for secret celebration. So, when she discovered the greenish discharge she was not at all alarmed. It reminded her of the sap that oozes from the barks of pine trees – strong, pungent, fertile. The workings of her own body were a mystery to her. She took great trouble with her appearance. Her chestnut hair, streaked here and there with grey, was swept back in a coil from her lightly lined face and pale green eyes. She had a slender neck, graceful shoulders, girlish hips. Yet of her innards she had only the vaguest notion – an impression of oiled, livid organs performing languid, primitive rituals unquestioningly – which was why the discharge did not at first bother her. She certainly didn't relate it to Lucas. Her body was merely dispelling something nasty and sharp-smelling which it needed to get rid of. She bowed to its wisdom.

She took to bathing more often, aware that the acrid odours of one's own body are always more pleasing to oneself than others. She dabbed lavender water on her wrists and behind her ears to distract attention. But as the weeks wore on she would panic if anyone so much as wrinkled a nose in her presence. Once, on a particularly muggy day in late August, Mr Weatherby paused in the middle of dictation and started sniffing noisily. 'Don't you get it?' he asked rising from the desk and wandering around the room.

'Get what?' she asked sliding her hand furtively into her handbag for the lavender water.

'That smell. Like seaweed, rotting seaweed.'

Grace sat in a damp pool.

'Perhaps it's the river,' she suggested, willing him to move away. He was poised like a hound. She was afraid he would catch the smell of fear from her which was now stronger than the other smell. 'It was at low tide this morning and it always stinks in the summer.'

'You must be right,' he said, 'it looks pretty foul from here with all that greenish stuff clinging to the banks. Ugh, disgusting . . . !'

Theodora Fitzgibbon

Potato Cakes

Traditional.
'. . . While I live I shall not forget her potato cakes. They came in hot, and hot from the pot oven, they were speckled with caraway seed, they swam in salt butter, and we ate them shamelessly and greasily, and washed them down with hot whiskey and water' ('The Holy Island', Experiences of an Irish R.M. – E. (E. Somerville and M. Ross).*

The three-legged iron pot is the origin of the term 'to take pot-luck'. In country districts it is used for roasting, stewing and for making cakes and bread. In counties Limerick and Cork it is also called a bastable oven, and the bread made in it a 'bastable cake'. Glowing turf (peat) sods are put on top when baking or roasting is being done to ensure even heat. The pot can be raised or lowered by a chain, and three short feet enable it to stand at the side of the hearth.

2 cups self-raising flour	¼ cup milk
2 heaped tablesp. butter or other fat	caraway seeds (optional)
1½ cups mashed potato	salt

Mix butter into the flour and add a good pinch of salt. Then mix in the mashed potato and pour in the milk to make a soft (not slack) dough. Roll out on a floured board and cut into rounds about 3 in. across. Sprinkle a few caraway seeds on top of each cake and bake in a hot oven (450°F. electric; gas regulo 6–7) for 20–30 minutes. Eat them hot, split across the middle and spread with butter. This dough can also be used to line a savoury flan tin. Makes about nine cakes.

WILLIAM TREVOR

from *Attracta*

English Girl's Suicide in Belfast the headline about Penelope Vade said, and below it there was a photograph, a girl with a slightly crooked smile and freckled cheeks. There was a photograph of her husband in army uniform, taken a few weeks before his death, and of the house in Belfast in which she had later rented a flat. *From the marks of blood on carpets and rugs*, the item said, *it is deduced that Mrs*

Vade dragged herself across the floors of two rooms. She appears repeatedly to have fainted before she reached a bottle of aspirins in a kitchen cupboard. She had been twenty-three at the time of her death.

It was Penelope Vade's desire to make some kind of gesture, a gesture of courage and perhaps anger, that had caused her to leave her parents' home in Haslemere and to go to Belfast. Her husband, an army officer, had been murdered in Belfast; he'd been decapitated as well. His head, wrapped in cotton-wool to absorb the ooze of blood, secured within a plastic bag and packed in a biscuit-tin, had been posted to Penelope Vade. Layer by layer the parcel had been opened by her in Haslemere. She hadn't known that he was dead before his dead eyes stared into hers.

Her gesture was her mourning of him. She went to Belfast to join the Women's Peace Movement, to make the point that somehow neither he nor she had been defeated. But her gesture, publicly reported, had incensed the men who'd gone to the trouble of killing him. One after another, seven of them had committed acts of rape on her. It was after that that she had killed herself.

A fortnight after Attracta had first read the newspaper item it still upset her. It haunted her, and she knew why it did, though only imprecisely. Alone at night, almost catching her unawares, scenes from the tragedy established themselves in her mind: the opening of the biscuit-box, the smell of death, the eyes, blood turning brown. As if at a macabre slide-show, the scene would change: before people had wondered about her whereabouts Penelope Vade had been dead for four days; mice had left droppings on her body.

MAIREAD DUNLEVY

from *Dress in Ireland*

Female Fashion 1840–1910

At the time of the Great Famine, 1845–7, the differences between the middle-class lady and the poor woman were dramatic. Reflecting the romantic attitudes of the earlier decades, the lady of fashion of the 1840s had become a pale, demure person – passive in mind and body. Physical activity was virtually impossible for her because she wore about a stone weight of underwear and tight, tiny shoes. Even the movement of her arms was restricted through a new method of setting-in sleeves. Her lower ribcage was compressed to the required shape through wearing stays (of different qualities) day and night from childhood. Some women went further and resorted to slimming to achieve the desired eighteen inch waist and trim ankles. Neatness and cleanliness were considered so important that the *Meath Herald and Cavan Advertiser* advised men to 'hang themselves' rather than marry a woman who dressed carelessly or who had shoes that were loose, or worn down at heel . . .

Dress of the Poor

In general, it can be said that the local traditional variations in dress seen in the early nineteenth century remained, although they were affected by changing economic factors. Striped red and blue petticoats were worn under gowns or skirts. Although madder-red dye was popular, indigo, shades of blue, green, brown and grey were used also. Full-skirted red petticoats were worn about ankle-length by mature women, and shorter by younger women. Skirts were often quilted, decorated with blue or black bands or a simple wide tuck above the hem. Early nineteenth century bodices were low-cut or rounded, with square or v-shaped necklines and elbow-length sleeves. High-necked fitted bodices, with or without small turned-down collars, evolved in the late nineteenth century and echoed the fashionable dress of the time: their sleeves were frequently long, tight and buttoned at the cuffs . . . When aprons were worn they were looped up along with the skirt and the ends tucked into the waist-band, thus exposing the petticoat . . . Traditional sole-less stockings known variously as troighthíní, lóipíní and mairtíní were worn particularly in Spring by women and boys as protection against 'the ire', a soreness and splitting of the skin caused by wet, cold work outside and exposure to hot fires in the home.

EMMA DONOGHUE

from *Stir Fry*

The door at the top of the stairs was swaying open, so she strolled in and glanced through the bead curtain.

It wasn't her fault; she was in no sense spying. She couldn't help but see the shape they made. Her eyes tried to untangle its elements. Ruth, crosslegged on the table, her back curved like a comma, and Jael, leaning into it, kissing her. There was no wild passion; that might have shaken her less. Just the slow bartering of lips on the rickety table where Ruth chopped garlic every night.

Maria clamped her eyes shut, as if they had not already soaked in the scene as blotting paper swallowed ink. When she raised her lids, the women had not moved. The kiss, their joint body, the table, all seemed to belong to a parallel world. She had the impression that no noise from behind the shifting skin of the bead curtain could reach them.

She doubled back to the door, making her brash boots land as softly as slippers. A count of ten, she gave them, as she leaned against the door frame. How long could a kiss last? Five more seconds. It occurred to her that they had no reason to stop. Nineteen hippopotamus, twenty hippopotamus . . . Perhaps they would go on all afternoon. The windows would darken around them, their faces would become silhouettes, the dinner would stay on the chopping board, and all this time Maria would be standing in the front door.

'I'm home, folks,' she yelled, loud and cheery as Doris Day. They behaved perfectly too, strolling out of the kitchen with armfuls of library books as if they had been rehearsing this little scene all their lives. Which, now she came to think of it, they probably had.

Five hours later was the earliest she could go to bed without having them worry that she was ill. She kept yawning heartily and explaining how her new job really took it out of her, what with the industrial vacuum cleaners and all.

At last she was under the covers, soft candlewick bunched in her fist. She concentrated on blacking out the tableau that was still flickering on the screen of her mind. What bothered her was that there was no distance. The topic had come up before, of course. Girls joked about it all the time in convent school; there'd even been rumours about the gym teacher. At parties, they swapped Freudian theories, and her friend Nuala had once claimed to have seen a French film with two women in bed in it. But it was never real. Now suddenly here were two friends of hers kissing on the table she ate at every night. Rapt faces and library books and garlic, how bizarre.

Liz McManus

from *Acts of Subversion*

After Oran had refilled the kettle and set it on the gas-ring he sat on the edge of his chair waiting for the Legion woman to leave. He enjoyed being with Mrs Gaughan. She had a simple gaiety and asked him questions about himself and seemed to find his answers absorbing. He was content to wait, listening to the sound of the sponge sloshing quietly over her wasted skin.

Once, without warning, the sheet slipped and her naked body lay exposed to his pop-eyed stare. Her swollen, shiny-skinned knees were bent up to frame the opening between her legs and he saw her other mouth, in its perpetual O, mirroring his astonishment. Her venus mount was bony and hairless. White as marble. And yet, between her skinny thighs as if a knife had broken the skin of a plum, there was a slit through which the insides of Mrs Gaughan throbbed lasciviously at him.

The low room brimmed with female flesh. The arms of the Legion woman swelled out of her cardigan, her massive breasts threatening to erupt shamelessly, as the buttons of her crimplene overall ached under the strain of her every movement. Unaware of his discomfiture, the Legion woman pulled the nightdress over Mrs Gaughan's head and lifted her up into a sitting position. Once she had her rosary-beads threaded between her fingers, Mrs Gaughan was ready to face another day, jammed in her nest of pillows and staring into space.

'Can't you hear the kettle, son?' she asked. Oran, his face burning and his cock bulging, stumbled into the kitchen and stood, appalled, in front of the gas-ring, while the air filled up with steam. He became aware of someone standing beside him.

'Ya feckin' eejit.' Casually the Legion woman stretched past him to turn off the gas. Her body was so close to him that his nostrils filled with the pungency of her sweat. 'D'you want to burn a hole in it or what?' Her expression slackened and she displayed her tongue, pink and quivering, within the lipsticked margins of her mouth.

From the bedroom Mrs Gaughan's voice came, thin and urgent. 'Come here to me, darling,' she entreated him but Oran couldn't. Trapped between her sick scrawniness and the steaming corpulence of the Legion woman he felt the breath was being squeezed out of his body. He made his escape, rushing past them both and plunging out the door.

2

Girly Years

MOLLY KEANE

from *Good Behaviour*

When we were children the food in the nursery was quite poisonously disgusting. None of the fruit juice and vitamins of today for us – oranges only at Christmastime and porridge every morning, variable porridge slung together by the kitchen maid, followed by white bread and butter and Golden Syrup. Boiled eggs were for Sundays and sausages for birthdays. I don't think Mummie gave us a thought – she left the ordering of nursery meals to the cook, who sent up whatever came easiest, mostly rabbit stews and custard puddings riddled with holes. No wonder the nannies left in quick succession.

Why do I hate the word 'crusted'? Because I feel with my lips the boiled milk, crusted since the night before, round the rim of the mug out of which I must finish my breakfast milk . . . I am again in the darkness of the nursery, the curtains drawn against the winter morning outside. Nannie is dragging on her corsets under her great nightdress. Baby Hubert is walking up and down his cot in a dirty nightdress. The nursery maid is pouring paraffin on a sulky nursery fire. I fix my eyes on the strip of morning light where wooden rings join curtains to curtain pole and think about my bantams . . . Even then I knew how to ignore things. I knew how to behave.

I don't blame Mummie for all this. She simply did not want to know what was going on in the nursery. She had had us and she longed to forget the horror of it once and for all. She engaged nannie after nannie with excellent references, and if they could not be trusted to look after us, she was even less able to compete. She didn't really like children; she didn't like dogs either, and she had no enjoyment of food, for she ate almost nothing.

She was sincerely shocked and appalled on the day when the housemaid came to tell her that our final nannie was lying on her bed in a drunken stupor with my brother Hubert beside her in another drunken stupor, while I was lighting a fire in the day nursery with the help of a tin of paraffin. The nannie was sacked, but given quite a good reference with no mention of her drinking; that would have been too unkind and unnecessary, since she promised to reform. Her next charge (only a Dublin baby) almost died of drink, and its mother wrote a very common, hysterical letter, which Mummie naturally put in the fire and forgot about. Exhausted, bored and disgusted by nannies, she engaged a governess who would begin my education and at the same time keep an eye on the nursery maid who was to be in charge of Hubert's more menial four-year-old necessities.

MOYA RODDY

from *The Long Way Home*

'What are you goin'ta be when you grow up Loretta?' Jo asked as they walked home.

'Dunno. What are you goin'ta be?' She pulled a long strip off the hot, fluffy loaf.

'I'm not gettin' married, that's for sure.' After a moment Jo added, 'I'd like to be a teacher.' Seeing a glitter in Loretta's eyes she hurried on, 'or a secretary or somethin'.' She hoped that put her off the scent. She didn't want Loretta guessing she'd sent Miss Kearns a Christmas card. She could hear her . . . . 'Teacher's pet, teacher's pet, teacher's pet with her knickers wet.'

But for once Loretta was too busy with her own thoughts to notice the redness creeping into Jo's face.

'I'm goin'ta get married and have loads of babies. Have you seen our new wan? She's gorgeous.'

'But wouldn't you like to travel round the world?'

'Whaa, and get eaten up by wild animals in the jungle,' she exclaimed, offering Jo the turnover loaf. Jo pulled a bit off. The loaf was getting thinner and thinner.

'That's only in the pictures.'

By now they'd reached their corner and Jo was hopping up and down and holding onto herself. She'd had to go since the bakery. But even though her house was only across the road she didn't want to go home. She liked being with Loretta more than anything even if she was always getting at her.

'Are ye comin' out later? I'm goin' in, me ma will be waitin' for the bread.'

'Don't go yet. Me da mightn't let me out again.'

'What are ye goin' red for?' Loretta demanded.

'I'm not.'

'You are so, Jo Nowd. You're as red as a beetroot.'

Jo held tighter to herself feeling the pee pee coming. She couldn't tell Loretta she'd gone red because she'd called her daddy 'da'. Loretta called her mammy and daddy 'ma' and 'da'. So did all the kids at school. Jo wasn't allowed to:

'We don't want you speaking like Dublin people. It's common. You'll never get on at school or get a good job if you don't speak properly.'

Jo wished magic could be done and she and Loretta could swop places and she could go home to Burns' even once.

JAMES STEPHENS

Miss Makebelieve of Dublin

Every morning about six o'clock Mary Makebelieve left her bed and lit the fire. It was an ugly fire to light, because the chimney had never been swept, and there was no draught. Also they never had any sticks in the house, and scraps of paper twisted tightly into balls with the last night's cinders placed on them and a handful of small coals strewn on the top were used instead. Sometimes the fire blazed up quickly, and that made her happy,

but at other times it went out three and four, and often half a
dozen times; then the little bottle of paraffin oil had to be
squandered – a few rags well steeped in the oil with a newspaper
stretched over the grate seldom failed to coax enough fire to boil
the saucepan of water; generally this method smoked the water,
and then the tea tasted so horrid that one only drank it for the sake
of economy.

Mrs Makebelieve liked to lie in bed until the last possible
moment. As there was no table in the room, Mary used to bring
the two cups of tea, the tin of condensed milk, and the quarter of a
loaf over to the bed, and there she and her mother took their
breakfast.

From the time she opened her eyes in the morning her mother
never ceased to talk. It was then she went over all the things that
had happened on the previous day and enumerated the places she
would have to go to on the present day, and the chances for and
against the making of a little money. At this meal she used to
arrange also to have the room re-papered and the chimney swept
and the rat-holes stopped up – there were three of these, one was
on the left-hand side of the fire grate, the other two were under the
bed, and Mary Makebelieve had lain awake many a night listening
to the gnawing of teeth on the skirting and the scamper of little
feet here and there on the floor. Her mother further arranged to
have a Turkey carpet placed on the floor, although she admitted
that oilcloth or linoleum was easier to clean, but they were not so
nice to the feet or the eye. Into all these improvements her
daughter entered with the greatest delight. There was to be a red
mahogany chest of drawers against one wall and a rosewood piano
against the wall opposite. A fender of shining brass with brazen
furniture, a bright, copper kettle for boiling water in, and an iron
for cooking potatoes and meat; there was to be a life-sized picture
of Mary over the mantelpiece and a picture of her mother near the
window in a golden frame, also a picture of a Newfoundland dog
lying in a barrel and a little wee terrier crawling up to make friends
with him, and a picture of a battle between black people and
soldiers.

Her mother knew it was time to get out of bed when she heard a heavy step coming from the next room and going downstairs . . . When the door banged she jumped up, dressed quickly, and flew from the room in a panic of haste. Usually then, as there was nothing to do, Mary went back to bed for another couple of hours. After this she arose, made the bed and tidied the room, and went out to walk in the streets, or to sit in the St Stephen's Green Park . . . She loved to watch the ducklings swimming after their mothers: they were quite fearless, and would dash to the water's edge where one was standing and pick up nothing with the greatest eagerness and swallow it with delight . . . Mary Makebelieve thought it was very clever of the little ducklings to be able to swim so well. She loved them and when nobody was looking she used to cluck at them like their mother, but she did not often do this because she did not know duck language really well, and feared that her cluck might mean the wrong things, and that she might be giving these innocents bad advice, and telling them to do something contrary to what their mother had just directed . . .

After that, growing hungry, she would go home for her lunch. She went home down Grafton Street and O'Connell Street. She always went along the right-hand side of the street going home, and looked in every shop window that she passed, and then, when she had eaten her lunch, she came out again and walked along the left-hand side of the road, looking at the shops on that side, and so she knew daily everything that was new in the city, and was able to tell her mother at night-time that the black dress with Spanish lace was taken out of Manning's window and a red gown with tucks at the shoulders and Irish lace at the wrists put in its place; or that the diamond ring in Johnson's marked One Hundred Pounds was gone from the case and that a slide of brooches of beaten silver and blue enamel was there instead.

In the night-time her mother and herself went round to each of the theatres in turn and watched the people going in and looked at the big posters. When they went home afterwards they had supper and used to try to make out the plots of the various plays from the pictures they had seen, so that generally they had lots to talk about

before they went to bed. Mary Makebelieve used to talk most in
the night-time, but her mother talked most in the morning.

MARGO HARKIN

from *Hush-a-Bye Baby*

DINKY. There's a letter for ye, ye wee bitch.

*She runs down awkwardly. It is tragic comedy after the sight of Goretti.
When she gets closer to Goretti she realises something is wrong.*

DINKY. What's wrong, Goretti what's wrong?

Goretti doesn't answer.

DINKY. Dear God, Goretti, tell me.

Goretti doesn't answer still.

DINKY. We can go back to Derry you know Goretti. I canny stick
it either having to talk Irish all the time. Here. At least you got a
letter. It's from Derry. Look Goretti. Go'ne open it. It'll cheer ye
up.

Goretti is incapable so Dinky opens the letter.

DINKY. Look, it's from your Mother. Oh look! There's another
letter inside.

*Goretti looks and she takes the letter. She finally realises that her Mother
has enclosed a letter from Ciaran. She pulls it out and reads it frantically.*

GORETTI. (*in bewilderment*) He doesn't know. He doesn't know
yet!

DINKY. Know what?
GORETTI. I'm pregnant, Dinky . . . Oh God I want to die.

Goretti is like a dam burst. She sobs uncontrollably. Dinky is taken aback. Eventually she puts her arm around her and tries to comfort her.

Scene 67 EXT. WALKING TO THE BUS STOP IN THE GAELTACHT, DAY

Goretti and Dinky are walking to the bus stop with their bags.

DINKY. You probably shouldn't be carrying that suitcase, Goretti.
GORETTI. I hope it makes me lose it . . . I don't want it.
DINKY. But maybe you're not pregnant.
GORETTI. I told ye, my period's overdue for three months now . . . Ciaran was the only one I told but he couldn't have got the letter.
DINKY (*gently*) I thought you knew they didn't allow letters in Irish into the prison . . . 'cause they don't know what you're saying I suppose.
GORETTI. That was the point.

They walk on.

GORETTI. I'm getting a visitor's pass for Saturday. He says he couldn't get me one before now with his family and all.

They pass the statue of the Virgin Mary again. Both look.

DINKY. (*to statue*) Don't you fucking move. I'm warning ye!

Goretti laughs with some relief.

Scene 68 INT. A VISITING CUBICLE IN CRUMLIN ROAD PRISON, DAY

This is a simple partitioned cubicle with two doors opposite each other. Ciaran is sitting on the far side of a small table. There are two chairs on the near side. He gets up and takes one of the chairs round to his side. The door behind him is open and we can see TWO PRISON WARDENS moving together to talk and parting again. They are chatty and joking with each other. Ciaran is nervous. The door opens and Goretti walks in. Ciaran jumps up. The door is locked behind Goretti.

CIARAN. Goretti.

He goes round and they hug each other tightly. Ciaran is overjoyed. The screw is watching them. They sit down, but on opposite sides of the table, holding hands across the top. The screw shuts the door.

CIARAN. I wasn't sure if you'd come. It's great to see you.
GORETTI. I didn't know what to think. I thought you didn't want to see me.
CIARAN. No way, Goretti, I thought about ye a lot . . . Me Ma took it while hard ye know, and what with our boys and all I couldn't get a pass out before now . . . When ye didn't write I thought . . .
GORETTI. But I did . . .
CIARAN. I never got it . . . Who did ye give it to?
GORETTI. It wasn't a 'com'. It went through the censors. Ye never got it because it was in Irish . . . I'm sure they had a good laugh translating it.
CIARAN. (*smiling*) Was it dirty?

Goretti takes her hand out of Ciaran's. She doesn't answer. The smile disappears off Ciaran's face.

CIARAN. Were ye trying to finish with me, Goretti?

Ciaran thinks this is the big shove-over. He takes her hand again.

GORETTI. I'm pregnant.

Ciaran can't believe his ears for a moment and then he falls back in his chair pulling his hands slowly out of Goretti's. She is left with her hands stretched across the table.

CIARAN. You're not serious?

Goretti doesn't answer.

CIARAN. Does anybody know?

Goretti starts to answer but she has barely opened her mouth when Ciaran interrupts her.

CIARAN. How can ye be sure? Have ye been to the doctor?
GORETTI. I haven't been to the doctor but I'm sure.

Ciaran stands up totally distracted.

CIARAN. Fuck me! . . . from the frying pan into the fire.

Goretti gets up and knocks quickly on the door. Ciaran realises what she is doing and he tries to get to her but the empty chair beside him gets in the way. As soon as she hears him getting up SHE SHOUTS.

GORETTI. You fucking bastard!
CIARAN. Goretti, I'm sorry.

The screw opens the door and she walks out without a backward glance, the door shuts. Ciaran is devastated at first, then he is angry at being mortified like that in front of the screws.

CIARAN. Fucking bitch!

Scene 70 EXT. OUTSIDE THE FRONT DOOR OF THE FRIELS' HOUSE, NIGHT

Goretti and Dinky are sitting on the step (or pavement). Dinky is smoking.

GORETTI. Swear to me, Dinky! Swear you'll tell nobody.
DINKY. I swear, Goretti! As God is me witness.

Silence. Dinky passes the cigarette to Goretti. She shakes her head in disgust.

DINKY. Will ye not go to the doctor?
GORETTI. No way! He'd only tell me Ma.

Silence.

DINKY. What are ye going to do?

Goretti doesn't answer. Eventually.

GORETTI. If I miscarry is that the same as an abortion?

Dinky looks hopelessly lost.

DINKY. I don't know, Goretti.

Pause.

DINKY. Are you sure, Goretti? About being pregnant? I mean ye don't look pregnant. Maybe you've got cancer or something.
GORETTI. I wish to God I had.

MARY KENNY

from *There's Something About a Convent Girl*

At school, I was frequently in trouble because I was a very difficult and troublesome child. I think it would now be said that I needed an educational psychologist. I was one of those mixed-up brats; but I guess I did have background problems. I lost my father when I was very young, and I was the last, by a long shot, of a family of four. In some ways, I think I started out as an unwanted child, though as I grew older I became rather the apple of Mama's eye; one of the reasons, I think, why I am against abortion is that in my own life, I know, emotionally, that you can be both an unwanted pregnancy, and subsequently, an adored child. But being both neglected and then indulged is not good for the character, and I think now I was neurotic. One of my fellow-classmates was Brenda Fricker, the actress, and we were, I seem to remember, the naughty girls of the form. She had lost her mother quite young, and I have a feeling that the nuns wanted to be kind to her on that account. She was a sweet, angelic-looking young girl, but, she was also seen as some sort of rebel or non-conformist. She was very popular; as a day-girl she would always do errands for the boarders.

Peig Sayers

from *Farewell to Youth*

Translated by Bryan MacMahon

The following day was a Sunday and everybody was doing his best to get ready for Mass, but when I got out of bed my father was nowhere to be seen. After we came home from Mass, dinner was ready, but there was still no trace of my father nor did anyone know where he had gone to. About six o'clock in the evening he strolled in the door.

'May the morning hoarseness catch you!' said my mother, 'Where were you all day?'

'In Dingle.'

'What did you want there for?'

'To get some place that'd suit that chubby lassie there!'

'And did you get it?'

'There's a place for her in Séamas Curran's house. Don't be a bit uneasy: Nell will be as good as a mother to her.'

'And God help me,' said my mother in a troubled tone of voice, 'what will *I* do?'

'The very best you can, my good woman,' said my father. 'And if there's peace when she's gone so much the better for everyone.'

My mother said no more but put down her head and cried bitterly.

Young as I was, my heart almost broke when I realized what she would have to go through when I was far away from her. I slipped out of the house and went back to the garden; there I sat down and cried my fill. I wasn't thinking of sport nor of play at that time but of the time that lay before me. I was jealous of Cáit-Jim and of the other girls who were as happy as the days are long, playing away for themselves. I thought that the turns of the world are very strange: some people sorrowful and others full of joy. At that particular moment the heart in my breast was broken with sorrow and dissatisfaction. I told myself that if everyone who had a brother's wife in the house was as heart-scalded as I was, then they were all very much to be pitied. My brother, Seán, was a good man but he wore only one leg of the britches.

It was getting late and I came in home; the food was on the table but I didn't eat much of it. Not a syllable out of anyone! They were all subdued, but when the time came for Muiris to arrive he came right in the door and Jim with him. They were chatting and making conversation for a while but they made no great delay because Muiris had a cold.

When my father got the house to himself and the rest were asleep: 'Go to school in the morning, child,' he told me, 'I have to talk to the schoolmaster about you.'

I didn't say a word but drew a sigh. I said my prayers and went to bed. But alas! I didn't get much sleep as I was weighing up the pros and cons of things the whole night long . . .

When I was dressed, I washed my face and hands. I hadn't broken my fast but that made no difference for it wasn't the first time I had gone to school on an empty stomach. When I was ready I took my little bag of books and went down the road. I was only barely in time for school as the Rolls were being called as I went in. The Master looked at me out of a corner of his eye but never said a word.

An hour afterwards the latch on the door was lifted and my father came in. I knew well that the time had come and cold sweat broke out through me. My schooldays were over.

My father had a chat with the Master; after a while the teacher came over to me.

'Your father wants you,' he said in a kindly tone. 'Good luck to you, girl!'

I couldn't speak a word because I was too lonely. My father went off out and I followed him. I'm telling you no lie when I say that there was a lump in my throat as I went home.

As soon as I went in – 'Put on your clothes now,' my father said.

'Wait until I eat a bite anyway?' I answered.

I took some food and then put on my clothes. I caught my shawl and looked up towards the corner at my mother who was seated by

the fire. Her body was huddled up and she was crying softly. I ran
towards her and put my two arms around her.

My father had to come and take me away.

KATE CRUISE O'BRIEN

from *The Homesick Garden*

'You're late, Antonia. What happened? I was *worried*.' I think I'd
prefer the old unworried Mum. Mum, worried, was just like all
the other mothers in the world. You've worried me, she seemed to
say.

'Antonia was knocked off her bike,' said Stephen in his deep
voice and then he squeaked, 'Someone interfered with her saddle.'

'This is Stephen, Mum. Stephen, this is Mum,' I said. Always
one for the formalities.

'How did they interfere with your saddle? How can you
interfere with a saddle?' Mum frowned at Stephen as if it was his
fault.

'They loosened it. It's a sort of joke. They think Antonia's bike
is funny, well that's the sort of childish sort of sense of humour
they have, so they loosened the saddle but they left it on so that
Antonia didn't know it was loose. So when a car knocked against
her, she went over.'

'Oh my God,' said Mum. 'Oh Antonia, oh I'm so sorry. Oh look
at your poor knees.'

'Well, I'll be going then,' said Stephen. He was brave enough
to instruct anyone, including A Mother, but an Emotional Mother
was another thing entirely. I could see that he wanted to run. So
very male. I couldn't help being pleased that there was something
predictable about him.

'Oh no you don't,' said Mum smartly as she pulled him in the door. 'You'll come right in here, Stephen, and tell me about it. And Antonia, go upstairs and wash your knees with Dettol.'

'That,' said Mum an hour later when Stephen had gone, 'is a very nice boy.' I was sitting at the kitchen table near the fire and my bandaged knees were stinging. I'd washed them and put Savlon on them – Dettol indeed – but Savlon wasn't serious enough for Mum, who had unearthed an incredibly ancient and possibly dangerous elastic bandage and bound my knees formally while Stephen declaimed about irresponsibility and schoolboy humour. They were both playing parts, of course, but I must say I enjoyed it enormously.

'A very nice boy,' said Mum. 'Why didn't you mention him before?'

'Well I didn't really know him before,' I said, loosening Mum's safety pins. They were rusty. 'At school they think he's peculiar.'

'Your school seems more than a little peculiar to me,' said Mum grimly. 'That's an expensive middle-class school and they behave like vandals. Fun, *fun* to bully and tease and put your life in danger.'

'All schools are like that, Mum,' I said. 'Most of them are worse. They don't think about danger. If they think it's funny, then you're a spoil-sport if you don't think so too.'

'And what do the teachers think?' asked Mum. 'Stephen said he thought they'd done this to your bike before. He said he thought you might have complained about it?'

'Well yes I did,' I said awkwardly. 'I told Mrs Davis and she said I should report it if it happened again.'

'Oh she did, did she?' said Mum. 'Well this time I'll report it. I'll write to Mrs Davis tomorrow. This WILL NOT DO! Still,' she said, calming down abruptly, 'still, he's a nice boy. I'm glad some good came of it.'

MAEVE BINCHY

from *A Portrait of the Artist as a Young Girl*

I wanted to be a saint. This was not just a childhood ambition: I wanted to be a saint until I was about twenty-two. It wasn't a question of 'I hope it will happen to me'; I was quite convinced that I would be a saint.

I had a very special relationship with God. I regarded him as a friend, and Irish, and somebody who knew me well. He had sent particular tortures my way – like not being good at games (until the marvellous netball 'discovery') and being fat at school. It was bad, very bad, to be fat, so these were the tortures that God was sending to try me. It was all very clear to me.

But I was hoping against hope that I wouldn't see a vision. People who saw visions very often ended up as martyrs; and although I was dead keen to be a saint, I wanted to be a non-martyred saint. Because of all the stories I had heard about the children of Fatima seeing Our Lady in a tree I always kept my eyes down on the road if I was walking anywhere with lots of trees. No visions for me! I had worked out this sainthood very well. You didn't have to be a martyr; you didn't even have to be a nun and devote your whole life to sanctity. You just had to have a special relationship with God and be a sort of intermediary between Him and the rest of the world.

I worried a lot about people who didn't keep up their own religion. I had a friend whose father was a Protestant – a lovely man whom we all adored because he used to give us fourpenny ice-creams when every other father only gave us twopenny ones. He used to drive his wife and children to Mass and then go for a walk on Dun Laoghaire pier. I would spend hours with his daughter wondering if he would be damned and roasted in hell. I felt that if he wasn't converted to Catholicism (which would be the ideal thing) he should at least be going to his own church (which would naturally not be as good as the *real* thing). Imagine this poor unfortunate man being harangued by his eight-year-old daughter and her friend saying, 'Honestly, Mr —, have you thought about it – the devil and the pain that goes on forever?' The more I look back on it, the more I realise what a poisonous little person I was – and having an over-developed imagination didn't help.

Part of the sainthood thing, too, was becoming a Child of Mary. This involved a combination of being in a sodality – a religious group – and being a prefect in school. You couldn't become a Child of Mary unless your peers and the nuns said that you were a person of great worth, high leadership quality and all the rest of it. I went off on my own to do a one-day retreat and then on 8 December I was made a Child of Mary. It was a lovely ceremony with candles all around, and I wore a veil and big blue ribbon with the Child of Mary medal on it. I was bursting with awareness of the importance of it all and always wore this big ribbon on my plump green chest.

But it was not to last. A very short time afterwards I was stripped of the medal, just like a soldier is cashiered from the army by having his buttons cut off. It happened like this. Most of the boarders had boyfriends. I didn't have any, but I became very popular by volunteering to post the boarders' letters to their boyfriends. I used to stuff the letters down the front of my gymslip and smuggle them out for posting. One evening, I was accosted by a nun, who kept talking to me and asking me if I was all right, because I looked as if I were dying of angina, clutching my chest. 'Oh, I'm fine, Mother, fine,' I blurted out, as one by one the letters slipped from under my gymslip. It was so humiliating as the nun picked up the letters addressed to Master Sean O'Brien, Master John Smith and so on. I really felt that the pit of hell was opening up in front of me.

'Isn't it very sad my dear,' she said icily, 'that you are not a person to be trusted? Tomorrow morning at assembly you will give your medal back.'

And so it was that, red-eyed, I handed back my Child of Mary medal. It was a bitter disappointment, particularly in the hot-house atmosphere that existed in a girls' school in those days. I did become a kind of heroine by refusing to disclose who had given me the letters, but if, like you, you were on the way to sainthood it wasn't enough being a popular heroine. I would have much preferred to have been a Child of Mary.

ESTHER JOHNSON

Stella To Dr Swift
on his birth-day, November 30, 1721

St Patrick's Dean, your Country's Pride,
My early and my only Guide,
Let me among the Rest attend,
Your Pupil and your humble Friend,
To celebrate in female Strains
The Day that paid your Mother's Pains;
Descend to take that Tribute due
In Gratitude alone to you.

When Men began to call me fair,
You interposed your timely Care:
You early taught me to despise
The Ogling of a Coxcomb's Eyes;
Show'd where my Judgment was misplaced;
Refined my Fancy and my Taste.
Behold that Beauty just decay'd,
Invoking Art to Nature's Aid:
Forsook by her admiring Train,
She spreads her tatter'd Nets in vain;
Short was her Part upon the Stage;
Went smoothly on for half a Page;
Her Bloom was gone, she wanted Art

As the Scene changed, to change her Part;
She, whom no Lover could resist
Before the second Act was hissed.
Such is the Fate of female Race
With no endowments but a Face;
Before the thirtieth Year of Life,
A Maid forlorn or hated Wife.

Stella to you, her Tutor, owes
That she has ne'er resembled those;
Nor was a Burthen to Mankind
With half her course of Years behind.
You taught how I might Youth prolong
By knowing what was right and wrong;
How from my Heart to bring Supplies
Of Lustre to my fading Eyes;
How soon a beauteous Mind repairs
The loss of changed or falling Hairs;
How Wit and Virtue from within
Send out a smoothness o'er the Skin;
Your Lectures could my Fancy fix,
And I can please at thirty-six.

The Sight of Chloe at fifteen
Coquetting, gives me not the Spleen;
The Idol now of every Fool
Till Time shall make their Passions cool;
Then tumbling down Time's steepy Hill,
While Stella holds her Station still.

O! turn your Precepts into Laws,
Redeem the Women's ruined Cause,
Retrieve lost Empire to our Sex,
That Men may bow their rebel Necks.
Long be the Day that gave you Birth
Sacred to Friendship, Wit and Mirth;

Late dying may you cast a Shred
Of your rich Mantle o'er my Head;
To bear with dignity my Sorrow,
One Day alone, then die Tomorrow.

MARY O'MALLEY

from *The Cloven Rock*

I. Ave

The little girl played
In her overturned boat,
Her church, her shop, her sailing ship.
The only architecture she knew
Had the vaulted roof
Of a sawn-in-two pucán.
She plainchanted with the cuckoo
And Ave, Ave, Ave Maria
Was the song she learned at school.

When they asked how many children
She could see the pained looks
Overcome the breeding.
She felt like scabies or the mange,
Infectious and poor.

II. The Visit

The little girl tightened
The belt on her skimpy
Home-made cotton dress,
Knowing her clothes marked her,
That even the polished shoes were wrong.

But she smiled as she burned,
Shame corseted her frame,
Buckled the words
Coming out of her mouth,
Making even her accent a misshapen thing.

She longed and she hated
But she spoke
Every time one of them came
Graciously, to visit her mother.

IV. Peasants

Her uncle said they were all
A crowd of English feckers
That should be shot. Useless
To the earth and all that walked it.
That shower
Thought we were still peasants.

Isn't a peasant a bird,
A lovely shiny bird
That lives in trees
And gets shot? Not far off
Her uncle said.

VII. Longing

They came in lovely leathery cars
From their big houses
Being nice. What was the evening line
Of roofless coastguard stations
Black against the bedtime sky
To them, or the round towers
Of Slyne Head?

They had pillars and porticoes
And Georgian houses where they sat
Speaking of Beethoven and Bach.
They listened to golden music
At nightfall, and they knew
What each instrument was called.

The little girl twisted.
When they were gone she asked God
For the gift of tongues.

Carraig Scaoilte (The Cloven Rock) is a rock at the edge of Bunowen Bay. When the fishing boats made it inside the Rock on a stormy day, the watching families knew they were safe.

Micheál mac Liammóir

from *All for Hecuba*

I meet suddenly a lanky, mysterious girl with slanting blue-green eyes; her name, she tells me, is Máire O'Keefe, and our youth, for we are both about fourteen, passes by for years in a dream. Some remote kinship is discovered between her father's family and my mother's, we talk of Ireland all day long; I play at night in the theatre and go to the art-school in the mornings, and at last we get back to Ireland together, she persuading her English mother that the air of Howth, near Dublin, is better for the chest than that of London and laying particular stress, for the benefit of an impressionable middle-age, upon the absence of Zeppelins, for this is the spring of 1917 and the daily talk is of raids and black-outs, and Russia has just overthrown the Tsars, and Ireland celebrates the first anniversary of Easter 1916 . . . Then when the war is over she falls ill; it is her lungs, the doctor says, and our dreams take an ugly turn; the air reeks of emulsion and creosote and she and her mother and I travel to Switzerland, and when she is a little better to Roquebrune in the south of France . . . And then in Mentone, Máire, who has battled successfully with tuberculosis for seven years, contracts pneumonia, and in a few days unbelievably, she is dead.

I have been struggling to write in Irish a romantic play on the legend of Diarmuid and Gráinne when her death wrought such havoc with me that to write or to paint any longer became impossible. We were sharing with Hubert Duncombe a flat in the Avenue de Verdun, and all through the brilliant December days that accompanied her last illness, and the unheeded gold of January that followed its conclusion, I would sit at the window watching the jewelled breathless circle of the mountains clambering to the sky; the Casino with its attenuated Baroque all in sparkling cardboard, the crinkled ochre roofs, the imperturbable violet sea, and above all the laughing young women in the streets, and I would think how strange it was that life still went on . . .

Standing now with my back to the window and the briefly twilit circle of the mountains and the sea, I looked again at the dead girl lying on the bed and began to dream about my life with her.

She and I are sitting in the Theatre at Monte Carlo, and Hubert Duncombe, elegant and cool as a fish, is leaning over her with a big light-blue programme, saying: '*Carnaval* to-night. And Biches, and *Tricorne*, and *Igor*. Of course *Igor*'s at the end, it always is,' and she answers, 'Well, where do you want them to put it? You can't begin a meal with *fine champagne*.'

And now we're walking slowly through a wood at home in Howth and she murmurs, 'The worst of having consumption is not that you're ill, but that you're perfectly well and can do nothing at all. Danger is so monotonous — you can't cough without knowing you're on the edge of an abyss. Even the wind is a menace,' and as she speaks we pass out of the wood, and a white gull wheels out of the mist and flies over the broken heather towards the sea.

And in Roquebrune a year ago in the garden over the sea with cypress and pomegranate trees above us, the senses lulled into security, the warm, translucent eyelids laced with blue and golden light, she had said suddenly, 'Have you ever noticed how in sunshine all the places one loves are the same? Howth and Roquebrune, the mountains and the desert, they're really all one, you see. What do these time theorists really mean? That all eternity is one enormous moment? Then all the earth is one great golden cup, a Noah's Ark in space, brimming with life. But you can only understand that through the sun.'

'And when it rains?' I asked, and she answered quite gravely, 'No, rain separates. It's the rain that isolates us in Ireland. When we have the sun, the hills in Connemara are those where Daphnis lived.'

. . . But she lived in Ireland and then in Switzerland, and fate had said she was to die in France.

And here she was very still and more lovely than she had been in life, although her wonderful eyes, her only claim to beauty, were closed for ever, and somehow I had to go. Life is like a waiting-room, sometimes. When people die it is like a waiting-room, dusty and interminable. And suddenly, lifting your head, you see a poster that attracts your attention. And then, as though you dreamed it all, you're in a train whistling away God knows where, smoking and talking, sharing your food with other passengers, and gazing out of the windows. But the waiting-room is in your soul and you never quite rid yourself of it. Oh no. You hardly, indeed, want to.

JOAN LINGARD

from *Sisters by Rite*

We stepped into the streets of Dublin. The bright lights astounded me.

'It's like daytime.'

'This is what it'll be like in Belfast,' said Aunt Belle, 'when the lights come on again.'

But I knew that it could never be quite like this. There was an excitement about the city that made me want to skip. The streets swarmed with people who looked as if they were enjoying themselves. Pub doors swung open spilling out light and noise. The restaurants were busy, the shop windows full. I was enthralled.

I told Rosie that I was going to live in Dublin when I grew up.

'But what about the nuns and priests?'

I hadn't noticed that many.

'Not noticed them? You must need glasses, Cora Caldwell?'

There had been so many other things to do, I retorted, like eating knickerbocker glories in Cafollas, drinking tea in Bewley's Oriental Tea Room, shopping in O'Connell Street, walking in the Phoenix Park, taking the tram to Dun Laoghaire and walking along the sea front; and there had been so many other things to look at, like chocolates piled up on shop counters, pounds and pounds of them, and silk stockings and diamond rings.

IVY BANNISTER

Roz, Danny, Henry and Mum

'Peace offering,' Henry says, holding out a mug of steaming coffee like a sacramental cup.

Doggie wags her tail at Henry, faithless bitch. Without a word, Roz pulls the duvet over her head. She'll take nothing that Henry has touched first.

He creaks backwards into the kitchen. In her imagination, Roz can see them there, snogging in the wicker breakfast chairs. Henry and Mum. Mum in the kitchen with her lover. The two of them, floating in a glass bubble.

Roz shivers. She hates the way Mum has changed since Henry. Mum has gone all soft and flabby. She has even stopped wearing a bra. Her breasts seem to spill out of her clothes, and when she wears a blouse with buttons up the front, you can see everything through the gaps. At her age, it isn't decent.

And all for Henry with his eyes that move in different directions, and a voice so soft you have to lean towards him to hear. Henry is old and he's bald, for Chrissake, so why should he be in Roz's kitchen, holding hands with her Mum? . . .

And yet . . . Roz can remember what it was like, when she was a little girl. Climbing into her mother's bed on a cold and shivery morning, after Daddy had gone to work. Then her mother's warm body would curl round hers to warm it.

There wasn't much point in getting into Mum's bed these days.

If only Henry would get run over by a car.

MAEVE KELLY

from *Orange Horses*

More trouble, Elsie thought. Someone had stolen the pony.

Then the door was pushed in and Johnny and Danny burst upon her, pulling at her blankets, crying, 'Get up, get up, Brigid has taken the pony.'

Fonsie was after them, face red with rage, shouting, 'That's your rearing for you, the little bitch has gone off riding like a tinker on the piebald.'

Well then, thought Elsie, stroking her wired up jaw, here's a right how do ye do. The little bitch is up on a pony and away like the wind.

'Wait till I lay hands on the little rap,' Fonsie said bitterly. 'Bringing disgrace unto the whole family. She's your daughter all right. But is she mine? Answer me that will you?'

'She is yours,' Elsie said. 'She didn't get that wild blood from me. Did you ever see one of my sisters up on a pony? Have any of my family got red hair? Every one of us has brown eyes. 'Twasn't from the wind she got the blue eyes and the hair.'

'She could be Danny's. From day one he was hanging around you. From the minute I brought you back.'

'He was twelve then,' Elsie said, wearily playing the chorus to an old tune.

'What has that got to do with it? You were fifteen. Brigid's near twelve now. She's not like a girl at all. There could be something wrong with her. When your jaw is better let you see to it and when she gets back here I'll give her a lesson she won't forget. Don't give me any of your old guff.' . . .

'I'm here, Mama,' Brigid was beside her, hopping up and down on the bed. 'Did you see me? I never fell off once. Did Dada see me?'

Exasperation filled every inch of Elsie's body. It took charge of the pain. She wanted to sit up and shake Brigid till her teeth rattled. She opened her mouth to say your father'll kill you and good enough for you when Brigid said, 'I wouldn't have done it if he hadn't turned orange. The sun turned him orange and I wanted to ride him while he was that colour.'

'He wasn't that colour at all,' Elsie said. 'You only thought he was that colour.'

'He was. I saw him,' Brigid insisted, her crossed eyes glinting with temper. 'Can I cuddle into you, Mama? Can I sleep here with you?' What was the use of anything, thought Elsie. The child was safe and sound and wanting to sleep beside her and she didn't want anyone in the bed with her. She wanted to toss and turn and groan in privacy.

'I might keep you awake.'

'You won't, Mama. And I'll get you anything you want. Will I make you a sup of tay? Did the fellas see me? What did they say?'

Elsie began to laugh. 'Oh my God,' she groaned, 'don't make me laugh. My jaw aches. They were raging. They'll kill you when they get their hands on you.'

'I don't care,' Brigid said. 'It was worth it. I'll kick them and I'll ride the pony again and again. I've him tethered now. I fell off loads of times but I got up again. It's easy. I'll practise. If they see I'm good, they'll let me do it. I'm not like you, Mama. I'm like my Dada and no one will bate me into the ground. You shouldn't let Dada hit you.'

DAISY FINGALL

from *Seventy Years Young*

My frock had come home, and if one should possess in time the wardrobe of the princess in the fairy tale, no other frock would be the same as that first ball dress for one's first Ball. How deliciously the paper rustled as one disturbed it! I lifted the frock out reverently, and laid it on the bed. Just white tulle, yards and yards of it. What more could any girl want? The full skirt was made over a stiffened foundation to make it stand out. I had no difficulty about the waist. I had as many inches then to mine as I had years, and while my contemporaries were being laced by exhausted mothers and maids into torturing corsets, I was only troubled as to how to make myself seem a little fatter. When I was dressed, I looked in the long solemn mirror, and of course did not recognise myself. I stared at a stranger whom I saw for the first and last time. Never again can one see oneself in one's first ball dress. As impossible to recapture one's first vision of a place afterwards grown familiar.

A mirror was a more magic thing before the days of electric light. Some one held a pair of candles high, and they glimmered in the glass like little distant stars. One of them was caught in my hair.

My face was very solemn and serious, as well it might be on such an occasion. I was seventeen and grown up. And it was a very much more serious and sudden matter, growing up, in those days than it is now. One became, or one tried to become, a young lady. I must say good-bye now to my races over the Dublin Mountains for which I had lifted my full long skirt over my knees, to the riding ponies astride up the mountain paths and, perhaps, to the sweet thing that had stirred only so faintly between boy and girl in the summer dusk.

I go very solemnly to my first Ball, in my whispering white tulle dress, with the scarlet berries in my hair. I had gone shopping deliciously beforehand in Grafton Street, buying long white gloves, open-work stockings, finest linen handkerchiefs with a little lace border, and other etceteras.

I did not always go to Grafton Street. Or perhaps I sometimes made a *détour*. For there was a bright autumn day when I walked back to Buswell's by way of Kildare Street. I wore a little fur jacket with the neatest of waists, and a tiny hat perched on the side of my hair, a little jaunty feather in it; altogether very like the hats that are worn to-day. I was quite unconscious and unaware of a young man who came out of the Kildare Street Club as I passed on the opposite side of the road, looked at me, and then, at a most discreet and courteous distance, followed me back to the hotel, into which I disappeared. That is how Fingall first saw me, and he declared afterwards that he fell in love with me at first sight . . .

My first meet

I was swung up on to an enormous horse, guaranteed wise and confidential enough to carry even a complete ignoramus across country . . .

My wise and confidential mount must be in the fashion, so he goes curvetting sideways with a great show of impatience. I hold the reins with small, incompetent, cold fingers. Sitting here by the fire talking, I can feel that coldness of a hunting morning, my first hunting morning, and of many such mornings to follow. Fingall has obviously forgotten me. Even his face looks chilly above his red coat. We move off slowly, down a lane, squelching in the mud, through a gate. Lifeboat, in his hurry, knocks me against the post. Has he broken my leg? No. I am still whole. But, of course, I shall be killed and no one will mind at all! There is nothing like going out hunting with your best friends, to teach you how little you matter to them.

Then we are galloping. Over the field, up the hill. I have ceased to be cold. How good the feeling of the ground under a horse's feet is! . . . Lifeboat is going like a wave. Oh, this is ecstasy! Almost better than the Blue Danube last night.

Although I had never hunted before that day, the trusty Lifeboat carried me safely over the most alarming country, until, taking a jump, he jerked up his head and hit me on the nose. I dropped the reins and fell off in agony. Fingall came galloping back. (After all I do matter to someone!) 'Are you hurt?' 'He has broken my nose,' I sobbed. And indeed I believe always that that accident did alter the shape of it. My fierce Irish-speaking nurse with her scrubbing had made it turn upwards. My friends assured me that the change was an improvement.

I spent that night with a large raw beefsteak over my nose to keep it from turning black. The remedy was evidently successful for I appeared at the Ball the following night apparently quite undamaged by my first hunting accident.

BERNADETTE DEVLIN

from *The Price of My Soul*

Faced with the police charge, the students' immediate reaction was to sit down. I had the loudhailer, and I shouted through it: 'Everybody sit down as quickly as possible, and then we'll see who's causing the violence!', and instead of running everybody just flopped to the ground. The police hadn't time to stop marching: they stumbled over the first rows, and it didn't improve their tempers to know that television photographers were filming the Royal Ulster Constabulary falling over students in their eager stomp forward in the interests of peace. Finally, the District Inspector (known from his PR visits to the university as 'Everybody's Friend DI Bradley') established some sort of order among his forces, got them all up on their feet again, and formed the cordon. Finding the whole thing hilarious, I turned round to one of the policemen in the cordon and said, 'There you are, you see! We're all sitting down comfortably!' I expected some kind of friendly sarcastic answer, but this fellow immediately threw his foot out in a most violent kick which landed on my ankle, and knocked the feet from under me. 'All but you, stupid bitch!' he said. And I found myself sitting very uncomfortably and very suddenly. Bernadette Devlin, poor creature, everybody's kid sister – immediately about twenty males were up and making for the constable, and I had to hobble up and get them to sit down again before the situation got out of control. We were a very self-disciplined lot: instead of giving the man a bashing, the students who had seen the incident began writing out reports of it, and getting other witnesses to sign. We'd been trained to do this by friends in the Society of Labour Lawyers. We knew more about legal evidence than the police did, we had more self-control, and we were better-humoured: whichever way they took us, we always had the upper hand.

We knew that according to the law we could refuse to give a policeman any information, unless he arrested us; and we also knew that if we challenged a policeman for his name or number, he was obliged to tell us one of them. I turned to the constable who had kicked me and asked him his name. He refused to answer. He didn't meet my eyes, but looked straight ahead and kept his mouth shut. I asked the policeman beside him. 'I don't know,' said he, 'I've never seen him before.'

'Does he come from Belfast?'

'I don't know. I'm not from Belfast.' This was a damaging admission: it meant that riot-squad policemen had been brought in from the countryside to deal with the non-violent students. We had all this immediately written down, witnessed and signed by the people who had heard it. Then I called the District Inspector over and said, 'This man refuses to give me his name,' and Mr Bradley knew enough of the law to oblige the man to give it. He was a constable from Queen Street Barracks, Belfast. The DI wouldn't let me have his number, so I said, 'Fair enough, I'll take my statement to the Queen Street Barracks and see what can be done about this disgusting behaviour, lowering the tone of our force.' We liked to make fun of them like that: they were the police who beat us, but when they behaved in an ignorant fashion we pulled them up for disgracing Northern Ireland. They couldn't win.

Later, when I went to the barracks, I found that this constable had apparently made a practice of kicking demonstrators and was so stupid he always got caught. My complaint, coming on top of several others, would be the last straw: out of the force he would go. And such was the extent of my political development at the time that, ignorant thug though he was, I couldn't see the point of adding to Northern Ireland's unemployed. I took my statement home again and, until such time as he kicked somebody else, he probably remained in the police force.

Emma Cooke

from *The Bridge*

About fifty yards up from the cove the river was spanned by the red iron railway bridge and whenever Laura and Catherine heard the whistle of a train in the distance they would race back to Elsie, and whoever got there first would hold the infant in her arms while the three of them gazed at the metal monster rattling across the bridge and Laura and Catherine would argue about whether it was going to Dublin where Auntie lived or to Tipperary where Granny lived or to 'somewhere else'.

Laura – who had been to Dublin once to visit Santa Claus and Toyland – claimed superior knowledge. The Dublin trains were the ones heading towards the chimneys of the electricity power station. She had seen them out of the carriage window on that magical morning, gleaming like some giant's castle through the raindrops slithering down the glass. And coming home in the evening – tired out, sticky, a damp patch on her new coat where she had dropped some ice cream in a big, bright parlour with loud music and shiny, coloured tables and millions of people she had never seen before in her life – the chimneys had welcomed her back with her present for Catherine, whose turn it would be next year, and the game of Ludo that Santa Claus in Snow White's Palace had pulled out of a big cardboard drum and a new elephant brooch bought in Woolworths pinned onto her stripy jumper . . .

Catherine never did go to Dublin after all. It should have been her turn before last Christmas. When the time came, and she should have been roaring away with Mummy in the big train, the money from her money-box safe in her Sunday shoulder bag, waving goodbye to Laura left on the station platform, they got baby Elsie instead, and Mummy said she was sorry, but no one from their house would be going anywhere for a long, long time.

Not that it really mattered. Baby Elsie was nicer than Santa Claus or Snow White's Palace. Nicer even than Rosabelle, the doll who could sleep and drink and wet her nappy. Elsie's blue eyes stared up at the grassy hills – which were not even proper hills, only small mounds – as if they were the biggest mountains in the world. Her pink face crumpled and silvery tears sailed down her cheeks like little fishes when a butterfly with orange-tipped wings landed on her nose. Lots of things surprised her. A blade of grass stroked under her fat chin made her legs wave in the air and her mouth open so that you could see her two new teeth. A cardigan dropped on her face for a second or two made her go all silent, and watching the pupils of her eyes contract when you lifted it up again reminded Catherine of the way her own night-time dreams vanished when she woke up and it was a school day.

And there were some good games they could play with her using the pram: racetrack – down the bank, round the next gap in the hills and back through the cowslip field. They took turns, Laura or Catherine sitting on the edge of the bank counting 'one-a-pecker . . . two-a-pecker', the way you did between lightning flashes and thunderclaps, while the other one galloped the pram around the route and Elsie bumped about on her pillows, fists waving and her solemn eyes encouraging the pusher to clippety-clop as fast as she possibly could.

SHEILA O'HAGAN

Going to the Gaiety

I thought of you as the hard man
ruling a house through the bottle
but when the opera opened
we climbed as one
up a hundred steps
and sat, dreamy from song
and the height of the gods,
to hear sad Traviata
peer down at Mimi in damson
Othello in saffron damask

and were lost in the lustre
of gaud and strut
as the scent of the heated crowd
rose in our faces like opium
and I squeezed close to your old serge
with its years of tobacco,
feeling emotion swell
with the taut of the long sweet note

releasing you
to be the father I loved
who wandered home
through the gold lit dark of Dublin
arm in arm with his daughter,
whistling the tune of your man
the Italian tenor.

JOAN O'NEILL

from *Daisy Chain War*

As we walked home slowly the sun went in, the light faded and it began to rain. Pauline Byrne and Tess Mathews came running up behind us just as the heavy drops fell wetting our thin summer frocks.

'Youse'll be drowned if youse go home. C'mon into our basement. We're starting a game of hospital,' Tess said.

'Her mother's out,' Pauline said. 'C'mon.'

May Tully was standing at a long scrubbed table in the middle of the big empty room of their disused basement.

'Hullo,' she said as I turned away.

'Aw c'mon Lizzie. Play with us,' Tess pleaded.

'I'm the surgeon,' May Tully addressed Vicky with a face that was ready to start a fight. She ignored me completely.

'I'd love to play. I'm going to be a doctor some day anyway.' Vicky's face was wreathed in smiles and I thought I'd better stay if it cheered her up.

'We're performing an operation. You Jimmy, strip off and lie up on the table. I'm going to scrub up.'

Jimmy made for the door.

Our hands reached out and grabbed him and pulled off his shirt. He was forced to lie on the table while Tess, Pauline and Vicky held him down. I kept nicks on the door.

'It's only a game, coward.' May returned covered in a white sheet, a pair of old gardening gloves on her hands.

She began to make imaginary cuts on his chest with a pencil and he groaned at suitable intervals, because she was tickling him. May was obsessed with bodies and bloodthirsty rituals. She had a glazed sadistic look in her eyes as she diagnosed Jimmy.

'Appendix,' she pronounced. 'It's about to burst. We'll have to remove the patient's trousers. Knife, Nurse,' she called to Vicky.

Jimmy went to leap off the table but Vicky, with a piece of a rag tied around her mouth, pushed him and held him down with a strength that belied her skinny appearance.

'Hold still,' her voice was muffled but insistent and he shivered as she reached out to open the buttons of his worn brown corduroy pants. May covered his mouth with her dirty hand to stifle his screams. The others snorted with suppressed laughter as Jimmy's grimy under-pants were revealed and examined closely by Vicky.

'Naked did you say Doctor?' she asked, a gleam in her eye, her small face flushed with delight.

'Correct, Nurse.'

Jimmy wriggled and squirmed, choking his protest, but there was no stopping Vicky.

'I've seen lots of naked men,' she declared. 'In the war you know,'

'Oh la de da I'm sure,' Tess mocked as Jimmy's pants fell to the floor.

'What's going on here?'

Mrs Mathews came thundering down the back stairs and into the room.

'I heard the commotion from upstairs. What in God's name are you doing lying there half-naked, Jimmy Scanlon? In front of all these girls. You ought to be ashamed of yourself.'

Jimmy half-rose from the table, purple with fear and embarrassment.

'Get dressed and get out of here. Go home all of you at once before I tell your mothers that you're up to no good.'

'We was having a game of hospitals, that's all,' chirped Vicky, looking as innocent as a baby.

ENID STARKIE

from *A Lady's Child*

My mother had been a pupil at Alexandra School, and some of the teachers who had taught her were still there when we arrived, and they had, with the intervening years, not modernised their methods of teaching or their ideas on education. The headmistress in my mother's time – and in our time as well – was Miss Mulvaney, LL.D., a woman of high intelligence and great force of character. She was in appearance the typical pioneer headmistress. She always dressed in Victorian, stiff, black clothes whose style she never changed and her straight grey hair was drawn into a tight knot at the back of her head. She always wore steel-rimmed glasses. She was of a colossal size, though she claimed, like so many excessively stout people, to have been as slim as a poplar when young. 'You should have seen me riding bareback!' she used often to say to us in class. But I used to think, when I was a child, that nothing smaller than an elephant could have carried her. In spite of her great bulk and weight she had a faculty, most distressing in a headmistress, of moving completely silently down the corridors and appearing unheard and unannounced when some unfortunate child was being guilty of some misdemeanour. She had regular classical features which some people might have thought handsome, though there was something too hard and intellectual, too inhuman, in her appearance to make a sympathetic appeal. But she was, in fact, like many people of rough exterior, very warmhearted, although she looked incapable of gentleness and weakness, and she certainly could not stand ordinary human folly, nor bear fools or dullards gladly. She was a woman of inflexible personality, as if hewn from a big block of granite, on large noble lines. Many people felt oppressed by her, for she had little patience with slowness and stupidity, very little patience indeed with women. Like most feminists, like most women who have struggled hard for intellectual liberty and recognition, she had a profound and unacknowledged contempt for women and much preferred the company of men. She often made mothers feel perfect idiots when they went to enrol their daughters at the school.

I can vividly recall the day when I was taken by my mother to be enrolled at the school. Dr Mulvaney was a friend of my father, whom she greatly admired, and she received us ahead of the other waiting mothers and children. I could see that my mother was not used to being treated in a summary fashion and that she did not like being hastily dismissed. She tried to lead the conversation herself, and she said, 'Her father wishes her to specialise in languages.' Dr Mulvaney took no notice and would certainly not have tolerated any interference in the curriculum or conduct of the school. 'Her father and I think that she shows special aptitude for languages,' my mother insisted, 'and we would like her to make them her special study.'

'I understand, Mrs Starkie, I understand perfectly,' answered Dr Mulvaney impatiently, because she hated people to waste time in repetition and she thought this a feminine trait. 'But I do not think it answers any purpose to discuss the child's attainments until these have been ascertained. I do not think I need detain you any longer, but I should like to put Enid through a short examination.'

My mother then departed and I was left to the mercies of Dr Mulvaney. After bowing my mother politely off the premises, she returned to her office puffing heavily from her exertions. 'Sit down while I read these letters,' she said to me in a kindly voice. 'Sit down, didn't I tell you!' she bellowed, when she saw me hesitate in the choice of a chair. 'And for God's sake don't twiddle your fingers like that, any one would think you had Saint Vitus's dance.' I was very frightened, but she was not angry and I was later to learn that her manner was largely bluster signifying nothing. I watched her read her letters rapidly, slitting them open with a quick movement of her gigantic paper-knife, and then throw them away into the waste-paper basket. 'Never be a parent, Enid,' she cried, 'and above all never be a mother!' She roared loudly with laughter at her own fun.

She was interrupted in her task by Gunning, the browbeaten porter, a poor rabbit of a man, who put his head round the door and said: 'There's a lady and a little girl to see ye, Doctor!'

'Didn't you know I was engaged, Gunning?' roared Dr Mulvaney. 'Put them in the waiting-room! Put them in the waiting-room!' But any brains poor Gunning may ever have possessed – and they can never have been many even in his hey-day – had long since been blasted out of his head by many years of service under Dr Mulvaney, and he stood fiddling with the knob of the door, looking at her blankly.

'Here, get out of my way!' she exclaimed impatiently, pushing past him into the hall. Then she drove the terrified mother and little girl before her into the waiting-room, saying, 'Dr Mulvaney will see you presently!' Then she returned to her study, laughing to herself, her anger and impatience now evaporated. 'The stupidity and slowness of Gunning sometimes drive me crazy,' she said, 'but he's a decent sort, a decent, willing sort, poor man, God help him!'

Then she bade me follow her to a classroom for my test. 'Have you a pen?' she asked as we walked along the corridors, but I could only shake my head. 'Whoever heard of going to an examination without a pen?' she said, and I tried to explain that I had not known that there was to be an examination. 'Don't answer me

back, child, it is not polite. And for God's sake hold up your head
or you'll grow up a hunch-back.'

OLIVER ST JOHN GOGARTY

Golden Stockings

Golden stockings you had on
In the meadow where you ran;
And your little knees together
Bobbed like pippins in the weather
When the breezes rush and fight
For those dimples of delight;
And they dance from the pursuit,
And the leaf looks like the fruit.

I have many a sight in mind
That would last if I were blind;
Many verses I could write
That would bring me many a sight.
Now I only see but one,
See you running in the sun;
And the gold-dust coming up
From the trampled butter-cup.

3

Love

J. M. SYNGE

from *The Playboy of the Western World*

PEGEEN (*looking at him playfully*) And it's that kind of poacher's love you'd make, Christy Mahon, on the sides of Neifin, when the night is down?

CHRISTY It's little you'll think if my love's a poacher's, or an earl's itself, when you'll feel my two hands stretched around you, and I squeezing kisses on your puckered lips, till I'd feel a kind of pity for the Lord God is all ages sitting lonesome in His golden chair.

PEGEEN That'll be right fun, Christy Mahon, and any girl would walk her heart out before she'd meet a young man was your like for eloquence, or talk at all.

CHRISTY (*encouraged*) Let you wait to hear me talking till we're astray in Erris, when Good Friday's by, drinking a sup from a well, and making mighty kisses with our wetted mouths, or gaming in a gap of sunshine, with yourself stretched back unto your necklace, in the flowers of the earth.

PEGEEN (*in a low voice, moved by his tone*) I'd be nice so, is it?

CHRISTY (*with rapture*) If the mitred bishops seen you that time, they'd be the like of the holy prophets I'm thinking, do be straining the bars of paradise to lay eyes on the Lady Helen of Troy, and she abroad pacing back and forward with a nosegay in her golden shawl.

PEGEEN (*with real tenderness*) And what is it I have, Christy Mahon, to make me fitting entertainment for the like of you, that has such poet's talking and such bravery of heart?

CHRISTY (*in a low voice*) Isn't there the light of seven heavens in your heart alone the way you'll be an angel's lamp to me from this out, and I abroad in the darkness spearing salmons in the Owen or the Carrowmore?

PEGEEN If I was your wife I'd be along with you those nights, Christy Mahon, the way you'd see I was a great hand at coaxing bailiffs, or coining funny nicknames for the stars of night.

CHRISTY You is it? Taking your death in the hailstones or in the fogs of dawn.

PEGEEN Yourself and me would shelter easy in a narrow bush (*with a qualm of dread*); but we're only talking, maybe, for this would be a poor, thatched place to hold a fine lad is the like of you.

CHRISTY (*putting his arm around her*) If I wasn't a good Christian it's on my naked knees I'd be saying my prayers and paters to every jackstraw you have roofing your head, and every stony pebble is paving the laneway to your door.

PEGEEN (*radiantly*) If that's the truth I'll be burning candles from this out to the miracles of God that have brought you from the South to-day and I with my gowns bought ready, the way that I can wed you, and not wait at all.

CHRISTY It's miracles and that's the truth. Me there toiling a long while and walking a long while not knowing at all I was drawing all times nearer to this holy day.

PEGEEN And myself a girl was tempted to go sailing the seas till I'd marry a Jewman with ten kegs of gold, and I not knowing at all there was the like of you drawing nearer, like the stars of God.

CHRISTY And to think I'm long years hearing women talking that talk to all bloody fools, and this the first time I've heard the like of your voice talking sweetly for my own delight.

PEGEEN And to think it's me is talking sweetly, Christy Mahon, and I the fright of seven townlands for my biting tongue. Well, the heart's a wonder; and I'm thinking there won't be our like in Mayo for gallant lovers from this hour today.

Hate Goes Just as Far as Love

(Seventeenth Century)

TRANSLATED BY BRENDAN KENNELLY

Woman full of hate for me
    Do you not recall the night
When we together, side by side,
      Knew love's delight?

If you remembered woman, how,
    While the sun lost its heat,
You and I grew hot —
      But why repeat?

Do you recall my lips on yours,
    Soft words you said,
And how you laid your curving arm
      Under my head?

Or do you remember, O sweet shape,
    How you whispered passionately
That God Almighty had never made
      A man like me?

I gave all my heart to you,
    Gave all, yet could not give enough;
Now, I've your hate. O skin like flowers,
      This hate goes just as far as love.

If a man believes he loves a woman
    And that she loves him too,
Let him know one thing for certain —
      It is not true.

Reconciliation

(Sixteenth Century)

TRANSLATED BY BRENDAN KENNELLY

Do not torment me, woman,
    Let our two minds be as one,
Be my mate in my own land
    Where we may live till life is done.

Put your mouth against my mouth
    You whose skin is fresh as foam,
Take me in your white embrace
    And let us love till kingdom come.

Slender graceful girl, admit
    Me soon into your bed,
Discord, pain will disappear
    When we stretch there side by side.

For your sweet sake, I will ignore
    Every girl who takes my eye,
If it's possible, I implore
    You do the same for me.

As I have given from my heart
    Passion for which alone I live,
Let me now receive from you
    The love you have to give.

The Coolun

(Seventeenth Century)

TRANSLATED BY SIR SAMUEL FERGUSON

O had you seen the Coolun
   Walking down by the cuckoo's street,
With the dew of the meadow shining
   On her milk-white twinkling feet!
My love she is, and my coleen oge,
   And she dwells in Bal'nagar;
And she bears the palm of beauty bright
   From the fairest that in Erin are.

In Bal'nagar is the Coolun,
   Like the berry on the bough her cheek;
Bright beauty dwells for ever
   On her fair neck and ringlets sleek;
Oh, sweeter is her mouth's soft music
   Than the lark or thrush at dawn,
Or the blackbird in the greenwood singing
   Farewell to the setting sun.

Rise up, my boy! make ready
   My horse, for I forth would ride,
To follow the modest damsel,
   Where she walks on the green hillside:
For ever since our youth were we plighted
   In faith, troth, and wedlock true –
She is sweeter to me nine times over,
   Than organ or cuckoo!

For, ever since my Childhood
   I've loved the fair and darling child;
But our people came between us,
   And with lucre our pure love defiled:

Ah, my woe it is, and my bitter pain,
    And I weep it night and day,
That the coleen bawn of my early love
    Is torn from my heart away.

Sweetheart and faithful treasure,
    Be constant still, and true;
Nor for want of herds and houses
    Leave one who would ne'er leave you.
I'll pledge you the blessèd Bible,
    Without and eke within,
That the faithful God will provide for us,
    Without thanks to kith or kin.

Oh, love, do you remember
    When we lay all night alone,
Beneath the ash in the winter storm,
    When the oak wood round did groan?
No shelter then from the blast had we,
    The bitter blast or sleet,
But your gown to wrap about our heads,
    And my coat around our feet.

MOYA CANNON

Afterlove

How could I have forgotten
the sickness,
the inescapability.
My strange love,
it frightens my life.
We sail high seas
and watch the voyages of stars.

Sometimes they collide.
Did you know, you make my head flame.
Blue flames and purple flames leap about my head.
I had once a thousand tongues,
but tonight,
my head is crashing through the sky,
my head is flaming on a dish.

My love,
carry it in carefully,
My love,
carry it in with trumpets.

ROSITA SWEETMAN

from *On Our Backs: Sexual Attitudes in a Changing Ireland*

MARIANNE New York was sex without any vibe at all. Just like putting it into a milk bottle or something.
CASS I always find it amazing if you go to bed with a guy and he turns out to be really gentle and affectionate. Being gentle is very intimate and personal, it throws me off my track! You know, the first night you're trying to prove something.
MARIANNE I used to feel if there was a really good sexual attraction everything else would flow. Now I don't think it works like that. For it to develop into a relationship you've got to get to know the person a bit rather than just hopping into a fucking thing. The really good relationships around now are ones that didn't just start on a fucking basis.
CASS I certainly feel ready for a steady relationship but I don't think it's going to be easy to find. The whole sexual make-up

doesn't allow for something deeper. And if you go out looking for it there's a sort of smell off you. A half starved look!

MARIANNE I want to get my career thing together so a relationship is out of the question. When I'm in one I get lost in a kind of dream.

CASS When I lived with Dick I hated all the shit of washing up and buying food and things. I had a big romantic idea about sitting up in a double bed with silk sheets, smoking big joints and watching telly.

MARIANNE But you're going to have to get into housework when you leave home anyway.

JOE You've got to work much harder at a relationship.

CASS You've got to make compromises and sacrifices.

MARIANNE That's exactly why I don't want it. I never want to compromise: I did it once, I craved a relationship but it was more the idea than the person that really mattered. Now it would have to be someone who fitted into my thing.

DAVID THOMSON

· from *Woodbrook*

I was completely innocent at first – to use the word in the Irish colloquial sense which is something between guileless and ignorant. I was so innocent in the year of the bees that I laid my happiness open for all to see – Phoebe on my lap at lessons, laughing by the open window of Aunt Nina's room, reciting Latin chants I had invented. 'Feles Felix, Felix Feles', cat happy, happy cat – Phoebe with her cheek resting on the open pages of *Heath's French Grammar* in the long grass by the tennis court and my arm about her and my wandering caress – Phoebe and me in the boat on the lake or walking home hand in hand, or bicycling with my arm round her shoulder pretending to help her up a hill. Her affectionate familiarity was unhidden too. When guests of the stiffer sort were expected, Ivy used to entreat her not to speak to me as though I was her favourite dog.

I judge my innocence by the spontaneous response I made a year later to Ivy's first expression of worry, so delicately put to me one rainy afternoon when she found me alone in the drawing-room. 'Phoebe's too taken up with you,' she said, and I answered at once, 'It's all right. You needn't worry, because I feel the same about her. But more so.'

I was startled and downhearted when I saw this did not reassure her. I meant that I would not suddenly leave Phoebe heartbroken, which was the only bad result I could foresee in the affair, which had inevitably, as Ivy must have known, developed into a state of passion too strong to be fulfilled by a light and loving kiss. It was fulfilled, though not in an adult way, and Ivy never spoiled it for Phoebe by inspiring her with guilt, although, when at last she grew frightened, she did find a way of separating us.

This 'innocence', or ignorance of the judgement of the world, allowed us into an exclusive state of grace that shut out guilt, from which I fell by stages. I remember for example a sense of relief when she became fourteen, because, although the law said sixteen, fourteen was I knew a normal age for marriage in some countries. No such thought would have entered my head in the state of grace. It was inspired by other people's anxiety. And when at last an open accusation came it fell like a blot of ink on a poem . . .

The honeymoon is said to have been the month in which hydromel, the wine of honey, was drunk after a wedding. Atilla the Hun drank so much after his that he died. There ought to be a ceremonial form of disengagement too, a specially chosen drink could be part of it, to be taken during the last month and used among other forms of diversion, as marriage games and whiskey were till recently used at wakes to dissipate some of the sorrows of death and construct a new life upon each grave.

DOROTHEA HERBERT

from *Retrospections of Dorothea Herbert* *1770–1806*

– Oh John Roe! Too adorable Man! These were the very Sentiments your looks expressed at that Moment – I could not be mistaken – Love helpd me to read your inmost Thoughts – Unkind John Roe! My Passion and Despair at that moment should have bound you to me for Ever! A poor timid Creature was I! Inexperienced in Worldly Craft, and bound down to Silence by Fear, Modesty, and Education! Alas I had then no Weapon, no Defence – Doom'd to suffer like a poor Dumb Brute whatever my severe Tyrant inflicted! He had me taken in inextricable snares! Nor had I yet learnd to Shun them or defend Myself – Ungratefull John Roe! – How terrible was the moment that joined us! and how terrible were we both to each Other at that black Instant when you Infamously resolved to forsake me and I as desperately Abandon'd Myself to Despair! I swear by the great God of Heaven I think that Hour united us in Bonds that were indissoluble – In an Eternal Union sacred and sure – That Bolt of Heaven or Hell struck him a determined Villain but all its Terrors lighted on me and left me as a stiffend Corpse – Blasted! – Undone for Ever!

Sure No Woman had ever such strong Claims to any Man's Love as I had to John Roe's for No Woman was ever so wrap'd up in One Man or so ruin'd by him.

Well might I that Night have cried to my Destroyer, How art thou fallen! Oh Lucifer! Son of the Morning! – No other Idea could be so applicable to his Conduct and Phisiognomy at that decissive Moment.

GEORGE EGERTON

from *Keynotes*

My dear woman, have you never dreamt, felt, had *intuitive experiences*? I have. I am not sure that I had not a keen sense of the ludicrous side of the whole affair, that one portion of my soul was not having a laugh at the other's expense. I do not quite know what I had been expecting. 'Tis true he had written me beautiful letters. You see he is too much of a word-artist to write anything else. Treated me badly?

No, I am not prepared to say that he did. I am glad he was too honest to hide his startled realisation of the fact that Autumn and Spring are different seasons, and that one's feelings may undergo a change in a winter. I do not see why I should resent that. Why, it would be punishing him for having cared for me. To put it in his words: 'I came as a strangely lovely dream into his life.' Probably the whole mistake lay in that. He thought of me as a dream lady with dainty hands, idealised me – and wrote to the dream creature. When I came back in the flesh, he realised that I was a prosaic fact, with less charming hands, a tendency to leanness, and coming crow's feet. His look of dismayed awakening was simply delicious. I wish I could catch and fasten the fleeting images that flit across my memory, you would grasp my mental attitude better. In the midst of all my pain, I was sitting next him, and he was stroking my hand mechanically, I noticed a glass case on the wall containing an Italian landscape with ball-blue sky and pink lakes. Pasteboard figures of Dutch-peasant build, with Zouave jackets, Tyrolese hats, and bandaged legs, figured in the foreground. You wound it up, and the figures danced to a *varsoviana*. I was listening to him, and yet at the same time I caught myself imagining how he and I would look dressed like that, bobbing about to the old-fashioned tune. I could hardly keep from shrieking with laughter. He had a turn-down collar on; he ought always to wear unstarched linen – it and his throat didn't fit. You cannot

understand me? Dearest woman, I do not pretend to understand
the thing myself.

Men and Women

TRANSLATED BY FRANK O'CONNOR

A Kiss

He's my doll!
    I'm so dim!
I send this
    Kiss for him.

The Goldsmith's Wife

The goldsmith's wife
    Is blacksmith-bred
With a face too white
    And a cheek too red.

Aideen

All are keen
To know who'll sleep with blond Aideen,
All Aideen herself will own
Is that she will not sleep alone.

No Names

There's a girl in these parts
    A remarkable thing!
But the force of her farts
    Is like stones from a sling.

Gold

Hero's daughter, Leinster's loveliest!
    Child of kings!
Mingling in one glow her ringlets
    And her rings.

Exile

What happier fortune can one find
Than with the girl who pleased one's mind
To leave one's home and friends behind
And sail on the first favouring wind?

W. B. YEATS

He Wishes for the Cloths of Heaven

Had I the heavens' embroidered cloths,
Enwrought with golden and silver light,
The blue and the dim and the dark cloths
Of night and light and the half-light,
I would spread the cloths under your feet:
But I, being poor, have only my dreams;
I have spread my dreams under your feet;
Tread softly because you tread on my dreams.

W.B. YEATS

Crazy Jane Talks with the Bishop

I met the Bishop on the road
And much said he and I.
'Those breasts are flat and fallen now,
Those veins must soon be dry;
Live in a heavenly mansion,
Not in some foul sty.'

'Fair and foul are near of kin,
And fair needs foul,' I cried.
'My friends are gone, but that's a truth
Nor grave nor bed denied,
Learned in bodily lowliness
And in the heart's pride.

'A woman can be proud and stiff
When on love intent;
But Love has pitched his mansion in
The place of excrement;
For nothing can be sole or whole
That has not been rent.'

JOHN FRANCIS WALLER

The Spinning Wheel

Mellow the moonlight to shine is beginning,
Close by the window young Eileen is spinning;
Bent o'er the fire her blind grandmother, sitting,
Is crooning and moaning and drowsily knitting.

Chorus

Merrily, cheerily, noiselessly, whirring,
Swings the wheel, spins the wheel, while the foot's stirring,
Sprightly and brightly and airily ringing
Thrills the sweet voice of the young maiden singing.

'Eileen, a chara, I hear someone tapping,'
''Tis the ivy, dear mother, against the glass flapping,'
'Eily, I surely hear somebody sighing,'
''Tis the sound, mother dear, of the summer winds dying.'

Chorus

'What's that noise that I hear at the window, I wonder?'
''Tis the little birds chirping the holly-bush under,'
'What makes you be shoving and moving your stool on,
'And singing all wrong that old song of "The Coolin"?'

Chorus

There's a form at the casement, the form of her true love,
And he whispers with face bent 'I'm waiting for you, love'
'Get up on the stool, through the lattice step lightly,
We'll rove in the grove while the moon's shining brightly.'

Chorus

The maid shakes her head, on her lips lays her fingers,
Steals up from her seat, longs to go and yet lingers;
A frightened glance turns to her drowsy grandmother,
Puts one foot on the stool, spins the wheel with the other.

Chorus

Lazily, easily, swings now the wheel round,
Slowly and lowly is heard now the reel's sound;
Noiseless and light to the lattice above her
The maid steps, then leaps to the arms of her lover.

Chorus

Slower, and slower, and slower the wheel swings,
Lower, and lower, and lower the reel rings;
Ere the reel and the wheel stopped their ringing and moving,
Through the grove the young lovers by moonlight are roving.

JAMES STEPHENS

from *The Crock of Gold*

While they rested the Thin Woman advised the children on many important matters. She never addressed her discourse to both of them at once, but spoke first to Seumas on one subject and then to Brigid on another subject; for, as she said, the things which a boy must learn are not those which are necessary to a girl. It is particularly important that a man should understand how to circumvent women, for this and the capture of food forms the basis of masculine wisdom, and on this subject she spoke to Seumas. It is, however, equally urgent that a woman should be skilled to keep a man in his proper place, and to this thesis Brigid gave an undivided attention.

She taught that a man must hate all women before he is able to love a woman, but that he is at liberty, or rather he is under express command, to love all men because they are of his kind. Women also should love all other women as themselves, and they should hate all men but one man only, and him they should seek to turn into a woman, because women, by the order of their beings, must be either tyrants or slaves, and it is better they should be tyrants than slaves. She explained that between men and women there exists a state of unremitting warfare, and that the endeavour of each sex is to bring the other to subjection; but that women are possessed by a demon called Pity which severely handicaps their battle and perpetually gives victory to the male, who is thus constantly rescued on the very ridges of defeat. She said to Seumas that his fatal day would dawn when he loved a woman, because he would sacrifice his destiny to her caprice, and she begged him for love of her to beware of all that twisty sex. To Brigid she revealed that a woman's terrible day is upon her when she knows that a man loves her, for a man in love submits only to a woman, a partial, individual and temporary submission, but a woman who is loved surrenders more fully to the very god of love himself, and so she becomes a slave, and is not alone deprived of her personal liberty, but is even infected in her mental processes by this crafty obsession. The fates work for man, and therefore, she averred, woman must be victorious, for those who dare to war against the gods are already assured of victory: this being the law of life, that only the weak shall conquer. The limit of strength is petrifaction and immobility, but there is no limit to weakness, and cunning or fluidity is its counsellor. For these reasons, and in order that life might not cease, women should seek to turn their husbands into women; then they would be tyrants and their husbands would be slaves, and life would be renewed for a further period.

I Shall Not Die for Thee

(Seventeenth Century)

TRANSLATED BY DOUGLAS HYDE

For thee I shall not die,
    Woman high of fame and name;
Foolish men thou mayest slay
    I and they are not the same.

Why should I expire
  For the fire of any eye,
Slender waist or swan-like limb,
  Is't for them that I should die?

The round breasts, the fresh skin,
  Cheeks crimson, hair so long and rich;
Indeed, indeed, I shall not die,
  Please God, not I, for any such.

The golden hair, the forehead thin,
  The chaste mien, the gracious ease,
The rounded heel, the languid tone,
  Fools alone find death from these.

Thy sharp wit, thy perfect calm,
  Thy thin palm like foam o' the sea;
Thy white neck, thy blue eye,
  I shall not die for thee.

Woman, graceful as the swan,
  A wise man did nurture me,
Little palm, white neck, bright eye,
  I shall not die for ye.

SIOBHAN CAMPBELL

By Design

While we stippled
my bedroom walls
two flies chased their pleasure
dizzy on the smells
of paint and love.

Later you slept
while I heard the creature
humming her low aftersong
like my own.

You woke
as the buzzing failed
and said her partner's neat escape
proved missionary is best.

I felt aggrieved
as if I had been left
in a bind of love
with warm beige
tightening to a gloss
about my knees.

Dear Dark Head

(*Eighteenth Century*)

TRANSLATED BY SIR SAMUEL FERGUSON

Put your head, darling, darling, darling,
    Your darling black head my heart above;
Oh, mouth of honey, with the thyme for fragrance
    Who, with heart in breast, could deny you love?

Oh, many and many a young girl for me is pining,
    Letting her locks of gold to the cold wind free,
For me, the foremost of our gay young fellows;
    But I'd leave a hundred, pure love, for thee!

Then put your head, darling, darling, darling,
    Your darling black head my heart above;
Oh, mouth of honey, with the thyme for fragrance,
    Who, with heart in breast, could deny you love?

SINÉAD O'CONNOR

The Last Day of Our Acquaintance

This is the last day of our acquaintance
I will meet you later in somebody's office
I'll talk but you won't listen to me
I know what your answer will be

I know you don't love me anymore
you used to hold my hand when the plane took off
two years ago there just seemed so much more
and I don't know what happened to our love

Today's the day
our friendship has been stale
and we will meet later to finalise the details
two years ago the seed was planted
and since then you have taken me for granted

You were no life-raft to me
I drowned in pain and misery
You did nothing to stop me
Now drown in your own self-pity

But this is the last day of our acquaintance
I will meet you later in somebody's office
I'll talk but you won't listen to me
I know your answer already

GERALDINE HAVERTY

The Story of Sarah Curran

It was at a ball given in her honor at the house of Mr Lambart of Rath Castle, in Wicklow, that Sarah Curran and Robert Emmet met. The meeting was signalized on his side by the sudden development of a passion that was as lasting as it was fiery. Sarah, on the contrary, was quite untouched. She was either indifferent to the handsome and dashing young patriot, or, else, was afraid of him. A delicate flower was she, pale and slender, with a crown of golden hair, a refined patrician style of face and manner. Barely seventeen, unused to the world, and much in awe of her father, it might be easily guessed that she hesitated to encourage the addresses of any suitor, especially one who would prove so unpleasing to her father, as a visionary, penniless, and extremely revolutionary young student.

In Trinity, where Emmet was a student, he was at this time somewhat under a cloud, on account of his known political opinions. A formal investigation had been made by the Chancellor (afterwards Lord Clare) in which all the students were examined under oath.

One writer says:

'There were a few — amongst the number poor Robert Emmet — whose total absence from the scene, as well as the silence that followed the calling out of his name, proclaimed how deep had been his involvement in the transactions now to be inquired into.'

It was just at this period of his career that he met Sarah Curran and another incentive to action was added to his violent patriotism in the shape of an ambition to win honors and triumphs which he could lay at the feet of his gentle lady. 'I must make myself worthy of the woman of my choice,' he said to a confidante, 'and the glory which sheds its lustre on the husband shall reflect its splendor on the wife.' . . .

If Sarah Curran had any ideas of patriotism, she never seemed to have expressed them. She was not the stuff of which patriots are made. The task of braving her lover's departure probably had far greater terrors for her than had the project of defying the whole British government for her lover. Yet her constancy was unswerving. She carried on a constant correspondence with him, through the medium of Miss Lambart, whose part in the matter was, to say the least, injudicious. Finally, the storm broke. The little insurrection, so excellently planned, so ill carried out, was soon over . . .

Sarah Curran failed, slowly but surely, after the tragic death of her lover. She left her father's house not as some have said, because ordered by him (Curran was not a hard-hearted man, and had been very fond of this delicate, timid child) but for various reasons – change of air, and separation from the scenes of so much sorrow. She stayed at Cork, with some Quaker friends named Penrose. She was petted and consoled by all who knew her, but the memory of the gallows and the nameless grave of her beloved seemed always before her mind. She moved like a shadow among the gayest scenes.

Washington Irving says: 'She did not object to frequent the haunts of pleasure but she was as much alone there as in the depths of solitude. She walked about in a sad reverie, apparently unconscious of the world about her.'

Donall Oge: Grief of a Girl's Heart

(Seventeenth Century)

TRANSLATED BY AUGUSTA GREGORY

O Donall Oge, if you go across the sea,
Bring myself with you and do not forget it;
And you will have a sweetheart for fair days and market days,
And the daughter of the King of Greece beside you at night.

It is late last night the dog was speaking of you;
The snipe was speaking of you in her deep marsh.
It is you are the lonely bird through the woods;
And that you may be without a mate until you find me.

You promised me, and you said a lie to me,
That you would be before me where the sheep are flocked;
I gave a whistle and three hundred cries to you,
And I found nothing there but a bleating lamb.

You promised me a thing that was hard for you,
A ship of gold under a silver mast;
Twelve towns with a market in all of them,
And a fine white court by the side of the sea.

You promised me a thing that is not possible,
That you would give me gloves of the skin of a fish;
That you would give me shoes of the skin of a bird;
And a suit of the dearest silk in Ireland.

O Donall Oge, it is I would be better to you
Than a high, proud, spendthrift lady:
I would milk the cow; I would bring help to you;
And if you were hard pressed, I would strike a blow for you.

O, ochone, and it's not with hunger
Or with wanting food, or drink, or sleep,
That I am growing thin, and my life is shortened;
But it is the love of a young man has withered me away.

It is early in the morning that I saw him coming,
Going along the road on the back of a horse;
He did not come to me; he made nothing of me;
And it is on my way home that I cried my fill.

When I go by myself to the Well of Loneliness,
I sit down and I go through my trouble;
When I see the world and do not see my boy,
He that has an amber shade in his hair.

It was on that Sunday I gave my love to you;
The Sunday that is last before Easter Sunday.
And myself on my knees reading the Passion;
And my two eyes giving love to you for ever.

O, aya! my mother, give myself to him;
And give him all that you have in the world;
Get out yourself to ask for alms.
And do not come back and forward looking for me.

My mother said to me not to be talking with you to-day,
Or tomorrow, or on Sunday;
It was a bad time she took for telling me that;
It was shutting the door after the house was robbed.

My heart is as black as the blackness of the sloe,
Or as the black coal that is on the smith's forge;
Or as the sole of a shoe left in white halls;
It was you put that darkness over my life.

You have taken the east from me; You have taken the west from
   me
You have taken what is before me and what is behind me;
You have taken the moon, you have taken the sun from me,
And my fear is great that you have taken God from me!

SAMUEL BECKETT

[*I would like my love to die*]

I would like my love to die
and the rain to be falling on the graveyard
and on me walking the streets
mourning she who sought to love me.

BERNARD MACLAVERTY

from *Cal*

Her erect nipples – 'It's the cold,' she said – the fragrance of her
juices on his hands, above all the awareness that he was giving her
pleasure, were almost too much for him. She made her noises and
he rose again and entered her, saying her name over and over again
as with light fingers she taught him to time his thrusts.

Afterwards he smiled and, leaning on one elbow, hawed on his
fingers and rubbed them on the imaginary lapel of his lean chest.

'Eventually,' she said, smiling.

They lay in each other's arms, eased and snug beneath the
blankets. Marcella said that she had to go back – just in case Gran
should phone or Lucy wake. They dressed and she said that they

should both go to the house. Cal kept kissing her and touching her even as she dressed.

Outside the snow had stopped falling and they walked, printing it with double tracks, she holding on to his elbow in case she should fall. Everything was still and crisp and bright as daylight. The snow squeaked dully as they pressed it with each step. Marcella looked back and said they were leaving clues. If there wasn't more snow they would be caught.

Cal said, 'What happens if you get pregnant?'

She smiled at him. 'I dusted off my diaphragm,' she said. He made a sound of amazement.

'Cal, I came to you hoping.'

In the house they drank more hot whiskeys and made love again on the rug in front of the fire, with the door held shut by an armchair against the possibility of Lucy coming down. When it was over they lay on their stomachs, their faces turned to each other. Cal's hand rested on her buttocks and she pushed his long hair behind his ear.

'You're such an attentive lover,' she said. 'You can see it in your eyes.'

'How do you mean?' His eyes flickered away from hers.

'Your attention to detail. You make me believe it's me.'

'I don't understand. It is you.'

'That's what I mean.'

'Isn't that how it always is?'

'Not always.'

'You're not making yourself very clear.'

She sat up and put her sheepskin coat round her shoulders and held her knees between her arms. Cal reached out beneath her ankles and delicately separated her labia with his fingers.

'A strawberry centre,' he said. 'My favourite.'

She ignored what he was doing to her and went on.

'I can't explain without talking about Robert – and that's not a very nice thing to do in the circumstances.'

Cal shrugged. 'I wish I'd met you before he did.'

She laughed. 'You'd probably have been in short trousers.' He looked hurt and she ruffled his hair. 'We had stopped making love

for a long time before he was killed. We had occasional sex but he
didn't make me realise I was me. He was having it off with some
creature of his imagination. God forgive me, I shouldn't speak ill
of the dead.'

'Were you in love with him?' Cal's voice still had echoes of a
shake in it.

'Love is a very strange idea. I never know what it is. When you
were young it seemed to be all intensity and no opportunity. Later
when you did get the opportunity the fire had gone out of it.'

'I still have it,' said Cal.

'You're still young. Anyway that's too simple. It must be a
mixture of friendship and desire. The friendship had gone out of
our marriage long ago and Robert's lust was for someone inside his
head – not me.'

ITA DALY

from *Ellen*

'I couldn't bring this up at home, not with Daddy around.'

'What?'

'I just wondered, it has to be gone into . . . Do you know all
about that side of marriage, Ellen?'

'What side?'

'Now you're trying to annoy me. I'm your mother and I have to
ask these things, it's my duty. Now, all I'll say is –'

'I know all about it, Mother, you don't have to tell me.'

'Nevertheless, I'm going to.' She sighed and looked at me, her
mouth drooping mournfully. 'Maybe women differ but I've never
enjoyed that side of marriage. And I'm quite sure you won't
either. But you have a duty, Ellen, you have to obey your husband
in that respect, even if you don't like it much. That's why
marriage is more of a sacrifice for women, but then they have the

children and that makes up for it. And anyway,' she added after a pause, 'they say that Protestant men have more self-control in that respect. I don't know why that should be, but I've often heard it said by them that should know. Funny, isn't it?'

'Inbreeding, I'd say.'

She nodded with complete seriousness. 'You could well be right.'

Adrien was showing no signs of wanting to ravish me but this was not due to his Protestant self-control, I believed, but rather to his state of being helplessly in love. Love had changed him, taking away his old bounce and assurance, and although I liked the new Adrien better, I could see that to the outside world he must seem a poor thing. He beseeched me with his eyes and sought to appease me with his smiles. He was incomplete, ego-less, looking out on the world with hesitation, without dash, without style.

I wondered at the perversity of love. Did Adrien's passion grow as he became more aware of my indifference towards him? And if I should suddenly fall in love with him, would I as suddenly see him reflate, like a pink balloon, as his voice increased by several decibels? Then he would fill his tweeds with that assurance that I remembered so well and treat me with the good-natured contempt that he had had for me in the past.

How pleased I was to be finished with love.

But, though I had no affection for Adrien, I could see that there was a bargain to be kept. He would provide me with a shelter so I must endeavour to provide him with whatever it was he needed in a wife. I was determined to play fair, and it must grow easier as, living together, he grew used to me and became less obsessed. I might even be able to revive his interest in cricket.

FRANCIS LEDWIDGE

The Death of Ailill

When there was heard no more the war's loud sound,
And only the rough corn-crake filled the hours,
And hill winds in the furze and drowsy flowers,
Maeve in her chamber with her white head bowed
On Ailill's heart was sobbing: 'I have found
The way to love you now,' she said, and he
Winked an old tear away and said: 'The proud
Unyielding heart loves never.' And then she:
'I love you now, tho' once when we were young
We walked apart like two who were estranged
Because I loved you not, now all is changed.'
And he who loved her always called her name
And said: 'You do not love me; 'tis your tongue
Talks in the dusk; you love the blazing gold
Won in the battles, and the soldier's fame.
You love the stories that are often told
By poets in the hall.' Then Maeve arose
And sought her daughter Findebar: 'Oh, child,
Go tell your father that my love went wild
With all my wars in youth, and say that now
I love him stronger than I hate my foes . . . '
And Findebar unto her father sped
And touched him gently on the rugged brow,
And knew by the cold touch that he was dead.

W.B. Yeats

Crazy Jane Grown Old Looks at the Dancers

I found that ivory image there
Dancing with her chosen youth,
But when he wound her coal-black hair
As though to strangle her, no scream
Or bodily movement did I dare,
Eyes under eyelids did so gleam;
Love is like the lion's tooth.

When she, and though some said she played
I said that she had danced heart's truth,
Drew a knife to strike him dead,
I could but leave him to his fate;
For no matter what is said
They had all that had their hate;
Love is like the lion's tooth.

Did he die or did she die?
Seemed to die or died they both?
God be with the times when I
Cared not a thraneen for what chanced
So that I had the limbs to try
Such a dance as there was danced —
Love is like the lion's tooth.

4

Marriage and Family

Pillow Talk

TRANSLATED BY JOSEPH DUNN

Once on a time, when Ailill and Medb had spread their royal bed in Cruachan, the stronghold of Connacht, such was the pillow-talk betwixt them:

Said Ailill, 'True is the saying, O woman, "She is a well-off woman that is a rich man's wife." '

'Aye, that she is,' answered the wife; 'but wherefore say'st thou so?'

'For this,' Ailill replied, 'that thou art this day better off than the day that first I took thee.'

Then answered Medb, 'As well-off was I before I ever saw thee.'

'It was a wealth, indeed, we never heard nor knew of,' said Ailill; 'but a woman's wealth was all thou hadst, and foes from lands next to thine were wont to carry off the spoil and booty that they took from thee.'

'Not so was I,' said Medb; 'the High King of Erin himself was my father, Eochaid Feidlich son of Finn son of Finnen son of Finnguin son of Rogen Ruad son of Rigen son of Blathacht son of Beothacht son of Enna Agnech son of Angus Turbech. Of daughters had he six: Derbriu, Ethne and Ele, Clothru, Mugain and Medb, myself, that was the noblest and seemliest of them all. It was I was the goodliest of them in bounty and gift-giving, in riches and treasure. It was I was best of them in battle and strife and combat. It was I that had fifteen hundred royal mercenaries of the sons of aliens exiled from their own land, and as many more of the sons of freemen of the land. These were as a standing household-guard,' continued Medb; 'hence hath my father bestowed one of the five provinces of Erin upon me, that is, the province of Cruachan: wherefore "Medb of Cruachan" am I called. Men came from Finn son of Ross Ruad, king of Leinster, to seek me for a wife, and I refused him; and from Cairbre Niafer son of

Ross Ruad, king of Tara, to woo me, and I refused him; and they came from Conchobar son of Fachtna Fathach, king of Ulster, and I refused him likewise. They came from Eochaid Bec, and I went not; for it is I that exacted a peculiar bride-gift, such as no woman ever required of a man of the men of Erin, namely, a husband without avarice, without jealousy, without fear. For should he be mean, the man with whom I should live, we were ill-matched together, inasmuch as I am great in largess and gift-giving, and it would be a disgrace for my husband if I should be better at spending than he, and for it to be said that I was superior in wealth and treasures to him, while no disgrace would it be were one as great as the other. Were my husband a coward, it were as unfit for us to be mated, for I by myself and alone break battles and fights and combats, and it would be a reproach for my husband should his wife be more full of life than himself, and no reproach our being equally bold. Should he be jealous, the husband with whom I should live, that too would not suit me, for there never was a time that I had not one man in the shadow of another. Howbeit, such a husband have I found, namely thyself, Ailill son of Ross Ruad of Leinster. Thou wast not churlish; thou wast not jealous; thou wast not a sluggard. So was I plighted thee, and gave purchase price to thee, which of right belongs to the bride – of clothing, namely, the raiment of twelve men, a chariot worth thrice seven bondmaids, the breadth of thy face of red gold, the weight of thy left forearm of white bronze. Whoso brings shame and sorrow and madness upon thee, no claim for compensation to satisfaction hast thou therefor that I myself have not, but it is to me the compensation belongs,' said Medb, 'for a man dependent upon a woman's maintenance is what thou art.'

'Nay, not such was my state,' said Ailill; 'but two brothers had I; one of them over Tara, the other over Leinster; namely Finn over Leinster and Cairbre over Tara. I left the kingship to them because they were older but not superior to me in largess and bounty. Nor heard I of a province in Erin under woman's keeping but this province alone. And for this I came and assumed the kingship here as my mother's successor; for Mata of Murese, daughter of Matach of Connacht, was my mother. And who could there be for me to

have as my queen better than thyself, being, as thou wert,
daughter of the High King of Erin?'
  'Yet so it is,' pursued Medb, 'my fortune is greater than thine.'
  'I marvel at that,' Ailill made answer, 'for there is none that
hath greater treasures and riches and wealth than I: indeed, to my
knowledge there is not.'

PAULA MEEHAN

The Pattern

Little has come down to me of hers,
a sewing machine, a wedding band,
a clutch of photos, the sting of her hand
across my face in one of our wars

when we had grown bitter and apart.
Some say that's the fate of the eldest daughter.
I wish now she'd lasted till after
I'd grown up. We might have made a new start

as women without tags like *mother*, *wife*,
sister, *daughter*, taken our chances from there.
At forty-two she headed for god knows where.
I've never gone back to visit her grave.

First she'd scrub the floor with Sunlight soap,
an armreach at a time. When her knees grew sore
she'd break for a cup of tea, then start again
at the door with lavender polish. The smell
would percolate back through the flat to us,
her brood banished to the bedroom.

And as she buffed the wax to a high shine
did she catch her own face coming clear?
Did she net a glimmer of her true self?
Did her mirror tell what mine tells me?
I have her shrug and go on
knowing history has brought her to her knees.

She'd call us in and let us skate around
in our socks. We'd grow solemn as planets
in an intricate orbit about her.

She's bending over crimson cloth,
the younger kids are long in bed.
Late summer, cold enough for a fire,
she works by fading light
to remake an old dress for me.
It's first day back at school tomorrow.

'Pure lambswool. Plenty of wear in it yet.
You know I wore this when I went out with your Da.
I was supposed to be down in a friend's house,
your Granda caught us at the corner.
He dragged me in by the hair – it was long as yours then –
in front of the whole street.
He called your Da every name under the sun,
cornerboy, lout; I needn't tell you
what he called me. He shoved my whole head
under the kitchen tap, took a scrubbing brush
and carbolic soap and in ice-cold water he scrubbed
every spick of lipstick and mascara off my face.
Christ but he was a right tyrant, your Granda.
It'll be over my dead body anyone harms a hair of your head.'

She must have stayed up half the night
to finish the dress. I found it airing at the fire,
three new copybooks on the table and a bright
bronze nib, St. Christopher strung on a silver wire,

as if I were embarking on a perilous journey
to uncharted realms. I wore that dress
with little grace. To me it spelt poverty,
the stigma of the second hand. I grew enough to pass

it on by Christmas to the next in line. I was sizing
up the world beyond our flat patch by patch
daily after school, and fitting each surprising
city street to city square to diamond. I'd watch

the Liffey for hours pulsing to the sea
and the coming and going of ships,
certain that one day it would carry me
to Zanzibar, Bombay, the Land of the Ethiops.

There's a photo of her taken in the Phoenix Park
alone on a bench surrounded by roses
as if she had been born to formal gardens.
She stares out as if unaware
that any human hand held the camera, wrapped
entirely in her own shadow, the world beyond her
already a dream, already lost. She's
eight months pregnant. Her last child.

Her steel needles sparked and clacked,
the only other sound a settling coal
or her sporadic mutter
at a hard part in the pattern.
She favoured sensible shades:
Moss Green, Mustard, Beige.

I dreamt a robe of a colour
so pure it became a word.

Sometimes I'd have to kneel
an hour before her by the fire,
a skein around my outstretched hands,
while she rolled wool into balls.
If I swam like a kite too high
amongst the shadows on the ceiling
or flew like a fish in the pools
of pulsing light, she'd reel me firmly
home, she'd land me at her knees.

Tongues of flame in her dark eyes,
she'd say, 'One of these days I must
teach you to follow a pattern.'

JONATHAN SWIFT

A Letter to a Very Young Lady on Her Marriage

The grand affair of your life will be to gain and preserve the friendship and esteem of your husband. You are married to a man of good education and learning, of an excellent understanding and an exact taste. It is true, and it is happy for you, that these qualities in him are adorned with great modesty, a most amiable sweetness of temper, and an unusual disposition to sobriety and virtue; but neither good nature nor virtue will suffer him to esteem you against his judgment; and although he is not capable of using you ill, yet you will in time grow a thing indifferent, and perhaps contemptible, unless you can supply the loss of youth and beauty with more durable qualities. You have but a very few years to be young and handsome in the eyes of the world, and as few months to be so in the eyes of a husband who is not a fool; for I hope you do not still dream of charms and raptures, which marriage ever did, and ever will, put a sudden end to. Besides, yours was a match of prudence and common good liking, without any mixture of that ridiculous passion which has no being but in playbooks and romances.

You must therefore use all endeavours to attain to some degree of those accomplishments which your husband most values in other people, and for which he is most valued himself. You must improve your mind by closely pursuing such a method of study as I shall direct or approve of. You must get a collection of history and travels, which I will recommend to you, and spend some hours every day in reading them, and making extracts from them if your memory be weak. You must invite persons of knowledge and understanding to an acquaintance with you, by whose conversation you may learn to correct your taste and judgment; and when you can bring yourself to comprehend and relish the good sense of others, you will arrive in time to think rightly yourself, and to become a reasonable and agreeable companion. This must produce in your husband a true rational love and esteem for you, which old age will not diminish. He will have a regard for your judgment and opinion in matters of the greatest weight; you will be able to entertain each other without a third person to relieve by finding discourse. The endowments of your mind will even make your person more agreeable to him; and when you are alone, your time will not lie heavy upon your hands for want of some trifling amusement.

As little respect as I have for the generality of your sex, it has sometimes moved me with pity to see the lady of the house forced to withdraw immediately after dinner, and this in families where there is not much drinking; as if it were an established maxim, that women are incapable of all conversation. In a room where both sexes meet, if the men are discoursing upon any general subject, the ladies never think it their business to partake in what passes, but in a separate club entertain each other with the price and choice of lace and silk, and what dresses they liked or

disapproved at the church or the playhouse. And when you are
among yourselves, how naturally after the first compliments do
you apply your hands to each other's lappets, and ruffles, and
mantuas; as if the whole business of your lives and the public
concern of the world depended upon the cut or colour of your
dress. As divines say, that some people take more pains to be
damned than it would cost them to be saved; so your sex employ
more thought, memory, and application to be fools than would
serve to make them wise and useful. When I reflect on this I
cannot conceive you to be human creatures, but a certain sort of
species hardly a degree above a monkey; who has more diverting
tricks than any of you, is an animal less mischievous and expensive, might in time be a tolerable critic in velvet and brocade, and
for aught I know, would equally become them.

I can give you no advice upon the article of expense; only I think
you ought to be well informed how much your husband's revenue
amounts to, and be so good a computer as to keep within it in that
part of the management which falls to your share; and not to put
yourself in the number of those political ladies, who think they
gain a great point when they have teased their husbands to buy
them a new equipage, a laced head, or a fine petticoat, without
once considering what long score remained unpaid to the butcher.

I desire you will keep this letter in your cabinet, and often
examine impartially your whole conduct by it; and so God bless
you, and make you a fair example to your sex, and a perpetual
comfort to your husband and your parent.

I am, with great truth and affection, Madam, your most faithful
friend and humble servant,

                        Dean Swift

Medbh McGuckian

Charlotte's Delivery

1

Summer never really came, its false hem
Beneath the quiet dress of shadow
Half-in, half-out of the rainwashed dream.

Something in its rounded winter power
Expanding for a bold internal minute
Made me decide on giving her a cold, short name.

Will it be stained as darkly as the last,
The tiny tapering of the inverted cup,
The faintly printed journey out of the mourning brooch?

2

Your morning sounds are a womb of roses,
Sinking into life and who-ness.
You collect yourself against me like a first book of time,
Dipping in and out of a coma.

You are a ring with a love-note hidden inside:
The us-ness in your eyes is what men, who are not us, go to find.
In the wrecked hull of the fishing-boat
Someone has planted a cypress under the ribs.

JONAH BARRINGTON

from *Elizabeth Fitzgerald*

After the victory the warders had a feast on the castle top, whereat each of them recounted his own feats. Squire Fitzgerald, who was a quiet, easy man, and hated fighting, and who had told my aunt at the beginning that they would surely kill him, having seated himself all night peaceably under one of the parapets, was quite delighted when the affray was over. He had walked out into his garden outside the walls to take some tranquil air, when an ambuscade of the hostile survivors surrounded and carried him off. In vain his warders sallied – the squire was gone past all redemption!

It was supposed he had paid his debts to Nature, if any he owed, when, next day, a large body of the O'Cahil faction appeared near the castle. Their force was too great to be attacked by the warders, who durst not sally; and the former assault had been too calamitous to the O'Cahils to warrant them in attempting another. Both were, therefore, standing at bay, when, to the great joy of the garrison, Squire Fitzgerald was produced, and one of the assailants, with a white cloth on a pike, advanced to parley.

The lady attended his proposals, which were very laconic. 'I'm a truce, lady! Look here (shewing the terrified squire), we have your husband in hault – yees have yeer castle *sure* enough. Now, we'll change, if you please: we'll render the squire and you'll render the keep; and if yees won't do that same, the squire will be throttled before your two eyes in half an hour.'

'Flag of truce!' said the heroine, with due dignity and without hesitation. 'Mark the words of Elizabeth Fitzgerald, of Moret Castle – they may serve for your own wife upon some future occasion. Flag of truce! I *won't* render my keep, and I'll tell you why – Elizabeth Fitzgerald may get another husband, but Elizabeth Fitzgerald may never get another castle; so I'll keep what I have; and if you can't get off faster than your legs can readily carry you, my warders will try which is hardest, your skull or a stone bullet.'

The O'Cahils kept their word, and old Squire Stephen Fitzgerald in a short time was seen dangling and performing various evolutions in the air, to the great amusement of the Jacobites, the mortification of the warders, and chagrin (which, however, was not without a mixture of consolation) of my great-aunt Elizabeth.

ANGELA GREENE

Terrorists's Wife

A phone-call takes him
into the dark for weeks.
In the mornings, his absence
fills me with dread. I thin my eyes
to watch for cars that come to wait
down in the street. All day
I move from room to room. I polish
each spotless place
to a chill shining. Fear tracks me
like hunger. In the silence,
the walls grow wafer-thin.
The neighbours wear masks –
tight lips, veiled looks, such
fine tissues of knowing.
My mother doesn't visit. I drag
my shopping from the next town.

Once, putting his clean shirts away,
my dry hands touched a shape
that lay cold and hard. I wept then,
and walked for hours in the park.
I listened for his name in the news.
When I looked at our sleeping son
my sadness thickened.

His comings are like his goings –
a swift movement in the night.
At times, he can sit here for days,
meticulously groomed; primed,
watching soccer games on T.V.,
our child playful in his lap.
But scratch the smooth surface
of his mood, and how
the breached defenses spit their fire.

Now, when he holds me to him,
I know I taste murder
on his mouth. And in the darkness,
when he turns from me, I watch him
light a cigarette. In his palm
the lighter clicks and flames.
Balanced, incendiary.

SAMUEL BECKETT

from *Happy Days*

WINNIE: Ah yes, if only I could bear to be alone, I mean prattle away with not a soul to hear. (*Pause.*) Not that I flatter myself you hear much, no Willie, God forbid. (*Pause.*) Days perhaps when you hear nothing. (*Pause.*) But days too when you answer. (*Pause.*) So that I may say at all times, even when you do not answer and perhaps hear nothing, something of this is being heard, I am not merely talking to myself, that is in the wilderness, a thing I could never bear to do – for any length of time. (*Pause.*) That is what enables me to go on, go on talking that is. (*Pause.*) Whereas if you were to die – (*smile*) – to speak in the old style – (*smile off*) – or go away and leave me, then what would I do, what *could* I do, all day long, I mean between the bell for waking and the bell for sleep? (*Pause.*) Simply gaze before me with compressed lips. (*Long pause while she does so. No more plucking.*) Not another word as long as I drew breath, nothing to break the silence of this place. (*Pause.*) Save possibly, now and then, every now and then, a sigh into my looking-glass. (*Pause.*) Or a brief . . . gale of laughter, should I happen to see the old joke again. (*Pause. Smile appears, broadens and seems about to culminate in laugh when suddenly replaced by expression of anxiety.*) My hair! (*Pause.*) Did I brush and comb my hair? (*Pause.*) I may have done. (*Pause.*) Normally I do. (*Pause.*) There is so little one *can* do. (*Pause.*) One does it all. (*Pause.*) All one can. (*Pause.*) 'Tis only human. (*Pause.*) Human nature. (*She begins to inspect mound, looks up.*) Human weakness. (*She resumes inspection of mound, looks up.*) Natural weakness. (*She resumes inspection of mound.*) I see no comb. (*Inspects.*) Nor any hairbrush. (*Looks up. Puzzled expression. She turns to bag, rummages in it.*) The comb is here. (*Back front. Puzzled expression. Back to bag. Rummages.*) The brush is here. (*Back front. Puzzled expression.*) Perhaps I put them back, after use. (*Pause. Do.*) But normally I do not put things back, after use, no, I leave them lying about and put them back all together, at the end of the day. (*Smile.*) To speak in the old style. (*Pause.*) The sweet old style. (*Smile off.*) And yet . . . I seem . . . to remember . . . (*Suddenly careless.*) Oh well, what does it matter, that is what I always say, I shall simply brush and comb them later on, purely and simply, I have the whole – (*Pause. Puzzled.*) Them? (*Pause.*) Or it? (*Pause.*) Brush and comb it? (*Pause.*) Sounds improper somehow. (*Pause. Turning a little towards* WILLIE.) What would you say, Willie? (*Pause. Turning a little further.*) What would you say, Willie, speaking of your hair, them or it? (*Pause.*) The hair on your head, I mean. (*Pause. Turning a little further.*) The hair on your head, Willie, what would you say speaking of the hair on your head, them or it? (*Long pause.*)

WILLIE. It.

WINNIE. (*Turning back front, joyful.*) Oh you are going to talk to me today, this is going to be a happy day! (*Pause. Joy off.*) Another happy day. (*Pause.*) Ah well, where was I, my hair, yes, later on, I shall be thankful for it later on. (*Pause.*) I have my – (*raise hands to hat*) – yes, on, my hat on – (*lowers hands*) – I cannot take it off now. (*Pause.*) To think there are times one cannot take off one's hat, not if one's life were at stake. Times one cannot put it on, times one cannot take it off. (*Pause.*) How often I have said, Put on your hat now, Winnie, there is nothing else for it, take off your hat now, Winnie, like a good girl, it will do you good, and did not. (*Pause.*) Could not. (*Pause. She raises hand, frees a strand of hair from under hat, draws it towards eye, squints at it, lets it go, hand down.*) Golden you called it, that day, when the last guest was gone – (*hand up in gesture of raising a glass*) – to your golden . . . may it never . . . (*voice breaks*) . . . may it never . . . (*Hand down. Head down. Pause. Low.*) That day. (*Pause. Do.*) What day? (*Pause. Head up. Normal voice.*) What now? (*Pause.*) Words fail, there are times when even they fail. (*Turning a little towards* WILLIE.) Is that not so, Willie? (*Pause. Turning a little further.*) Is not that so, Willie, that even words fail, at times? (*Pause. Back front.*) What is one to do then, until they come again? Brush and comb the hair, if it has not been done, or if there is some doubt, trim the nails if they are in need of trimming, these things tide one over.

BIDDY JENKINSON

Silence

TRANSLATED BY PÁDRAIGÍN RIGGS

How I welcome you, little salmon
who leapt the womb, impatient to commence life.
I undertake to be a river to you
as you follow your course from the haven of
    my belly to far distant seas.

Let yourself go, and drink up your fill.
Suck sleep from me. By the terms of the breast-contract
I'll suck back from your puckered lips
love, with which I'll suckle another time, and for that
    I'm grateful.

How I welcome you, salmon of sleep
who made a tranquil pool in my life-stream.
In the rhythm of your heartbeat
I hear the music of the Heavens,
    and it guides my way.

JAMES STEPHENS

The Red-haired Man's Wife

I have taken that vow!
And you were my friend
But yesterday – Now
All that's at an end;
And you are my husband, and claim me, and
    I must depend!

Yesterday I was free!
Now you, as I stand,
Walk over to me
And take hold of my hand;
You look at my lips! Your eyes are too
    bold, your smile is too bland!

My old name is lost;
My distinction of race!
Now, the line has been crossed,
Must I step to your pace?
Must I walk as you list, and obey, and smile
        up in your face?

All the white and the red
Of my cheeks you have won!
All the hair of my head!
And my feet, tho' they run,
Are yours, and you own me and end me,
        just as I begun!

Must I bow when you speak!
Be silent and hear;
Inclining my cheek
And incredulous ear
To your voice, and command, and behest;
        hold your lightest wish dear!

I am woman! But still
Am alive, and can feel
Every intimate thrill
That is woe or is weal:
I, aloof, and divided, apart, standing far,
        can I kneel?

Oh, if kneeling were right,
I should kneel nor be sad!
And abase in your sight
All the pride that I had!
I should come to you, hold to you, cling to
        you, call to you, glad!

If not, I shall know,
I shall surely find out!
And your world will throw
In disaster and rout!
I am woman, and glory, and beauty; I,
      mystery, terror and doubt!

I am separate still!
I am I and not you!
And my mind and my will,
As in secret they grew,
Still are secret; unreached, and untouched,
      and not subject to you.

The Snoring Bedmate

(Seventeenth Century)

Translated by John V. Kelleher

You thunder at my side,
Lad of ceaseless hum;
There's not a saint would chide
My prayer that you were dumb.

The dead start from the tomb
With each blare from your nose.
I suffer, with less room,
Under these bedclothes.

Which could I better bide
Since my head's already broke –
Your pipe-drone at my side,
Woodpecker's drill on oak?

Brass scraped with knicky knives,
A cowbell's tinny clank,
Or the yells of tinkers' wives
Giving birth behind a bank?

A drunken, braying clown
Slapping cards down on a board
Were less easy to disown
Than the softest snore you've snored.

Sweeter the grunts of swine
Than yours that win release.
Sweeter, bedmate mine,
The screech of grieving geese.

A sick calf's moan for aid,
A broken mill's mad clatter,
The snarl of flood cascade . . .
Christ! now what's the matter?

That was a ghastly growl!
What signified that twist? –
An old wolf's famished howl,
Wave-boom at some cliff's breast?

Storm screaming round a crag,
Bellow of raging bull,
Hoarse bell of rutting stag,
Compared with this were lull!

Ah, now a gentler fall –
Bark of a crazy hound?
Brats squabbling for a ball?
Ducks squawking on a pond?

No, rough weather's back again.
Some great ship's about to sink
And roaring bursts the main
Over the bulwark's brink!

Farewell, tonight, to sleep.
Every gust across the bed
Makes hair rise and poor flesh creep.
Would that one of us were dead!

WINIFRED LETTS

Prayer for a Little Child

God keep my jewel this day from danger;
From tinker and pooka and black-hearted stranger.
From harm of the water, from hurt of the fire.
From the horns of the cows going home to the byre.
From the sight of the fairies that maybe might change her.
From teasing the ass when he's tied to the manger.
From stones that would bruise her, from thorns of the briar.
From red evil berries that wake her desire.
From hunting the gander and vexing the goat.
From the depths o' sea water by Danny's old boat.
From cut and from tumble, from sickness and weeping;
May God have my jewel this day in his keeping.

HUGH LEONARD

from *Home Before Night*

My grandmother made dying her life's work. I remember her as a vast malevolent old woman, so obese that she was unable to wander beyond the paved yard outside her front door. Her pink-washed cottage had two rooms and she agonized her way through and around them, clutching at the furniture for support and emitting heart-scalding gasps, as if death was no further off than the dresser or the settle bed where my uncle Sonny slept himself sober. In those days people confused old age with valour; they called her a great old warrior. This had the effect of inspiring her to gasp even more distressingly by way of proving them right and herself indomitable. In case her respiratory noises should come to be as taken for granted as the ticking of the clock (which at least stopped now and then), she provided a contrapuntal accompaniment by kicking the chairs, using the milk jugs as cymbals and percussing the kettle and frying pan.

To be fair, it was her only diversion. The rent-man, peering in over the half-door, would suffer like a damned soul as she counted out three shillings and ninepence in coppers, threepenny bits and sixpences, wheezing a goodbye to each coin, and then began her tortured *via dolorosa* towards him, determined to pay her debts before dropping dead at his feet, a martyr to landlordism. Even Dr Enright was intimidated. When he had listened to her heartbeats it was not his stethoscope but her doomed slaughterhouse eyes imploring the worst which caused him to tell her: 'Sure we've all got to go some day, ma'am.' That pleased her. Privately, she saw no reason why she should go at any time, but she liked to nod submissively, essay a practice death-rattle and resignedly endorse the will of the Almighty.

She dressed in shiny black and wore a brooch inscribed 'Mother'. Her girth almost exceeded her stature, and her pro-digious appetite amazed me, for her cooking verged on the poisonous: in fact, I have known no other woman who could make

fried eggs taste like perished rubber. On the occasions when my
mother deposited me at Rosanna Cottage for the day, the midday
meal consisted unvaryingly of fried egg and potatoes. I was too
afraid of her baleful eyes to refuse to eat, so would get rid of the
accursed egg by balancing it on the blade of my knife and
swallowing it whole. This she came to interpret as a tribute to her
culinary powers and, as my eyes streamed and gorge rose, would
set about frying me another egg.

DERRY JEFFARES

Devoted Mothers

I still feel angry when I recollect
How my father, offered a contract by La Scala
At seventeen, felt the powerful effect
Of Edwardian possessiveness: a heart attack
Threatened by his widowed mother,
Who, like Mrs Synge, just three roads away,
Attended Zion Church, wanted to smother
Anything artistic. Mrs Synge was sure
Musicians were not nice: besides, they drank.

JUNE LEVINE

from *Sisters*

The night I became engaged to a Canadian Jewish medical
student, I knew I had pulled It off. My father, especially, would be
well pleased with me, and he was. So were my Jewish grand-
parents (the others were dead by now), my aunts, uncles, brothers,

sisters, perhaps even my mother. To have done something so right, by accident as I thought, was very exciting. It was wonderful to float around in a cloud of tribute for months until the wedding, feeling approval everywhere, the fulfilment of everyone's expectations.

What, I asked my father, would I do about the job I had got myself in Fleet Street? Ah, forget that nonsense, he said, this was worth more. I never asked how he meant that. Did he really see marriage as such an opportunity for a woman, the ideal for his daughter? Years later, when I got divorced, he advised me: 'What you should do now is look for a husband . . .' To this day, there is still no greater joy a daughter could give my father than to tell him she was getting married, especially to a nice Jewish boy. Other good news would be pregnancy, a husband achieving something, sons doing well, news of somebody else's daughter getting married. The solid achievement of looking so well that you deserved a good husband came high on his list, as in: 'She's a beautiful-looking girl, is there no sign of her getting married?'

'Daddy, she's a surgeon . . .'

'You'd think that girl would have lots of fellows after her. Maybe she's too particular.'

PATRICK C. POWER

from *The Book of Irish Curses*

Near Inistioge one can still see the ruins of Brownsford Castle which formerly belonged to a family of FitzGeralds. The last FitzGerald to live there was known as 'the Baron'. Tradition states that one of his tenants, a widow, had some problems trying to keep her only son under control and she complained of him to the 'Baron'. FitzGerald unwisely heeded her and remarked grimly: 'He'll be quiet from now on!' He then took the young fellow and beat him so badly that he killed him. This drew on the 'Baron' the curse of the bereaved widow who called down misfortune on the killer and said that the four winds of heaven would blow through his castle in Brownsford. It is an historical fact that this FitzGerald was a casualty at the Battle of Aughrim in 1691. It is also a fact that Brownsford Castle was forsaken and that its walls stood naked under the skies. This, it was said, was the result of a widow's curse . . .

One hears of some IRA men raiding a house in south Tipperary in 1921 to take the son of a widow for execution because it was understood that he had passed important information to the British authorities. Not only his mother, but also his sister confronted the armed men and they also shot her in their nervous reaction to her tirade of abuse. The mother solemnly cursed them. She said that the arm which fired the shot at the girl would rot on the man who killed her. Strangely enough the gunman died in great pain from some disease which affected his arm and the others who were there that night died afterwards in rather unpleasant and unusual ways. Was it all a coincidence?

JOHN MCGAHERN

from *Amongst Women*

For five whole glaring days they worked away like this, too tired and stiff at night to want to go anywhere but to bed. They had all the hay won except the final meadow when the weather broke. The girls never thought they would lift their faces to the rain in gratitude. They watched it waste the meadows for the whole day.

'To hell with it. We're safe now anyhow. If we don't get the last meadow itself it will do for bedding. Only for the whole lot of you we'd not be near that far on,' Moran was able to praise.

'It was for nothing, Daddy.'

'It was everything. Alone we might be nothing. Together we can do anything.'

Rose put down a big fire against the depression of the constant rain. Everybody in the house loved to move in the warmth and luxury of it, to look out from the bright room at the rain spilling steadily down between the trees. When they moved away from the fire to the outer rooms the steady constant drip of rain from the eaves in the silence was like peace falling . . .

By the time Maggie had to go back to London they had never felt closer in warmth, even happiness. The closeness was as strong as the pull of their own lives; they lost the pain of individuality within its protection. In London or Dublin the girls would look back to the house for healing. The remembered light on the empty hayfields would grow magical, the green shade of the beeches would give out a delicious coolness as they tasted again the sardines between slices of bread: when they were away the house would become the summer light and shade above their whole lives . . .

'What would you study at university?'

'I'd like to do medicine.'

'How long would that take?'

'The most of seven years.'

'Physician heal thyself,' he muttered in a half-overheard aside and went out.

Sheila could not have desired a worse profession. It was the priest and doctor and not the guerrilla fighters who had emerged as the bigwigs in the country Moran had fought for. For his own daughter to lay claim to such a position was an intolerable affront. At least the priest had to pay for his position with celibacy and prayer. The doctor took the full brunt of Moran's resentment.

Sheila withdrew into angry silence. There were moments when she thought of looking for outside help but there was really no one she could turn to. Maggie had barely enough to live on. She considered writing to Luke in London – she had even taken notepaper out – but realized that it would be directly confronting Moran. She could not bring herself to do it.

Throughout, Moran did not attempt to influence Sheila directly but his withdrawal of support was total.

After two days Sheila anounced truculently, 'I'm not going to the university. I'll take the civil service.'

'I didn't want to stand in your way, that's why I said nothing but I can't help thinking it is closer to your measure.'

'How?' Her anger brought out his own aggression.

'How, what? How, pig, is it?' he demanded.

'What do you mean, Daddy? I didn't understand what you said, that's all,' she was quick to change but she refused to withdraw.

'You'd understand quick enough if you wanted to. You know the old saying there's none more deaf than those who do not want to hear.'

'I'm sorry. I just didn't understand, Daddy.'

'Going for medicine is a fairly tall order, isn't it? Even with scholarships it takes money. I consider all my family equal. I don't like to see a single one trying to outdistance another.'

'I didn't say anything like that. I just said what I'd like to do,' she said brokenly, with bitterness.

'That's right. Blame me because the world isn't perfect,' Moran complained equally bitterly. 'Blame, blame. No matter what you do. Blame is all you get in this family.'

ELIZABETH RIVERS

from *Stranger in Aran*

'Hurry and come down, Padraig is at the house and he'll be asking for you.' 'What!' I cried and not a stir out of me. 'Will you want to get married?' she asked. 'I am too young,' I said. 'No, I won't get married.' 'Oh, get married,' Katy begged me. 'We'll have a fine time and when you're married I'll come over to your house where you'll go. Morning and evening I'll be in talking to you and we'll have fun!' Well, I put an old shawl around me and I went with Katy and hurried to come down to my mother's house. Padraig wasn't there at all yet. He'd sent his brother in first and he waited at Katy's house till he'd hear how it would go. My mother was there. 'Will you get married, Brigid?' she says. 'I will not,' I said. Then I went to speak to my father. He was in bed in the room. 'Do you want me to get married?' I asked him. 'I do,' he says, 'it is a nice house and he is a nice man, and I'd like you to be married near us, but it is for yourself to decide.' 'Well, if you like me to go in in it, and if my mother would like me to go in in it, I will go in it,' I said, and I came out in the room. 'Will I send word for Padraig to come?' my mother asked. 'Yes, send word,' I said to her. So Padraig came. He sat down and his brother sat down and they were talking. My father came out in the room. 'Padraig wants to know will you be married to him?' my mother says, 'are you satisfied to take him?' And I looked over the room and Padraig was laughing. The word came up in my mouth.' Brigid turned and looked at me as we walked along. 'And, "I will be married", I said, and they all clapped hands and called out. His brother went out and got horses and they went to Kilronan for whiskey. I went out to houses in the village to call people and I borrowed a gramophone. They all came back then and they all drank whiskey and we danced until nine o'clock in the morning. And then I went to bed, and I cried,' Brigid sighed, 'I don't know how it was, that was all – to say the word. There was no going back then.'

FRANCES SHERIDAN

from *The Dupe*

ROSE. Here's Mr Brilliant, Madam.
MRS ETHERDOWN. Bid him come in.
SIR JOHN. Mr Brilliant! who the d—l's he?
ROSE. My lady's jeweller, Sir.

SIR JOHN. My lady's jeweller, quotha? – Well, I'll treat you with a ring, since you put me in mind of it.

(*Enter Jeweller.*)

MRS ETHERDOWN. Servant, Mr Brilliant – What have you got there?

JEWELLER. I made bold to bring your ladyship a few things, that I fancy will please you.

MRS ETHERDOWN. Let's see.

JEWELLER. Here's a pair of ear-rings will come cheap; I can let your ladyship have them for two hundred and eighty pound.

MRS ETHERDOWN. Baubles! How do you like them, Sir John?

SIR JOHN. 'Pshaw! – If you have got ever a neat diamond hoop, of about nine or ten guineas, my wife may be a purchaser.

JEWELLER. None so low as that, Sir; I have from fifteen to twenty – will your ladyship please to look at these?

SIR JOHN. No, no; you have nothing here that we want.

JEWELLER. I have brought a bill, according to your orders, Madam.

MRS ETHERDOWN. Give it to Sir John.

SIR JOHN. I have no occasion for it, Sir; I suppose I can furnish myself at any other shop as well as at yours. (*Throws down the bill, without looking at it.*)

MRS ETHERDOWN. That's no reason you should not pay him, Sir John.

SIR JOHN. Pay him! for what?

MRS ETHERDOWN. A few trifles that I have had of him.

JEWELLER. You'll find my charges very reasonable, Sir.

SIR JOHN. Well, well, Sir, you may carry your trinkets away.

JEWELLER. If Sir John doesn't like the jewels, Madam, I shall be very ready to take them again, with some allowance.

MRS ETHERDOWN. Sir, I shall keep them – and Sir John will pay you for them another time – Next week you shall have your money.

JEWELLERY. It's very well, Madam. (*Exit Jeweller.*)

SIR JOHN. So Bab! egad, this was a good bold push – and you really thought I was to be drawn in to buy you some of these gym-cracks!

MRS ETHERDOWN. No, no; I know you too well for that; but I think you ought to be ashamed not to pay your honest debts.

SIR JOHN. Debts!

MRS ETHERDOWN. Ay, there are all the people's bills.

SIR JOHN. Bills! (*He takes them up.*)

MRS ETHERDOWN. And vastly reasonable they are, in my mind – I don't suppose the whole (*He examines them.*) amount to above fifteen hundred pounds – You find I have not been extravagant, Sir John.

SIR JOHN. Why, what! – you don't mean, I suppose, that these are debts!

MRS ETHERDOWN. Real debts – contracted by me your lawful wife.

SIR JOHN. And that I am to pay them! you don't mean that?

MRS ETHERDOWN. Undoubtedly – who else should pay a woman's debts, but her husband?

SIR JOHN. And I am *your* husband, and you are *my* wife; and all these are real, actual debts, you say?

MRS ETHERDOWN. All reality, substantial truth, as you will find to your cost – Ha, ha, ha! the farce is at an end between us; and you will find me quite a different creature from what you supposed, I assure you.

SIR JOHN (*Stands and stares at her.*). Why – why – why – what the devil are you? a woman or a fiend?

MRS ETHERDOWN. Ha, ha, ha! a woman, a woman of spirit, a woman of fashion, a woman of pleasure, expence, profusion, luxury! what do you think of me now?

SIR JOHN. Why, you are an imp of hell, I believe; where's your sawcer eyes, and your cloven feet – and, and, and, and – your horns, pray?

MRS ETHERDOWN. Oh, I leave *them* for you, my dear Sir John.

SIR JOHN. Dear! damnable!

MRS ETHERDOWN. Why, do you fancy I could ever have any regard for such a *thing* as you are?

SIR JOHN. Curse me, but I have a good mind to – to –

MRS ETHERDOWN. To beat me, I hope: ha, ha, ha! do, at your peril! Who is it that you threaten with your anger? Do you take me for the tame fool I have appeared all this while? And do you fancy I'll submit to your absurd humours, merely for a maintenance? No, no, Sir; let me tell you, I shall enter upon a new system; I must have my separate purse, separate chariot, separate bed, my morning concerts, routs, visiting days – and if you expect I should live with you –

SIR JOHN. Live with me! fire and sulphur! I'd as soon – I'll lock you up in a dungeon – feed you on bread and water – bastinado you!

MRS ETHERDOWN. Ha, ha, ha, ha!

SIR JOHN. Starve you – make you lie on straw –

MRS ETHERDOWN. I despise your menaces: I am your wife, acknowledged in the face of the world; and I'll make you know it too.

MARIA EDGEWORTH

from *Castle Rackrent*

There were no balls, no dinners, no doings, the country was all disappointed – Sir Kit's gentleman said, in a whisper to me, it was all my lady's own fault, because she was so obstinate about the cross – 'What cross? (says I) is it about her being a heretic?' – 'Oh, no such matter, (says he) my master does not mind her heresies, but her diamond cross, it's worth I can't tell you how much, and she has thousands of English pounds concealed in diamonds about her, which she as good as promised to give up to my master before he married, but now she won't part with any of them, and she must take the consequences.'

Her honey-moon, at least her Irish honey-moon, was scarcely well over, when his honour one morning said to me – 'Thady, buy me a pig!' – and then the sausages were ordered, and here was the first open breaking out of my lady's troubles – my lady came down herself into the kitchen to speak to the cook about the sausages, and desired never to see them no more at her table. – Now my master had ordered them, and my lady knew that – the cook took my lady's part, because she never came down into the kitchen, and was young and innocent in house-keeping, which raised her pity; besides, said she, at her own table, surely, my lady should order and disorder what she pleases – but the cook soon changed her note, for my master made it a principle to have the sausages, and swore at her for a Jew herself, till he drove her fairly out of the kitchen – then for fear of her place, and because he threatened that my lady should give her no discharge without the sausages, she gave up, and from that day forward always sausages or bacon, or pig meat, in some shape or other, went up to table; upon which my lady shut herself up in her own room, and my master said she might stay here, with an oath; and to make sure of her, he turned the key in the door, and kept it ever after in his pocket – We none of us ever saw or heard her speak for seven years after that – he carried her dinner himself – then his honour had a great deal of company to dine with him, and balls in the house, and was as gay and gallant, and as much himself as before he was married – and at dinner he always drank my Lady Rackrent's good health, and so did the company, and he sent out always a servant, with his compliments to my Lady Rackrent, and the company was drinking her ladyship's health, and begged to know if there was any thing at table he might send her; and the man came back, after the sham errand, with my Lady Rackrent's compliments, and she was very much obliged to Sir Kit – she did not wish for any thing, but drank the company's health. – The country, to be sure, talked and wondered at my lady's being shut up, but nobody chose to interfere or ask any impertinent questions, for they knew my master was a man very apt to give a short answer himself, and likely to call a man out for it afterwards – he was a famous shot – had killed his man before he came of age, and nobody scarce dare look at him whilst at Bath. – Sir Kit's character was so well known in the county, that he lived in peace and quietness ever after, and was a great favourite with the ladies, especially when in process of time, in the fifth year of her confinement, my Lady Stopgap fell ill, and took entirely to her bed, and he gave out that she was now skin and bone, and could not last through the winter. – In this he had two physicians' opinions to back him (for now he called in two physicians for her), and tried all his arts to get the diamond cross from her on her death bed, and to get her to make a will in his favour of her separate possessions – but she was there too tough for him – He used to swear at her behind her back, after kneeling to her to her face, and call her, in the presence of his gentleman, his stiff-necked Israelite, though before he married her, that same gentleman told me he used to call her (how he could bring it out I don't know!) 'my pretty Jessica'.

The Mothers' Lament at the Slaughter of the Innocents

(Eleventh Century)

TRANSLATED BY KUNO MEYER

Then as the executioner plucked her son from her breast one of the women said:

Why do you tear from me my darling son,
The fruit of my womb?
It was I who bore him,
My breast he drank.
My womb carried him about,
My vitals he sucked,
My heart he filled.
He was my life,
'Tis death to have him taken from me.
My strength has ebbed,
My speech is silenced,
My eyes are blinded.

Then another woman said:
It is my son you take from me.
I did not do the evil,
But kill me – me!
Kill not my son!
My breasts are sapless,
My eyes are wet,
My hands shake,
My poor body totters.
My husband has no son,
And I no strength.
My life is like death.
O my own son, O God!
My youth without reward,
My birthless sicknesses
Without requital until Doom.
My breasts are silent,
My heart is wrung.

Then said another woman:
Ye are seeking to kill one,
Ye are killing many.
Infants ye slay,
The fathers ye wound,
The mothers ye kill.
Hell with your deed is full,
Heaven is shut,
Ye have spilt the blood of guiltless innocents.

And yet another woman said:
O Christ, come to me!
With my son take my soul quickly!
O great Mary, Mother of God's Son,
What shall I do without my son?
For Thy Son my spirit and sense are killed.
I am become a crazy woman for my son.
After the piteous slaughter
My heart is a clot of blood
From this day till Doom.

MARY BECKETT

from *The Excursion*

Both the men wiped their foreheads and cleared their throats and then one of them said, 'He'll be all right after a while, Mrs Teggart. Don't worry about him. We were all hot after the train when we got to Dublin and we went into a pub opposite the station in Amiens Street. The rest of us went out after a drink or two but he stayed on. Some of the men looked in before the train in the evening and the barman said he had been there all the time. He's not used to drink – that's why he's so far gone.'

Eleanor thanked them coldly and politely though her lips were so stiff that each word was an effort. The men slipped out, closing the door after them.

She sat down slowly, without taking her eyes off him as he slumped with his mouth open and one leg stuck straight out in front of him. She could do nothing for him; she couldn't go near him although she knew he ought to be helped to bed. Then he got up suddenly and began to lurch about the kitchen.

As she watched him her numbness gave place to violent choking rage. He hadn't seen Dublin at all. He had sat drinking in one public house opposite the station for hours, seeing nothing, hearing nothing. There would be no conversation to be made out of that. What right had he to take the day and waste it when she could have made such good use of it. He staggered towards the fireplace, groping blindly for the mantelpiece. She watched him, tightlipped, and then a wild urge made her push him furiously in front of the fire. He threw up his hand, grabbing at the mantelpiece as he fell, and pulled himself into the chair.

Her legs felt weak and she sat down slowly, one hand on her cheek and the other holding the table. She couldn't look at him anymore. What had possessed her to try and push him into the fire? That was murder – she might have killed him. That was what she had come to – murder. Or maybe she had imagined it all.

She turned round quickly and looked at him. He was half-lying in the chair with his eyes open, staring at the ceiling. His cap was

lying at the side of the fire. It was scorching slightly. It made her
head swim as she smelled it. She got up and went slowly to bed,
holding on to every article of furniture on the way.

MOIRA O'NEILL

Her Sister

'Brigid is a Caution, sure!' – What's that ye say?
Is it my sister then, Brigid MacIlray?
Caution or no Caution, listen what I'm telling ye . . .
Childer, hould yer noise there, faix! there' no quellin' ye! . . .
Och, well, I've said it now this many a long day.
'Tis the quare pity o' Brigid MacIlray.

An' she that was the beauty, an' never married yet!
An' fifty years gone over her, but do ye think she'll fret?
Sorra one o' Brigid then, that's not the sort of her.
Ne'er a *hate* would *she* care though not a man had thought of her.
Heaps o' men she might 'a had . . . *Here, get out o' that,*
Mick, ye roguel deshroyin' o' the poor ould cat!

Ah, no use o' talkin! Sure a woman's born to wed,
An' not go wastin' all her life by waitin' till she's dead.
Haven't we the men to mind, that couldn't for the lives o' them
Keep their right end uppermost, only for the wives o' them? –
Stick to yer pipe, Tim, an' give me no talk now!
There's the door fore'nenst ye, man! out ye can walk now.

Brigid, poor Brigid will never have a child,
An' she you'd think a mother born, so gentle an' so mild . . .
Danny, is it puttin' little Biddy's eyes out ye're after,
Swishin' wid yer rod there, an' splittin' wid yer laughter?
Come along the whole o' yez, in out o' the wet,
Or may I never but ye'll soon see what ye'll get!

She to have no man at all . . . *Musha, look at Tim!*
Off an' up the road he is, an' wet enough to swim,
An' his tea sittin' waitin' on him, there he'll sthreel about now, —
Amn't I the heart-scalded woman out an' out now?
Here I've lived an' wrought for him all the ways I can,
But the Goodness grant me patience, for I'd need it wid that man!

What was I sayin' then? Brigid lives her lone,
Ne'er a one about the house, quiet as a stone . . .
Lave a-go the pig's tail, boys, an' quet the squealin' now,
Mind! I've got a sally switch that only wants the peelin' now . . .
Ah, just to think of her, 'deed an' well-a-day!
'Tis the quare pity o' Brigid MacIlray.

GEORGE MOORE

from *A Drama in Muslin*

Mrs Barton, like a coaxing cat, glided up to the marquis and led him into the adjoining room.

'The season is now drawing to its close,' she said winningly, 'we shall be soon returning to Galway. We shall be separating. Olive thinks there is no one like *le marquis*. I know she likes you, but if there is no – no – if it is not to be, I should like to tell her not to think about it any more.'

The marquis felt as if the earth were gliding beneath his feet. What could have tempted the woman to speak like this to him? What answer was he to make her? He struggled with words and thoughts that gave way, as he strove to formulate a sentence, like water beneath the arms of one drowning.

'Oh, really, Mrs Barton,' he said, stammering, speaking like one in a dream, 'you take me by surprise. I did not expect this; you certainly are too kind. In proposing this marriage to me, you do me an honour I did not anticipate, but you know it is difficult off hand, for I am bound to say . . . at least I am not prepared to say that I am in love with your daughter . . . She is, of course, very beautiful, and no one admires her more than I, but −'

'Olive will have twenty thousand pounds paid down on her wedding day; not promised, you know, but paid down; and in the present times I think this is more than most girls can say. Most Irish properties are embarrassed, mortgaged,' she continued, risking everything to gain everything, 'and twenty thousand pounds would be a material help to most men. At my death, she will have more, I −'

'Oh, Mrs Barton, do not let us speak of that!' cried the little man.

'And why not? Does it prove that because we are practical, we do not care for a person? I quite understand that it would be impossible for you to marry without money, and that Olive will have twenty thousand paid down on her wedding day will not prevent you from being very fond of her. On the contrary, I should think −'

'Twenty thousand pounds is, of course, a great deal of money,' said the little man, shrinking, terror-stricken, from a suddenly protruding glimpse of the future with which milord had previously poisoned his mind.

'Yes, indeed it is, and in these times,' urged Mrs Barton.

The weak grey eyes were cast down, abashed by the daring determination of the brown.

'Of course Olive is a beautiful girl,' he said.

'And she is so fond of you . . . she is so nice and so full of affection . . . '

The situation was now tense with fear, anxiety, apprehension; and with resolute fingers Mrs Barton tightened the chord until the required note vibrated within the moral consciousness. The poor marquis felt his strength ebbing away; he was powerless as one lying in the hot chamber of a Turkish bath. Would no one come to help him? The implacable melody of 'Dream Faces,' which Olive hammered out on the piano, agonised him. If she would stop for one moment he would find the words to tell her mother that he loved Violet Scully and would marry none other. But bang, bang, bang the left hand pounded the bass into his stunned ears, and the eyes that he feared were fixed upon him. He gasped for words, he felt like a drunkard who clutches the air as he reels over a precipice, and the shades of his ancestors seemed to crowd menacingly around him. He strove against his fears until a thin face with luminous eyes broke through the drifting mists like a star.

'But we have seen so little of each other,' he said at last; 'Miss Barton is a great beauty, I know, and nobody appreciates her beauty more than I, but I am not what you call in love with her.' He deplored the feebleness of his words, and Mrs Barton swooped upon him again.

'You do not love her because, as you say, you have seen very little of each other. We are going down to Brookfield to-morrow. We shall be very glad if you will come with us, and there you will have an opportunity of judging, of knowing her: and she is such an affectionate little thing.'

Appalled, the marquis sought again for words, and he glanced at his torturer timidly, as the hare looks back on the ever-nearing hounds. Why did she pursue him, he asked, in this terrible way? Had she gone mad? What was he to say? He had not the courage to answer 'No' to her face. Besides, if Violet would not have him, he might as well save the family estates. If Violet refused him! Ah, he did not care what became of him then!

Ten minutes after he said good-night. To get out of the light into the dark, to feel the cool wind upon his cheek, oh! what a relief it was! 'What could have persuaded that woman to speak to me as she did? She must be mad.' He walked on as if in a dream;

the guineas she had promised him chinking dubiously through his
brain. Then stopping suddenly, overcome by nerve excitement, he
threw his arms in the air: his features twitched convulsively. The
spasm passed; and, unconscious of all save the thoughts that held
and tore him – their palpitating prey – he walked onwards. . . .
Black ruin on one side, and oh! what sweet white vision of
happiness on the other! Why was he thus tortured – why was he
thus torn on the rack of such a terrible discussion? He stopped
again, and his weak neck swayed plaintively. Then, in the sullen
calm that followed, the thought crossed his mind: – If he only
knew . . . She might refuse him; if so, he did not care what
became of him. . . . He would accept the other willingly . . . But
would she refuse him? That he must know at once . . . he could
not return to his hotel, the uncertainty was more than he could
bear . . . If she did refuse, he would, at all events, escape the black
looks of his relations. In the cowardice of the thought the weary
spirit was healed, assuaged, as tired limbs might be in a bath of
cool, clear water. Darkness faded, and the skies seemed to glow as
if with a double dawn. Why lose a moment? It was only half-past
ten – an 'outside' would take him in less than two minutes to
Fitzwilliam Place. Yes, he would go.

And as the car clattered he feasted on the white thin face and the
grey allurements of the bright eyes. He would not think – it was
paradise to banish thought.

He was shown upstairs. The ladies were alone, talking over the
fire in the drawing-room. Nothing could be more propitious, but
his fears returned to him, and when he strove to explain the
lateness of his visit, his face had again grown suddenly haggard
and worn. Violet exchanged glances, and said in looks, if not in
words, 'It is clear they have been hunting him pretty closely
to-day.'

'I must apologise,' he said, 'for calling on you at such an hour; I
really did not think it was so late, but the fact is I was rather
anxious to see . . . '

'But won't you sit down, Lord Kilcarney?' said Violet. 'I assure
you we never go to bed before twelve; and sometimes we sit up
here until one – don't we, mamma?'

Mrs Scully smiled jocosely, and the marquis sat down. In an instant his fate was decided. Overcome by the girl's frail sweetness, by the pellucid gaiety of her grey eyes, he surrendered; and his name and fortune fluttered into her lap, helplessly as a blown leaf. He said –

'I came to see you to-night . . . I took the liberty of calling on you at this late hour, because things had occurred that . . . well, I mean . . . you must have observed that I was attached to you. I don't know if you guessed it, but the fact is that I never cared for anyone as I do for you, and I felt I could bear with uncertainty no longer, and that I must come to-night, and ask you if you will have me.'

Violet raised her eyes – 'Say yes,' murmured the marquis, and it seemed to him that in the words life had fallen from his lips.

'Yes,' was the answer, and he clasped the thin hand she instinctively extended to him.

'Ah, how happy you have made me, I never thought such honours were in store for me,' exclaimed Mrs Scully. The discipline of years was lost in a moment; and, reverting to her long-buried self, she clasped the marquis to her agitated bosom with all the naturalness of a Galway shopgirl. Violet looked annoyed, ashamed, and Mrs Scully, whom excitement had stripped of all her grand manners, said –

'And new, me dear children, I'll leave yeu to yerselves.'

The lovers sat side by side. Violet thought of how grand it would be to be a marchioness, of her triumph over the other girls; the marquis of his long years of happiness that would – that must now be his, of the frail grace that as a bland odour seemed to float about his beloved.

Maire Mhac an tSaoi

The Hero's Sleep

Little clustered head sweet as the blackberry,
Little foreign son, my part of this world,
Welcome and nest in my heart,
Welcome under the rafters of this house,
Little morning star come from a long way off.

Blood from without is good;
Look at my little bull calf of a man;
Head him off from the doorway
Or wedge him in a tub:
As healthy as a trout, I swear it!
And every limb prospering:
Beauty a crown for strength –

You took your colour from the autumn
And from the dun rose;
Every yellow is beautiful from its relationship with you.
See Conor our son
Not as was planned, but as
The higher powers willed his coming
Come to my arms, little barley hen,
The lamp is lighting and the night is threatening;
The fox is walking the road;
May no cat from the sea lead him snapping in your direction,
Since you are the candle of the household on a little golden
    candlestick.

When you are asleep under my breast
My love is a wall about you –
But when you set out on your kingly progress
It is in vain for me to spy on you:

What defence will you bring with you?
A charm? A talisman? Or a taboo?
'Never trust the white',
Is the proper prayer for your race.

Like every mother at times
I turn over thoughts in my mind,
And while I dwell on them,
Suddenly you have caught up a wooden spoon!
On the instant as in a dream I see
The hero's light over your countenance,
As though coming towards me there were
The little boy from Eamhain, the Hound of Feats.

MRS KATHLEEN BEHAN

The Family Breaks Up

All our relations were Republicans – to understand Brendan you
have to understand that. My first husband's mother was an even
greater Republican than myself. I saw her in 1939, just before she
went to England – she was about eighty then. I had had measles as
a child, which had permanently damaged my sight, and she
thought I was great – an old blind woman, as she called me, to get
two husbands, where good-looking women could only get one if
they were lucky.

Her house was full of papers – she had one of Lenin and the
Russian Revolution, and then alongside that a copy of the *Catholic
Herald*. She told me she was going to England in a few months.

'You giving up this grand house?' said I. (She lived out along
the Clontarf Road, you know.)

'I am,' says she.

'Well, that's a queer thing,' says I. 'You wanting to go to England after all you've said about them over the years. You to go and live amongst them at the end of your life!'

'I am going,' she says, 'to strike a blow for Ireland, and even if I am at the end of my life I am going to strike it.'

I burst out laughing, God forgive me. The sight of this poor old woman going off to fight the Empire would make a cat laugh.

Well, off she went, and her two daughters, Evelyn and Emily, with her, just before Christmas – we had a party the night before she left. She was as good as her word – it was a bomb from her house that started the bombing campaign in England in 1939. Some people over here were delighted: one man said in the Dail that every bomb that exploded over there raised his heart. Wasn't that a terrible thing to say? I said to that man when I met him at a party, 'You should remember that every British soldier is some poor mother's son.'

Still, Shaw said that a baby carriage couldn't afford to be too gentlemanly if it had to fight a fifteen-ton lorry. Old Mrs Furlong used to bless every bomb. Peggy legs, the old woman used to call the sticks of explosive – you know, after the sticks of sweets that we used to eat when we were children. Queer old peggy legs. One of her daughters let a stick of gelignite fall out of a box and it blew up.

They were all arrested, along with a man – it was all in the papers. He was condemned to twenty years, Emily to five years, Evelyn to two years and Mary Ann Furlong herself to three years. She was muttering to herself when the judge called her to stand up so that he could read her penalty.

'Stand up for His Lordship,' said the court clerk.

'Wait a minute,' said she. 'I'm saying the Angelus, if you ever heard of it.'

'Now,' said she when she was ready. 'What do you want to say to me?'

He said that he had to condemn her to three years of penal servitude, and that she was as bad as the men.

'That's what I always heard,' said she, turning away without looking at him at all.

'Up the Republic,' said Martin, wrestling with the keepers.

'Encore, encore, after that,' said the old woman, walking proudly down the stairs to begin her three years.

It was after that that Brendan went off to England himself and followed in her footsteps. Do you know he said a funny thing to me one time? All his life he had been taught to hate the English, yet later on he wouldn't hear a bad word spoken against them. He claimed they were the finest people he ever had the pleasure to live among.

KATHARINE TYNAN

Any Woman

I am the pillars of the house;
    The keystone of the arch am I.
Take me away, and roof and wall
    Would fall to ruin utterly.

I am the fire upon the hearth,
    I am the light of the good sun,
I am the heat that warms the earth,
    Which else were colder than a stone.

At me the children warm their hands;
    I am their light of love alive.
Without me cold the hearthstone stands,
    Nor could the precious children thrive.

I am the twist that holds together
    The children in its sacred ring,
Their knot of love, from whose close tether
    No lost child goes a-wandering.

I am the house from floor to roof,
    I deck the walls, the board I spread;
I spin the curtains, warp and woof,
    And shake the down to be their bed.

I am their wall against all danger,
    Their door against the wind and snow,
Thou Whom a woman laid in manger,
    Take me not till the children grow!

5

The Bit O' Strange

from *The Exile of the Sons of Usnach*

TRANSLATED BY A. H. LEAHY

Now once it chanced upon a certain day in the time of winter that the foster-father of Deirdre had employed himself in skinning a calf upon the snow, in order to prepare a roast for her, and the blood of the calf lay upon the snow, and she saw a black raven come down to drink it. And 'Levorcham,' said Deirdre, 'that man only will I love, who hath the three colours that I see here, his hair as black as the raven, his cheeks red like the blood, and his body as white as the snow.' 'Dignity and good fortune to thee!' said Levorcham; 'that man is not far away. Yonder is he in the burg which is nigh; and the name of him is Naisi, the son of Usnach.' 'I shall never be in good health again,' said Deirdre, 'until the time come when I may see him.'

It befell that Naisi was upon a certain day alone upon the rampart of the burg of Emain, and he sent his warrior-cry with music abroad: well did the musical cry ring out that was raised by the sons of Usnach. Each cow and every beast that heard them, gave of milk two-thirds more than its wont; and each man by whom that cry was heard deemed it to be fully joyous, and a dear pleasure to him. Goodly moreover was the play that these men made with their weapons; if the whole province of Ulster had been assembled together against them in one place, and they three only had been able to set their backs against one another, the men of Ulster would not have borne away victory from those three; so well were they skilled in parry and defence. And they were swift of foot when they hunted the game, and with them it was the custom to chase the quarry to its death.

Now when this Naisi found himself alone on the plain, Deirdre also soon escaped outside her house to him, and she ran past him, and at first he knew not who she might be.

'Fair is the young heifer that springs past me!' he cried.

'Well may the young heifers be great,' she said, 'in a place where none may find a bull.'

'Thou hast, as thy bull,' said he, 'the bull of the whole province of Ulster, even Conor the king of Ulster.'

'I would choose between you two, ' she said, 'and I would take for myself a younger bull, even such as thou art.'

'Not so, indeed,' said Naisi, 'for I fear the prophecy of Cathbad.'

'Sayest thou this, as meaning to refuse me?' said she.

'Yea indeed,' he said; and she sprang upon him, and she seized him by his two ears. 'Two ears of shame and of mockery shalt thou have,' she cried, 'if thou take me not with thee.'

'Release me, O my wife!' said he.

'That will I.'

Then Naisi raised his musical warrior-cry, and the men of Ulster heard it, and each of them one after another sprang up: and the sons of Usnach hurried out in order to hold back their brother.

'What is it,' they said, 'that thou dost? let it not be by any fault of thine that war is stirred up between us and the men of Ulster.'

Then he told them all that he had done; and 'There shall evil come on thee from this,' said they; 'moreover thou shalt be under the reproach of shame so long as thou dost live; and we will go with her into another land, for there is no king in all Ireland who will refuse us welcome if we come to him.'

Then they took counsel together, and that same night they departed, three times fifty warriors, and the same number of women, and dogs, and servants, and Deirdre went with them. And for a long time they wandered about Ireland, in homage to this man or that; and often Conor sought to slay them, either by ambuscade or by treachery; from round about Assaroe, near to Ballyshannon in the west, they journeyed, and they turned them back to Benn Etar, in the north-east, which men today call the Mountain of Howth. Nevertheless the men of Ulster drave them from the land, and they came to the land of Alba, and in its wildernesses they dwelled. And when the chase of the wild beasts of the mountains failed them, they made foray upon the cattle of the men of Alba, and took them for themselves; and the men of Alba gathered themselves together with intent to destroy them.

Then they took shelter with the king of Alba, and the king took them into his following, and they served him in war. And they made for themselves houses of their own in the meadows by the king's burg: it was on account of Deirdre that these houses were made, for they feared that men might see her, and that on her account they might be slain.

Now one day the high-steward of the king went out in the early morning, and he made a cast about Naisi's house, and saw those two sleeping therein, and he hurried back to the king, and awaked him: 'We have,' said he, 'up to this day found no wife for thee of like dignity to thyself. Naisi the son of Usnach hath a wife of worth sufficient for the emperor of the western world! Let Naisi be slain, and let his wife share thy couch.'

'Not so!' said the king, 'but do thou prepare thyself to go each day to her house, and woo her for me secretly.'

Thus was it done; but Deirdre, whatsoever the steward told her, was accustomed straightway to recount it each evening to her spouse; and since nothing was obtained from her, the sons of Usnach were sent into dangers, and into wars, and into strifes that thereby they might be overcome. Nevertheless they showed themselves to be stout in every strife, so that no advantage did the king gain from them by such attempts as these.

The men of Alba were gathered together to destroy the sons of Usnach, and this also was told to Deirdre. And she told her news to Naisi: 'Depart hence!' said she, 'for if ye depart not this night, upon the morrow ye shall be slain!' And they marched away that night, and they betook themselves to an island of the sea.

Now the news of what had passed was brought to the men of Ulster. ''Tis pity, O Conor!' said they, 'that the sons of Usnach should die in the land of foes, for the sake of an evil woman. It is better that they should come under thy protection and that the (fated) slaying should be done here and that they should come into their own land, rather than that they should fall at the hands of foes.' 'Let them come to us then,' said Conor, 'and let men go as securities to them.' The news was brought to them.

'This is welcome news for us,' they said; 'we will indeed come, and let Fergus come as our surety, and Dubhtach, and Cormac the son of Conor.' These then went to them, and they moved them to pass over the sea.

But at the contrivance of Conor, Fergus was pressed to join in an ale-feast, while the sons of Usnach were pledged to eat no food in Erin, until they had eaten the food of Conor. So Fergus tarried behind with Dubhtach and Cormac; and the sons of Usnach went on, accompanied by Fiacha, Fergus' son; until they came to the meadows around Emain.

Now at that time Eogan the son of Durthacht had come to Emain to make his peace with Conor, for they had for a long time been at enmity; and to him, and to the warmen of Conor, the charge was given that they should slay the sons of Usnach, in order that they should not come before the king. The sons of Usnach stood upon the level part of the meadows, and the women sat upon the ramparts of Emain. And Eogan came with his warriors across the meadow, and the son of Fergus took his place by Naisi's side. And Eogan greeted them with a mighty thrust of his spear, and the spear brake Naisi's back in sunder, and passed through it. The son of Fergus made a spring, and he threw both arms around Naisi, and he brought him beneath himself to shelter him, while he threw himself down above him; and it was thus that Naisi was slain, through the body of the son of Fergus. Then there began a murder throughout the meadow, so that none escaped who did not fall by the points of the spears, or the edge of the sword, and Deirdre was brought to Conor to be in his power, and her arms were bound behind her back.

. . . Deirdre lived on for a year in the household of Conor; and during all that time she smiled no smile of laughter; she satisfied not herself with food or with sleep, and she raised not her head from her knee . . .

'Whom dost thou hate the most,' said Conor, 'of these whom thou now seest?'

'Thee thyself,' she answered, 'and with thee, Eogan the son of Durthacht.'

'Then,' said Conor, 'thou shalt dwell with Eogan for a year;' and he gave Deirdre over into Eogan's hand.

Now upon the morrow they went away over the festal plain of

Macha, and Deirdre sat behind Eogan in the chariot; and the two
who were with her were the two men whom she would never
willingly have seen together upon the earth, and as she looked
upon them, 'Ha, Deirdre,' said Conor, 'it is the same glance that a
ewe gives when between two rams that thou sharest now between
me and Eogan!' Now there was a great rock of stone in front of
them, and Deirdre struck her head upon that stone, and she
shattered her head, and so she died.

A Learned Mistress

TRANSLATED BY FRANK O'CONNOR

It is part of the legend of Irish history that the Renaissance missed
Ireland completely, but Ireland was a part, however minute, of
Europe, and in their dank and smoky castles, the Irish and Anglo-
Irish aristocracy lived a life that fundamentally differed little from
the life that went on in the castles of the Loire. Isobel Campbell,
the great Countess of Argyle, wrote a poem to her chaplain's – but
really, I can't say what – and the joke was taken up by her
Campbell kinsmen, who still wrote classical Irish. She might have
written this little poem, and who will dare to say that it does not
breathe the whole spirit of the Renaissance?

> Tell him it's all a lie;
>   I love him as much as my life;
> He needn't be jealous of me –
>   I love him and loathe his wife.

> If he kill me through jealousy now
>   His wife will perish of spite,
> *He*'ll die of grief for his wife –
>   Three of us dead in a night.

All blessings from heaven to earth
        On the head of the woman I hate,
And the man I love as my life,
        Sudden death be his fate.

John B. Keane

from *Letters of an Irish Parish Priest*

The High Valleys,
Lochnanane.

Dear Father O'Mora,

I am a married woman whose family is done for and all gone their ways abroad in the world from their home in the High Valleys. My husband and I were always united and happy until two months ago he got a parcel from his brother Martin in Chicago. First I thought the contents was a rubber boat or the like but I found out in time it was a rubber woman that could be pumped up with air or filled with warm water until it became the size and shape and colour of a fine figure of a young woman exactly the same in appearance as Dolores Viago, the famous film star that was in voyage to mars. She has glass eyes, dark with long lashes exactly the same as the real Dolores and when she is squeezed she sighs like a real person from some gadget under her oxter. My husband has gone crazy over her, taking her to bed and talking to her and buying the like of a watch for her and some nice clothes and underwear. I do not know what to do Father. There are more cases than me here in the High Valleys which was always a holy and contented place where the Rosary is never missed in any house even still but he puts Dolores Viago in the trimmings and puts her alongside him and says a decade in a woman's voice, by the way it would be her talking. He answers in his own voice and I answer too for the sake of quietness. Others have their false women too but it was my brother-in-law Martin that sent the first one. Then they all started writing for one. I only saw one other. She is the image of Mrs Freddie Fox-Pelley who rides the horses on T.V. except she hasn't a stitch of clothes on her.

Will you guide us Father out of this evil pass. Pray for us Father. Our men are shoving into the years and are turning a bit foolish. Frighten them Father know would they forget this nonsense.

Yours faithfully,
Noreen Hannassy (Mrs).

JULIA O'FAOLAIN

from *No Country for Young Men*

Honesty and mate-jettisoning horrified Grainne. Yet she felt prepared to believe the part of the message which said that good sex made you a healthier and better-balanced person. Her balance was bad. She didn't need anyone to tell her that. But you had to decide how you were going to play things. As this fellow had said, choice caged you and the best choice, she felt, was a charitable hypocrisy. It was easier on families, more exciting for the hypocrite. She had seen the new, frank mode in operation among foreign friends. Married or not, according to this formula, you brought your bed companion to dinner and acknowledged him. This revived the matter of social definitions and table manners and the discredit he might reflect on you if he didn't have them. But where then was the romance of finding a creature uniquely appropriate to night, intimacy and bed? Someone as anonymous as a merman or satyr with furry, frondy thighs. Asocial and outside time. She had seen paintings of these lewd creatures of old fantasy when she was in Italy and they had taken her breath away. Right in the museums, framed in ornate gilt: a publicly acknowledged, ancient dream of pastoral bliss and folly. Naked girls in forests, minotaurs and goatmen licking at them. Frondy wetnesses, clear streams, pink nipples, mouths open down to their tonsils. She forgot the names of the painters, remembering only Raphael who painted virgins, God help us, with prim little mouths. She hadn't profited from that year at all. It had been the wrong time for her, and the men were terrifying. She remembered their eyes X-raying her clothes. She had been innocent but had understood. You couldn't fail to. Their thighs pressed against the cloth of their trousers and so did their genitals. Was it all an act, you wondered, or were they really that mad for it? That great at it? You'd like to know. To have tried just once. Instead, she'd married Michael and after a while she'd given up wanting it. Maybe an emotional duct dried up on you. Like religion: use it or lose it. Of course there *had* been — no, don't think of *him*! That had been a case, if ever there was one, of falling between the old and the new. 'Make yourself cheap,' warned the old ethic, 'and men will take you lightly.' She had and he had. Very. But with a stranger, an anonymous man of the night, you didn't care about being taken lightly. You *wanted* to be wanton like witches who, in nocturnal orgies, did the opposite of everything they did by day. It would purge and renew you. Surely it would.

She had been reminded of her ancient female dream by this man's electric look. Was she counting her chickens before they were hatched? Was she even sure that she had a hold of an egg? Maybe this fellow didn't even know he was looking? Had a cast in his eye? Dare she ask: 'Sir, is yours an anthropologist's or a tourist's scrutiny? Are your intentions reliably dishonourable? Do you realize that you've shaken a decent wife and mother out of her ethical corsettings? Do you know the responsibilities that that entails? She needs a new shape: needs the surround of a new presence, like a cuckoo's egg, in the nesty warmth of some unknown bird.'

David Greene

from *The 'Act of Trust' in a Middle-Irish Story*

There was a fine, firm, righteous, generous princely king ruling over Ireland, Niall Frassach, son of Fergal. Ireland was prosperous during his reign. There was fruit and fatness, corn and milk in his time, and he had everyone settled on his own land. He called a great assembly (oenach) in Tailtiu once, and had the cream of the men of Ireland around him. Great kings and wide-eyed queens and the chiefs and nobles of the territories were ranged on the stately seats of the assembly. There were boys and jesters and the heroes of the Irish in strong eager bands racing their horses in the assembly.

While they were there, a woman came to the king carrying a boy child, and put him into the king's arms. 'For your kingship and your sovereignty,' said she, 'find out for me through your ruler's truth (fir flatha) who the carnal father of this boy is, for I do not know myself. For I swear by your ruler's truth, and by the King who governs every created thing, that I have not known guilt with a man for years now.'

The king was silent then. 'Have you had playful mating with another woman?' said he, 'and do not conceal it if you have.' 'I will not conceal it,' said she; 'I have.' 'It is true (is fir),' said the king. 'That woman had mated with a man just before, and the semen which he left with her, she put it into your womb in the tumbling, so that it was begotten in your womb. That man is the father of your child, and let it be found out who he is.'

LETITIA PILKINGTON

from *Memoirs of Mrs Letitia Pilkington*

So, it seems, I was to be the bait wherewith he was to angle for gold out of a rival's pocket – a scheme which had a twofold prospect of gain annexed to it; for while a lover has hope, he seldom quits the chace and will even thank the husband for taking the friendly freedom of using his purse; and yet should the gallant be detected in taking any friendly freedoms with the wife in return, the law is all against him; damages and imprisonment must ensue – which considerations may serve as a warning to all men not to invade properties, or commit wilful trespass on their neighbour's ground.

If my readers are by this time the least acquainted with my spirit, they may judge, I looked on this project with the contempt it deserved; however, I promised complaisance, which indeed Mr Worsdale's seeming merits might well deserve . . .

Mr Pilkington and Mr Worsdale were at the play; they met us going out, and Mr Pilkington committed me to the care of his friend, who had a coach waiting to convey me home; but Mr Pilkington went to his old rendezvous to the actress, to my very great mortification, because I really preferred his conversation to any other in the world. However, he was so complaisant, he used every evening to send Mr Worsdale to keep me company while he pursued his pleasures; and, as I shall answer it to Heaven, he did everything in his power to forward and encourage an amour between his friend and me . . .

Another instance either of his extraordinary confidence in my fidelity to him, or rather indifference about it, was that he obliged me to go alone with his friend to Windsor, though, as it was winter, there was no possibility of going there and returning the same day, it being twenty miles distant from London; so that we had not only two days but a night also to pass together. Could any husband be more obliging to his rival than to give him such an opportunity to accomplish his wishes? Had mine but concurred, I had then been undone; for truly the gentleman tried every argument to win me to them; but in vain. My husband's misconduct in exposing me to such temptation stung me to the quick; nay, I could not help believing they were both in a plot to betray me to ruin; and, as we were at the top Inn in the town, I started at every noise of horsemen who stopped there; and concluded, though falsely I believe, that Mr Worsdale had given Mr Pilkington a direction where to find us; and, as this imagination wholly possessed me, I little regarded either the elegance of our entertainment or the tenderness and passion the gentleman expressed in every word and look: his soft endearments were all lost on one who regarded him as an enemy. I was obstinately sullen, and pretended weariness on purpose to quit his company; but I lost all patience when, calling to the maid to show me to my chamber, I found there was but one – nay, and but one bed too – provided for two guests; for, it seems, my gentleman had so ordered it, hoping, no doubt, to supply my husband's place.

I was now in a manner convinced there was treachery intended against me, and reproached my desiring swain in such bitter terms that he had no way to prove his innocence but by retiring, though very reluctantly, to another apartment; and I took special care to barricade my own, not only double-locking it but also placing all the chairs and tables against the door, to prevent a possibility of being surprised.

Sam Hanna Bell

from *December Bride*

The days that followed in Rathard were tense and silent. Hamilton proved fiercely adamant, determined to give up nothing: yet he lacked the courage to ask the woman to give up Frank. There was nothing further to be hidden now from any one of them. The brothers moved warily in each other's presence, knowing that a sudden action was fraught with violence. And Sarah went about the house, eyes and ears strained to catch every word and gesture. Sometimes when her mind became tired and numb, she felt that she was watching a scene and she had neither sympathy nor blame for the woman she saw. Yet when she was nakedly conscious of what was happening to her she never wavered in her calm attention to the men, never setting one above the other. And all the time her fear was being dissipated by a mounting pride fed by all the humiliating years when she was a girl. She had two men . . .

Although there was sufficient passion and confusion present, which, in a more inactive and leisured household might have broken out in violence, the insistent demands of the farm took them away from each other for long periods . . . These communal activities made it necessary for decisions to be taken in the evenings, at the fireside, and advice offered and considered. And as the outside world thawed and the sound of running water was heard once more in the dykes, so speech began to move again, sluggishly at first, between the brothers.

Yet, in the end, Frank and Hamilton fought. They had left the house after the midday meal and as Sarah went to the door to empty a basin, she heard the heavy breathing of men. There was something evil and deliberate about the sound. Then there came a hoarse grunt and the thud of a falling body. She flew to the byre and saw them on the ground between the stalls. The animals were tossing their heads in fear and crowding away from the struggling men. Hamilton knelt on his brother's chest, his fist raised like a hammer and his head nodding patiently as he timed his blow on the face jerking from side to side beneath him. The woman screamed and lifting a graip, struck Hamilton on the back. The brothers rose slowly, picking the filth from their clothes. They stared at each other like men who had wakened from a nightmare. 'You fools!' shouted Sarah. They did not even turn to look at her. They stood there, their hands moving mechanically over their bodies, gazing into each other's faces. Hamilton closed his fist and stared at it dumbly. Is this the fist I meant to smash you with, brother? his eyes asked. Slowly the woman felt their hurt bewilderment: she knew that at that moment she did not exist. She was alien, barred, shut away from them. And the knowledge of her own guilt quelled any rebellion in her. She turned away, her head lowered, and left them. Yet before she had reached the house, her instinct was stirring in revolt against this bond between the men.

W.B. YEATS

from *Deirdre*

CONCHUBAR. One woman and two men; that is the quarrel
            That knows no mending.

AMANDA MCKITTRICK ROS

from *Thine in Storm and Calm*

She knew all the forms of vice to which the human flesh and mind are heir and to continue a career of evil she bought Modesty Manor, adopting the nom-de-guerre of Pear. It was soon visited by all the swanks of seekdom within comfortable range of her rifling rooms of ruse and robbery, degradation and dodgery.

She had a swell staff of sweet-faced helpers swathed in stratagem, whose members and garments flowed with the lust of the loose, sparkled with the tears of the tortured, shone with the sunlight of bribery, dangled with the diamonds of distrust, slashed with sapphires of scandal and rubies wrested from the dainty persons of the pure.

Always on the alert for attractive magnets whose characters had still to be moulded by artful manoeuvres, she found the rosy little rural ruby, Helen Huddleson, would add considerably in advocating her accursed object. With this thought haunting her she had succeeded so far by intriguing Helen to her house of dissipation, damnation, disorder and distrust.

Anon

from *The History of Betty Ireland*

There was no woman of the sisterhood who knew how to behave herself as Betty did; she jilted the gentlemen, and prostituted herself to those of an inferior rank, if she liked their persons. She would drink like a fish-woman, and her company was coveted by men of every degree; for she adapted her discourse to the capacity of those that came to her house. If they did not approve the doxies which she constantly retained, they were at liberty to send for or bring others with them; and her house was the rendezvous of many ladies and merchants' wives. . . .

A warrant being obtained, she gave bail; and having traversed the indictment, was tried at the next session after.

Her counsellors pleaded very strenuously, that allowing what had been said to be true, yet it could not affect her so far as to prove her a bawd; and the informing constables deposed that they never heard any complaint made against her keeping a disorderly house, or found any lewd persons in it.

The justices were divided in their opinions; however, the majority over-ruled the rest, and ordered Betty to be carted from the Gate-house in Westminster, to Charing Cross, which sentence she suffered.

She soon broke up house-keeping, and resolved to be revenged of one of the justices who exerted himself against her more haughtily than the rest.

She was informed that he loved a pretty girl in a corner as well as the most demure sinner; and after some small time had passed, she took a fine lodging, and dressing herself in rich apparel, she flung herself one day in his way, who could not resist the temptation.

She kept him at a distance for some time, which made him the more eager, and during that time she looked out for one of the pockiest fellows she could get to lie with her. Being now deeply pickled, she admitted his worship to her embraces, who soon found he had met a hotter reception than he expected.

The next day she left her lodgings, and hired an apartment in an apothecary's house, by whom she was salivated, and the justice was necessitated to go into the powdering tub. But her revenge ended not here, for she wrote a smart account of what had befallen him, of the presents he had made her, and what he suffered; wherein she set him forth in such lively colours, that everybody knew his person by his picture. This was a second mortification to him, and he used all the means imaginable to find out Betty, but all to no purpose.

It has been a general observation, which time and experience have evinced to be true, that women are endearing, indulgent, and compassionate by nature; but when they become apostates from virtue, divesting themselves of chastity, and embrace vice, they degenerate from bad to worse, till at last their endearments are changed into rage, their indulgence into hatred, and their compassion into cruelty. They will stick at nothing to gratify their revenge, lust, and barbarity; and when they have contracted such vicious habits, they become more implacable, more barbarous, than the most savage Indians. They triumph in acts of inhumanity, and take a pleasure in putting their fellow creatures to the severest torments.

KATE O'BRIEN

from *Mary Lavelle*

'Do you know that you're seducing me?' he asked her.

She leant forward, and pulled him down so that he lay with his head in her lap. 'I can't go away until – until I've been your lover.'

He turned in her lap and took her in his arms, drew her down until they lay together, face to face. Holding her thus, very close to his breast, he spoke with urgent clarity, in the slow Spanish she always understood.

'I'm only twenty-five,' he said, 'and only two years married. I have always sneered at the vulgarity of infidelity. I have never given a snap for any other woman but Luisa. Now at the first test I am undone. Since my first sight of you I have lived in bitter unfaithfulness and coldness. You seem so terrifyingly beautiful, you're so artless and innocent and heavenly that I have fooled myself that you are the sort of myth that might ruin any man, however true, however virtuous! But is that so? Are you a fatal exception that makes splinters of everything normal? Or am I just vulgarly infatuated, and is this a showing-up? Are you my true love – or an illusion?'

She kissed him, very gently.

'I'm an illusion. So are you. But there's nothing to be afraid of in that.'

'You're very young. Much younger than me. You know nothing about love.'

'Only what it feels like.'

'You don't know that.'

'Oh, I know what you're thinking – but I'm not afraid. I know you'll hurt me, and that what I'm asking for will be painful and unhappy for me now. I know the risk too. I'm not a fool at all, Juanito. I've grown up very fast since meeting you. But if I think all that unimportant, so that no one else can ever have from me what I want you to have – oh, dear love!'

'Ah, darling! Darling!'

They clung together trembling. Juanito kissed her eyes and ears and throat and though Mary burned to kiss him too, intuition told her to lie still awhile, to let him love her. She lay under his hands and marvelled at her peace. She thought of school and home, of John, of God's law and of sin, and did not let herself discard such thoughts. They existed, as real and true as ever, with all their traditional claims on her − but this one claim was his, and she would answer it, taking the consequences. And as to John, she reflected with casuistic pity that what she was about to do now would make things easier for him. A moony story about being in love with a Spaniard would render him prolongedly unhappy and half-hopeful − but this other news, revolting him, would turn his heart away from her, and cure it.

'Dear love, I love you,' she whispered to Juanito's whispers.

'I'm going to take you,' he said. 'I'm going to make you my lover, but not, believe me, on your silly terms.' He smiled at her.

'Yes, on my terms.'

'No, sweet. Love is not so easy as that. But we won't talk now − we're lovers now.'

He began to undress her, gently and kindly.

'Aphrodite!' he said, when she gleamed white and shivered in the moonlight. 'Ah, you're too beautiful! You'll blind me! Mary, I love you, I love you!'

He took her quickly and bravely. The pain made her cry out and writhe in shock, but he held her hard against him and in great love compelled her to endure it. He felt the sweat of pain break over all the silk of her body. He looked at her face, flung back against the moss, saw her set teeth and quivering nostrils, beating eyelids, flowing, flowing tears. The curls were clammy on her forehead now, as on that day when she came into Luisa's drawing-room from the bullfight. She was no longer Aphrodite, but a broken, tortured Christian, a wounded Saint Sebastian. He held her still and murmured wild Spanish words of love. His heart hurt him as if it might in fact break. How grotesquely we are made, he thought, how terrible and insane are our delights and urgencies. I love her, love her, and yet I tear and break her for my pleasure, because I must, because I love her, because she loves me. Oh love, forgive me! Oh, forgive me, love!

She opened her eyes and smiled a little at him.

'It's all right now,' she said. 'Oh, it's better now.'

'No,' he said, 'you must have patience. Love takes a lot of learning.'

She drew his head down to hers.

'Not such a terrible lot – honestly. I love you, I love you.'

JENNIFER JOHNSTON

from *The Invisible Worm*

'Daddy did something dreadful to me.'

She hung the towel neatly on the wooden towel horse and then bent to pull the plug from the bath.

'What was that, dear?' Her voice was reasonably uninterested.

'In the summerhouse. He . . . '

She straightened up and looked at me, her face suddenly worried.

' . . . did something . . . '

'What? What sort of thing?'

'Dreadful.'

The words I had thought of wouldn't come out of my mouth.

'The most dreadful . . . '

'What are you talking about?'

'You know. That thing. I don't know the name for it. He did that thing to me. That's why I fell into the sea. I wanted to drown. I tried to and then I . . . couldn't. Please don't be angry. Please don't kill me.'

'I'm not sure what you're trying to say, Laura, but you're frightening me. I wish you would be more clear.'

I just shook my head.

'I can't,' I whispered.

'Of course you can.'

'I haven't the words.'

She took a step towards me and I thought for a moment that she was going to hit me.

'Don't . . . '

I put my hands up to protect my face.

'Of course you have the words, Laura! What did he do that was so dreadful?'

'Rape.' I whispered the terrible word, and I felt myself blushing as I said it – as if I were lying, I thought, blushing as if I were lying.

'I'm not lying,' I said to her. 'I promise you I'm not lying.' There was just the cheerful sound of the bath water running, gurgling down through the pipes.

'Do you know what that word means?' she asked me at last.

'Yes.'

'If I thought you were telling the truth, I'd kill him,' she said.

'I am telling the truth. Why do you think I wanted to go away to boarding school?'

'You mean he's been doing this for ages?'

'Not this. Not exactly that . . . thing, but he's been . . .' The words dried up again.

'Sometimes,' she said, 'girls invent this sort of thing. Boys do, too . . . children . . . for some purpose of their own. Sometimes that happens. Children who are, perhaps, slightly mad or perhaps vindictive. Something like that . . .'

'I was never mad before now,' I said, and walked past her out of the bathroom.

Sean O'Faolain

from *The Faithless Wife*

Adding it all up (he was a persistent adder-upper), only one problem had so far defeated him: that he was a foreigner and did not know what sort of women Irish women are. It was not as if he had not done his systematic best to find out, beginning with a course of reading through the novels of her country. A vain exercise. With the exception of the Molly Bloom of James Joyce the Irish Novel had not only failed to present him with any fascinating woman but it had presented him with, in his sense of the word, no woman at all. Irish fiction was a lot of nineteenth-century *connerie* about half-savage Brueghelesque peasants, or urban *petits fonctionnaires* who invariably solved their frustrations by getting drunk on religion, patriotism or undiluted whiskey, or by taking flight to England. Pastoral melodrama (Giono at his worst). Or pastoral humbuggery (Bazin at his most sentimental). Or, at its best, pastoral lyricism (Daudet and rosewater). As for Molly Bloom! He enjoyed the smell of every kissable pore of her voluptuous body without for one moment believing that she had ever existed. James Joyce in drag.

'But,' he had finally implored his best friend in Ailesbury Road, Hamid Bey, the third secretary of the Turkish embassy, whose amorous secrets he willingly purchased with his own, 'if it is too much to expect Ireland to produce a bevy of Manons, Mitsous, Gigis, Claudines, Kareninas, Oteros, Leahs, San Severinas, what about those great-thighed, vast-bottomed creatures dashing around the country on horseback like Diana followed by all her minions? Are they not interested in love? And if so why aren't there novels about them?'

His friend laughed as toughly as Turkish Delight and replied in English in his laziest Noel Coward drawl, all the vowels frontal as if he were talking through bubble gum, all his r's either left out where they should be, as in *deah* or *cleah*, or inserted where they should not be, as in *India-r* or *Iowa-r*.

'My dear Ferdy, did not your deah fatheh or your deah mamma-r eveh tell you that all Irish hohsewomen are in love with their hohses? And anyway it is well known that the favourite pin-up gihl of Ahland is a gelding.'

'Naked?' Ferdinand asked coldly, and refused to believe him, remembering that his beloved had been a hohsewoman, and satisfied that he was not a gelding. Instead, he approached the Italian ambassador at a cocktail party given by the Indonesian embassy to whisper to him about *l'amore irlandese* in his best stage French, and stage French manner, eyebrows lifted above fluttering eyelids, voices as hoarse as, he guessed, His Excellency's mind would be on its creaking way back to memories of Gabin, Jouvet, Brasseur, Fernandel, Yves Montand. It proved to be another futile exercise. His Ex groaned as operatically as every Italian groans over such vital, and lethal, matters as the Mafia, food, taxation and women, threw up his hands, made a face like a more than usually dessicated De Sica and sighed, *'Les femmes d'Irlande? Mon pauvre gars! Elles sont d'une chasteté . . . '* He paused and roared the adjective, ' . . . FORMIDABLE!'

Ferdinand had heard this yarn about feminine chastity in other countries and (with those two or three exceptions already mentioned) found it true only until one had established the precise local variation of the meaning of 'chastity'. But how was he to discover the Irish variation? In the end it was Celia herself who, unwittingly, revealed it to him and in doing so dispelled his last doubts about her susceptibility, inflammability and volatility – despite the very proper Sisters of the Spanish Steps.

The revelation occurred one night in early May – her Meehawl being away in the West, presumably checking what she contemptuously called his Gaelic-squeaking scissors . . .

'My dearest and perfect love, you have told me everything about Irishwomen that I need to know. None of you says what you think. Every one of you means what you don't say. None of you thinks about what she is going to do. But every one of you knows it to the last dot. You dream like opium eaters and your eyes are as calm as resting snow. You are all of you realists to your bare backsides. Yes, yes, yes, yes, yes, you will say this is true of all

women, but it is not. It is not even true of Frenchwomen. They
may be realists in lots of things. In love, they are just as stupid as
all the rest of us. But not Irishwomen! Or not, I swear it, if they
are all like you. I'll prove it to you with a single question. Would
you, like Mimi, live for the sake of love in a Paris garret?'

She gravely considered a proposition that sounded delightfully
like a proposal.

'How warm would the garret be? Would I have to die of
tuberculosis? You remember how the poor Bohemian dramatist
had to burn his play to keep them all from being famished with the
cold.'

'Yes!' Ferdy laughed. 'And as the fire died away he said, "I
always knew that last act was too damned short." But you are
dodging my question.'

'I suppose, dürling, any woman's answer to your question
would depend on how much she was in love with whoever he was.
Or wouldn't it?'

Between delight and fury he dragged her into his arms.

'You know perfectly well, you sweet slut, that what I am asking
you is, "Do you love me a lot or a little? A garretful or a
palaceful?" Which is it?'

Chuckling she slid down low in the settee and smiled up at him
between sleepycat eyelashes.

'And you, Ferdy, must know perfectly well that it is pointless
to ask any woman silly questions like that. If some man I loved
very much were to ask me, "Do you love me, Celia?" I would
naturally answer, "No!" in order to make him love me more. And
if it was some man I did not like at all I would naturally say, "Yes,
I love you so much I think we ought to get married," in order to
cool him off. Which, Ferdy, do you want me to say to you?'

'Say, ' he whispered adoringly, 'that you hate me beyond the
tenth circle of Dante's hell.'

She made a grave face.

'I'm afraid, Ferdy, the fact is I don't like you at all. Not at all!
Not one least little bit at all, at all.'

At which lying, laughing, enlacing and unlacing moment they
kissed pneumatically and he knew that if all Irishwomen were

Celias then the rest of mankind were mad ever to have admired women of any other race.

Their lovemaking was not as he had foredreamed it. She hurled her clothes to the four corners of the room, crying out, 'And about time too! Ferdy, what the hell have you been fooling around for during the last six weeks?' Within five minutes she smashed him into bits. In her passion she was more like a lion than a lioness. There was nothing about her either titillating or erotic, indolent or indulgent, as wild, as animal, as unrestrained, as simple as a forest fire. When, panting beside her, he recovered enough breath to speak he expressed his surprise that one so cool, so ladylike in public could be so different in private. She grunted peacefully, and said in her muted brogue, 'Ah, shure, dürling, everything changes in the beddaroom.'

DERMOT BOLGER

from *The Woman's Daughter*

I always promised myself afterwards that it would be the last time. I was so resolute that it seemed nothing he could do in the future would break my grip. I remember how the moonlight would slant into the room and I'd lie here occasionally hearing footsteps. I'd think anyone out at that time of night must be embarked on some sort of adventure. Johnny would be curled up back in his pyjamas beside me with his body so hot it was like a furnace to touch. He always fell asleep immediately afterwards, mumbling a few words as he untangled himself and turned to the wall. It wasn't long after my eleventh birthday, and I'd think of our two guardian angels hovering, wounded and disappointed, on both sides of the bed. Daddy thought nothing of us sharing the one bed, especially after the nightmares I used to have. It was as a badge of courage that I'd first undressed, like in all the other games of dares. Johnny'd saved up his pocket money to buy a packet of birthday candles. He'd light one on the dressing table to make it exciting. In the half light it was just like those old games of marriage. I'd imagine him as my husband coming home tired from work. In the darkness it was more sinister, his actions more frightening, more like a stranger. One step, two step, the bogeyman is coming, his hands pushing mine downwards towards that hard and slippery thing. I'd enjoy the excitement then, his breath coming fast against my ear, his hands never still. It was afterwards that I'd lie awake, knowing that what I was doing was wrong, and terrified that there might be some way for people to guess my sin. I'd think of my father in the next room, how his face would crumble in if he ever knew. I knew that I had let him down, and grew more guarded now and withdrawn in school.

The single candle is stuck with wax onto the top of the chipped dresser. Its small flame lengthens and draws in the shadows along the walls of the room. They lie curled together against the cool sheet below and the rough warmth of blankets above, her feet drawn up into his stomach as she allows him to peel each nail on her toes, just the scratch of nail cutting through nail filling the silence. Then the light clicks in their father's room and they pause for a few moments before they tentatively begin. The blankets are tossed down below their knees, her nightdress slipped up above her head. His hand stroking across her thigh, he suppresses her giggles with his lips. Both close their eyes, retreat into their separate illicit fantasies: *her husband coming home to her from work*, he draws her hand down to the rigid penis, *his own girl in a doorway down the dark side entrance of the Casino*, where the first light hairs cluster around its base. Stiff with the thrill of fear and excitement they lie, afraid to creak the bed springs, until he grimaces in his cramped position, his mouth pushed into her hair to stifle the panting as his limbs overspill with pleasure. She watches the white stains settle over her naked stomach, feels his body relax as he turns and drifts towards sleep. The cloth is tucked beneath the mattress, she shivers as she wipes herself, the husband's knock, his bicycle ticking down towards the shed, the first kiss on her lips in the sparkling kitchen, all gone, all gone.

POLLY DEVLIN

from *Dora*

The truth was that before she met her lover Dora had become accustomed to living her life in a state of boredom, anxiety, and obsessive love for her children, a cocktail of some potency and one, she felt, that many women drank daily. After a day's inbibing of these spirits, husbands might well wonder why their wives were not themselves, the young, nubile nannies they thought and hoped they had married. No one, Dora thought, could get through the violent tedium of young, daily married life, without becoming angry, so that the very way a husband ate a meal could become a matter for thought-murder. She wondered how many husbands found their wives lovable and exciting after they had borne their children. Life as a single parent is the daily state of many married women and their husbands become interruptions. She imagined thousands of husbands seeking each night among the bedclothes and the duvets for the bodies they once found so exciting and coming instead upon the stony thighs of the women they find they have married.

There was no doubt if Dora was being honest that before she met her lover she was up on some crow's nest in the structure of her life, on the lookout. Dora knew that at certain times in any woman's life, the treasure chest that is her feminity, her sexuality is battened down, and Nature, sly old brute, pretends to be quiescent, to be soothed. You might as well be a block of wood as be a woman, thought Dora. She looked at the other women of her age with young children whom people in shops called dear and whose husbands, at certain kinds of gathering, were asked what the wife did. Then one day, when the children had become less demanding, having grown out of the stage where their well-being was a biological imperative, the same young women, well not so young now, sent out a message, just the faintest signal, hardly discernible one might think, that famous bat squeak, the merest whiff of musk, and the men came, dropping out of the trees or

from behind the wheels of their cars or from behind their office
desks or their dry martinis, hairs on the palms of their hands or
their buttocks, swarthy or white-skinned, crew-cut or curly-
haired, appearing like the annunciation with no sense of their own
ridiculousness, from all kinds of unlikely vestries, certain, so as far
as Dora could see, of their welcome, all of them, no matter how
dunce-like, or complacent.

Dora watched. At work, at parties, at gatherings, she saw that
the woman would almost certainly know more about the verities of
life than the person who moved across the ground towards her, but
that would not occur to him. The odds are that she would even be
grateful for the approach of the male creature as he sidled up. At
least in the decades of the sixties and seventies, Dora's time for
these observances, this all seemed true, though it also seemed to
Dora in her older age that things hadn't much changed, and that
wise, good, young women were as foolish as ever. And the truth,
she had to admit, was that the young man had not sidled up to
her – he had come running across her garden like Mercury, and
she, intoxicated by his speed and her own upsurge of adrenalin,
had welcomed him.

BRID MAHON

from *A Time to Love: The Life of Peg Woffington*

'You are a fool and a failure, Patrick Taafe,' she said in a passion.
'God's truth, if I were a man I swear I'd go into that gaming room
and sweep the boards.'

He started to laugh and she lashed out at him in her rage.

'Listen to me, Peg.' He caught her fists, held them in an iron
grip. 'You've given me an idea. Whaley has arranged a gambling
session tonight in Squire Connolly's lodge.'

'The Hellfire Club,' she shuddered. 'Where you expect to recoup your losses. I don't want to hear any more.'

'For Christ's sake, listen. I'll wager Whaley that a lady will suddenly materialise in our midst. It's an unwritten rule that no female crosses the threshold of the lodge. Old Nick swears he can smell women a mile off. Like his master Whaley, he hates your sex.'

'I'll not hear any more of your crazy schemes.' She was shouting and he was ordering her to keep her voice down.

'All you have to do is wear the breeches. Dress up as Sir Harry Wildair. I'll introduce you as my nephew, Peter, lately arrived from London. Whaley likes them young and fresh. Then we'll reveal all, collect the winnings and I'll take you home.'

'The whole of town saw me play Wildair.' He was driving her mad with his talk.

'Whaley has never been known to put a foot inside the Playhouse. He has no interest in actresses. He wouldn't know you from his washerwoman.'

'And what of the rest?'

'Ely is a sportsman. He'll be glad to see Whaley bested.'

'And what about Dashwood? He's a known satanist. It's common gossip he poisoned five wives.'

Taafe smiled grimly. 'Dashwood may have his quirks and fancies but he believes in neither God nor the devil.'

She knew she was insane to listen to him but things were desperate and the gamble just might pay off. 'What if they rape me?'

'Whaley's too depraved for such simple pleasures, my pet.' His blue eyes had the look of a gambler willing to stake his soul in the hope of a win. 'I might borrow more. Raise the stakes. Two hundred guineas at ten to one. It would net us two thousand. God's guts, Whaley will be the laughing-stock of the town when word gets around.'

Her lips trembled. 'Will you promise to take me away the moment the wager is paid?'

'Will you promise to lie with me at least once before the bell tolls for me?'

She softened. 'Don't talk like that. When all this is over we'll plan something. Maybe we'll go to America.'

'I'd go to hell and back with you,' he said, hugging her so fiercely that she was sure every bone in her body would break.

She was out of her body, suspended in air, looking down on a small, fat figure bent over a naked woman spread on a cruciform table which was covered with a black cloth. Black candles flickered and the idiot acolyte waved his censer. Monkish figures were prostrate before the altar before the terrible rite of the black mass. The satanic priest raised a chalice and drank, then kissed the breasts and genitals of the naked woman, cold serpent's tongue, drove her back into her body. In the candlelight something glinted. His penis was swollen, ringed with spikes. He was mounting her and she braced herself for the thrust, and was filled with such pain, revulsion, that she screamed, went on screaming, though she made no sound.

A hooded figure watched through a drugged mist. Insanely the old servant giggled, swung the censer in a circle, loosing coals that perfumed the air, burned the vestments, the altar cloth. Above her the satanic priest moved, took a candle, set fire to the acolyte's hair, turning flesh and bones into a burning torch. A scream of agony ended in a sobbing wail and the room was filled with the horrifying stench of burning flesh. Patrick Taafe, shocked sober, jumped up, knocking over chairs and kneeling figures in his frenzied dash to where Peg lay. She saw his wild eyes and glistening forehead as he gathered her up in his arms. After that she remembered no more.

from *Encounter*

TRANSLATED BY PATRICK C. POWER

(Iubhdan, the king of the little people, and Bebo his wife, are brought into the presence of the king of Ulster, Fergus. Iubhdan introduces himself and his queen.)

Said Fergus: 'Take him out to the common household and hold him carefully.' Iubhdan was brought out after that and Bebo was left inside with Fergus and he fell in love with her and made love to her. When he was having intercourse with her he placed his hand on the top of her head. The queen inquired why he did this. 'I shouldn't be surprised,' said he, 'if my penis which is seven fists long, didn't go through your head and you only three fists high. For that reason I put my hand on your head.'

'Desist from it Fergus,' said the queen, 'it's many a thing that a woman's loins absorb.'

Fergus went then to where Iubhdan was. 'I went into your wife, Iubhdan,' said Fergus.

'She liked that,' said Iubhdan.

'I went again,' said Fergus.

'You enjoyed that,' said Iubhdan.

'I went the third time,' said he.

'Both of you liked that,' said Iubhdan.

'I went into her a fourth time,' said Fergus.

'Shit in her from this out! If you'd care to do me some good,' said Iubhdan, 'don't leave me among these people here. The breath of the big men is making a corrupt corpse of me . . . '

Patricia Burke Brogan

from *Eclipsed*

MANDY. I could write to Elvis in Hollywood!

BRIGIT. No! Not again!

(*Nellie-Nora blesses herself.*)

MANDY. Juliet! Will you give me a pencil! Quick!

JULIET. You're going to write to a filmstar in America? Will he get the letter?

MANDY. Of course he will! Elvis gets all my letters!

MANDY. Now! (*Slowly as she writes*) 'My dearest Elvis,
Thank you for your beeeautiful wonderful photo! I'll keep it under my pillow! Please send me more photos of yourself for my scrapbook too. You're gorgeous! All my love and – a hundred kisses!'

JULIET. A hundred kisses?

MANDY. Yours forever! – No! Yours forever and ever and ever! Your darling Mandy! Kiss! Kiss! Kiss!

NELLIE-NORA. Your sweetheart sounds nicer!

JULIET. Maggie Brennan was writing a letter to a boy and she wrote S.W.A.L.K. – sealed with a loving kiss! Will you put that in too, Mandy?

MANDY. Yes! That's a great idea!

(*Mandy writes S.W.A.L.K. She and Juliet giggle. Brigit is scornful.*)

BRIGIT. Yours until Hell freezes! And now the address! Your address, Mandy? Your address?

(*Brigit snaps letter from Mandy and reads.*)

BRIGIT. Saint Paul's Home for Penitent Women! Home for the unwanted. The outcasts! Saint Paul's Home for the women nobody wants!

MANDY. No, Brigit! No! Give me my letter! . . .

Mandy hugs mannikin which the others have dressed up as Elvis. Women watch her, then return to work. Lights are rose-coloured.

BRIGIT. He's askin' you to marry him, Mandy!

MANDY. I will! Oh, yes! I will!

NELLIE-NORA. I've a great idea! We'll dress Mandy for her

weddin'! Hurry! Hurry! Mother o' God! He might change his mind!

(*Cathy takes off Mandy's white apron and fastens it veil-like on her hair, then drapes a long white sheet over her shoulders as a train. Juliet helps.*)

CATHY. A pure white veil! A long satin train!

JULIET. You're very posh, Mandy!

NELLIE-NORA. You look gorgeous, Mandy!

MANDY. I am! I'm gorgeous!

BRIGIT. Remember! I'm the Bishop! I'll do this important wedding!

(*Brigit jumps onto table up right and dresses in crimson soutane. She puts surplice/mitre on her head while women finish dressing Elvis . . . Brigit deepens her voice and says:*)

BRIGIT. Silence!

(*The women push basket towards Bishop/Brigit. Juliet holds long train.*)

BRIGIT. Do you, Mandy Prenderville, take this Elvis Presley as your lawful husband to have and to hold in sickness and in health until death do you part?

MANDY. I do! Oh, yes! I do!

BRIGIT. And now, Elvis Presley, do you –

MANDY. But, Brigit, his real name is Elvis Aron Garon Presley!

BRIGIT. Do you, Elvis Aron Garon Presley, take Mandy Prenderville –

NELLIE-NORA. He does! He does!

BRIGIT. Don't interrupt, Nellie-Nora! Do you, Elvis Aron Garon Presley, take Mandy Prenderville as your lawful wedded wife to have and to hold in sickness and in health until death do you part?

(*Nellie-Nora rocks Elvis's head in assent. Cathy is in tears. Sister Virginia stands at doorway in background, but the women do not notice her.*)

BRIGIT. I now pronounce you man and wife. Bless you!

NELLIE-NORA, BRIGIT AND CATHY. Congratulations, Mandy!

(*Mandy begins to kiss Elvis, but Brigit interrupts.*)

BRIGIT. You – may kiss the bride, Elvis Aron Garon Presley!

(*Mandy kisses Elvis. The women cheer.*)

NELLIE-NORA. Have as many babies as you want now, Mandy!

ANNE ENRIGHT

from *The Portable Virgin*

Dare to be dowdy! that's my motto, because it comes to us all – the dirty acrylic jumpers and the genteel trickle of piss down our support tights. It will come to her too.

She was one of those women who hold their skin like a smile, as if she was afraid her face might fall off if the tension went out of her eyes.

I knew that when Ben made love to her, the thought that she might break pushed him harder. I, by comparison, am like an old sofa, welcoming, familiar, well-designed.

This is the usual betrayal story, as you have already guessed – the word 'sofa' gave it away. The word 'sofa' opened up rooms full of sleeping children and old wedding photographs, ironic glances at crystal wine-glasses, BBC mini-series where Judi Dench plays the deserted furniture and has a little sad fun.

It is not a story about hand-jobs in toilets, at parties where everyone if in the van-rental business. It is not a story where Satan turns around like a lawyer in a swivel chair. There are no doves, no prostitutes, no railway stations, no marks on the skin. So there I was knitting a bolero jacket when I dropped a stitch. Bother. And there was Ben with a gin and tonic crossing his legs tenderly by the phone.

'Thoroughly fucked?' I asked and he spilt his drink.

Ben has been infected by me over the years. He has my habit of irony, or perhaps I have his. Our infections coincide in bed, and sometimes he startles me in the shops, by hopping out of my mouth.

'Thoroughly,' he said, brushing the wet on his trousers and flicking drops of gin from his fingertips.

There was an inappropriate desire in the room and a strange dance of description as I uncovered her brittle blonde hair, her wide strained mouth. A woman replete with modified adjectives, damaged by men, her body whittled into thinness so unnatural you could nearly see the marks of the knife. Intelligent? No. Funny? No. Rich, with a big laugh and sharp heels? No. Happy? Definitely not. Except when he was there. Ben makes me too sad for words. I finished the row, put away my needles and went to bed.

6

Money and Power

JULIE O'CALLAGHAN

Pep-Talk to Poets from Their Sales Manager

Alright, you Irish guys –
first off – I love ya – got it?
Hey – where's the blarney?
Quit looking like you were just included
in a 'Contemporary British Poetry' anthology
or something; we got books to sell!
Now, what abouta few Volkswagons in bogs
or grey streets with graffiti on the walls –
scenes like that;
you haven't been turning it out lately.
How come? I need stuff with slogans, guys.
Folksy stuff – know what I mean?
I'm doin my best but it's all lookin
a little like a yawner at this stage.
That's all, lads – keep at it.

I wanna see all a you extra-terrestrials
gravitating over here double quick, fellas.
'Take me to yer reader' – right, guys?
Now let's get serious – huh?
Here's your sales chart – up, up, up!
Kinda like a flying saucer discovering
new universes of humanoids who wanna book of poetry.
We're gonna capture new markets, aren't we,
and no more traitors writing
transvestite translations or we'll zap them
with our lazer gun – right?
Goils! Move yer feminist little butts over here.
Yer doin terrific. Lots of sarcasm
about what termites we guys are, lots of PMT,
lots of mothers acting square – magnificent!

My god, you're going great guns, ladies.
OOPS! I mean WOMEN don't I?
We want a lot of hype comin up to Christmas
so those cash registers keep singing.
Just one word of advice: see if you can
Virginia Woolf-up your images a bit
and who knows what we can do?
Sisterhood is powerful!

All miscellaneous misfits, up front please.
Lookit pals, *you* want an easy life,
I wanta easy life and *we all* want super-sales,
so why not give up this poetic individuality baloney
and get yourselves an angle, join a group.
My job is tough enough
without you weirdos
lousing it up even more!

W. R. O'HEGARTY

Two letters Regarding the Treatment of Women in De Valera's Constitution

JOINT COMMITTEE OF WOMENS' SOCIETIES AND SOCIAL WORKERS

9 Ely Place,
Dublin, Oct. 10 1936....

Dear Mrs Concannon,

The Joint Committee asked the President to receive a deputation on matters affecting women, in view of the possibility of the new Constitution. The President has refused for the second time to give us a personal interview and has asked for a Memorandum, which we are sending, re-iterating our request to be received.

We are sure you will appreciate our feeling that a memorandum on such a matter is not adequate, and may not even be seen by the President. The Committee feel that a similar request from a body representing sixteen men's associations would not be refused.

We should be most grateful if you, the only woman representative on the Second Chamber Commission, used your influence with the President to induce him to receive a deputation.

The Committee greatly appreciated your kindness and helpfulness in putting their views before the Commission.

Yours faithfully,

W.R. O'Hegarty

(Hon. Sec.)

Mrs Concannon TD
Dail Eireann
Leinster House
Kildare Street
Dublin

JOINT COMMITTEE OF
WOMENS' SOCIETIES AND SOCIAL WORKERS

9 Ely Place,
Dublin, Nov. 11 1936.....

Dear Sir,

With regard to the request for a further memorandum, S. 9278, the Committee has never seen any results achieved from the sending of a memorandum not followed by a personal interview. We should have felt encouraged to send a second memorandum if we had received any queries concerning, or criticism of the first. The Constitution is being changed, and amendments may be inserted which might vitally affect the interests of women, and it seems to us to be grossly unjust that a Committee representing 16 women's societies will not be accorded an hour of the President's time.

An emergency meeting of all the affiliated societies is being called for next Monday to put the President's refusal before them and decide what further action should be taken.

It may be pointed out that on the question of the Women Police the President referred us to the Minister for Justice. A detailed scheme, which had previously been submitted to the Heads of the Garda Síochána was sent to the Minister for Justice, and he, like the President, was unable to find time to receive a deputation. (A copy of his reply is enclosed.) The ignoring of women and their interests would seem to be a concerted policy of the Government.

Yours faithfully,
W.R. O'Hegarty

(Hon. Sec.)
The Private Secretary to the President
Government Buildings
Upper Merrion Street
Dublin

DR YVONNE SCANNELL

The Constitution and the Role of Women

Women had no part in framing Bunreacht na hÉireann. Not one woman took part in drafting it. Of the 152 TDs who had an opportunity to comment on the draft, only three were women. These three, known sorrowfully as the 'Silent Sisters', made no meaningful contribution whatever to the debate on the draft.

Outside the Dáil, a number of women's organisations protested in
vain against certain articles – so much so that de Valera admitted
knowing that he had a 'bad reputation with women'.

The article in the Constitution that attracted the fiercest
opposition from women at the time was article 41.2 This article
reads:

1. In particular, the State recognises that by her life within
the home, woman gives to the State a support without which the
common good cannot be achieved.

2. The State shall, therefore, endeavour to ensure that *mothers*
shall not be obliged by economic necessity to engage in labour to
the neglect of their duties in the home. [Emphasis added.]

There are two ways of looking at this article. The first is to take
de Valera at his word and to regard the first paragraph as a tribute
to the work that is done by women in the home as mothers. The
second paragraph, if it is to be regarded as anything other than a
paternalistic declaration, can be read as a constitutional guarantee
than no *mother* is to be *forced* by economic necessity to work outside
the home to the neglect of her duties there. The mothers covered
by this guarantee would include widows, unmarried mothers,
mothers whose husbands are unable or unwilling to support their
families, even relatively rich mothers with heavy expenses such as
those necessitated by caring for ill or handicapped children.

The second way of looking at article 41.2 is different. To some,
it is grossly offensive to the dignity and freedoms of womanhood.
It speaks of woman's *life* within the home (not just her work
there), implying that the natural vocation of woman (the generic is
used, so it means *all* women) is in the home. It is the grossest form
of sexual stereotyping. It can be regarded as an implicit denial of
freedom of choice to women in personal matters, a freedom taken
for granted by men. It speaks of *mothers* neglecting their duties,
but omits to mention the duties of fathers. It fails to recognise that
a woman's place is a woman's choice.

Despite the protests about article 41.2, de Valera refused to
delete it. His reasons for refusing show that his vision of the role of
woman in Irish society was that of a full-time wife and mother in
an indissoluble marriage, having a 'preference for home duties'

and 'natural duties' as a mother. This protected creature is to be supported by 'a breadwinner who is normally and naturally in these cases when he is alive, the father of the family . . . able by his work to bring in enough to maintain the whole household'.

De Valera's defence of article 41.2 can be rationalised by an attitude of romantic paternalism, which, as a famous American judge has said, 'in practical effect puts women, not on a pedestal, but in a cage'.

Constitutional history shows that it is the second and less positive interpretation of article 41.2 that de Valera's successors in office have almost invariably adopted. Lawyers for the state tried to rely on article 41.2 to justify tax discriminations against married women in the Murphy case, and social welfare discriminations against women in the recent Hyland case. They successfully relied on it to justify social welfare discriminations against deserted husbands obliged to assume full-time child care duties in *Dennehy* v. *Minister for Social Welfare*.

The Oireachtas in its legislation continued to assume that the normal vocation of women was in marriage, motherhood and the home. In particular, the social welfare system until very recently was founded on the philosophy that women are dependent on men and that society must only support them when this dependence (for one reason or another) ceases. The women of 1937 were right to fear that the state would give article 41.2 the most restrictive interpretation of their rights.

JONATHAN SWIFT

from *Directions to the Waiting-Maid*

If you are in a great Family, and my Lady's Woman, my Lord may probably like you, although you are not half so handsome as his own Lady. In this Case, take Care to get as much out of him as you can; and never allow him the smallest Liberty, not the squeezing of your Hand, unless he puts a Guinea into it; so, by degrees, make him pay accordingly for every new Attempt, doubling upon him in proportion to the Concessions you allow, and always struggling, and threatning to cry out or tell your Lady, although you receive his Money: Five Guineas for handling your Breast is a cheap Pennyworth, although you seem to resist with all your Might; but never allow him the last Favour under a hundred Guineas, or a Settlement of twenty Pounds a Year for Life.

I must caution you particularly against my Lord's eldest Son: If you are dextrous enough, it is odds that you may draw him in to marry you and make you a Lady: If he be a common Rake, (and he must be one or t'other) avoid him like *Satan*; for he stands less in awe of a Mother, than my Lord doth of a Wife; and, after ten thousand Promises, you will get nothing from him, but a big Belly or a Clap, and probably both together.

NELL MCCAFFERTY

In View of the Circumstances

The woman was married and expecting her 14th child. Her husband was unemployed.

'Fourteen children' said the justice, looking down at the woman. She pulled her coat nervously around her swollen belly. 'Well, what do you have to say for yourself? This is the fourth, no fifth offence of shop-lifting,' continued the justice.

'The last time was for my children,' whispered the woman.

'I beg your pardon?' asked the justice.

'And this time my husband was getting a chance of a job,' continued the woman. 'He's been idle this two years, and I was trying to steal a pair of overalls to make him presentable.'

'But this is your fifth offence,' said the justice.

'The other times it was for my children,' said the woman.

'You've certainly brought a lot of children into the world. Fourteen,' said the justice.

'Thirteen,' said the woman, 'I'm expecting the 14th.'

'You present a problem to me,' said the justice.

'I owe £100 rent and the light's about to be cut off,' said the woman, crying now.

'Does your husband know?' asked the justice.

'No,' she said, 'he doesn't know about any of them. I get belted around for less.'

'You mean if he knew, there'd be trouble?' translated the justice. 'What does he work at?'

'Any kind of work,' she said, still crying. 'A couple of months ago he got three days' work and –'

'You look young. How old are your children?' interrupted the justice.

'The eldest is 15 and the youngest is 12 months,' said the woman.

'You know, this is your fifth offence. What am I going to do with you? Can you help me out yourself? You're going to have another child shortly,' said the justice.

'You'd do anything when your children are hungry,' whispered the woman.

'I know that. Are you short of money?' the justice asked this pregnant mother of thirteen, whose husband was unemployed.

'I owe £100 in rent,' the woman said.

'What happened on the four previous occasions?' the justice turned to the ban garda.

'She appealed and got the three months' sentence suspended,' said the ban garda.

'You see, you've been given a chance,' said the justice . . .

Had the woman's solicitor represented her, he might or might not have told the justice how she squatted into a two-bedroom Corporation flat from a one-bedroom Corporation flat; how her previous home had been destroyed by fire; how she suffered from anaemia. And other details.

It might or might not have made a difference.

Iris Murdoch

from *The Red and the Green*

But of course these explanations, upon which he himself later meditated, were in a way otiose. Millie was a gorgeous desirable object. He wondered why all men were not in love with her, and soon began to suspect that they were. She was an over-flowing vessel, a plump, gay, generous woman. There was some coldness, some shivering, shrewd thinness in Christopher which needed her desperately, which clung to her as to a source of warmth and life. He only half concealed his need, watching her with a large affectation of detachment, and enraptured by the cool amused gaze which, in the formality of their new relationship, she with equal affectation adopted. He remembered how, in the old quarrelling days, Millie would sometimes shout out, 'But I adore Christopher!' Now, as their poker-faced relation gradually broke down into tenderness and laughter, he realized that Millie was not only grateful, she was prepared in effect to adore him. This made Christopher very happy indeed.

Time passed, and Millie's affairs became more involved and difficult. Christopher lent her more money. He gave her advice too, but he was a prudent rather than an original capitalist and an ineffective helper. Millie took advice in other quarters, without revealing the seriousness of the situation, and merely increased the muddle she was in. She was incapable of economies. Christopher watched these developments with mixed feelings, and gradually an idea which seemed to him both sinister and delightful formulated itself in his mind. Millie's difficulty would be Christopher's opportunity.

That he might ever ask Millie to marry him was a notion which, after he had fallen in love with her, he had early dismissed. He wanted to be happy, to enjoy the deliciousness of her company, not to ask too much; and it seemed clear that she could not possibly want to marry him. She was a spoilt girl, he was not by any means her only admirer, and she ostentatiously enjoyed her freedom. She 'adored' him, but she was not in the least in love with him. 'Adoration' was something different. Millie skipped about, bounded like a dog, shouted more than usual when Christopher arrived. But she let him depart without repining. She liked the intermittent character of their converse. He would have wished to be with her day and night. He coveted her body with a passion which his shrewd hedonism constantly quieted and checked. He did not care, at his age, to suffer the sleepless nights of unsatisfied desire, and he did not in fact suffer them. But he wanted Millie; and he knew that she did not, in that way, want him.

Discretion about money had somehow cast a veil of secrecy over their whole relationship. It was not generally known that they were fond of each other or that they met so often; and Christopher kept up for the benefit of some of his relations the fiction that he found Millie 'trying'. He did this partly out of an innate taste for the clandestine, partly because of the money question, and partly because Millie wanted it that way. Christopher was realistic and resigned about Millie's desire for secrecy. A popular woman who enjoys her admirers and is also kind-hearted will naturally want to keep her friendships strictly sealed off from each other. To each man Millie seemed available with an undivided attention and a full heart. Christopher was consoled by being more in her confidence than most. He at least knew about the others; and he was fairly certain that, at present at any rate, these 'relationships' which Millie cultivated remained at a level of innocuous flirtation, although hearts other than hers were sometimes cracked in the process.

E.B. d'Auverge

from *Wanderjahre*

While Lola Montez (then twenty-six) was on a visit to Madame Steinkiller, the wife of the principal banker of Poland, the old viceroy sent to ask her presence at the palace one morning at eleven o'clock. She was assured by several ladies that it would be neither politic nor safe to refuse to go; and she did go in Madame Steinkiller's carriage, and heard from the viceroy a most extraordinary proposition. He offered her the gift of a splendid country estate, and would load her with diamonds besides. The poor old man was a comic sight to look upon – unusually short in stature, and every time he spoke, he threw back his head and opened his mouth so wide as to expose the artificial gold roof of his palate. A death's-head making love to a lady could not have been a more disgusting or horrible sight. These generous gifts were most respectfully and very decidedly declined. But her refusal to make a bigger fool of one who was already fool enough was not well received . . . Now when Lola Montez appeared that night at the theatre, she was hissed by two or three parties who had evidently been instructed to do so by the director himself. The same thing occurred the next night; and when it came again on the third night, Lola Montez, in a rage, rushed down to the footlights, and declared that those hisses had been set at her by the director, because she had refused certain gifts from the old prince, his master. Then came a tremendous shower of applause from the audience; and the old princess, who was present, both nodded her head and clapped her hands to the enraged and fiery Lola.

Here, then, was a pretty muss. An immense crowd of Poles, who hated both the prince and the director, escorted her to her lodgings. She found herself a heroine without expecting it, and indeed without intending it. In a moment of rage she had told the whole truth, without stopping to count the cost, and she had unintentionally set the whole of Warsaw by the ears.

The hatred which the Poles intensely felt towards the govern-

ment and its agents found a convenient opportunity of demon-
strating itself, and in less than twenty-four hours Warsaw was
bubbling and raging with the signs of an incipient revolution.
When Lola Montez was apprised of the fact that her arrest was
ordered, she barricaded her door; and when the police arrived she
sat behind it with a pistol in her hand, declaring that she would
certainly shoot the first man dead who should break in. The police
were frightened, or at least they could not agree among themselves
who should be the martyr, and they went off to inform their
masters what a tigress they had to confront, and to consult as to
what should be done. In the meantime, the French Consul
gallantly came forward and claimed Lola Montez as a French
subject, which saved her from immediate arrest; but the order was
peremptory that she must quit Warsaw.

FRANK MCGUINNESS

from *The Factory Girls*

ELLEN. Right. Stage one completed. Now Major Tom to ground
control.

ROSEMARY. There are two phones, do you notice?

ELLEN. I don't mean the phones, you stupid bitch. I meant the
call system.

(Ellen *goes to the desk and switches on the system. She reads prepared
statement.*)

ELLEN. Good afternoon, ladies. This is the representative of the
action committee, consisting of the examiners and their message
girl. We have decided to take action over proposed unfair working
conditions. Our first step is the takeover of the office until such
times as better conditions are offered. This is our last communication with the outside world until then. Good afternoon and good
luck. (*She switches off the system.*) Well, with luck, one or two
people will have shit themselves in the rush to get to Rohan.

REBECCA. How long will it take?

ELLEN. Not long I imagine. Come on. All hands start getting the stuff out.

(*The women begin to unpack making improvised conversation. Food, clothes, cigarettes, crockery, cutlery, pots, a kettle, two small gas canisters and a stove. Rosemary has brought an inordinate amount of clothes, some of which she holds up against herself, admiring them in an imaginary mirror. Out of Una's case may appear any variety of objects, the only specifics being those mentioned.*)

REBECCA. Why did you bring an electric fire, Una?

UNA. It still gets very cold at nights, Rebecca.

ELLEN. Woman, did you ever realise why you don't bring a fire to work with you? This place is heated by oil, central heating. Have you heard of it?

UNA. I've heard of it well enough to know central heating can go wrong. I'm glad I brought my fire.

ROSEMARY. Two hot water bottles?

UNA. Quite sensible as well. One's for my bad stomach and nobody's borrowing it.

VERA. Oh sweet Jesus, she's brought a chip-pan.

UNA. You'll thank me when you're dying for a chip.

REBECCA. We are not frying chips in this place and that is that.

ELLEN. Rosemary, what exactly or where exactly do you think you are? Standing there admiring yourself, do you think this is a bloody fashion show?

ROSEMARY. I'm just looking at this skirt. I don't suit blue as a rule but I think this is very nice. My mother bought it for me this morning when she heard I was definitely going with yous. Isn't she not right in the head? I said to her who would see me locked in Rohan's office, but she said you could always have an accident.

(*Rosemary and Vera talk, Una has started to remove at least two bottles of Bushmills interspersed with large packs of toilet rolls.*)

REBECCA. The bare necessities of life I see.

UNA. Mock on. I'll have the best laugh. I know yous are all hiding the drink you brought. I didn't expect to see that. But if this is a long stay, I notice there's a dire shortage of the other lady (*pointing to toilet rolls*). Don't come crying to me when yous are skiptipaloor-ing from the shithouse.

(*A loud rattle is heard.* Rohan's *voice is heard off.*)

ROHAN. Ellen?

ELLEN. Hold it.

ROHAN. Ellen, are you in there?

ELLEN. Yes, Mr Rohan. I've come up as you asked me.

ROHAN. What in Christ's name are you about?

(*Pause*)

ROHAN. Ellen, what are you doing?

(*Pause*)

ROHAN. What in hell's name are you up to?

ELLEN. Our purpose has already been made clear.

ROHAN. Our? How many of you are in there?

ELLEN. One

VERA. Two.

UNA. Three.

REBECCA. Four.

ROSEMARY. Five.

(*Pause*)

ROHAN. Now ladies, be sensible, open the door.

(*Pause*)

ROHAN. Open the door.

(*Pause*)

ROHAN. I warn you to leave this office.

ELLEN. You leave.

ROHAN. Right, you're out of a job, each and every one of you.

ELLEN. OK. We'll take yours.

ROHAN. You're out of your minds, do you hear me, you're mad.

ELLEN. Aah, is your head beginning to go?

ROHAN. Jesus Christ, what are you trying to do?

(*Pause*)

ROHAN. Now look, I'll ring Mr Bonner, we'll reason this out around a table. Open the door.

VERA. Go to hell.

ROHAN. I ask you calmly once more, get out of my office.

ELLEN. That's right, calm down. Even men your age can get heart attacks. Don't die on us, that would be too easy. We're not leaving until you improve your offer.

ROHAN. You stupid bitches.

UNA. Good evening, Mr Rohan, and good night.

ROHAN. You leave me with no alternative.

ELLEN. You left us with no alternative.

ROHAN. Oh no. You're going to find out who gives orders here. Christ, damn you, I tried to be fair all along, but now the kid gloves are off. You're going to learn the hard way who you're up against.

ELLEN. I'm trembling with fear.

ROHAN. Every worker in this factory is being sent home now. If I can't get into work there, nobody else will.

VERA. That doesn't make much of a difference, does it? When you could work here there still wasn't many working.

ROHAN. Laugh on, we'll see who has the last laugh.

ELLEN. I'm bursting my sides. Go home and get your nappies changed.

MAY MORTON

Spindle and Shuttle

And good was twined with ill
When spinning yarn and weaving linen were
Still country crafts. The old blind woman with
Her spinning-wheel beside the open door
Would spin and spin with finger-tips for eyes
Matching the spindle's hunger to her own
Till each was satisfied; but she could feel
The warm sun on her face, the kindly wind
Lay gentle hands upon her faded hair.

The cottage weaver cramped and stiff from toil
That made a convict's treadmill of his loom
Could run a mile around his one green field
To flex his muscles; and could pause a while
To hear the blackbird's song, or sing his own.

Back and forth
Warp and Woof;
Wing of angel,
Devil's hoof:

The hand-loom turns to lumber and the wheel
Becomes a thing to win a tourist's glance
When far from field and bird the factories rise,
A myriad spindles and a maze of looms
Cradled within four walls. On every side
Thin streets of small brick houses spawn and sprawl
Though none could give its neighbour elbow-room.
Sleep flies each morning at the siren's shout
And women hurry, shapeless in their shawls,
In multitudes made nameless, to the mill,
Some young, some old, and many great with child:
All wage slaves of the new industrial age,
All temple vestals of the linen god.
Some will put off their shoes from off their feet
And barefoot serve the spindles all day long,
Some will keep constant vigil where the looms
Like giant nightmare spiders pounce and crawl
With spider skill across the tethered web
While captive shuttles darting to and fro
Will weave, not hare and hounds, but shamrock sprays
To tempt nostalgic exiles. None may rest
Till day ends and the siren sets them free.
Even the children, sad as wilting flowers
Plucked in the bud, must give their days to toil,
Their nights to weariness and never know
How morning comes with laughter to a child.

But linen prospers and the linen lords
Build fine town mansions for their families
And plan a city hall whose splendid dome
Will soar above the long lean streets and look
Beyond them to the green encircling hills.

> Back and forth
> Warp and woof:
> Wing of angel,
> Devil's hoof:

Young men see visions and old men dream dreams:
Their beacons lit on summits far away,
Their faith entangled in the baffling rope,
Good twined with evil, evil twined with good.
Strand upon strand with whiter strands for some;
The spinner and the weaver in the mill
Now earn a living and have time to live,
Children whose mothers were half-timers once
Untouchables in factory and school
May learn to play and even play to learn
And think of spindle as a word to spell.
Mill-girls have shed their shawl-cocoons and shine
Brighter than butterflies. With gleaming hair
And ankles neat in nylon each can look
Into her mirror with a practised smile
And see herself the reigning linen queen.
The great domed hall four-square in stubborn stone
With polished marble floors magnificent
As any Rajah's palace has stood now
For nearly half a century. Strange how
The little laurel hedge that hems its lawns
Reveals we still are country-folk at heart
Deep-rooted in the fields our fathers tilled.

> Back and forth
> Warp and woof:
> Wing of angel,
> Devil's hoof:

The white strands catch the moment's light, and show
A pattern in the fabric, damask smooth.
We spin and weave, with yarns and years and tears
Our webs of linen and of destiny:
A people's life is netted in the loom
Their story echoes in the spindle's song.

EILIS DILLON

from *Across the Bitter Sea*

Samuel was five years old when Mary moved into the big house. In theory she was his nurse but no nurse wears a red silk dress and dines at the master's table. George had looked so old – to an eighteen-year-old girl he became old George at once – but he was only fifty then, tall and thin and athletic, with dark weather-beaten skin and iron-gray hair. He treated her like a lady, so successfully that she could refuse him nothing. After her first night in his bed, she ran home to her mother, trailing her red dress in the grass and ruining her London shoes.

'Didn't you know that was what he wanted?' her mother said. 'You're spoiling your good dress. Now that it's done you may as well go back. You won't mind the next time. It's like that always.'

'But it's a sin.'

'And what are we to eat?' her mother asked tersely.

'You fixed it with him!' Mary said in horror.

'I did,' said Mrs Hogan. 'We're alive and we'll stay that way if you have sense. He won't see us in want. He's a decent man. We're the one age. I know him all my life. He'll treat you right. Don't let him know you got such a fright. Men don't like that. Was he rough?'

'No.'

Mary felt ashamed, for some reason, and could not look at her mother.

'Then you're all right. It's not in him to be rough. He'll never marry again. He won't risk another of his own class after that Sylvia and he's a strong, healthy man that needs a wife.'

'You know a lot about him,' Mary said sourly.

'I do. I'm the one age with him, I tell you.' She stopped suddenly and then said fiercely, 'Get back at once. The child might come to harm while you're gone.'

So Mary had never complained to her mother again, though seven years later she had had satisfaction in hearing her uncle, her mother's brother Andrew, tell his sister that she had acted disgracefully.

'You sold your own daughter,' he said. 'You gave her to that landlord as a tallywoman when you should have been fighting to your last breath for her.'

'We're not all fighters,' Mrs Hogan said, but sounding frightened, as well she might since Andrew was standing over her with his fists clenched and his face like thunder.

'You're no fighter, though all belonging to you were,' Andrew said bitterly, sounding all the stronger because of the slight American intonation that he had picked up. 'Hadn't you any respect for the rest of us that you saw striking a blow for Ireland in '98? Don't you remember that we had to clear out for fear of the likes of George Flaherty?'

'George Flaherty is a decent man,' Mrs Hogan said faintly.

It was her last protest. Andrew withered her with a blast of words in which he accused her of betraying the whole country as well as her own daughter. In the end Mrs Hogan was in an agony of tears and agreeing that Mary must be got out of old George's clutches at once. Her child was dead, and Andrew had the delicacy not to say that this made things easier. He had a fine man eager to have her, Thomas MacDonagh of Cappagh, whose brother had travelled all the way to Chicago from Boston to tell Andrew of Mary's position and to make an offer for her.

So Mary had left George and Samuel, half bewildered with grief, for though she knew that they represented the sins of lust and luxury, still she loved them both with all her heart. George had aged a lot in the seven years and had developed a few old-

mannish mannerisms that were a warning of coming decay, but
still she hated leaving him. She was used to his ways and afraid of
what she would encounter with Thomas, whom she had seen only
once. He had come over from Cappagh to a funeral in Moycullen
and had met her with Samuel at the edge of the lake.

'Mary Hogan.' He repeated her name when she had said it to
him. 'And you're nurse to George Flaherty's child.'

Samuel was too far away to hear. He was skimming stones very
skillfully on the smooth water of the lake. Mary cast her eyes
down. Anyone could see that Samuel was too old for a nurse.
Thomas had heard the whole story, of course, as it was a scandal in
the parish.

He said delicately, 'I'd like to see you again, Mary.'

She said, not more than half meaning it, 'I'd like it too.'

He sent a message to his brother in Boston and got her for
himself. Such decisive action was frightening. It might denote a
bully, or at least a man who would always be congratulating
himself on having rescued her from a sinful state.

SEAN O'CASEY

from *The Plough and the Stars*

THE COVEY. There's only one freedom for th' workin' man:
contrhol o' th' means o' production, rates of exchange an' the
means of disthribution. (*Tapping* Rosie *on the shoulder*.) Look here,
comrade, I'll leave here to-morrow night for you a copy of
Jenersky's *Thesis on the Origin, Development an' Consolidation of the
Evolutionary Idea of the Proletariat*.
ROSIE. (*throwing off her shawl on to the counter, and showing an
exemplified glad neck, which reveals a good deal of a white bosom*). If y'ass
Rosie, it's heartbreakin' to see a young fella thinkin' of anything,
or admirin' anything, but silk thransparent stockin's showin' off
the shape of a little lassie's legs!

(The Covey, *frightened, moves a little away*.)

ROSIE. (*following on*) Out in th' park in th' shade of a warm summery evenin', with your little darlin' bridie to be, kissin' an' cuddlin' (*she tries to put her arm around his neck*), kissin' an' cuddlin', ay?

THE COVEY. (*frightened*). Ay, what are you doin'? None o' that, now; none o' that. I've something else to do besides shinannickin' afther Judies!

(*He turns away, but* Rosie *follows, keeping face to face with him.*)

ROSIE. Oh, little duckey, oh, shy little duckey! Never held a mot's hand, an' wouldn't know how to tittle a little Judy! (*She clips him under the chin.*) Tittle him undher th' chin, tittle him undher th' chin!

THE COVEY. (*breaking away and running out*) Ay, go on, now; I don't want to have any meddlin' with a lassie like you!

ROSIE. (*enraged*) Jasus, it's in a monasthery some of us ought to be, spendin' our holidays kneelin' on our adorers, tellin' our beads, an' knockin' hell out of our buzzums!

MARIA LUDDY

Prostitution and Rescue Work in Nineteenth-Century Ireland

For the poorer prostitutes conditions could be miserable. The 'Bush' was a wooded place near Cobh, Co. Cork, where ' . . . 20 to 25 to 30 women . . . lived all the year round under the furze . . . like animals.' Many prostitutes also followed soldiers around from one depot to another. Dr Curtis, who gave evidence to a select committee on the operation of the Contagious Diseases Act, stated 'they (the prostitutes) are always moving about from Fermoy to Kinsale, and the garrison towns . . . and sleeping under forts, and behind the barracks.' The 'Wrens of the Curragh' were a notorious band of prostitutes who lived primitively in makeshift huts on the

perimeters of the Curragh army camp in Co. Kildare. The number
of women living in these conditions varied but up to sixty women
were stated to live there at any one time. Many of these were
undoubtedly prostitutes but it is probable that some, at least,
were also involved in long standing common law relationships
with some of the soldiers, since it was the practice of the army
authorities at this time not to recognise soldiers' marriages unless
they were living in married quarters in the camp. Even living in
such conditions there was a certain bond of solidarity amongst the
fifty or sixty women who occupied the 'nests'. The women pooled
their meagre financial resources and lived off it. The 'colony' was
also 'open to any poor wretch who imagines that there she can find
comfort'. 'The poor women who followed soldiers to the camp
were . . . made as welcome amongst the wrens as if they did not
bring with them certain trouble and an inevitable increase to the
common poverty.' These women appear to have been badly treated
by the local population and Charles Dickens, writing of a visit he
had made to the area in the 1840s, stated that it was ' . . . quite
common for the priest, when he met one of them ('wrens') to seize
her and cut her hair off close.'

Julia Carlson

from *Edna O'Brien Interview*

**You mentioned that everyone in your village was appalled.
Exactly how did people respond to the banning of your
books?**

I'm sure if I'd lived in Dublin, let's say, or come from Dublin, the
reaction might have been a little more mixed because Dublin's full
of contrary people for a start, and they would just take sides. In my
own village one person would tell me what another person had
said. They'd pass on the bad news about how dirty it was. There's

one little joke, however. The first book was banned, and all were duly horrified. The second book came, and they had apoplexy. One woman said to me, 'You know,' she said, 'we're beginning to think that the first book was a prayer book by comparison.' Some woman who had read it got terribly ill and felt she was possessed by the devil, and the priest had to come to her house. There were a few copies of it burned in the chapel grounds. It all belongs to the Middle Ages, don't you think?

SEAMUS KAVANAGH

Biddy Mulligan – The Pride of the Coombe

One of the best known of Dublin songs made famous by Jimmy O'Dea but sung by others and predating his many theatre performances as the eponymous heroine.

> I'm a buxom fine widow, I live in a spot,
> In Dublin they call it the Coombe;
> My shops and my stalls are laid out on the street,
> And my palace consists of one room.
> I sell apples and orange, nuts and split peas,
> Bananas and sugar-stick sweet,
> On Saturday night I sell second-hand clothes
> From the floor of my stall on the street.

Chorus

> You may travel from Clare
> To the County Kildare,
> From Francis Street on to Macroom,
> But where would you see me
> A fine widow like me?
> Biddy Mulligan, the pride of the Coombe.

I sell fish on a Friday, spread out on a board
The finest you'd find in the sae,
But the best is my herrings, fine Dublin Bay herrings,
There's herrings for dinner to-day.
I have a son Mick, and he's great on the flute
He plays in the Longford Street Band,
It would do your heart good to see him march out,
On a Sunday for Dollymount strand.

Chorus

In the Park on a Sunday, I make quite a dash,
The neighbours look on with surprise,
With my Aberdeen shawlie thrown over my head,
I dazzle the sight of their eyes.
At Patrick Street corner for sixty-four years,
I've stood and no one can deny,
That while I stood there, no person could dare
To say black was the white of my eye.

Chorus

Rita Ann Higgins

Some People Know What It Is Like

to be called a cunt in front of their children
to be short for the rent
to be short for the light
to be short for school books
to wait in Community Welfare waiting rooms full of smoke
to wait two years to have a tooth looked at
to wait another two years to have a tooth out (the same tooth)
to be half strangled by your varicose veins, but you're 198th on
    the list

to talk into a banana on an S.E.S. scheme
to talk into a banana in an S.E.S. dream
to be out of work
to be out of money
to be out of fashion
to be out of friends
to be in for the Vincent De Paul man
to be in space for the milk man
(sorry, mammy isn't in today she's gone to Mars for the weekend)
to be in Puerto Rico this week for the blanket man
to be in Puerto Rico next week for the blanket man
to be dead for the coal man
(sorry, mammy passed away in her sleep, overdose of coal in
    the tea-pot)
to be in hospital unconscious for the rent man (St Judes ward
    4th floor)
to be second hand
to be second class
to be no class
to be looked down on
to be walked on
to be pissed on
to be shat on

and other people don't.

Dympna McLoughlin

from *Workhouses and Irish Female Paupers 1840–70*

Pauper women were not vulnerable in the sense of being timid
individuals seeking only to be placed under the protection of a
husband or father. Many of them, after leaving or being left by

their men, lived for long years on their own, often bringing up large families unaided. Yet there was a certain vulnerability about these pauper women though it was not the artificial vulnerability of timid, weak and helpless women written about in romantic journals of the time. Rather it was their vulnerability to unscrupulous men in positions of power – to masters who overworked them until they were ill and then got rid of them, to workhouse functionaries who abused them physically and sexually and Boards of Guardians who were deaf to their complaints of cruelty and abuse. They were vulnerable also in that, whilst burdened with the lethargy of pregnancy and the weakness of childbirth and nursing, the fathers of their children were not obliged to pay anything towards their maintenance.

The reasons why women entered the workhouse were many. It is suggested here that there was a major disparity between the stated reasons for entry and the actual ones. According to the Poor Law Act, relief was only to be given to individuals who were unable to support themselves or their families. Not surprisingly then many female inmates stated themselves incapacitated through injury or sickness, or rendered destitute and friendless on the death of a parent or relative. None mentioned the fact that they wished to participate in one of the proposed workhouse emigration schemes or that they needed shelter and sustenance on their travels from one part of the country to another. Most times they entered the workhouse along with their children not when destitute, but when the subsistence nature of the family economy was in crisis, such as the 'hungry month' of May, before the potatoes were ready for eating, or during particularly bad winter weather when they could no longer travel, sell or beg.

Aileen O'Meara

from *Woman and Poverty*

The scale of women's poverty is enormous. Extrapolating from the comprehensive survey of income in households carried out by the Economic and Social Research Institute (ESRI) in 1988, the Combat Poverty Agency revealed that there are over a quarter of a million women living in poverty in Ireland . . .

Less than one-third of Irish women earn an independent income through paid work, compared to 60% of men. Over six in ten – 61% – of women who work outside the home are low paid.

The low paid part time workers are mainly women, unskilled manual workers, clerical workers in low grades and shop assistants.

The biggest demographic area of growth is also the one with the highest poverty risk: the single parent family. At least 80,000 such families existed in the 1986 census, most of them headed by a woman. Most of these are dependent on social welfare, or on private maintenance from their husbands or partners. Those depending on private maintenance are particularly insecure: a study of 1,127 maintenance orders made through the courts between 1976 and 1986 found only 13% fully paid up, and amounts awarded were very low.

Women are living longer, and as they get older, the more likely they are to be poor.

And for those with jobs, there is an increased reliance in the economy on part-time and service sector jobs, both categories low paid, and typically associated with women.

Surveys of poverty amongst women point to one central fact: women's responsibility to care for children reduces their access to an income of their own, and therefore heightens their risk of poverty.

As the groups working with women in poor areas have increasingly found, in order to get women out of the isolation of homes and to become aware of their problems and its solutions, the first thing needed is childcare facilities.

These figures measure the extent of financial poverty. They do not measure the extent of the other dimensions of poverty in society, which are clear to anyone who has been in the featureless estates of outer Dublin, the inner city deprivation of run-down flat complexes, who has sat in a crowded and stuffy health centre, queued in a dole office with a leaky roof, or walked long distances because they could not afford a bus.

The physical surroundings of poverty are dismal. The emotional ones can also be deprivatory, the stresses and pressures of coping alone or without support, as well as reducing nutrient intake to ensure that the rest of the family have enough.

Dr Pauline Lee and Dr Michael Gibney of the Department of Clinical Medicine in Trinity College's Medical School produced startling results in a report on patterns of food and nutrient intake in a suburb of Dublin with chronically high unemployment, published in June 1989.

The diets of women were characterised by low intakes of fibre, low intakes of iron, low intakes of vitamin C.

Looking more closely at the findings for women, the researchers found a large variation in energy and nutrient intakes with energy intakes being lowest in the group of single mothers and deserted wives, and highest in the group of married women with three or four children. Single mothers, for example, had a considerably lower intake of meat, resulting in markedly low iron and zinc intakes.

With regard to inadequate nutrient intakes, women always fared worse than men, with about three times as many women having less than 75% of the Recommended Dietary Allowance (RDA) for vitamin C. Amongst single mothers, only half the women achieved even half the RDA for iron.

However, no differences whatever were seen between children from single or two-parent families, suggesting that women do without in order for their children to eat properly.

MARY DORCEY

Songs of Peace

for a young woman marching against war in the streets of Dublin

Women in the streets again,
hundreds in the streets again,
marching, holding hands,
singing frail songs against
death and destruction.
We don't want to die in your nuclear war.
At every barrier we stand and chant
into the visored eyes,
when they link arms against us we call
nuclear bombs kill gardai too.

We have turned full circle
to the sixties and hippies
scattering flowers for peace.
Nuns have joined us now —
changed their habits for tracksuits,
white masks on their faces
they bear black coffins
for sisters killed by soldiers.
We shall overcome, they sing:
Fifteen years ago I did not ask,

What or when or whom?
And you tell me with pride
you will stay all night in the park,
in the wet and the dirt and the dark,
laying your body down
between life and their weapons.
And yet you confide with the
injured eyes of a child
refused, that when they arrested
you at the gate,

They shoved and taunted and abused.
And I have been told
that the women at Greenham wept
when they woke to find missiles
brought in while they slept,
as though patient protest
might establish a claim
to codes of war and fair warning.
And I wish you were right,
I wish it were true that

If women enough would gather,
women enough, would leave
husbands and children and sing,
laying their bodies down in the muck.
Yet how often before
have we offered our flesh, in hope,
in barter, in supplication?
And who will it please, if they come
for us, to find this time
we have made our own camps

Unarmed in the dirt and dark?
And I wish you were right
that songs and kisses could do,
hold back bullet and bomb,
loose power, reclaim the night.
But soldiers have always liked songs of peace,
and women have sung them to war before this.
And on return they have paid their respects,
have buried us bravely, buried us well,
with love and flowers and songs of peace.

EILIS NI DHUIBHNE

from *The Flowering*

Sally Rua. She went mad because she could not do the work she loved, because she could not do her flowering. That can happen. You can love some kind of work so much that you go crazy if you simply cannot manage to do it at all. Outer or inner constraints could be the cause. Sally Rua had only outer ones. She was so good at flowering, she was such a genius at it, that she never had any inner problems. That was the good news, as far as she was concerned.

Sally Rua. Lennie's ancestor. Of course, none of that is true. It is a yarn, spun out of thin air. Not quite out of thin air: Lennie read about a woman like Sally Rua. She had read, in a history of embroidery in Ireland, about a woman who had gone mad because she could not afford to keep up the flowering which she loved, and had to go into service in a town house in the north of Ireland. The bare bones of a story. How much of that, even, is true? She might have gone mad anyway. She might have been congenitally conditioned to craziness. Or the madness might have had some other cause, quite unconnected with embroidery. The son of the house might have raped her. Or the father. Or the grandfather or the hired man. People go mad for lots of reasons, but not often for the reason that they haven't got the time to do embroidery.

Still and all. The woman who wrote the history of embroidery, an excellent, an impassioned book, the name of which would be cited if this were a work of scholarship and not a story, believed that that was the cause of the tragedy. And Lennie believes it. Because she wants to. She also wants to adopt that woman, that woman who was not, in history, called Sally Rua, but some other, less interesting name (Sally Rua really was the name of Lennie's great grandmother, but what she knows about her is very slight) as her ancestor. Because she does not see much difference between history and fiction, between painting and embroidery, between either of them and literature. Or scholarship. Or building houses. The energies inspiring all of these endeavours cannot be so separate, after all. The essential skills of learning to manipulate the raw material, to transform it into something orderly and expressive, to make it, if not better or more beautiful, different from what it was originally and more itself, apply equally to all of these exercises. Exercises that Lennie likes to perform. Painting and writing, embroidering and scholarship. If she likes these things, someone back there in Wavesend must have liked them too. And if someone back there in Wavesend did not, if there was no Sally Rua, at all, at all, where does that leave Lennie?

ELIZABETH MALCOLM

from *Women and Madness*

John Murray, an apothecary, died in 1835 of a fever, leaving his widow to bring up seven children, ranging in age from 11 months to 11 years. She was assisted financially by her two brothers and also by her brother-in-law, Denis Murray, an army surgeon who had served in the East Indies for many years. In the mid-1840s, however, the family was hit by a series of disasters. One of Elizabeth Murray's brothers died, as did one of her sons after a long illness. Eleanor, the eldest daughter who was 22, also became seriously ill. This occurred during the black famine year of 1847: a tragic time for many Irish families. Eleanor did recover, but, according to her uncle Surgeon Murray, she was immediately afflicted with 'dementia'. For two years her mother looked after her at home. By May 1850, however, she had become so unmanageable that she had to be committed to the county jail as a dangerous lunatic; and from there in October she was transferred to St Patrick's. She was admitted as the highest category of paying patient, with a fee of 40 guineas a year, for although she had no resources of her own, she was entitled to £400 upon her mother's death. But in 1854 Surgeon Murray, who was then living on half pay in Enniskerry, County Wicklow, petitioned the hospital to have his niece's fee reduced 'to the cheapest class of paid patient'. After consideration, the governors agreed to reduce the sum to £30 a year. In his petition the surgeon said that he had hoped St Patrick's might be able to cure Eleanor, but, on the contrary, 'the complaint appears to have settled down into confirmed idiocy leaving no room for hope of recovery'. Eleanor Murray died in St Patrick's of 'senile decay' in 1903. Casebooks, begun in 1899, record her as suffering from 'melancholia and dementia' and as living 'a very automatic life': eating when food was placed in front of her, sleeping when put to bed, and spending most days sitting beside the fire staring vacantly in front of her. After 53 years in the institution, it is hardly to be wondered at that Eleanor Murray's life had become 'automatic'.

These women are typical of female patients admitted to St Patrick's during the 1840s in a number of respects, notably in the fact that they all experienced a family breakdown resulting in financial hardship. Such cases would seem to underline the crucial role of the father in the nineteenth-century, Irish, middle-class family and to suggest that the younger, female members were utterly unprepared to cope with the consequences of his unexpected death. These women were not expected nor trained to work and only undertook employment when forced to do so by dire necessity. But jobs like governessing, music teaching or dressmaking, though relatively 'respectable', were insecure and poorly paid and hardly amounted to a satisfying career. The accounts of the lives of governesses contained in the hospital admission forms particularly portray loneliness, poverty and uncertainty. If an orphaned young woman did not work, however, then she became a financial burden upon her family. Fathers of course were expected to support unmarried daughters, but other relatives were less willing, and often less able, to do so. Brothers, for instance, demonstrated a greater readiness than any other single relative to commit family members to St Patrick's. Among the admission documentation surviving from the 1840s are letters from the brothers of female patients, complaining of the financial difficulties attendant upon raising their own families while having, at the same time, to support a mad sister. On the other hand, however, there are a few cases which look suspiciously as though brothers were trying to rid themselves of unwanted female dependants by having them committed. Admittedly the evidence is suggestive rather than conclusive, but wrongful committals certainly were a problem in nineteenth-century private asylums.

What emerges most forcefully though from the correspondence accompanying admission forms is a picture of women struggling to cope with familial and economic misfortune, with insecurity and with powerlessness in a society that allowed them little scope for self-expression or independence. These letters and petitions reveal a complex and problematical socio-economic context which is almost totally absent from the theoretical literature on the subject. One inevitably wonders what a study of the surviving admission forms from the public asylums would reveal about the lives and problems of Irish rural and working-class women. Unfortunately to date, except for one brief article, no such study has been attempted.

VICTORIA WHITE

from *Mr Brennan's Heaven*

The door had begun to swing almost continuously, for it was five-thirty and wave after wave of people were converging on Brennan's as if they had made a secret arrangement. Their movements seemed as mechanical as genuflections in a church. What are they doing, I wondered, why don't they stop it? What is it makes them do this? I had no answer, but a face came into my mind, the face of a woman so beautiful that only the richest man in the world could have her for his own. Suddenly I realised that no-one would ever ask me to be more than an approximation to that face, that I would never get any thanks or appreciation for being anything else. And I felt giddy and sick, the voices slurred together, I couldn't stand it, the faces around me seemed completely foreign. Tony leant towards me saying something to me, but I put my hands to my ears. I thought I was going to faint and I slid off my stool and pushed through the people to the Ladies. Miraculously, there was no-one there, and I clicked on the latch. The silences and the white surfaces calmed me. I bent down and washed my face and then looked up at myself. I had never been more struck by my beauty. My eyes were like sapphire against the soft bronze of my skin, and my hair hung round me in a great gold mass. I could hear Tony knocking at the door but I ignored him. I started to smile and the face in the mirror smiled and nobody else could see it, only me. Nobody else could have it. This was what I wanted then, I thought, and I felt happy for the first time since my marriage. Tony was trying to force the door but I pushed my back against it and I could see my strength reflected in the face in the mirror. I could hear lots of voices, and Tony's voice above them all, but I was smiling, and I didn't let them in.

And later when I miscarried and Tony came to see me I kept my eyes and my mouth shut.

I must hurry this now. I must close my book and wait for the nurse to bring in my tea. The Angelus sounds and the nuns and nurses shuffle through the long corridors. The Virgin's face is calm.

CHARLOTTE GRACE O'BRIEN

from *The Feminine Animal*

We have now come to it that through the classes in which life is artificial the term 'old maid' is no longer one of reproach, whereas one daily hears teeming motherhood lamented almost as a scandal. A woman in herself, and by herself alone, is required to be as hard and as well able to combat with the world as man. Half the female world in London society is running a race with old maidhood; half the male world, on the other hand, is looking on cheerfully and speculating. They say, 'It's a pity, but it can't be helped.' Now, I believe that to a large extent it can be helped, and will be helped, and that, in the natural course of things, women are being rapidly compelled to see that the chances of marriage are becoming fewer and fewer in society; they are forced to face the necessity of making their own lives, and I believe it is the best thing that could possibly happen to them, and that, instead of making them harder and more manlike, it will restore to them the womanhood they are in danger of losing, in their present time of waiting on the men who do not come and that, as every one knows, shameful though it may be to say, is exactly what all the idle girls in London and elsewhere are doing. How *can* they do it? Idling, amusing themselves, with their senses perfect and their youth and their education and strength, and all the work of the world crying to them. It is enough to make the blood flame to think of it, and to see what women are making of this society they create – for it is their creation, this artificial society. A man wants to be well fed and well clothed, and with that most men are content. But women! What will satisfy them? – servants and carriages, silks and satins. The actual thing they possess is nothing, but they must equal or exceed their neighbour in every ridiculous display. They make marriages impossible by their vanity and emulation.

Now, I picture to myself a state of things when a young and strong woman shall be ashamed of a life of idleness and self-indulgence, or even want of definite work as a man is or ought to be – when, instead of the present division between the sexes, both shall be workers, going in and out together – when men shall meet and respect women in professional life, when they shall see women able to live alone and poorly in lodgings or chambers – then, once again, the woman will become, as she is now among the poor, a help-meet for man, not a burden. Then women will go out to lands where men are now brutalised by their absence. Then the balance of the sexes will recover itself as the dangers and hardships of life are shared more equally, for more men are actually born into the world than women, though boys are more hard to rear than girls. Every symptom that I can see of the increasing freedom of the young woman reassures me that we are only in a transition stage. Would to God that with their desire of freedom their sense of responsibility for the gift of life were also increasing! but freedom is the first step to all progress, national or individual

K. W. Nicholls

from *Irish Women and Property in the Sixteenth Century*

On the dissolution of the marriage by annulment or the husband's death the wife was entitled (unless disqualified by her adultery), to the repayment of the dowry she had brought. In such a case, she had no other claim on her husband's property, either outright or in life interest, in contrast to the Germanic systems of community of property described above. This situation for Ireland is expressed in the statement of Gráinne ní Mháille that:

Among the Irishry the custom is, that wives shall have but her first dowry without any increase or allowance for the same, time out of mind it hath been so used, and before any woman so deliver up her marriage [dowry] to her husband she receives sureties for the restitution of the same in manner and form as she hath delivered it, in regard that husbands through their great expenses, especially chieftains, at the time of their deaths have no goods to leave behind them, but are commonly indebted. At other times they are divorced upon proof of precontracts; and the husband now and then without any lawful or due proceeding do put his wife from him, and so bringeth in another so as the wife is to have sureties for her dowry for fear of the worse.

These sureties for repayment of the dowry are authenticated in sixteenth century records. Margaret Tobin brought on her marriage to Thomas fitz Richard (MacThomas Geraldine) a dowry of 80 cows, 24 stud mares, five riding-horses, a pair of backgammon tables and a harp, 'besides household goods'. Four years later MacThomas put her away, 'without divorce, aid or consent of Holy Church', and afterwards married another wife, whereupon Margaret's father sued Lord Power, who had gone surety for MacThomas's performance of the marriage contract. This case, like others, shows how real was the need for the reasons adduced by Gráinne, for security for the repayment of the dowry, especially the frequency of annulments ('divorces') and the simple repudiation of wives in Gaelic society. In such an eventuality, the wife might find it very difficult to recover her dowry, and several surviving Elizabethan chancery bills are those of divorced wives seeking redress in such cases. Owny (Úna) Mageoghagan brought her husband, also a Mageoghagan, Feagh, a dowry of 18 cows, five work-horses, 24 swine, 24 sheep, a pan worth 20 shillings and an iron griddle with a 'barnis' (trivet), also worth 20 shillings; after their divorce 'according the laws of the church', Feagh and a certain Hugh Mageoghagan (perhaps his father) who had engaged to repay the dowry on such an eventuality failed to do so, and Una and her new husband (yet another Mageoghagan) were forced to sue them, successfully, in chancery (1592).

MARIE JONES

from *The Hamster Wheel*

KENNY. Do you ever stop to think what you're doing to me.
JEANETTE. What?
KENNY. It's hard enough having to be washed and dressed . . . but that's not enough . . . I'm parcelled off to a crazy club so you

can take away the last bit of independence I had. Could you not at least have waited till I'm better?

JEANNETTE. What about *my* independence . . . why can't I have any?

KENNY. You were happy enough before to sit back and let me do it all for you . . . you didn't cry for your independence then.

JEANETTE. Because there wouldn't have been any point . . . you knew it all . . . I was too stupid to do anything . . . maybe if you had given me a bit of encouragement before I wouldn't be in such a bloody mess . . . have you forgotten that . . . Oh don't you do that Jeanette, you'll make a balls of it . . . leave it until I come home . . . leave that to me you don't know nothing about money . . . but who has to do it now?

KENNY. What do you have to do now?

JEANETTE. Alright do you want to know? . . . I'll bloody tell you then . . . in case you haven't noticed, I have no job at the moment . . . in two months' time you will be dependent on invalidity and I will be dependent on you and the mortgage will be dependent on God because there will be nobody else to pay it. . . . We have a washing machine that is held together with sticky tape . . . a biscuit tin full of bills that I'm frightened to pay . . . but you haven't noticed any of these things have you . . . because I didn't want you to worry.

KENNY. All the more reason why you shouldn't be wasting money on driving lessons.

JEANETTE. You bastard . . . you selfish bastard . . . I have had it with you . . . I'm sick of you feeling sorry for yourself. Tired of being taken for granted. Me . . . me . . . me . . . you can't get any further than that can you . . . you were the same before and you haven't changed one bit . . . well you listen here . . . I am the one who is taking charge and if you don't like it you can go wherever the hell you like, but believe me nobody else would take the gift of you. (*She kicks the wheelchair and exits.*)

ROSITA SWEETMAN

from *On Our Backs: Sexual Attitudes in a Changing Ireland*

Diane, age 26: Initially, we thought the main work in the Rape Crisis Centre would be providing medical and legal aid for rape victims but the more we got briefed the more we realized counselling would be the main thing, helping women get over the shame, get back into normal life. At first we didn't realize how big the problem of rape was. There are two factors: society's attitude to rape and helping rape victims. Rape isn't just a guy who gets a sexual urge and jumps on a woman passing by. We want to show that the way people are brought up, the way women are objectified in films and books, is all part of rape. Also that it's not the woman's fault: *any* woman can be raped. That often only comes home to people when someone they know is raped.

The London Centre say the number of reported rapes is only the tip of the iceberg, we feel it's the same here but haven't got statistics yet; also in London they say over fifty per cent of rape victims know their attackers and we've certainly found the same. The 'date rape' is really common: a guy meets a girl at a dance, gives her a lift home, then rapes her. It starts as an attempt at seduction, which fails, so the guy just goes ahead and rapes. We tend to think there's more sexual violence here within families, rape and incest, than in England.

The one hundred per cent increase in rape last year is probably partly to do with rising urban violence, and partly that more women are reporting rape. It's part of a change in attitudes, women recognize rape for what it is, they know they haven't led the man on or provoked him.

The Centre will consist of a room with a twenty-four hour telephone service. We'll keep records but they'll be anonymous in case anyone breaks in. If someone rings they can come to the Centre, or a woman can go and talk to them at home, or outside if they want that.

We have a group of women doctors who'll attend to victims, lawyers who'll give legal advice and help, someone to accompany the woman to the police station to make a statement, and we'd advise them to keep notes because there's often a two year time lag before the case comes up in court.

The laws on rape are so bad that even the Department of Justice and the police want them changed. The Council for the Status of Women have made a submission to the Law Reform Commission on rape; while we support it, we feel they didn't go far enough. They didn't recognize marital rape; obviously if you do you're challenging the whole system whereby the husband has complete control over his wife. Then there's the whole thing of the woman's past sexual history being brought up in court which they want changed, as we do. In any other normal criminal case if the defendant tries to discredit the witness by bringing up the past he loses the protection of the court; in a rape case the woman's past sexual history can be brought up but not the man's.

We're not looking for fifteen year sentences for rapists, none of us are great believers in the prison system, but we do feel while rapists are often given psychiatric treatment or help, the victims are left with nothing, and obviously they need it very badly. So we feel there should be psychiatric help for them, particularly for younger women who've been brutally attacked, or attacked within the family.

The Woman of Three Cows

(Seventeenth Century)

TRANSLATED BY JAMES CLARENCE MANGAN

O Woman of Three Cows, *agra*![1] don't let your tongue thus rattle!
Oh, don't be saucy, don't be stiff, because you may have cattle.
I have seen – and, here's my hand to you, I only say what's true –
A many a one with twice your stock not half so proud as you.

Good luck to you, don't scorn the poor, and don't be their
    despiser;
For worldly wealth soon melts away, and cheats the very miser;
And Death soon strips the proudest wreath from haughty human
    brows —
Then don't be stiff, and don't be proud, good Woman of Three
    Cows!

See where Momonia's heroes lie, proud Owen Mór's descendants,
'Tis they that won their glorious name, and had the grand
    attendants;
If *they* were forced to bow to Fate, as every mortal bows,
Can *you* be proud, can *you* be stiff, my Woman of Three Cows?

The brave sons of the Lord of Clare, they left the land to mourning;
Mavrone![2] for they were banished, with no hope of their returning.
Who knows in what abodes of want those youths were driven to
    house?
Yet *you* can give yourself these airs, O Woman of Three Cows.

O, think of Donnell of the Ships, the Chief whom nothing
    daunted,
See how he fell in distant Spain unchronicled, unchanted!
He sleeps, the great O'Sullivan, where thunder cannot rouse —
Then ask yourself, should *you* be proud, good Woman of Three
    Cows?

O'Ruark, Maguire, those souls of fire, whose names are shrined in
    story;
Think how their high achievements once made Erin's greatest
    glory.
Yet now their bones lie mouldering under weeds and cypress
    boughs —
And so, for all your pride, will yours, O Woman of Three Cows.

Th' O'Carrolls, also, famed when fame was only for the boldest,
Rest in forgotten sepulchres with Erin's best and oldest;
Yet who so great as they of yore in battle or carouse?
Just think of that, and hide your head, good Woman of Three
  Cows.

Your neighbour's poor; and you, it seems, are big with vain ideas,
Because, forsooth, you've got three cows – one more, I see, than
  she has;
That tongue of yours wags more at times than charity allows;
But if you're strong, be merciful – great Woman of Three Cows.

Avran[3]
Now, there you go; you still, of course, keep up your scornful
  bearing,
And I'm too poor to hinder you; but, by the cloak I'm wearing,
If I had but *four* cows myself, even though you were my spouse,
I'd thwack you well, to cure your pride, my Woman of Three
  Cows.

[1]*a grádh*: my love
[2]*mo bhrón*: my sorrow
[3]*amhrán*: song

KATHARINE SIMMS

from *Women in Gaelic Society During the Age of Transition*

There are hints that women had not always been excluded from the
upper echelons of the bardic orders: for instance the notice in the
Annals of Inisfallen of the death in 934 of Uallaige daughter of
Muinechán, 'poetess of Ireland', or allusions in the literature of
legendary or fictitious figures such as the poetess Liadán, who

abandoned the poet Cuirithir to become a nun and Feidelm the poetess of Connacht who encounters Queen Medb in the Old Irish Saga *Táin Bó Cuailgne* while on her way back 'from Albion after learning the art of *filidecht*' (or poetry). However it appears that from about the eighth century onwards, a distinction grew up in the poetic order between the honoured ranks of the *filid* who were distinguished by book-learning, and the humbler bards, who were illiterate. Since the monastic schools had a monopoly of book learning in early Ireland, it was inappropriate for women to receive the more advanced training, and in this respect the secular schools of post-Norman Ireland seem to have followed the example of their monastic predecessors. The Middle Irish retelling of the *Táin Bó Cuailgne* found in the twelfth century Book of Leinster describes Feidelm as a bondmaid and prophetess (*banchumal, banfáid*) with no reference to her learning. Similarly in bardic poetry of the thirteenth and fourteenth centuries there are derogatory references to women fortune-tellers, *mná mana*, and to women balladeers, who composed the popular *abhran* verse in praise of the Irish nobility in return for food and lodging:

'Their prizes, namely the getting food by means of their doggerel(?), are their very nature; there is a great demand for their wares, they seek not gold or kine.'

The early sixteenth century Scottish Book of the Dean of Lismore, among other miscellaneous pieces of medieval Gaelic verse, contains a poem of 'hates', in which a 'poet-band that includes a woman' is considered as detestable as 'sadness in a drinking house' or 'a host that would make no foray'.

The medieval Irish scholars who so heartily despised such uneducated women entertainers were organised into hereditary professions and consequently had womenfolk of their own. There are 44 entries in the post-Norman annals concerning female members of clerical or bardic families. Seven of these simply name daughters of important men without reference to their husbands, but there was a tendency for the daughter of one learned man to marry another, particularly noticeable with the poetic family of O hUiginn and the O Duibhgeannáin historians. The wife – or in the case of a clerical household, the concubine – of a scholar had an honoured role in Gaelic society, but earned the annalists' admiration by a display not of learning but of piety and hospitality, particularly towards the learned classes themselves.

EAVAN BOLAND

from *A Kind of Scar*

The tendency to fuse the national and the feminine, to make the image of the woman in the pretext of a romantic nationalism – these have been weaknesses in Irish poetry. As a young poet, these simplifications isolated and estranged me. They also made it clearer to me that my own discourse must be subversive. In other words, that I must be vigilant to write of my own womanhood – whether it was revealed to me in the shape of a child or a woman from Achill – in such a way that I never colluded with the simplified images of woman in Irish poetry.

When I was young all this was comfortless. I took to heart the responsibility of making my own critique, even if for years it consisted of little more than accusing Irish poetry in my own mind of deficient ethics. Even now I make no apology for such a critique. I believe it is still necessary. Those simplified women, those conventional reflexes and reflexive feminisations of the national experience; those static, passive, ornamental figures do no credit to a poetic tradition which has been, in other respects, radical and innovative, capable of both latitude and compassion.

But there is more to it. As a young poet I would not have felt so threatened and estranged if the issue had merely been the demands a national programme makes on a country's poetry. The real issue went deeper. When I read those simplifications of women I felt there was an underlying fault in Irish poetry; almost a geological weakness. All good poetry depends on an ethical relation between imagination and image. Images are not ornaments; they are truths. When I read about Cathleen Ni Houlihan or the Old

Woman of the Roads or Dark Rosaleen I felt that a necessary
ethical relation was in danger of being violated over and over
again; that a merely ornamental relation between imagination and
image was being handed on from poet to poet, from generation to
generation; was becoming orthodox poetic practice. It was the
violation, even more than the simplification, which alienated me.

No poetic imagination can afford to regard an image as a
temporary aesthetic manoeuvre. Once the image is distorted the
truth is demeaned. That was the heart of it all as far as I was
concerned. In availing themselves of the old convention, in using
and re-using women as icons and figments, Irish poets were not
just dealing with emblems. They were also evading the real
women of an actual past: women whose silence their poetry should
have broken. They ran the risk of turning a terrible witness into an
empty decoration. One of the ironic purposes of my argument has
been to point out that those emblems are no longer silent. They
have acquired voices. They have turned from poems into poets.

EILÉAN NÍ CHUILLEANAÍN

Those People

When the four women tramp in sight
Dragging their children round the corner,
All the dolls in the shop windows look askance.
The shopkeepers know these people,
They are not going to leave,
They will remain visible,
Still there at three in the afternoon
When the shops are closed and the bars
Shutter their darkness, they will be
Out on the cobbles, beside the abandoned
Slimy fountain, hardly moving at all
But showing no definite signs of sleep.

At night their campfire will glow
– They will be cooking that stew,
Lifting the lid to stir it, and
The smell will blow all over
As it reeks now from their skirts.

The man at the cash-register
Beside the looped bead curtains says
I think myself it's the goat's milk.

Una Claffey

from *The Women Who Won*

It was the Women's Political Association (WPA) which brought
Frances Fitzgerald into the limelight of the women's movement.
She became a member of the association and within a short time
was elected chairwoman. Like many women it was motherhood
which provoked in her an intense interest in the organisation of
society. 'The division of labour really hits you,' she says. She
describes this as an intensely political issue. But why did it take
her so long to join a political party? It was no secret in political
circles that she was seen by many politicians and party organisers
as an ideal candidate.

In the particular strands of the women's movement in which she
was involved there is neither a history nor a culture of women
being highly involved in party politics. And even in the WPA at
committee level she says there is almost a kind of veto on party
politics. 'I think it's very much a disadvantage. It's not a good
idea.' She points to the Three Hundred Group in England where
there are Tory women and Labour women involved in a committee
and going their separate ways at election time. This she sees as a
much better model. She'd like to see that here and feels it's more
politically grounded. But she doesn't see it happening – though

she has already taken an active role in the Group 84 in the Dáil, where women from all parties are invited to work on issues in a cross-party fashion.

When Frances Fitzgerald decided to run for the Dáil there were women in the women's movement who felt she was careerist and had used her position to promote her own ambition. Frances insists she didn't come across this a lot. She got a standing ovation from the CSW following her election. This gave her fantastic encouragement. 'I think we've got to the stage of maturity where I won't be lashed for personal ambition. What I heard more than anything was "you're very brave". Maybe there is some bravery in standing out and going for election.'

She knows she's been lucky but she's astute enough to also be a little worried. She's used to working with women and has found them very supportive. She's worried about keeping up contacts and maintaining the encouragement she got from other women and the clear vision she's developed and shared with them. But she has no worries about being ghettoised or seen as 'a one issue' person. 'I'm happy to identify with women's issues because I think women's issues are *all* issues and I'm proud to be associated with them.' In spite of whatever misgivings Frances Fitzgerald may have about Leinster House she feels a fantastic sense of delight and pride at having been elected. She describes the election of twenty women as a small step. 'In terms of influencing the agenda or the style of debate it's really only when there are eighty or ninety women that will happen. It's early days yet.'

ANTHONY BLINCO

Career Girl

Lightly frocked typist Sally
Forever lost in the sun and gloom
Of glossy office windows

Tracing thoughts of someone's dismal work
In neat fingered patterns of un-understanding
Indent and paragraph.
There, fresh as powdered rose each dawn,
(Except when flushed and red fortells a moody day).
Sitting, chatting, typing to herself –
With Molly's baby on her knee
And Mother's second pregnancy –
In mind of tomorrow and yesterday.
Sometimes overtiming, and sometimes
Wishing on a diamond ring;
Waiting for a kingdom on a shoestring,
Though shoes are mostly pointed high
And heeled.
There Sally will winter each year
And only the shades of her clothes and her eyes
Will weather the change in her age;
Everyone knowing her a pillar
Of secret chastity, magazine reading
And Saturday shopping
With friends of her own to meet for afternoon tea.

Eileen Evason

from *Community Women's Action*

Women have been increasingly visible at the grass roots in Northern Ireland. Many women were forced into more active, public roles as a result of the conflict. It was women who broke the Falls Curfew to take food into the area when it was illegally cordoned off for house-to-house searches by the British army in 1970. Women filled the gap in, for example, the civil rights movement when men were interned. Women were at the forefront

of the rent and rates strike and campaign against the Payment For
Debt Act which followed. Women married to internees and
prisoners had to learn how to deal with officialdom in their day-
to-day lives and to become spokespersons and activists at a
broader level.

For some this may be seen purely and simply as women finding
their strength. The reality has been more complex as such changes
need not entail a drastic revision of the role of wives. It may be
acceptable for women to take on new responsibilities when men
are absent but assumed that things will revert to 'normal' when
the men return. As Lynda Edgerton (1986) has noted, husbands
may be less enthusiastic when notions of equality and challenging
authority in the political arena intrude into the domestic sphere.
The pressure on women to 'stand by their men' and to be faithful
and supportive, regardless, is also not suggestive of radical
change. The actual extent and effects of all these strains and
pressures on women in both communities has still to be
researched.

Similar questions are raised, though in a less dramatic sense, by
women's involvement in community action over the past twenty
years. Here women have won some remarkable victories. In the
1970s women played a significant part in the rapid expansion of
tenant and community groups that occurred across Northern
Ireland. Women dominated some of the most militant and
successful housing campaigns, most notably the campaign in the
late 1970s for the demolition of flats and maisonettes in Turf
Lodge in West Belfast and the campaign for the demolition of the
Divis flats in the 1980s. Women have also been to the forefront in
the many campaigns over the past twenty years relating to the
high levels of poverty in Northern Ireland. In 1971 one of the very
first public actions by women in Belfast, organised by women on
the Ormeau Road, was to protest against the withdrawal of school
milk by the then Minister of Education – Margaret Thatcher.
Women marched to Stormont, addressed the City Council and
organised a march to the city hall with two cows at the head of the
march . . . Moreover some developments in the 1980s, notably

the Women's Information Days, have had a major benefit in allowing women to start questioning the divisive myths and stereotypes cultivated by local politicians. Women from East Belfast have had the opportunity to discover that Poleglass (the new estate built to take the over-spill of population from West Belfast) 'is not a paradise for Roman Catholics' and women from West Belfast have learned of poverty and poor services in East Belfast.

LELAND BARDWELL

Them's Your Mother's Pills

They'd scraped the top soil of the gardens
and every step or two they'd hurled a concrete block
Bolsters of mud like hippos from the hills
rolled on the planters plantings of the riff-raff of the city.

The schizophrenic planners had finished off their job
folded their papers, put away their pens –
The city clearances were well ahead.

And all day long a single child was crying
while his father shouted: Don't touch them,

Them's your mammie's pills.

I set to work with zeal to play 'Doll's House',
'Doll's Life', 'Doll's Garden', while my adolescent sons played
'Temporary Heat'

in the sitting room out front
and drowned the opera of admonitions:

Don't touch them, them's your mammie's pills.

Fragile as needles the women wander forth
laddered with kids, the unborn one ahead
to forge the mile through mud and rut
where mulish earth-removers rest, a crazy sculpture.

They are going back to the city for the day
this is all they live for –
Going back to the city for the day.

The line of shops and solitary pub
are camouflaged like check points on the border
the supermarket stretches emptily
a circus of sausages and time
the till-girl gossips in the veg department
Once in a while a woman might come in
to put another pound on
the electronic toy for Christmas.

From behind the curtains every night
the video lights are flickering, butcher blue
Don't touch them, them's your mammie's pills

No one has a job in Kilenarden
nowadays they say it is a no-go area
I wonder, then, who goes and does not go
in this strange forgotten world
of video and valium

I visited my one time neighbour
not so long ago. She was sitting
in the hangover position
I knew she didn't want to see me
although she'd cried when we were leaving

I went my way
through the quietly rusting motor cars and prams
past the barricades of wire, the harmony of junk.
The babies that I knew are punk-size now
and soon children will have children
and new voices ring the *leit motif*:

Don't touch them, them's your mammie's pills.

JOYCE CARY

from *To Be a Pilgrim*

Last month I suffered a great misfortune in the loss of my
housekeeper, Mrs Jimson. She was sent to prison for pawning
some old trinkets which I had long forgotten. My relatives
discovered the fact and called in the police before I could inter-
vene. They knew that I fully intended, as I still intend, to marry
Sara Jimson. They were good people. They saw me as a foolish old
man, who had fallen into the hands of a scheming woman. But
they were quite wrong. It was I who was the unfaithful servant,
and Sara, the victim. It was because I did not give Sara enough pay
and because she did not like to ask me for money that she ran into
debt, and was tempted to take some useless trifles from the attic.

I was very ill on account of this disaster to my peace of mind,
and the family put me in charge of my niece Ann. I say in charge,
because Ann is a qualified doctor, and has power over me. People
boast of their liberties nowadays, but it seems to me that we have
multiplied only our rules. Ann, aged 26, could lock me up for the
rest of my life, if she chose, in an asylum. This would not alarm
me so much if I could make out what goes on in the girl's head.

When I asked her to be allowed to see Sara in prison, she
answered only, 'We must see how you are.'

And the very next day she said: 'What you really want, uncle, is a change at the seaside.'

'What, at this season?' I was startled by such a suggestion. The girl kept silence. She had no more expression, behind her round spectacles, than a stone ink bottle.

I do not like this girl. I prefer my other niece and several of my honorary nieces. I haven't seen Ann since she was a child. She has lived much abroad, and she never troubled, during her medical training, to visit me.

She has been chosen to take care of me because she is a doctor. But she is a stranger, and I can't tell how dangerous she is, how obstinate. Old men don't like strangers. How can they? For how can strangers like old men? They know nothing of them but what they see and imagine; which in an old man, cannot be very pleasant or entertaining.

'If you take me to the seaside,' I said to Ann, 'I shall go mad. Or perhaps that is the family's plan of campaign.'

'You must have a change, uncle.'

'Do you think I am mad?'

'No.'

'It wasn't you who tried to get me shut up?'

'Cousin Blanche may have – no one else.'

'Why? Because I wear a queer hat? To me, you know, it isn't a queer hat – it's a sensible hat.'

'I think you're quite right to stick to your own fashions.'

But I could see very well that she doesn't like to go out with me.

This is a small point, of course, but it shows the peculiar difficulties of my position, as an old man suspected of being insane. If I ordered tomorrow a young man's suit, with enormous trousers and a tight waist, and put on my head a little American hat like a soup plate, or one of those obscene objects called a Tyrolese hat, I should look and feel so disgusting to myself that life would not be worth living. Yet when I examine myself, as now, in a long glass, with Ann's eyes, I see that I must be a queer object to a stranger, and a young stranger.

My hatter tells me that there is only one man in England beside myself, who still wears a curly-brimmed bowler. But he agrees

with me that there has never been a better hat, that hats, in fact,
since the last war, have gone to the devil. And are getting more
degenerate, more slack, more shapeless, every day.

'If you don't like going out with me,' I told Ann, 'you can walk
behind or on the other side of the street and watch me from there.'

But this suggestion was badly received. The girl did not answer
at all. The effect was quite that of a keeper in an asylum. I was
upset and after a little consideration, I said that I should go to the
seaside if she insisted.

AILBHE SMYTH

from *A Great Day for the Women of Ireland*

Women's representation in electoral politics, whether of the Left
or the Right, is low in Ireland (just 7.8% of TDs are women) and
no woman had ever run for President before. This candidate was
not 'merely' a woman but one who had consistently challenged the
institutions of the State to achieve justice, equality and autonomy
for women. She was identified, through her work in the courts, in
the Senate and with a variety of women's groups, with the most
controversial issues to have surfaced in Irish social and political life
during the 1970s and 1980s: contraception, divorce, abortion,
the rights and status of single mothers, social welfare, employment equality rights and so on. Furthermore, independence,
fluency and exceptional intelligence, qualities abundantly possessed by Mary Robinson, are not necessarily assets in a culture
which has systematically constructed 'woman' as passive depend-
ant, and which suffers from a historically rooted suspicion of
radicalism. She won nonetheless. And convincingly . . .

The women's vote was seen as crucially significant in swinging
the election in Mary Robinson's favour. More or less absent in

general elections during the 1980s, it surfaced substantially, apparently taking Fianna Fail and Fine Gael by surprise: it was as if women voters had simply been waiting for the opportunity to make their presence felt. They broke the rules, crossed party lines and, it is reckoned, were a key factor in encouraging male voters to do likewise. As Mary Maher commented:

> 'Much has been made of the way the women's vote went to her. I suspect that what was so evident as to draw comment was the proud jubilance of women voters at having a splendid candidate to vote for who also happened, icing-on-cake fashion, to be a woman. That was one in the eye for the ah-ya-boy-ya crowd, all right. But what's truly significant is that she got the men's vote. . . . The men of Ireland went unhesitatingly out and voted for a woman President because she represented their views.'
>
> (*The Irish Times*, 12/11/90)

Was Mary Robinson elected despite the defeats and hardship of the 1980s or precisely because those years had been so utterly intolerable? The result has been explained as signalling either the death throes of Old Ireland or the birth pangs of New Ireland. It seems to me there is but a hair's breath between the two interpretations. One way and another, it constituted both a smart slap in the face for the old order, ineffectual and inappropriate and, paradoxically perhaps, an indisputable demonstration of the depth and breadth of social and cultural transformation that had already occurred. A declining birthrate, rapidly growing numbers of married women in the workforce, the increasing entry of women into third-level education – these are only some of the more visible signs of the extent to which women's life options, attitudes and expectations have been changing over the past twenty years. . . .

Working for radical change substantially from within the judicial and legislative systems, Mary Robinson was at once centrally involved, as politician and lawyer, with the major feminist challenges to the State, yet not perceived by the Establishment as a 'dangerous subversive'. She thus succeeded in gaining the support of both radical and reformist elements in the Women's Movement without jeopardising 'mainstream' respect for her extraordinary and ground-breaking achievements. Most significantly, as a woman – the unknown quantity in the public arena – she was sign and carrier of renewal. . . .

Mary Robinson's very presence is a refutation of stereotypical notions of feminine 'passivity'. She presents an image of ourselves, as women and indeed as Irish, that is positive, modern, sophisticated, independent, and capable of making sense of differences without erasing them. Exploding myths and shibboleths, she allows us to break free of constraints and to set about re-creating ourselves.

MARY ROBINSON

from *The Inaugural Speech*

The Ireland I will be representing is a new Ireland, open, tolerant, inclusive. Many of you who voted for me did so without sharing all my views. This, I believe, is a significant signal of change, a sign, however modest, that we have already passed the threshold to a new, pluralist Ireland. . . .

My primary role as President will be to represent this State. But the State is not the only model of community with which Irish people can and do identify. Beyond our State there is a vast community of Irish emigrants extending not only across our neighbouring island – which has provided a home away from home for several Irish generations – but also throughout the continents of North America, Australia and of course Europe itself. There are over 70 million people living on this globe who claim Irish descent. I will be proud to represent them. And I would like to see Áras an Uachtaráin, my official residence, serve – on something of an annual basis – as a place where our emigrant communities could send representatives for a get-together of the extended Irish family abroad.

There is yet another level of community which I will represent. Not just the national, not just the global, but the local community. Within our State there are a growing number of local and regional communities determined to express their own creativity, identity, heritage and initiative in new and exciting ways. In my travels throughout Ireland I have found local community groups thriving on a new sense of self-confidence and self-empowerment. Whether it was groups concerned with adult education, employment initiative, women's support, local history and heritage, environmental concern or community culture, one of the most enriching discoveries was to witness the extent of this local empowerment at work.

As President I will seek to the best of my abilities to promote this growing sense of local participatory democracy, this energising movement of self development and self expression which is surfacing more and more at grassroots level. This is the face of modern Ireland. . . .

The best way we can contribute to a new integrated Europe of the 1990s is by having a confident sense of our Irishness. Here again we must play to our strengths – take full advantage of our vibrant cultural resources in music, art, drama, literature and film; value the role of our educators; promote and preserve our unique environmental and geographical resources of relatively pollution-free lakes, rivers, landscapes and seas; encourage and publicly support local initiative projects in aquaculture, forestry, fishing, alternative energy and small scale technology.

Looking outwards from Ireland, I would like on your behalf to contribute to the international protection and promotion of human rights. One of our greatest national resources has always been, and still is, our ability to serve as a moral and political conscience in world affairs. We have a long history of providing spiritual, cultural and social assistance to other countries in need – most notably in Latin America, Africa and other Third World countries. And we can continue to promote these values by taking principled and independent stands on issues of international importance.

If it is time, as Joyce's Stephen Dedalus remarked, that the Irish began to forge in the smithy of our souls 'the uncreated conscience of our race' – might we not also take on the still 'uncreated conscience' of the wider international community? Is it not time that the small started believing again that it is beautiful, that the periphery can rise up and speak out on equal terms with the centre, that the most outlying island community of the European Community really has something 'strange and precious' to contribute to the sea-change presently sweeping through the entire continent of Europe? As a native of Ballina, one of the most western towns in the most western province of the most western nation in Europe, I want to say – 'the West's awake'.

I turn now to another place close to my heart, Northern Ireland. As the elected choice of the people of this part of our island I want to extend the hand of friendship and of love to both communities in the other part. And I want to do this with no strings attached, no hidden agenda. As the person chosen by you to symbolise this Republic and to project our self image to others, I will seek to encourage mutual understanding and tolerance between all the different communities sharing this island.

In seeking to do this I shall rely to a large extent on symbols. But symbols are what unite and divide people. Symbols give us our identity, our self image, our way of explaining ourselves to ourselves and to others. Symbols in turn determine the kinds of stories we tell; and the stories we tell determine the kind of history we make and remake. I want Áras an Uachtaráin to be a place where people can tell diverse stories – in the knowledge that there is someone there to listen.

I want this Presidency to promote the telling of stories – stories of celebration through the arts and stories of conscience and of social justice. As a woman, I want women who have felt themselves outside history to be written back into history, in the words of Eavan Boland, 'finding a voice where they found a vision'.

May it be a presidency where I the President can sing to you, citizens of Ireland, the joyous refrain of the 14th century Irish poet as recalled by W.B. Yeats:

'I am of Ireland . . . come dance with me in Ireland'.

7

Shapechangers

from *The War for the Bull of Cuailgne*

TRANSLATED BY AUGUSTA GREGORY

Then Maeve bade her chariot-driver to yoke her horses, that she might go and consult with her Druid and ask a prophecy from him, to foretell for her if the army she was bringing out would get the victory, and would come back safely. And she said to the Druid: 'There are many that will part here to-day from their companions and their friends, from their country and their lands, from their father and their mother. And if it happens that the whole of them do not come back again safe and sound, it is on me the complaints and the curses will fall. And besides that,' she said, 'there is no one that goes out or that stops behind, that is dearer to us than we are to ourselves. So find out for us now whether we shall return, or not return.' And the Druid said: 'Whoever returns or does not return, you yourself will return.'

Her chariot was turned then, and she went back again homeward. But presently she saw a thing she wondered at, a woman sitting on the shaft of the chariot, facing her, and this is how she was: a sword of white bronze in her hand, with seven rings of red gold on it and she seemed to be weaving a web with it; a speckled green cloak about her, fastened at the breast with a brooch of red gold; a ruddy, pleasant face she had, her eyes grey, and her mouth like red berries, and when she spoke her voice was sweeter than the strings of a curved harp, and her skin showed through her clothes like the snow of a single night. Long feet she had, very white, and the nails on them pink and even; her hair gold-yellow, three locks of it wound about her head, and another that fell down loose below her knee.

Maeve looked at her, and she said: 'What are you doing here, young girl?' 'It is looking into the future for you I am,' she said, 'to see what will be your chances and your fortunes, now you are gathering the provinces of Ireland to the war for the Brown Bull of Cuailgne.' 'And why would you be doing this for me?' said Maeve.

'There is good reason for it,' she said, 'for I am a serving-maid of your own people.' 'Which of my people do you belong to?' said Maeve. 'I am Fedelm of the Sidhe, of Rath Cruachan.' 'It is well, Fedelm of the Sidhe; tell me what way you see our hosts.' 'I see crimson on them, I see red.' 'Yet Conchubar is lying in his weakness at Emain; my messengers are come back from there, and we need not be in dread of anything from Ulster,' said Maeve. 'But look again, Fedelm of the Sidhe, and tell me the truth of the matter.' 'I see crimson on them, I see red,' said the girl. 'Yet Eoghan, son of Durthacht, is in his weakness at Rathairthir; my messengers are come back from him; we need not be afraid of anything from Ulster. Look again, Fedelm of the Sidhe; how do you see our hosts?' 'I see them all crimson, I see them all red.' 'Celtchair, son of Uthecar, is lying in his weakness within his fort; my messengers are come back from him. Tell me again, Fedelm of the Sidhe, how do you see our hosts?' 'I see crimson on them, I see red.' 'There may be no harm in what you see,' said Maeve, 'for when all the men of Ireland are gathered together in one place, there will surely be quarrels and fights among them, about going first or last over fords and rivers, or about the first wounding of some stag or boar, or such like. Tell me truly now, Fedelm of the Sidhe, what way do you see our hosts?' 'I seem crimson on them, I see red. And I see,' she said, 'a low-sized man doing many deeds of arms; there are many wounds on his smooth skin; there is a light about his head, there is victory on his forehead; he is young and beautiful, and modest towards women; but he is like a dragon in the battle. His appearance and his courage are like the appearance and the courage of Cuchulain of Muirthemne; and who that Hound from Muirthemne may be I do not know; but I know this much well, that all this host will be reddened by him. He is setting out for the battle; he will make your dead lie thickly, the memory of the blood shed by him will be lasting; women will be keening over the bodies brought low by the Hound of the Forge that I see before me.'

This is the foretelling that was made for Maeve by Fedelm of the Sidhe, before the setting out of the hosts at Cruachan for Ulster.

*

Now, when Maeve told Fedelm of the Sidhe that there need be no fear of the men of Ulster coming out to attack the army, for they were lying in their weakness, she meant that they were under the curse and the enchantment that was put on them one time by a woman they had ill-treated. And the story of it is this:

There was a man of the name of Crunden, son of Agnoman, that lived in a lonely part of Ulster, among the mountains, and he had a good way of living; but his wife had died, and he had the care of all his children on him. One day he was sitting in the house, and he saw a woman come in at the door, tall and handsome, and with good clothes on her, and she did not say a word, but she sat down by the hearth and began to make up the fire. And then she went to where the meal was, and took it out and mixed it, and baked a cake. And when the evening was drawing on, she took a vessel and went out and milked the cows, but all the time she never spoke a word. Then she came back into the house, and took a turn to the right, and was the last to stop up and to cover over the fire.

She stayed on there, and Crunden, the man of the house, married her, and she tended him and his sons, and everything he had prospered.

It happened, one day, there was to be a great gathering of the men of Ulster, for games and races and all sorts of amusements, and all that could go, both of men and women, used to go to that gathering. 'I will go there to-day,' said Crunden, 'the same as every other man is going. 'Do not,' said his wife, 'for if you so much as say my name there at the fair,' she said, 'I will be lost to you for ever.' 'Then indeed I will not speak of you at all,' said Crunden. So he set out with the others to the fair, and there was every sort of amusement there, and all the people of the country were at it.

At the ninth hour, the royal chariot was brought on the ground, and the king's horses won the day. Then the bards and poets, and the Druids, and the servants of the king, and the whole gathering, began to praise the king and the queen and their horses, and they cried out: 'There were never seen such horses as these; there are no better runners in all Ireland.'

'My wife is a better runner than those two horses,' said

Crunden. Then the king was told of that he said: 'Take hold of the man, and keep him until his wife can be brought to try her chance and to run against the horses.'

So they took hold of him, and kept him, and messengers were sent from the king to the woman. She bade the messengers welcome, and asked what brought them. 'We are come, by the king's order,' they said, 'to bring you to the fair, to see if you will run faster than the king's horses; for your husband boasted that you would, and he is kept prisoner now until you will come and release him.'

'It is foolish my husband was to speak like that,' she said; 'and as for myself, I am not fit to go, for I am soon going to give birth to a child.'

''Tis a pity,' said the messengers, 'for if you do not come, your husband will be put to death.'

'If that is so, I must go, whatever happens,' she said.

So with that she set out for the gathering, and when she got there all the people were crowding about her to see her. 'It is not fitting to be looking at me, and I the way I am,' she cried; 'and what have I been brought here for?'

'To run against the two horses of the king,' the people called out.

'Ochone!' she said, 'do not ask me, for I am close upon my hour.'

'Take out your swords and put the man to death,' said the king.

'Give me your help,' she said to the people, 'for every one of you has been born of a mother.' And then she said to the king: 'Give me even a delay until my child is born.'

'I will give no delay,' said the king.

'Then the shame that is on you will be greater than the shame that is on me,' she said, 'it is a heavier punishment will fall on you than has fallen upon me. And bring out the horses beside me now.'

Then they started, and the woman outran the horses and gained the race; and at the goal the pains of childbirth came on her, and she bore two children, a boy and a girl, and she gave a great cry in her pain.

And a weakness came suddenly on all that heard the cry, so they had no more strength than the woman as she lay there. And it is what she said: 'From this out, and till the ninth generation, the shame that you have put on me will fall on you; and at whatever time you most want your strength, at the time your enemies are closing on you, that is the time the weakness of a woman in childbirth will come upon all men of the province of Ulster.'

And so it happened; and all of the men of Ulster that were born after that day, there was no one escaped that curse and that enchantment but only Cuchulainn.

Eiléan Ní Chuilleanáin

Pygmalion's Image

Not only her stone face, laid back staring in the ferns,
But everything the scoop of the valley contains begins to move
(And beyond the horizon the trucks beat the highway.)

A tree inflates gently on the curve of the hill;
An insect crashes on the carved eyelid;
Grass blows westward from the roots,
As the wind knifes under her skin and ruffles it like a book.

The crisp hair is real, wriggling like snakes;
A rustle of veins, tick of blood in the throat;
The lines of the face tangle and catch, and
A green leaf of language comes twisting out of her mouth.

Edmund Lenihan

from *Alice Kyteler*

'Force not my hand, madam, for if once I pronounce you witch, your doom is sealed. Admit to your evil-doing while yet you may. Then perhaps may you be admitted to mercy and forgiveness.'

It was a fair plea on his part, clearly in deference to her rank. A lesser person – or maybe one more guilty – would have grasped the opportunity willingly. But not Dame Alice. Her only acknowledgement that she had even heard his words was a slight smile.

Scarcely able to hide his irritation, the Judge, very deliberately, so that all might see, placed the black cloth on his head.

'So be it,' he said grimly. And thus he pronounced his sentence: that the prisoner be brought forth from the jail one week from that day, and taken to the place of public execution, there to receive the full rigours of the law.

A like sentence was passed on Petronilla by the angry Judge, despite all her protests of innocence. . . .

He began: 'Be it known to all that I, by the grace of God Mayor of this town of Kilkenny, do hereby order, in the name of the powers spiritual and temporal of this kingdom, that Dame Alice Kyteler and Petronilla of Meath be brought forth and conveyed to the place of execution, that the sentence of the court may be carried out. Guards! Bring forth Petronilla of Meath!'

The guards clanked into the dark interior of the jail, ordered the jailer to give up the prisoner. 'Prepare yourself, Dame Kyteler,' they gibed as they led the wretched servant out. But Alice paid them not the slightest heed, only gazed intently at the barred window, as if meditating.

Pale as death Petronilla was, but through all her ordeal she would never once cry for mercy or speak ill of her mistress. They led her to where the stakes stood like the doorjambs of eternity, and bound her quickly and securely. A spark, a wisp of smoke, and in a few moments the flames were crackling through the dry wood piled around, feeling their hungry way towards her. To the very limit of human endurance she clenched her teeth and suffered in silence, but at last she could bear it no further, and her agonised screams echoed through the narrow streets, re-echoed from the walls of St Canice's Cathedral, and off across the pleasant waters of the Nore. Many a secret listener shuddered, hearing in her awful shrieks the terror of a lost soul falling into eternal darkness. Others, more fastidious, felt a twinge of disgust at the barbarousness of the proceedings – could she not merely have been kept in jail, where she would speedily be forgotten about, as many another had?

Soon enough, Petronilla's hard passage from this world was over. Only the smell of cooking flesh lingered on in the still air for some time longer while the fire was allowed to burn itself into embers. Some of those who watched could not help but pray. Petronilla had been no stranger to them. Had they not met her almost daily, hurrying about her mistress' business in the town? Or seen her, head bowed, praying in the cathedral of a Sunday? A few had even known her well. Now she was dead. Most horribly dead. . . .

'Guards! Bring forth Alice Kyteler.' . . .

'In God's name, Captain, what delays you? His Worship awaits, and the Lord Bishop.'

Of a sudden, one of the iron hinges sprang from the massive jamb and the door slewed drunkenly inward. With a yell of triumph, the soldiers surged forward into the little chamber, weapons at the ready. They were unnecessary. The cell was empty of all but the charred remnants of the stool and a handful of smouldering straw in its corner. Of Alice Kyteler there was nothing.

SEAMUS HEANEY

Act of Union

I

To-night, a first movement, a pulse,
As if the rain in bogland gathered head
To slip and flood: a bog-burst,
A gash breaking open the ferny bed.
Your back is a firm line of eastern coast
And arms and legs are thrown
Beyond your gradual hills. I caress
The heaving province where our past has grown.
I am the tall kingdom over your shoulder
That you would neither cajole nor ignore.
Conquest is a lie. I grow older
Conceding your half-independent shore
Within whose borders now my legacy
Culminates inexorably.

II

And I am still imperially
Male, leaving you with the pain,
The rending process in the colony,
The battering ram, the boom burst from within.
The act sprouted an obstinate fifth column
Whose stance is growing unilateral.
His heart beneath your heart is a wardrum
Mustering force. His parasitical
And ignorant little fists already
Beat at your borders and I know they're cocked
At me across the water. No treaty
I foresee will salve completely your tracked
And stretchmarked body, the big pain
That leaves you raw, like opened ground, again.

LADY WILDE

The Horned Women

A rich woman sat up late one night carding and preparing wool, while all the family and servants were asleep. Suddenly a knock was given at the door, and a voice called: 'Open! Open!'

'Who is there?' asked the woman of the house.

The mistress, supposing that one of her neighbours had called and required assistance, opened the door, and a woman entered, having in her hand a pair of wool carders, and bearing a horn on her forehead, as if growing there. She sat down by the fire in silence, and began to card the wool with violent haste. Suddenly she paused and said aloud: 'Where are the women? They delay too long.'

Then a second knock came to the door, and a voice called as before: 'Open! Open'

The mistress felt herself constrained to rise and open to the call, and immediately a second woman entered, having two horns on her forehead, and in her hand a wheel for spinning the wool.

'Give me place,' she said, 'I am the Witch of the Two Horns,' and she began to spin as quick as lightening.

And so the knocks went on, and the call was heard, and the witches entered, until at last twelve women sat round the fire – the first with one horn, the last with twelve horns. And they carded the thread, and turned their spinning wheels, and wound and wove, all singing together an ancient rhyme, but no word did they speak to the mistress of the house. Strange to hear and frightful to look upon were these twelve women, with their horns and their wheels; and the mistress felt near to death, and she tried to rise that she might call for help, but she could not move, nor could she utter a word or cry, for the spell of the witches was upon her.

Then one of them called to her and said: 'Rise, woman, and make us a cake,'

Then the mistress searched for a vessel to bring water from the well that she might mix the meal and make the cake, but she could find none. And they said to her: 'Take a sieve and bring water in it.'

And she took the sieve and went to the well, but the water poured from it, and she could fetch none for the cake, and she sat down by the well and wept. Then a voice came by her and said: 'Take yellow clay and moss and bind them together and plaster the sieve so that it will hold.'

Nuala Archer

Ordinary Dragonfly Flicks

Another year of dragonflies
A drop in the bucket for these fairies
that have survived 300 million years.

An early one there – hovering.

Now leaping into air.
Un-Stephening the Green.

Framing in the minute windows
of her wings the topsy-turvy
water-wrinkled trees.

like some far-out flick

featuring jazzy celluloids of turquoise and jade
with a *da capo* feminine ending –

unstressed and ongoing –

hovering among the uncertain sound tracks
of children sending vowels
ballooning into air like coloured dots of silence

where pixilated directions drift
into each other and spark off lightning –

purple and pink – over a disco lake
of memory and through

a flower wilderness.
a fierce, unfathered woman

palpating noon's brief lunch break.
transfusing its pale shadows
and razored rainbows

with her own holograms of words
beaming her into a body of profound balance

merging with the laughter
and singing voices
coming from the loo labelled *mna*.

ANON

The Gay Old Hag

Will you come a boating, my gay old hag,
Will you come a boating, my tight old hag,
Will you come a boating, down the Liffey floating?
I'll make a pair of oars of your two long shins.

Crush her in the corner the gay old hag,
Crush her in the corner the tight old hag,
Crush her in the corner and keep her snug and warm,
Put powder in her horn, she's a fine old hag.

Napoleon's on dry land, says the gay old hag,
Napoleon's on dry land, says the tight old hag,
Napoleon's on dry land, with a sword in his right hand,
He's a gallant Ribbon man, says the gay old hag.

My mother's getting young, says the gay old hag,
My mother's getting young, says the gay old hag,
My mother's getting young and she'll have another son
To make the orange run, says the gay old hag.

Remember '98, says the gay old hag,
When our Boys you did defeat, says the gay old hag,
Then our Boys you did defeat, but we'll beat you out compleat,
Now you're nearly out of date, says the fine old hag.

BRENDAN KENNELLY

Bread

Someone else cut off my head
In a golden field.
Now I am re-created

By her fingers. This
Moulding is more delicate
Than a first kiss,

More deliberate than her own
Rising up
And lying down.

Even at my weakest, I am
Finer than anything
In this legendary garden

Yet I am nothing till
She runs her fingers through me
And shapes me with her skill.

The form that I shall bear
Grows round and white.
It seems I comfort her

Even as she slits my face
And stabs my chest.
Her feeling for perfection is

Absolute.
So I am glad to go through fire
And come out

Shaped like her dream.
In my way
I am all that can happen to men.
I came to life at her fingerends.
I will go back into her again.

ANON

The Shannon Mermaid

'Sure, [said the old woman], 'twas over there beyond the corner where the river is that the mermaid was caught, and Deny Duggan described her to me, and he the oldest man in Foynes. The man that caught her was one of those who watched the weir over on the

Island. They were forever seeing a woman on the point, and they knew it was the mermaid that was ever living in the river, and one day the man saw her sitting on a big stone on the point and she a-combing her fine golden hair back from the forehead of her, and combing it from the rack. And he faced round and crept up behind her when she was not knowing it, and caught her by the two shoulders of her, and brought her to his house, where his mother lived.

'It was the beautifullest woman ever you see'd, with the golden hair and fair skin of her. Now after a time he took her as his wife, and she had three children to him, and all the time she was doing all the work a woman might do, but never a smile or a laugh out of her, except one day when he was a-doing something with the child on the floor, playing with it, and then she let the sweetest laugh out of her that ever you heard. Now the man had taken the covering from her that she had the day sitting on the rock, a sort of an oily skin, and he had been told to keep it from her and put it away by way of luck.

'And the house was built so that the fireplace had piers like on each side of it, as in the country houses, and on the top a shelf, and 'twas on this that the man had put away the covering among the nets and sacks. For – she was going about the house doing all the work that a woman might do, but that she could never climb up on a thing, and she afeared even to stand on a chair to reach a thing as might be. But one day – it was seven years from the day he had caught her on the stone and brought her home – she was sitting by the fire with the child, and he just able to walk. He was on her knee sitting, when the man came in looking for the net, and he began to throw things on the shelf looking for it. Well, he threw down an old sack out way of him, and with it sure the covering fell down, and her seeing it, and it fell behind her so as she couldn't lay hand to the child on her knee; so she looked over her shoulder and saw she put the child to stand with the chair, went and took the covering and out of the door with it before the man had time to get down stop her, and down to the shore she went with a laugh as never heard with the ringing in it, and into the sea, and she never come back again.

'And the three children of her were reared on the island beyond Deny Duggan's, and 'tis three ages [generations] ago now. Deny he is the oldest man in Foynes, and when he was young heard of the children of her, and heard of her from a friend of the man worked with him on the weir.'

W.B. YEATS

The Song of Wandering Aengus

I went out to the hazel wood,
Because a fire was in my head,
And cut and peeled a hazel wand,
And hooked a berry to a thread;
And when white moths were on the wing,
And moth-like stars were flickering out,
I dropped the berry in a stream
And caught a little silver trout.

When I had laid it on the floor
I went to blow the fire aflame,
But something rustled on the floor,
And some one called me by my name.
It had become a glimmering girl
With apple blossom in her hair
Who called me by my name and ran
And faded through the brightening air.

Though I am old with wandering
Through hollow lands and hilly lands,
I will find out where she has gone,
And kiss her lips and take her hands;
And walk among long dappled grass,
And pluck till time and times are done
The silver apples of the moon,
The golden apples of the sun.

JOHN BOYLE O'REILLY

The Lure

'What bait do you use,' said a Saint to the Devil,
'When you fish where the souls of men abound?'
'Well, for special tastes,' said the King of Evil,
'Gold and Fame are the best I've found.'
'But for common use?' asked the Saint. 'Ah then,'
Said the Demon, 'I angle for Man, not men,
     And a thing I hate
     Is to change my bait,
So I fish with a woman the whole year round.'

DEIRDRE BRENNAN

Purgation (Saorghlanadh)

I don't remember now
How often our love was made flesh
I don't remember how often
In the dead of night
Squatting on my hunkers
I gave birth to babies
In fields, in bogs
In abandoned houses,
On rubbish dumps
With the ground oozing under me.

I scarcely remember their gluey bodies
Under the moon
How I drowned them
In drains and bogholes,

How I threw them from me
Without a screed of clothes
Over the slope of the gorge
Or how I left them rolled up like snails
At the bottom of ditches
Amidst the pecking of birds.

Nights recently they take possession of me
Coming unexpectedly and without invitation
They close in on me
Until my body is filled with them
And I'm deafened with the noise
Of their sucking
With their newborn cries
Their whingeing calls
That I baptize them.

A fever on my skin
From morning to evening
I run along the edge of the gorge
Listening to the echoes
Of their voices from its depths;
I wade every pond
Every muddle puddle in search of them
And I dig in ditches
Untangling their fingers
From roots of ivy
And honeysuckle
That I may make a posy
From their bones.

W.B. Yeats

from *Cathleen Ni Houlihan*

BRIDGET. (*to the Old Woman*). Will you have a drink of milk, ma'am?

OLD WOMAN. It is not food or drink that I want.

PETER. (*offering the shilling*). Here is something for you.

OLD WOMAN. This is not what I want. It is not silver I want.

PETER. What is it you would be asking for?

OLD WOMAN. If any one would give me help he must give me himself, he must give me all.

(*Peter goes over to the table staring at the shilling in his hand in a bewildered way, and stands whispering to Bridget.*)

MICHAEL. Have you no one to care you in your age, ma'am?

OLD WOMAN. I have not. With all the lovers that brought me their love I never set out the bed for any.

MICHAEL. Are you lonely going the roads, ma'am?

OLD WOMAN. I have my thoughts and I have my hopes.

MICHAEL. What hopes have you to hold to?

OLD WOMAN. The hope of getting my beautiful fields back again; the hope of putting the strangers out of my house.

MICHAEL. What way will you do that, ma'am?

OLD WOMAN. I have good friends that will help me. They are gathering to help me now. I am not afraid. If they are put down to-day they will get the upper hand to-morrow. (*She gets up.*) I must be going to meet my friends. They are coming to help me and I must be there to welcome them. I must call the neighbours together to welcome them.

MICHAEL. I will go with you.

BRIDGET. It is not her friends you have to go and welcome, Michael; it is the girl coming into the house you have to welcome. You have plenty to do; it is food and drink you have to bring to the house. The woman that is coming home is not coming with empty hands; you would not have an empty house before her. (*To the Old Woman.*) Maybe you don't know, ma'am, that my son is going to be married to-morrow.

OLD WOMAN. It is not a man going to his marriage that I look to for help.

PETER (*to Bridget*). Who is she, do you think, at all?

BRIDGET. You did not tell us your name yet, ma'am?

OLD WOMAN. Some call me the Poor Old Woman, and there are some that call me Cathleen, the daughter of Houlihan.

PETER. I think I knew some one of that name, once. Who was it, I wonder? It must have been some one I knew when I was a boy. No, no; I remember, I heard it in a song.

OLD WOMAN (*who is standing in the doorway*). They are wondering that there were songs made for me; there have been many songs made for me. I heard one on the wind this morning. (*Sings*).

> Do not make a great keening
> When the graves have been dug to-morrow,
> Do not call the white-scarfed riders
> To the burying that shall be to-morrow.
>
> Do not spread food to call strangers
> To the wakes that shall be to-morrow;
> Do not give money for prayers
> For the dead that shall die to-morrow . . .

They will have no need of prayers, they will have no need of prayers.

MICHAEL. I do not know what that song means, but tell me something I can do for you.

PETER. Come over to me, Michael.

MICHAEL. Hush, father, listen to her.

OLD WOMAN. It is a hard service they take that help me. Many that are red-cheeked now will be pale-cheeked; many that have been free to walk the hills and the bogs and the rushes will be sent to walk hard streets in far countries; many a good plan will be broken; many that have gathered money will not stay to spend it; many a child will be born and there will be no father at its christening to give it a name. They that have red cheeks will have pale cheeks for my sake, and for all that, they will think they are well paid.

(*She goes out; her voice is heard outside singing*).

> They shall be remembered for ever,
> They shall be alive for ever,
> They shall be speaking for ever,
> The people shall hear them for ever.

BRIDGET (*to Peter*). Look at him, Peter; he has the look of a man that has got the touch. (*Raising her voice.*) Look here, Michael, at the wedding clothes. Such grand clothes as these are! You have a right to fit them on now; it would be a pity to-morrow if they did not fit. The boys would be laughing at you. Take them, Michael, and go into the room and fit them on.

(*She puts them on his arm.*)

MICHAEL. What wedding are you talking of? What clothes will I be wearing to-morrow?

BRIDGET. These are the clothes you are going to wear when you marry Delia Cahel to-morrow.

MICHAEL. I had forgotten that.

(*He looks at the clothes and turns towards the inner room, but stops at the sound of cheering outside.*)

SUSAN MITCHELL

To the Daughters of Erin

> Year after year, from south and north,
>   From east and west the tramp of men
> Rang on our mother's land, and forth
>   To battle marched her sons again.
> Year after year we raised the keen
>   For heroes of our name and race.

We knelt and wept for what had been,
   All Ireland was a keening place.

The nations saw our mother shamed,
   The nations saw our heads bent low.
Nor knew that in our hearts untamed
   Fire still unquenchable could glow.
With downcast eye and shrouded head,
   Kathleen Ni Houlihan, have we
Showed to the world thy glory fled,
   Our beauty marred betraying thee.

Rise from your knees, O daughters, rise!
   Our mother still is young and fair,
Let the world look into your eyes
   And see her beauty shining there.
Grant of that beauty but one ray,
   Heroes shall leap from every hill,
To-day shall be as yesterday,
   The red blood burns in Ireland still.

EDNA LONGLEY

from *From Cathleen to Anorexia*

Gonne, Markievicz and Maeve the warrior-queen have enjoyed a new lease of life in Northern Republican ideology. Perhaps Feminists too readily assume that it's *always* a good thing when passive versions of women are transformed into active ones. Both have political uses.

   Two passive images are the vulnerable virgin and the mourning mother: images that link Cathleen with Mary. They project the self-image of Catholic Nationalism as innocent victim, equally oppressed at all historical periods. (Is there a subconscious admission that Irish men victimise women?) This assigns to Britain the

perpetual role of male bully and rapist. In Seamus Heaney's
'Ocean's Love to Ireland': 'The ruined maid complains in Irish.' In
the mid-1970s Heaney could still symbolise the Northern conflict
as 'a struggle between the cults and devotees of a god and a
goddess'; between 'an indigenous territorial numen, a tutelar of
the whole island, call her Mother Ireland, Kathleen Ni Houlihan
. . . the Shan Van Vocht, whatever' and 'a new male cult whose
founding fathers were Cromwell, William of Orange and Edward
Carson'. To characterise Irish Nationalism (only constructed in the
nineteenth century) as archetypally female both gives it mythic
pedigree and exonerates it from aggressive and oppressive intent.
Its patriarchal elements also disappear. Here, perhaps, we glimpse
the *poetic* unconscious of Northern Nationalism. At the same time,
Heaney's mouldering 'Bog Queen' in *North* may indirectly represent the cult of Cathleen as a death-cult. The book contains an
unresolved tension between two Muses: a symbolic mummified or
mummifying woman (not yet Anorexia) and the warmly creative,
life-giving aunt who bakes scones in the poem 'Sunlight'.

While Virgin-Ireland gets raped and pitied, Mother Ireland
translates pity into a call to arms and vengeance. She resembles the
white-feather-bestowing 'Little Mother' in First-World-War recruiting. Traditionally, it is her *sons* whom Mother Ireland recruits
and whose *manhood* she tests. More recently, some of her daughters
have also become 'freedom-fighters'. In *Mother Ireland* Bernadette
Devlin and Mairead Farrell differed in their attitudes to the
personification. Devlin felt that Mother Ireland had empowered
her as a strong woman; Farrell said: 'Mother Ireland, get off our
backs.' But did she? Is there not collusion between all feminine-
Nationalist images, between Queen Maeve and Mother Ireland,
between the feminine-pathetic and the feminine-heroic? The
latter too disguises or softens aggression: the looks and dress of
Gonne and Markievicz were propaganda-assets. On the cover of
the biased *Only the Rivers Run Free: Northern Ireland: The Women's
War* a glamorous young paramilitary woman fronts a desperate-
looking Sean Bhean.

Such images of Irish women are among those selectively
approved by Anorexia. The cover of *Spare Rib* (August 1989)

features another: a West Belfast Mother Courage with child in pram, smoke and flames behind her, and insets of a British soldier and 'Stop Strip Searches'. Of course there are many courageous working-class mothers on the Falls, ditto on the Shankill. But does it help them if this magazine distorts the profile of Irish women to include no police or UDR widows; no non-aligned social-workers, doctors or teachers; no members of the DUP; no Belfast or Dublin yuppies; no Southern feminists; no TDs? There are also articles with titles like 'Britain's War on Ireland' and 'Irish in Britain – Living in the Belly of the Beast' (an interesting variation on rape-images: cannibalism? Jonah and the whale?). And a literary section, among other poetic sentimentalities, reprints Susan Langstaff Mitchell's 'To the Daughters of Erin': 'Rise from your knees, O daughters rise!/Our mother still is young and fair . . . Heroes shall leap from every hill . . . The red blood burns in Ireland still'. (Feminism, where are you?) *Spare Rib* has certainly provided the most ludicrous instance yet of the British Left's anachronistic and self-righteous pieties on Ireland. But it's up to Irish women themselves to expose the loaded terms in a statement like: 'In the *Six Counties Irish* women experience *oppression* both as women and as members of a *colonised people*' (my italics). I attended a *Time to Go* conference in London which offered a seminar on 'Ireland in Feminism'. I think Feminism in Ireland should have something to say about that.

During the Irish revolution Nationalist women discovered – though not all acknowledged or cared – that their oppression as women did not end with the Dawning of the Day. The briefly eulogised 'Dáil Girl . . . wielding a cudgel in one hand and a revolver in the other' soon gave way to Dev's ideal of 'life within the home'. Nor had the Dáil girl necessarily taken up her cudgel for Feminism. As a general rule: the more Republican, the less Feminist. The ultra-Nationalism of the six women deputies who opposed the Treaty was, in Margaret Ward's words, governed by the 'ghosts of dead sons, husbands, and brothers'. Theirs were 'opinionated minds' with no – female? – capacity for compromise, and they set a pattern for the limited participation of women in the Free State/Republic's political life: almost invariably licensed by male relatives, by dynastic privilege. Rosemary Cullen Owens in *Smashing Times* (less romantic than Ward's *Unmanageable Revolutionaries*) brings out the tension between Nationalism and Suffragism: 'From 1914 onwards, with Home Rule on the statute book, it was the growing separatist movement which created the greatest obstacle to a united women's movement'.

Sinn Féin women (the only women quoted in *Spare Rib*) have recently adopted some Feminist ideas. But they cling, like their elder sisters, to the prospective goodwill of Republican men, and to the fallacy that: 'there can't be women's liberation until there's national liberation'. Devlin in *Spare Rib* seems significantly wary of 'the gospel according to the Holy Writ of Feminism'. What a woman 'needs to know is that we, her sisters, will catch her if she stumbles, help her find the questions – the answers she must find herself'. Who are 'we, her sisters'? And what kind of elitism lurks in Devlin's assertion (in *Mother Ireland*) that 'the best young feminist women today are those who have come through the experience of the Republican movement'?

While admiring the bonding that tough circumstances beget, and perceiving these circumstances as tragic, I do not accept that either the supportiveness of the ghetto or the essential survival-strategy in Armagh Gaol affords a model for Irish women in general. The basis of such bonding is tribal rather than sisterly. It remains true that the vast majority of Republican women come from traditionally Republican families – recruited by and for a patriarchal unit. The Irish Women's Movement, instead of walking away or vaguely empathising, might examine the role of Nationalist conditioning in all this: the ideological forces which played a part in sending out Mairead Farrell to be shot.

Contrary to Nell McCafferty, I think that 'Feminism and Physical Force' is self-evidently a contradiction in terms. Years ago a member of the Irish Women's Franchise League said: 'It is our conviction feminism and militarism are natural born enemies and cannot flourish in the same soil'. Militarism, that touch of Madame Defarge, gives the Sinn Féin sisterhood its faintly chilling aura. In *The Demon Lover: On the Sexuality of Terrorism*, Robin Morgan argues that revolutionary terrorism inevitably involves a death-cult. It enacts the quest of the male hero who already 'lives as a dead man'. She asks: 'Why is manhood always perceived as the too-high price of peace?' and notes that when men take over any movement: 'what once aimed for a humanistic triumph now aims for a purist defeat. Martyrdom'. The same syndrome can be detected in Protestant anticipations of Armageddon, apocalypse, their last stand (the ghosts of religious wars walk on both sides). Morgan's conclusion mirrors the Irish Nationalist historical pattern: 'The rebel woman in a male-defined State-that-would-be is merely acting out another version of the party woman running for office in the State-that-is'. Unionist party-women have been equally acquiescent in militarism.

Cathleen-Anorexia encourages women to join a male death-cult which has a particularly masochistic martyrology. This cult's rituals deny the 'connectivity' which Morgan sees as the 'genius' of feminist thought: 'In its rejection of the static, this capacity is witty and protean, like the dance of nature itself . . . It is therefore a volatile capacity – dangerous to every imaginable status quo, because of its insistence on *noticing*. Such a noticing involves both attentiveness and recognition, and is in fact a philosophical and activist technique for being in the world, as well as for changing the world'. In 'Easter 1916' Yeats understands that 'Too long a sacrifice/Can make a stone of the heart', and contrasts that stone with 'the living stream'. Surely the chill, the stone, the self-destructiveness at the heart of Irish Nationalism shows up in its abuse of women and their gifts of life.

from *The Story of Eochaid's Sons*

Translated by Standish H. O'Grady

When they ceased from their wandering they kindled themselves a fire; they cooked them somewhat of the game, and ate till they were satisfied. But then, by operation of their meal, they were affected with great drouth and thirst, and 'let us send one to look for water,' said they. 'I will go,' said Fergus. Away the young fellow goes in quest of water; and he lights on a well, over which he finds an old woman standing sentry. The fashion of the hag was this: blacker than coal every joint and segment of her was, from crown to ground comparable to a wild horse's tail the grey wiry mass of hair that pierced her scalp's upper surface; with her sickle of a greenish looking tusk that was in her head, and curled till it touched her ear, she could lop the verdant branch of an oak in full bearing (i.e. acorn-laden); blackened and smoke-bleared eyes she had; nose awry, wide-nostrilled; a wrinkled and a freckled belly, variously unwholesome; warped crooked shins, garnished with massive ankles and a pair of capacious shovels; knotty knees she had, and livid nails. The beldame's whole description in fact was disgusting. 'That's the way it is, is it?' said the lad, and: 'that's the very way', she answered. 'Is it guarding the well thou art?' he asked, and she said: 'it is.' 'Dost thou license me to take away some water?' 'I do,' she consented, 'yet only so that I have of the one kiss on my cheek.' 'Not so,' said he. 'Then water shall not be conceded by me.' 'My word I give,' he went on, 'that sooner than give thee a kiss I would perish of thirst!' Then the young man departed to the place where his brethren were, and told them that he had not gotten water.

Ailill started to look for some, duly reached the same well and denied the *cailleach* a kiss. He besought her for water but she granted him not access to the spring.

Brian, eldest of the sons, then went on the quest, and equally attained to the identical well; he solicited the old thing for water, but denied her a kiss.

Fiachra went now; the spring and the *cailleach* he found both, and petitioned for water. 'I will give it,' she said, 'and give me a kiss for it.' He bestowed on her a bare touch of a kiss, and she said: 'have thou but mere contact of Tara!' and it came true: of his seed two ruled Ireland, *Dathí* and *Ailill molt* namely, but of the others' seed: of Brian's, Ailill's, Fergus's, not one.

Niall went in search of water, and came to the very well: 'Let me have water, woman!' he cried. 'I will give it,' said she, 'and bestow on me a kiss.' He answered: 'Forby giving thee a kiss, I will even hug thee!' then he bends him to embrace, and gives her a kiss. Which operation ended, and when he looked at her, in the whole world was not a young woman of gait more graceful, in universal semblance fairer than was she; to be likened to the last-fallen snow lying in trenches every portion of her was, from crown to sole; plump and queenly forearms, fingers long and taper, straight legs of a lovely hue she had; two sandals of the white bronze betwixt her smooth and soft white feet and the earth; about her was an ample mantle of the choicest fleece, pure crimson, and in the garment a brooch of white silver; she had lustrous teeth of pearl, great regal eyes, mouth red as the rowan-berry. 'Here, woman, is a galaxy of charms' said the young man. 'That is true indeed.' 'And who are thou?' he pursued.

' "Royal Rule" am I,' she answered and uttered this:-
'King of Tara. I am "Royal Rule" . . . '

Sara Berkeley

The Beach

If I could only be that milky stretch
Arms stuck with clams
Flung open to the sea, generous-limbed,
My pale hair in fronds
Uncombed by every salt-toothed wind,
Armed with a frailty of shells
Wrists of coral,
Stippled,
Duned.

My people
Would bring fine dogs
To run the tides, excited, worrying my brow
Burying their bones between my barnacled ribs.

My time would be
Time of the storm,
The sea winded, throwing herself headlong
Spreading herself over the boulders
Tangling in my hair; and in the calm
Of a dawn great with beached whale
I would shake out the loosened shale
My back mildly to the shore,
My face awash –
Loveless.

JAMES JOYCE

from *Finnegans Wake*

Yes, you're changing, sonhusband, and you're turning, I can feel you, for a daughterwife from the hills again. Imlamaya. And she is coming. Swimming in my hindmoist. Diveltaking on me tail. Just a whisk brisk sly spry spink spank sprint of a thing theresomere, saultering. Saltarella come to her own. I pity your oldself I was used to. Now a younger's there. Try not to part! Be happy, dear ones! May I be wrong! For she'll be sweet for you as I was sweet when I came down out of me mother. My great blue bedroom, the air so quiet, scarce a cloud. In peace and silence. I could have stayed up there for always only. It's something fails us. First we feel. Then we fall. And let her rain now if she likes. Gently or strongly as she likes. Anyway let her rain for my time is

come. I done me best when I was let: Thinking always if I go all
goes. A hundred cares, a tithe of troubles and is there one who
understands me? One in a thousand of years of the nights? All me
life I have been lived among them but now they are becoming
lothed to me. And I am lothing their little warm tricks. And
lothing their mean cosy turns. And all the greedy gushes out
through their small souls. And all the lazy leaks down over their
brash bodies. How small it's all! And me letting on to meself
always. And lilting on all the time. I thought you were all
glittering with the noblest of carriage. You're only a bumpkin. I
thought you the great in all things, in guilt and in glory. You're
but a puny. Home! My people were not their sort out beyond there
so far as I can see. For all the bold and bad and bleary they are
blamed, the seahags. No! Nor for all our wild dances in all their
wild din. I can seen meself among them, allaniuvia pulchrabelled.
How she was handsome, the wild Amazia, when she would seize
to my other breast! And what is she weird, haughty Niluna, that
she will snatch from my ownest hair! For 'tis they are the stormies.
Ho hang! Hang ho! And the clash of our cries till we spring to be
free. Auravoles, they says, never heed of your name! But I'm
loothing them that's here and all I lothe. Loonely in me loneness.
For all their faults. I am passing out. O bitter ending! I'll slip away
before they're up. They'll never see. Nor know. Nor miss me. And
it's old and old it's sad and old it's sad and weary I go back to you,
my cold father, my cold mad father, my cold mad feary father, till
the near sight of the mere size of him, the moyles and moyles of it,
moananoaning, makes me seasilt saltsick and I rush, my only, into
your arms. I see them rising! Save me from those therrble prongs!
Two more. Onetwo moremens more. So. Avelaval. My leaves have
drifted from me. All. But one clings still. I'll bear it on me. To
remind me of. Lff! So soft this morning, ours. Yes. Carry me
along, taddy, like you done through the toy fair! If I seen him
bearing down on me now under whitespread wings like he'd come
from Arkangels, I sink I'd die down over his feet, humbly
dumbly, only to washup. Yes, tid. There's where. First. We pass
through grass behush the bush to. Whish! A gull. Gulls. Far calls.
Coming, far! End here. Us then. Finn, again! Take. Bussoftlhee,

mememormee! Till thousendsthee. Lps. The keys to. Given! A
way a lone a last a loved a long the

AUGUSTA GREGORY

from *The Golden Apple*

WITCH. My name is Sighing and Sorrow, Black Night of Winter,
White Night of Snow; Grief, Groaning, Keening, and a Grave!
RURY. What is it ails you?
WITCH. Sit down till I will tell you. Twelve sons I had and they
are all after being brought away to their death.
RURY. What way can I help you?
WITCH. Go back, bring the armies of the King of Ireland, till
they will go against the armies of the Dogheads that brought them
away.
RURY. I cannot do that. I must go on until my business will be
done. I will come then and help you.
WITCH. You are deceiving me.
RURY. I never left a lie after me in any place.
WITCH. Take this bone in your hand; put this flesh I offer you in
your mouth.
RURY. I will not deny you because you are in trouble and grief.
(Rury *is putting a bit in his mouth when* Pampogue *comes behind him
and snatches it from him.*)
PAMPOGUE. Use none of her food or you are a gone man! It is best
throw it in the fire. (*She throws it away.*)
WITCH. My seven curses upon you, you have freed him when I all
but had him in my hands!
RURY. You are lying to me, and deceiving me! You are no lone
woman wanting help.
WITCH. I will get you yet! I will tear the heart out of you! I swear
it by the earth that holds the graves of the dead!

RURY. There is no fear on me. I know who you are. You are the Hag of Slaughter.

WITCH. I am that! And I tell you I myself will set the ravens croaking over your grave.

RURY. They will never croak and call out in Connacht that I was brought down by a hag! Have a care now! I am loth to shed the blood of a woman, but it would be right for me to strike at a witch!.

(*He takes* Simon *by the shoulder and goes off waving a sword.*)

WITCH. (*to* Pampogue). That is what you have done with your meddling and your want of wit.

PAMPOGUE. You lied to me! He is a king's son. I would not give you leave to put poison in his mouth.

WITCH. Fool! You think to manage me and to set yourself over me! It was no poison. It was the food that would put him under my power for ever, and he taking and eating it from my hand.

PAMPOGUE. Get him into your power again and put the seven spells of love on him. I will have nothing to do with your Giants and Grugachs, it is with that man only I will wed.

WITCH. You are on the path of destruction now. My grief that I let you leave the garden!

PAMPOGUE. Go, get me that king's son!

WITCH. Have you no thought at all for her who cared and reared you, and gave in to everything you would ask?

PAMPOGUE. Get me what I want! You filled me with the things I did not want. It is my own way I will go now!

WITCH. It will be a bad way for you and for yourself. But take your own way. I will get him for you, if striving will do it. I will give him the golden apple. It will buy for you his love. But I thought the man was not born in Ireland that would stand against my spells as he did.

JOHN MONTAGUE

Sheela-na-Gig

The bloody tent-flap opens. We slide
into life, slick with slime and blood.
Cunt, or Cymric *cwm*, Chaucerian *quente*,
the first home from which we are sent
into banishment, to spend our whole life
cruising to return, raising a puny mast
to sail back into those moist lips
that overhang *labia minora* and *clitoris*.
To sigh and die upon the Mount of Venus,
layer after layer of warm moss,
to return to that first darkness!
Small wonder she grins at us, from gable
or church wall. For the howling babe
life's warm start: man's question mark.

CECIL FRANCES ALEXANDER

Dreams (written for children)

Beyond, beyond the mountain line,
The greystone and the boulder,
Beyond the growth of dark green pine,
That crowns its western shoulder,
There lies that fairy land of mine,
Unseen of a beholder.

Its fruits are all like rubies rare,
Its streams are clear as glasses;
There golden castles hang in air,
And purple grapes in masses,

And noble knights and ladies fair
Come riding down the passes.

Ah me! they say if I could stand
Upon these mountain ledges,
I should but see on either hand
Plain fields and dusty hedges:
And yet I know my fairy land
Lies somewhere o'er their edges.

JUSTICE LUKE GERNON

Ireland Delineated

'Ireland is at all poynts like a young wench that hath a green sickness . . . She is very fayre of visage, and hath a smooth skinn of tender grasse. Indeed she is somewhat freckled (as the Irish are) some partes darker than others. Her flesh is of a softe and delicate mould of earth, and her blew vaynes trayling through every part of her like rivulets. She hath one master vayne called the Shannon, which passeth quite through her, and if it were not for one knot (one mayne rock) it were navigable from head to foot. She hath three other vaynes called the sisters – the Suir, the Nore and the Barrow which, rising at one spring, trayle through her middle parts and joyne together in their going out.

Her bones are of polished marble, the grey marble, the black, the redd, and the speckled, so fayre for building that their houses show like colledges, and being polished, is most rarely embellished. Her breasts are round hillockes of milk-yielding grasse, and that so fertile, that they contend with the vallyes . . . Of complexion she is very temperate, never too hott, nor too could, and hath a sweet breath of favonian winde.

She is of gentle nature. If the anger of heaven be agaynst her, she will not bluster and storme, but she will weep many days

together, and (alas) this summer she did so water her plants that
the grass and the blade was so bedewed, that it became unprofit-
able, and threatens a scarcity.

AE

A Priestess of the Woods

The young priestess stood up before them; she was pale from vigil,
and the sunlight coming through the misty evening air fell upon
her swaying arms and her dress with its curious embroidery of
peacock's feathers; the dark hollows of her eyes were alight and as
she spoke inspiration came to her; her voice rose and fell,
commanding, warning, whispering, beseeching; its strange rich
music flooded the woods and pierced through and through with
awe the hearts of those who listened. She spoke of the mysteries of
that unseen nature; how man is watched and ringed round with
hosts who war upon him, who wither up his joys by their breath;
she spoke of the gnomes who rise up in the woodland paths with
damp arms grasping from their earthy bed.

'Dreadful' she said 'are the elementals who live in the hidden
waters: they rule the dreaming hart; their curse is forgetfulness;
they lull man to fatal rest, with drowsy fingers feeling to put out
his fire of life. But most of all, dread the powers that move in air;
their nature is desire unquenchable; their destiny is – never to be
fulfilled – never to be at peace . . . She paused for a moment; her
terrible breath had hardly ceased to thrill them, when another
voice was heard singing; its note was gay and triumphant, it broke
the spell of fear upon the people,

> I never heed by waste or wood
> The cry of fay or faery thing
> Who tell of their own solitude;
> Above them all my soul is king.

The royal robe as king I wear
　　Trails all along the fields of light;
Its silent blue and silver bear
　　For gems the starry dust of night.

The breath of joy unceasingly
　　Waves to and fro its folds star-lit,
And far beyond earth's misery
　　I live and breathe the joy of it.

The priestess advanced from the altar, her eyes sought for the singer; when she came to the centre of the opening she paused and waited silently. Almost immediately a young man carrying a small lyre stepped out of the crowd and stood before her: he did not seem older than the priestess; he stood unconcerned though her dark eyes blazed at the intrusion; he met her gaze fearlessly; his eyes looked into hers – in this way all proud spirits do battle. Her eyes were black with almost a purple tinge, eyes that had looked into the dark ways of nature; his were bronze, and a golden tinge, a mystic opulence of vitality seemed to dance in their depths; they dazzled the young priestess with the secrecy of joy; her eyes fell for a moment. He turned round and cried out, 'Your priestess speaks but half truths, her eyes have seen but her heart does not know. Life is not terrible but is full of joy. Listen to me. I passed by while she spake, and I saw that a fear lay upon every man, and you shivered thinking of your homeward path, fearful as rabbits of the unseen things, and forgetful how you have laughed at death facing the monsters who crush down the forests. Do you now know that you are greater than all these spirits before whom you bow in dread: your life springs from a deeper source. Answer me, priestess, where go the fire-spirits when winter seizes the world?'

'Into the Fire-King they go, they dream in his heart.' She half chanted, the passion of her speech not yet fallen away from her. 'And where go the fires of men when they depart?' She was silent; then he continued half in scorn, 'Your priestess is the priestess of ghouls and fays rather than a priestess of men; her wisdom is not for you; the spirits that haunt the elements are hostile because they

see you full of fear; do not dread them and their hatred will vanish.
The great heart of the earth is full of laughter, do not put
yourselves apart from its joy, for its soul is your soul and its joy is
your true being.'

He turned and passed through the crowd; the priestess made a
motion as if she would have stayed him, then she drew herself up
proudly and refrained. They heard his voice again singing as he
passed into the darkening woods,

> The spirits to the fire-king throng
>   Each in the winter of his day:
> And all who listen to their song
>   Follow them after in that way.
>
> They seek the heart-hold of the king,
> They build within his halls of fire,
> Their dreams flash like the peacock's wing,
> They glow with sun-hues of desire.
>
> I follow in no faery ways;
> I heed no voice of fay or elf;
> I in the winter of my days
> Rest in the high ancestral self.

The rites interrupted by the stranger did not continue much
longer; the priestess concluded her words of warning; she did not
try to remove the impression created by the poet's song, she only
said, 'His wisdom may be truer; it is more beautiful than the
knowledge we inherit.'

Edmund Lenihan

from *Aoibheall the Banshee*

In Ireland long ago every family that had the least pretension to respectability had a banshee of its own. Without one its members would be regarded as not Irish at all, only upstarts, vagabonds and 'sprus'.

Now, the men of Dál gCais, the Dalcassians, were different from most other Irish clans in one thing: they took immense pride in the fact that their banshee was one of the handful of such spirit women in all of Ireland whose name was known. It had been discovered, so family tradition had it, in the distant past by Seanchán, one of their most powerful druids, but so many generations had in the meantime passed away that though she was universally respected, even feared, among them there was now no agreement on what the original form of that name had been when the minds of men were undimmed by the pettinesses of everyday living. Aoibheall some called her. Others, in the best Clare fashion, refused to accept that. 'No,' they said. 'That isn't it, at all! Her right name is Aoibhinn, the lovely One.' Maybe they were merely trying to keep on the right side of her, for she was one who had many unearthly powers and was not at all loath to invoke them against those whom she judged to have injured her good repute within the clan. Also, since she was a sister of the terrible Áine, whose fairy palace was at Knockainey in County Limerick, there was a double incentive to speak well of her.

It was she who, in withered and ancient form, led the twenty-five banshees of Clare to Rath Lake the night before the Battle of Dysert O'Dea in July of 1318. Imagine the shock to Richard de Clare, that proud, fearless Norman lord, whose intent was to snatch for himself the lands of Inchiquin, when he and his men came on these haggish women just before dawn, scrubbing rich robes and armour till the water boiled and ran red with blood! He recovered himself quickly, though.

'Out of our way, filthy crones, or by God's bones we'll trample ye.'

They ignored him, as if he and his army were mere shadows. Incredulous, he halted his progress. Accustomed to having his every whim obeyed without question, he could only stare at these weird figures and their frantic labours. His next words, when they came, were an anti-climax, almost forlorn: 'What devilment are ye doing there, anyway?'

Aoibheall it was who approached him with his answer, seeming to reach it to him with the dishevelled garments she offered.

'Washing *your* clothes and the clothes of your men. Hah-haaaaah!' Her laugh chilled them to the bone, far more intensely than the early coolness of that fatal day. Aghast, they stood transfixed as the terrible figures slowly dissolved into the lakeside mist, and many a flinty warrior, men who had faced Turks and heathen hordes unafraid, threw furtive glances towards their leader then. We will never know what De Clare thought, whether he hesitated in face of this evil omen, for at that moment a messenger tore up, gasped out his news – that the Irish forces were mustering on the Hill of Scool and haste was of the essence. In the flurry which followed to reach the high ground at Tullyo-dea, to the north-east, the warning of Aoibheall was forgotten, and so it came to pass that later in the day, his customary arrogance now in full flow again, he forced a passage of the little stream at Macken Bridge but was ambushed a short distance away and cut down, together with several of his chief commanders. Thus began a rout, which developed into a bloody massacre. The bodies of De Clare's Normans and their Irish allies were scattered for miles and only a battered and scarred remnant reached the relative safety of Burnratty castle – relative, because less than a week later De Clare's widow, in her despair and anguish, burned it and set sail down the Shannon for England, never to see the land of which her husband had intended her to be mistress.

Nuala Ní Dhomhnaill

Kundalini

Don't unblock your heart —
in there a serpent
lies in loops.

Who explores this cave
will find asleep
a grim Medusa.

She rises up behind you
sharp and terrible her voice
throughout the land.

Hot coals and glowing fires
her swollen candle eyes
freezing your pulse's blood.

No good, St Cuan
putting the meal-tub on her head.
She is too tall.

And you cannot blind her eyes
as once before you did,
with punning sentences.

She swells, spines on her back:
she'd eat five-sixths of the world
without permission.

She's there indeed —
sempiternally.
Ay! Senor — c'est la vie.

8

Practical Heroism

The Agricultural Irish Girl

If all the women in the town were bundled up together,
I know a girl could beat them all, in any kind of weather;
The rain can't wash the powder off, because she does not wear it,
Her face and figure's all her own: it's true, for I declare it!

Chorus

For she's a big stout, strong lump of an agricultural Irish girl,
She neither paints nor powders and her figure is all her own,
And she can strike that hard that you'd think that you'd been
struck by the kick of a mule,
It's 'the full of the house' of Irish love is Mary Ann Malone.

She was only seventeen last grass, and still improving greatly;
I wonder what she'll be at all when her bones are set completely,
You'd think your hand was in a vice the moment that she shakes it.
And if there's any cake around, it's Mary Ann that takes it.

Chorus

For she's a big stout, strong lump of an agricultural Irish girl,
She neither paints nor powders and her figure is all her own,
And she can strike that hard that you'd think that you'd been
struck by the kick of a mule,
It's 'the full of the house' of Irish love is Mary Ann Malone.

BEATRICE GRIMSHAW

from *From Fiji to the Cannibal Islands*

Another day I went up to Imale, where there was rumour of serious
fighting. It was thought that an attack – or something as near to
an attack as the Tannese ever make – would be made on this place

in the course of the day, for the Lowinnie men, who were hostile, knew that a meeting of two tribes was to be held at Imale that morning, and it was probable that they would try to take advantage of the occasion. My host, the missionary of the district, went with me. We carried no arms, as there may be risk in doing so in Tanna, and there cannot be much protection. As in Malekula, absence of firearms at once proclaims the peacefulness of the visitor's errand, so that he can approach a fighting village safely, as a general rule. If the natives had any grudge against him, and wished to kill him, he would be shot from ambush in the back, so that firearms, even if carried, would not be much use.

The walk up from the beach where we left our boat to the hill village of Imale was exceedingly hot, as there was a very steep rise, and no air circulated through the tremendous reeds – over fifteen feet high – that shut in the track. Here and there these had been cut away so as to give a clear view ahead, and prevent surprise from any one creeping softly along the open path round a corner. We advanced quickly and rather noisily to the village, and found a score or two of men sitting about the square, nursing their guns. Right across the centre of the open space lay an immense branch, cut down from the great banyan overhead – a sign of vengeance and a call for blood. The chief of the village had been killed by the enemy, and this bough had been cast across the village square to symbolise his fall, and act as a continual reminder. To-day it was to be burned, for a friendly tribe from the other side of the bay had killed the slayer of the chief, and his spirit was avenged. A dozen or two of this tribe had slipped away at dead of night in their boat, and come up to Imale. They were now going to receive their reward from the new chief of the village, who was the brother of the man that had been slain.

No objection was made to our presence, and while the missionary engaged in a little conversation with a man he was hoping eventually to convert from heathenism, I roamed about the square, photographing and talking. I was not understood, but I did not understand the replies I received either, so things were even.

Neither in Lamanian nor here had a white woman ever been

seen, and the villages were almost unknown even to the few white men of the island. Little interest, however, was excited by my appearance. What feeling there was seemed to be equally compounded of reserve and mistrust, and even the women made no advances.

There was a good deal of military science, in a small way, about the disposition of the fighting men. The women they had placed in an enclosure behind a high reed fence. Some of their own number were perched in high trees overlooking the approaches to the village; others were squatted down on their heels, gun in hand, at the two entrances. The rest sat or lay about the village, keeping an intermittent lookout while they talked, or stared at us with a kind of sullen curiosity.

I was sitting on the fallen banyan log, and watching the villagers set fire to the far end of it, when two or three men came hurriedly into the square, and rushed up to an ugly old chief, who seemed to have quite as much influence as the titular head of the village. They carried a small green parcel, wrapped in banana leaf and neatly tied with native fibre. Everybody wanted to see it at once; all heads were bent over it, and all eyes strained, while the old man untied the parcel, and disclosed – a lump of fresh yam!

The celebrated footprint in 'Robinson Crusoe' could not have caused more excitement. To whom did the yam belong? Whence had it come? How had it been dropped where it was found, right in the middle of a track leading up to the village? No one knew anything about it. It seemed obvious that 'an enemy had done this thing', and an enemy who must be unpleasantly near to the village at that minute.

Nothing could be done; so, after a good deal of chatter, the old man merely told his followers to keep a good lookout, and went on with his conversation, which chiefly concerned the disposal of an enemy's body supposed to have been partly eaten by him a few days before. The missionary and I both wanted to know about it – he because he wished to discourage this sort of festivity; I because I wanted to get a thigh-bone as a curiosity. It could not have hurt the gentleman who had been made a *rôti* of, and it would have been very valuable to me. But the old chief was 'foxing'; he had never heard of cannibalism, not he; the man hadn't been eaten at all – he wasn't even sure that he had been killed.

Such an innocent, amiable old man as he looked! Such a simple, childlike smile as he put on! His grey hair, tied up in a red and white pocket-handkerchief, looked wonderfully venerable and reverend, and he himself everything that was respectable – an impression hardly detracted from by the circumstances that he wore no other clothes save the head-dress referred to. And yet – his fox-like old eye, shifting and twinkling under those pent-house brows . . .

'Now, look here, you know you did!' says the missionary plumply.

The nice old gentleman's smile takes on a different character – becomes, in fact, a giggle, like that of a schoolgirl caught eating surreptitious chocolates.

'Well – I eatum jus' little fellow bit!' he allows.

At this naïve admission (based on a model that most people will recall) I cannot help laughing irreverently; and just at that moment, as Rider Haggard would say, 'a strange thing happens'. The fifteen warriors squatting at the other side of the square suddenly rise as one man to their feet, and point their guns straight at us. We are, in fact, in the position of a couple of deserters facing a firing-party. There might be pleasanter situations.

'Stop that!' yells the missionary in Tannese; and the natives lower their guns, looking a trifle astonished. The old chief explains. It is quite a simple explanation, as he puts it – they saw a head moving some way behind us in the scrub, so they were going to fire at it; that is all. The circumstance of our heads – and bodies – being equally in the line of fire is evidently not regarded as pertinent to the matter in hand.

. . . Was it an accident, or what schoolboys call an 'accidental-done-on purpose'? We never knew.

MARY LEADBEATER

from *The Annals of Ballitore*

Everyone seemed to think that safety and security were to be found in my brother's house. Thither the insurgents brought their prisoners, and thither, also, their own wounded and suffering comrades. It was an awful sight to behold in that large parlour such a mingled assembly of throbbing, anxious hearts – my brother's own family, silent tears rolling down their faces, the wives of the loyal officers, the wives of the soldiers, the wives and daughters of the insurgents, the numerous guests, the prisoners, the trembling women – all dreading to see the door open, lest some new distress, some fresh announcement of horrors should enter. It was awful, but every scene was now awful, and we knew not what a day might bring forth.

Young girls dressed in white, with green ribbons, and carrying pikes, accompanied the insurgents. They had patrols and a countersign, but it was long before they could decide upon the password. At length they fixed upon the word 'scourges'. Sentinels were placed in various parts of the village. One day, as I walked to my brother's, a sentinel called to a man who walked with me not to advance on pain of being shot. The sentinel was my former friend 'the Canny'. I approached him and asked would he shoot me if I proceeded. 'Shoot you!' exclaimed he, taking my hand and kissing it, adding a eulogium on the Quakers. I told him it would be well if they were all of our way of thinking, for then there would be no such work as the present.

I thought the bitterness of death was passed, but the work was not yet begun. Colonel Campbell's men, who had impatiently rested on their arms several hours, marched out of Athy. They took Narraghmore in their way, and directed their mistaken rage against the newly erected house of Colonel Keatinge, planting cannon to destroy the dwelling so much worth had inhabited. They mortally wounded John Carroll, cousin to the Colonel. This party of soldiers entered Ballitore exhausted by rage and fatigue;

they brought cannon. Cannon in Ballitore! The horse and foot had now met. Colonel Campbell was here in person and many other officers. The insurgents had fled on the first alarm, the peaceable inhabitants remained. The trumpet was sounded, and the peaceable inhabitants were delivered up for two hours to the unbridled licence of a furious soldiery! How shall I continue this fearful narrative?

My mind never could arrange the transactions which were crowded into those two hours. Every house in the Burrow was in flames; a row of houses opposite the school was also set on fire; none others were burnt immediately in the village, but a great many windows were broken, and when I heard this crash I thought it was the cannon. We saw soldiers bending under loads of plunder. Captain Palmer came in to see me, and was truly solicitous about us, and insisted on giving us 'a protection'. Soldiers came in for milk; some of their countenances were pale with anger, and they grinned at me, calling me names which I had never heard before. They said I had poisoned the milk which I gave them, and desired me to drink some, which I did with much indignation. Others were civil, and one enquired if we had any United Irishmen in the house. I told them we had. In that fearful time the least equivocation, the least deception appeared to me to be fraught with danger. The soldier continued his enquiry: 'Had they plundered us?'

'No, except of eating and drinking.'

'On free quarters,' he replied, smiling, and went away.

A fine looking man, a soldier, came in, in an extravagant passion; neither his rage nor my terror could prevent me from observing that this man was strikingly handsome; he asked me the same question in the same terms – and I made the same answer. He cursed me with great bitterness, and, raising his musket, presented it to my breast. I desired him not to shoot me. It seemed as if he had the will, but not the power to do so. He turned from me, dashed pans and jugs off the kitchen table with his musket, and shattered the kitchen window. Terrified almost out of my wits, I ran out of the house followed by several women almost as frightened as myself. When I fled, my fears gained strength, and I believed my enemy was pursuing; I thought of throwing myself into the river at the foot of the garden, thinking the bullet could not hurt me in the water. One of our servants ran into the street to call for help. William Richardson and Charles Coote, who kindly sat on their horses outside our windows, came in and turned the ruffian out of the house.

MARGARET BARRINGTON

from *My Cousin Justin*

No one ever entered the kitchen without receiving either a warning or a reprimand. No sooner was your hand on the latch than her voice boomed out:

'Mind and wipe your feet on the mat. I won't have ye sheddin' yer clabber all over my clean kitchen.'

Her conversation was shrewd and racy. She could curse fluently, so she boasted, in four languages – in the English, the Gaelic of Donegal, the Gaelic of Rachery, and the Gaelic of the Isles.

On the occasions when Wattie, as she put it, 'made a holy show of himself', Bella always took him in hand. If he were past reason or scorn, she would hoist him on the broad of her back like a sack of oats and bear him out to the stables where she bedded him in the straw and left him until such time as he sobered up. On re-entering the kitchen she would wash her hands with a Pilate-like gesture and smooth her black hair behind her ears with her damp palms. Then, patting herself all over, she would remark to Theresa who sat warming her shins at the fire:

'What can ye expect from a pig but a grunt.'

She treated Wattie with the contempt she felt for all men, pouring forth her scorn at every opportunity and accusing him of all manner of misdemeanours. He paid no more heed to her nagging than a duck does to water. He accepted the position of unofficial husband with equanimity. Every Saturday morning she would rout him out of bed at five o'clock to whitewash the kitchen. When he had finished she would stand looking at it and remark:

'Lord of Creation! Isn't it a queer thing but no man alive can do anything without making a dirt? Look at the floor, will ye? By rights I should make ye go down on yer marrow bones and scrub it. Heth! Since ever the curse of Adam fell on us, a man's no more use than a bull calf. What he does he has til be driven to, and when that's done, a woman must needs run after him, reddin' up.'

MARY O'DONNELL

Cot Death

When I turned her over,
what I saw was a changeling's mask,
mauve and mottled, like old lilac,
her lips purpled shut.

No flutter from her eyelashes
that always quivered
like down on a young bird,
and I knew how her nostrils,

the pink-edged membranes
were inhabited by death,
how the sculpting of her ears
had nothing to do with sound.

Since then, I am haunted awake,
a wailing behind my temples,
and I grit my teeth each time
I see dolls in snug shop windows,

their glassy eyes accusatory,
knowing them to be corpses
subpoenaed for a public enquiry
into some woman's unmotherly neglect.

I will always wonder if
those matrons who shun me lest
I conjure a changeling to their doors,
are not correct, I will wonder

if I invoked some blood-curdling sprite
to suffocate the child before she
suffocated me. And wondering,
I am haunted, I am unstill,

my days waxing, murderously.

SEAN O'CASEY

from *Juno and the Paycock*

MRS BOYLE. Oh, it's thrue, then; it's Johnny, it's me son, me own son!

MARY. Oh, it's thrue, it's thrue what Jerry Devine says – there isn't a God, there isn't a God; if there was He wouldn't let these things happen!

MRS BOYLE. Mary, you mustn't say them things. We'll want all the help we can get from God an' His Blessed Mother now! These things have nothin' to do with the Will o' God. Ah, what can God do agen the stupidity o' men!

MRS MADIGAN. The polis want you to go with them to the hospital to see the poor body – they're waitin' below.

MRS BOYLE. We'll go. Come, Mary, an' we'll never come back here agen. Let your father furrage for himself now; I've done all I could an' it was all no use – he'll be hopeless till the end of his days. I've got a little room in me sisther's where we'll stop till your throuble is over, an' then we'll work together for the sake of the baby.

MARY. My poor little child that'll have no father!

MRS BOYLE. It'll have what's far bether – it'll have two mothers.

A rough voice shouting from below. Are yous goin' to keep us waitin' for yous all night?

MRS MADIGAN. (*going to the door, and shouting down*). Take your hour, there, take your hour! If yous are in such a hurry, skip off, then, for nobody wants you here – if they did yous wouldn't be found. For you're the same as yous were undher the British Government – never where yous are wanted! As far as I can see, the Polis as Polis, in this city, is Null an' Void!

MRS BOYLE. We'll go, Mary, we'll go; you to see your poor dead brother, an' me to see me poor dead son!

MARY. I dhread it, mother, I dhread it!

MRS BOYLE. I forgot, Mary, I forgot; your poor oul' selfish mother was only thinkin' of herself. No, no, you mustn't come – it wouldn't be good for you. You go on to me sisther's an' I'll face th' ordeal meself. Maybe I didn't feel sorry enough for Mrs Tancred when her poor son was found as Johnny's been found now – because he was a Diehard! Ah, why didn't I remember that then he wasn't a Diehard or a Stater, but only a poor dead son! It's well I remember all that she said – an' it's my turn to say it now: What was the pain I suffered, Johnny, bringin' you into the world to carry you to your cradle, to the pains I'll suffer carryin' you out o' the world to bring you to your grave! Mother o' God, Mother o' God, have pity on us all!

MARY HOLLAND

Unforgettable Meeting of Life and Art

'English audiences cry during the performance. Here people sit very still and lean forward as though they want to hear every word. Afterwards, when they talk to you, they often start to weep.'

Fiona Shaw stands, sipping a glass of red wine, surrounded by some of the audience who have come to see her in the Royal Shakespeare Company's touring production of 'Electra' at the Templemore sports stadium and leisure complex in Derry. The main hall, usually marked out as a basketball pitch, has been transformed with tiered seating and banks of powerful lights. Below us, the set is a landscape of bare stone slabs, the house of Agamemnon at Mycenae, overlooking the plain of Argus.

We have just been watching Ms Shaw play the title role in Sophocles' tragedy, consumed with a grief that cannot be assuaged, driven by the desire for revenge. Her whole body, it seemed, had become an instrument for expressing these emotions. Her eyes blazed from sunken sockets and her hands scraped frantically at her flesh, as though the only way she found it possible to dull the pain was by doing physical damage to herself.

Much has been written about Deborah Warner's production of 'Electra', *The Irish Times* described it as 'awe-inspiring'. It is probably impossible for me to convey what the play meant in Derry last week, as each night brought news of more murderous attacks, carried out in vengeance for killings committed days and weeks before.

It stripped away the comforting words and phrases with which for so long we have tried to make death less dreadful, forced us to realise that in the first six weeks of this year, 27 families have had to deal, as best they could, with terrible primitive emotions – grief, hatred, the desire for revenge.

I had thought myself lucky to take three or four performances seen in the theatre, most of them long ago, to my grave. Paul Scofield in 'King Lear'. Peter Brook's production of 'A Mid-

summer Night's Dream', a couple of others, maybe. What happened
in Derry last week was on a par with these, but in some ways went
beyond them.

Consider the theme of the play and the time and place of the
performance. Queen Clytemnestra, together with her lover Aegis-
thus, murdered her husband Agamemnon when he returned
victorious from the war with Troy. The queen claims that she
killed him because he had sacrificed their daughter, Iphigenia, in
order to secure a fair wind for the Greek fleet.

Many years later, the murder of her father is still an open wound
to Electra. She spurns all offers of comfort and reproaches her
sister, who has come to terms with the loss, as little better than a
collaborator with his killers. Her only reason for living is the hope
that her brother Orestes, whom she smuggled to safety as a baby,
will return as a grown man to avenge their father's death.

This play and the questions it raises about justice, retribution,
the violence of human feelings and the need to moderate them,
was performed last week in a city, and before an audience, which
for the past 20 years has had to confront all these things on an
almost daily basis.

Those who were lucky enough to see Fiona Shaw in 'Hedda
Gabler' at the Abbey know the power of her work and the fierce,
committed intelligence which Deborah Warner brings to inter-
preting the classics. Talking to friends since last weekend, it seems
likely that this production of 'Electra' will sweep the board when
it comes to this year's theatrical awards in Britain.

It came to Derry as part of Impact 92, the year-long festival
which has already set the city buzzing. Just prior to that, the
company was in Paris for 11 sell-out performances. Deborah
Warner said to me: 'One week there are receptions at which people
want to discuss the aesthetic of the production. Here a woman said
to me: "The queen was quite right to kill her husband. He
sacrificed his daughter so his side could win".'

At one level, last week was an awesome vindication of those
who believe that this is what the arts should be about, and where
they should be – close to the cutting edge of political argument.

Fiona Shaw said: 'I do believe we must use the theatre to debate these dangerous issues – justice, retribution, violence.'

One woman spoke of the actress's performance as Electra: 'I thought of Mrs Kelly, whose son was killed on Bloody Sunday, and the way they would find her, even years afterwards, lying on his grave with her face smeared with earth.' Another talked of Electra's sister begging her to bow to the inevitable: 'I kept remembering the hunger strikers, when their families were trying to persuade them to give up the fast and accept the prison system.'

Such meetings of life and art are rare enough. But last week was as bleak and frightening a time in Northern Ireland as anyone could remember. Church leaders and politicians seemed to be at a loss for anything to say which might give some reassurance about the present situation.

Into this situation came a group of actors, with a play written in another country long ago, which showed that a society can be poisoned by war and grief and revenge, that this can last for generations, but finally the cycle of violence is broken and justice prevails.

The actors were telling a story about one of the school groups that came to the performance, boys of 11 and 12 years old. One of them, reading from the programme note, was heard saying to his friends: 'This play was first performed 2,400 years ago,' to which his companion replied: 'How come it's taken so long to get to Derry?'

Maybe it took a long time to travel from the great amphitheatre on the slopes of the Acropolis to the Templemore sports stadium, but 'Electra' arrived just when it was needed. Those of us who saw it will not forget the experience.

CHARLOTTE GRACE O'BRIEN

from *Care of the Emigrants*

'Then I realised,' she says, in her own account which I have already quoted, 'I could do nothing unless I seized the ropes into my own hands. This I knew was possible owing to the confidence of the Irish people in my father's name, William Smith O'Brien. I took a large house in Queenstown, and had myself registered as an ordinary lodginghouse keeper, licensed for 105 lodgers, and then the play began in earnest. The Board of Trade and the Ship Companies, my first foes, when they saw I was in real earnest, determined upon improving the condition of things in Queenstown, helped me all they could.

'I visited the ships along with a medical officer day after day, often beginning at six o'clock in the morning and going through three or four ships. In the meantime more or less of my 105 lodgers had to be looked after in the house. It was a rough life. I had not even a bedroom, but slept in my sittingroom. Having been at the work more than a year, I saw clearly that no permanent good could be done in Ireland; and that New York was to be my next point. The White Star Line took me over free of cost in the autumn of 1882. When I arrived, instead of going to a hotel or fashionable boardinghouse, I took a room in a tenement house in Washington Street. I spent some time there with a porter, a longshoreman, and their wives. A month spent in New York gave me a full insight into the lives of the Irish emigrants and the fate of the innumerable unprotected girls who were swarming through my own hands in Queenstown. . . .

'About three thousand people passed through my lodginghouse this year, but when I came to America I determined to close it altogether and to re-open it on my return. I established the house partly because there was great need of such a place and partly because I knew it would give me a direct and strong influence over all the Queenstown steamship lines. I knew I could force almost any reform I wanted if I put myself directly in relationship with the emigrants. I did not attempt to influence their choice of lines, but to any who spoke to me I expressed myself openly. I was most anxious not to injure any line, but to work upon, write to, and visit the heads of the companies, and urge strongly what reforms I thought were needed. I went over eleven ships in May 1881, with the Board of Trade officer, and then none until January, 1882, since which time I have seen them all constantly. I have paid them over one hundred visits this year. I have visited every nook and corner of them. I have had frequent letters from emigrants describing the treatment they received, and also a number of emigrants passing through my hands returning from America. Thus I have gained as thorough a knowledge of the subject as I could obtain.

'And what has been the result? As to lavatories and sanitary arrangements, the Board of Trade, after my letters, and what was brought out in Parliament, took action, and there has been a great improvement in this respect, and in the addition of a number of staircases and entrances, so as to give separate access to the different classes of steerage passengers. In my opinion all sanitary arrangements ought to be, as they are in the White Star vessels, so arranged that there shall be no excuse for the women to leave their steerage at night. This is not attainable in many of the old vessels, but in all new built ships I have no doubt it will be studied and brought forward. As Mr Rogers said in his letter to the *Sun*, the White Star Line has given the married people separate private rooms, while the lavatories are provided on this and other lines with soap, washbowls, and towels. This is a step beyond even my anticipation. I should like to see them provide the bedding and utensils that constitute a steerage outfit, but the fact is that no member of the Conference lines can take any step of that kind unless all do it together. Mirrors are permitted, because there were no Conference rules against them. Nobody ever thought of such a thing being done or dreamed of as the provision of towels and bowls, to enable steerage folks to wash.

'Did you ever travel as a steerage passenger?'

'Yes, twice from Queenstown to Liverpool. I should not have the slightest objection now to travel in that way. I asked to be allowed to on this last trip, but they would not permit me to. I wanted to find out about the ventilation. I was told that nothing could be more horrible than the experiences in the steerage a few years ago. Now those who travelled then and have since recrossed the ocean say they were treated well, and were very comfortable.'

JO SLADE

In Fields I Hear Them Sing

They were two strong mountain women
They came the long way round.
It was said they'd never die
But carry on even when
The crows had picked them
And the village dogs had licked
And chewed their bones.

Long winters follow through
From when I'd hardly top the wall
Of the graveyard or stop the standing
In pews and kneel like the rest;
I won't forget – I remember each look,
Faces that stare from ivory buckets
And big hairy arms like a man's.

All the houses humped under winter's
Cloven hoof. Inside my brothers
Wrestled on the bed, banging and choked
As if the whole village were cheering
Their strength – as if I'd care which
One was strongest,
Or who to fear the most.

I couldn't have cared then and
Now it occurs to me how they grew
Taller and stronger and how they acquired
That outward air of pride – riding down
The wide road their high boots like
The slick hairs of a black cat
Their heads high as the trees,
Ancient and overbearing.

They made of my mother a kind
Of ill-planted vine, twisted in her barrage
Of nitter-natter, never truly human
But more a pedigree sow
And all women were seen the same,
As interferers with eyes that coloured
The foreground in ambiguity, rumor
And swift potions for the sick.

With me it was different
Because I wandered – because the seasons
Drew me to the woods to watch the dressing
And the undressing, limb logs stretched
As the sky descended its dark mouth
Closed on my lips.

White sister mountain on your shoulders
The women came singing.
These who came from another side, so far
Off, so far away, some other country
Where none of us had ever been
But I knew existed for even then we
Stayed put on our own,
Steeped in the mountain's shadow.

When the strangeness of their presence
Had passed and we'd finished staring
Men started to jeer their independent ways.

How it was that they could perform
The same hard duties on the land
No men around to move the yellow ricks?

Often I went over their way, passed
The railway that runs a giant zip
Through the cornfield and they'd talk
To me of what it is to be a woman,
Of giving birth and dying.
Now I know all this
And I am quiet since.

My father poked the fire
That dry September night I felt his eyes
Burn inside me, like my own candle,
As if I had swallowed it entirely
And the flame so hot my belly became
Like a pyre outstripping me.

I, told him what I knew,
How those women could tell of bad times
Coming 'cause no sight was made
Of small swallows and how when
I was ill they gathered berries
And crushed them into strong booze.

He kept me inside our house.
For weeks I watched from my window
Autumn tint the trees in blood colours.
Days dragged on
My mother told me they'd gone,
That on their breath men smelt a burning.

Now I think back
And I wish those women were here
In this place and I wish the other people
Had seen it then the way I saw it

But they didn't.
Still in fields I hear them sing,
Across grass their shadows linger

And if I dream it is of faded things,
Of the sun sinking in their eyes,
Of a red sky leaning against their breath.

Mrs Kathleen Behan

from *The Move to Crumlin*

As I told you, Crumlin was a cold place and it got colder still with hunger. By the latter part of the thirties, it was hard to manage. More and more people were out of work, and everything in Crumlin was dear. In Russell Street you could have lived for years on tick. If you went to the Fat Man's shop he would put it in the book till next week. Then again, in Russell Street you were near all the markets and secondhand shops. In Crumlin we had none of that. Only long lines of thousands of houses, each and every one the same. No buses either, and if you walked down to Dolphin's Barn there was a long, expensive tram ride into the city.

I had to make ends meet. Many's the time I thought I would run away and do something else, but there was nowhere to run to. You had to stand your ground, though many a poor working woman ended up in a mental home. If there is a Heaven, it must be for working women. It won't be for nuns – they have no strain compared with a woman running a family. It was Hell on earth telling all my sons, 'You can't eat this or that, because it has to be left for your father.' But what else could we do? Occasionally I would cook an egg for Da's breakfast and I would watch him eat it. Sometimes he would lop the top off the egg and give it to one of the lads. Then again they could dip their bread in it. Looking back, in Russell Street we had years of plenty.

We were so poor that the lads would go on to the Corporation rubbish dump and salvage apples or anything. One day they brought home a great box of chocolates. Then they would start digging for old coal and cinders in the hot ash. One lad was buried alive, because they built great tunnels down into the dump to get at the cinders, and one of them collapsed on him. You couldn't believe how poor we were. I tried to sell two old vases to a friend for a shilling, just to buy a bit of tea and that. Mind you, one advantage we had then over people now was that you could buy everything in ounces: tea, sugar, anything. There were little amounts for poor people. Even cigarettes you could buy one for a penny. Of course, it was dearer buying things that way, but if that was all you had, that was what you had to do. I always tried to send the children to bed full no matter how I did myself. But it was an awful time trying to manage on half nothing.

Yes, poverty laid a heavy hand on my family in the late thirties. It shook our house and started to beat the lard out of us. A family can only stand the grinding so long, and then something has to give. Da never missed an hour's work in his life when he could get it. But it wasn't that plentiful, and then the strike lasting nine months put us back years. The working man never recovers from a long strike. Everything you have saved, every penny you have spared, has to go.

And then in our greatest hour we had no Russell Street to fall back on. We had new houses, but rent to pay. In the old slums we wouldn't pay God Almighty. The neighbours in the Street were kindness itself, too. But then we had the open hall doors, and everyone lived within a stone's throw of each other, some of them just next door in the tenement. Dominic has written a history of the Street, called *Teems of Times*, and it has been on the television. He showed that they would put their eyes out on sticks for you in Russell Street – they would do *anything* for a body. The neighbours in Crumlin were good people but they were isolated and scattered, and it takes years to get to know anyone in an estate, if you ever do. In our little boxes in Crumlin all we knew in the first years was poverty, hunger and rent.

Christina Reid

from *Joyriders*

SANDRA. I stole a car once . . . all by myself . . . I never told nobody, doin' it was enough . . . I just drove it roun' them posh streets in South Belfast until it ran outa petrol, an' then I walked home. Didn't need to boast about it the way the fellas do . . . just doin' it was enough . . . When the careers' officer come til our school, he asked me what I wanted to do, an' I says, 'I wanna drive roun' in a big car like yer woman outa Bonnie an' Clyde, an' rob banks,' an', he thought I was takin' a hand out him, so I says, 'All right then, I'll settle fer bein' a racin' driver.' An' he says, 'I'd advise you to settle for something less fantastic Sandra.' . . . They're all the same. They ask ye what ye wanta be, an' then they tell ye what yer allowed to be . . .

Eva Bourke

For D.W.

I would trade any Scala singer's
glacial heights
for the warm sandpaper
of her voice's gladly obeyed commands.
Daughter of ballad singers
and instrument makers
from the Liberties,
in her Ballyfermot back-garden
full of Jerusalem artichokes,
Rhenish vines, Siberian rabbits,
Chinese quail and crowds
of local children.

I slept beside her
in her wide strawberry bed,
felt the rasp of her rough shins
and listened to her heave deep breaths
from her smoke-corroded lungs,
knowing that inside her fifteen stone body
was the delicate girl of fourteen
that grew fat after a night of rape,
putting layer upon protective layer
around her,
until the princess left
and the jester was born.
But she never fooled me –
her body had to grow
to accommodate her generous heart,
and to this day
she walks in beauty
on feet of size three.

ALICE TAYLOR

from *The Chapel Woman*

Old Mrs McCarthy had been the chapel woman all her life, and when she died her daughter Nonie took over, regarding it as a family inheritance rather than a job. Nonie carried around in her head the history of the graveyard which surrounded the church. She knew who was buried in every corner, even those who had left no address or who lay beneath the small rock-like marking stones without inscription. These marking stones were the forerunner of headstones; people knew their family graves by measuring the distance of these rocks from each other, from the nearby church, or even from the nearest ditch.

She was a soft-spoken, stooped little lady who arranged weddings, funerals and christenings, and she was a reference book on all church events past and present. She did everything but say Mass and hear confessions – though with her in-depth knowledge of the parish she probably had a good idea of what went on in the confessionals as well. She did the church laundry and counted the collections. The village shops and pubs came to her for change, so the brown pennies collected on Sunday often found their way back during the following week to their original owners.

To supplement her income she looked after the dispensary, and she had a little sweet shop simply called 'Nonie's', which was so small that it could be filled by just one customer. The children on their way up and down to school popped in and out to her clutching their pennies. The cream-coloured counter topped with a piece of frayed brown lino was very high, and Nonie's customers were very small, so she recognised them all by the tops of their heads. To the left of her slatted front door was one small window packed with jars and flat boxes of all kinds of sweets. The children pressed their faces against the glass while making their selections, their heads blocking the light and darkening the little shop. They squeezed inside and bartered at the counter, then left with strings of Black Jack hanging from their jaws and sticks of Peggy's Leg clenched between their teeth like long white cigars. They bought hard penny-bars and fists of Cleeves toffees that gave hours of sticky sucking for one penny.

As she grew older, Nonie became crippled with arthritis. Her older sister Ellie came back to look after her and to take over all her duties. But while small, frail Nonie seemed bowed beneath the weight of her responsibilities, Ellie was a big woman who took everything in her stride. Nonie regarded her church work as an inherited honour while to Ellie it was something that circumstances had thrust upon her. Nothing excited her. Christenings, funerals, weddings, parish priests and bishops all blew across her path, but she continued on her original course with calm determination.

HUBERT BUTLER

from *Aunt Harriet*

Aunt Harriet was the strictest sort of Christian Scientist. She never admitted to any illness. She never went to a dentist but let her teeth fall out so that her cheeks contracted round three or four solitary tusks. This did nothing for her appearance. Aunt Florence had frequent small illnesses and many visits from the doctor. There must have been some snappishness between the sisters but we children never heard a word of it. We squabbled as much as most families do, but confronted by the outside world we were loyal to each other.

In those days, the Sinn Feiners were in the habit of visiting people, two by two and often by night, asking them for money for 'dependents of the Irish Republicans'. They went to Lavistown one night and Aunt Harriet had looked out of her bedroom window and said reproachfully that she would give them nothing, that she had given up the Gaelic League when it had become political and when the Sinn Feiners had started a campaign of violence. After this little lecture they went away. . . .

In the days before the War and the 1916 Rising, the more enlightened of the Anglo-Irish were trying desperately to identify themselves with Ireland. Aunt Harriet organized the first local Feis, an ancient festival of song and dance and miscellaneous junketting which centuries before took place at Tara. At the Kilkenny Feis there were competitions for Irish dancing and singing, lace-making, cake, jam, section honey and craft work. When it was all over, Aunt Harriet was presented by the committee with a 'Tara' brooch, a richly ornamented safety pin with which the ancient Irish held their clothes together, mass produced from originals in the National Museum.

The Gaelic League was not 'political' in those days and even the British saw nothing against it. When Lady Aberdeen, Ireland's all but last Vice-Reine, came down to open our local concert hall, she defied the ridicule of the Anglo-Irish neighbours by dressing herself and the ladies of the party in emerald green with Tara brooches. She and her husband were very Scottish; he wore the Gordon tartan and they wrote a book called *We Twa*. They bred Aberdeen terriers and were Aberdonianly thrifty, and it was one of their aims to show how very Scottish one could be and yet loyal to the Crown. Why could not the Irish be the same? She entertained very little in the Vice-Regal Lodge, but started a campaign against tuberculosis with no political overtones, and motored all over Ireland trying with some success to introduce village nurses into every community.

Elizabeth Bowen

from *The Most Unforgettable Character I've Met*

When Sarah, then Sarah Cartey, first arrived at Bowen's Court, County Cork, she was a girl of fourteen. She left her home in County Tipperary to become a kitchenmaid in my grandfather's house. Taking her place in the trap beside her new Master, she had set out one morning upon the fifty-mile drive. She did not know when, if ever, she would see home again. Ireland looks so small from the outside, it is hard to realize how big the distances feel: for the simple people, each county might be a different continent – and way back in the last century this was even more so. Young Sarah, face set towards County Cork, might have been driving off into Peru. Mr Bowen, towering beside her in his greatcoat, and keeping his horse along at a saving trot, was for her the one tie between the old and the new – she already knew him by sight, and by awesome name, for the Master owned large estates in both counties, and drove to and fro weekly between the two. It was on the return from one of these trips that he was bringing back with him Sarah Cartey. In his part of Tipperary, as in his part of Cork, everyone went in dread of Mr Bowen. He was a just man, but he was hard: to his wealth was added the weight of his character – choleric, dynamic and overbearing. In those days, the Protestant Irish landlord exercised more or less absolute power, and was, if he misused it, hated accordingly. Tall and heavy, bearded, genially ruddy but with rather cold blue eyes, my grandfather was typical of his class. Unlike some, he ran his estates like a man of business. Few loved him, but he was a big gun.

But so, in her way, was Sarah. From the first, it seems, they recognized this in each other, which was the reason why they got on so well. Driving along that day, she sat fearlessly upright. When he spoke she answered, cheerfully and forthright. The tears that kept pricking her violet-blue eyes were blinked back: she did not let one fall. At home, her mother and all the neighbours had told her she was a lucky girl, to get such a start – legends of Bowen's Court grandeur were current in Tipperary. So she kept her chin high, as befitted a lucky girl. If this were life, she was going to live it well. It was in the dusk, at the end of the day-long journey, that Sarah saw Bowen's Court for the first time.

When Sarah, as an old woman, told me this story, she looked at me with eyes that had never changed. Their character and their colour were set off by jet-black lashes. Laughing and ageless, these were the most perfect Irish eyes in the world. . . .

Though hers was the most independent mind I have known, Sarah did not question the social order. The injustices (as they would appear now) of my grandfather's household did not strike her. Out of what might have been servitude she made for herself a creative career. Her whole personality went into what she did. I believe that 'class' to Sarah meant simply this – the division of people according to their different duties. Thus, she worked alongside the Bowens, rather than for them. She respected the Bowens because, as she saw it, they played their allotted parts in the proper way. She perceived that the Master, in his estate management, spared himself no more than he spared his men; that the Mistress's life, with so many demands upon it, was selfless; that the young gentlemen lived under discipline like cadets; that the young ladies studied, and practised the piano, as industriously as she, Sarah, scrubbed at the pots and pans. If downstairs you worked like a black, upstairs you had to 'behave' like a Spartan. Life evened up, in the long run. She envied no one, and only pitied those to whom God had given nothing to do. When she was nearly eighty, I told her she worked too hard. 'Thank God, I always enjoy myself!' she flashed out.

CHARLOTTE BROOKE

from *Preface to Reliques of Ancient Irish Poetry*

With a view to throw some light on the antiquities of this country, to vindicate, in part, its history, and prove its claim to scientific as well as to military fame, I have been induced to undertake the following work. Besides the four different species of composition which it contains (the Heroic Poem, the Ode, the Elegy and the Song) others yet remain unattempted by translation:- the Romance, in particular, which unites the fire of Homer with the enchanting wildness of Ariosto. But the limits of my present plan have necessarily excluded many beautiful productions of genius, as little more can be done, within the compass of a single volume, than merely to give a few specimens, in the hope of awakening a just and useful curiosity, on the subject of our poetical compositions.

Unacquainted with the rules of translation, I know not how far those rules may censure, or acquit me. I do not profess to give a merely literal version of my originals, for that I should have found an impossible undertaking. – Besides the spirit which they breathe, and which lifts the imagination far above the tameness, let me say, the *injustice*, of such a task, – there are many complex words that could not be translated literally, without great injury to the original – without being 'false to its sense, and falser to its fame.'

I am aware that in the following poems there will sometimes be found a sameness, and repetition of thought, appearing but too plainly in the English version, though scarcely perceivable in the original Irish, so great is the variety as well as beauty peculiar to that language. The number of synonima[1] in which it abounds, enables it, perhaps beyond any other, to repeat the same thought, without tiring the fancy or the ear.

It is really astonishing of what various and comprehensive powers this neglected language is possessed. In the pathetic, it breathes the most beautiful and affecting simplicity; and in the bolder species of composition, it is distinguished by a force of expression, a sublime dignity, and rapid energy, which it is scarcely possible for any translation fully to convey; as it sometimes fills the mind with ideas altogether new, and which, perhaps, no modern language is entirely prepared to express. One compound epithet must often be translated by two lines of English verse, and, on such occasions, much of the beauty is necessarily lost; the force and effect of the thought being weakened by too slow an introduction on the mind; just as that light which dazzles, when flashing swiftly on the eye, will be gazed at with indifference, if let in by degrees.

But, though I am conscious of having, in many instances, failed in my attempts to do all the justice I wished to my originals, yet still, some of their beauties are, I hope, preserved; and I trust I am doing an acceptable service to my country, while I endeavour to rescue from oblivion a few of the invaluable reliques of her ancient genius; and while I put it in the power of the public to form some idea of them, by clothing the thoughts of our Irish muse in a language with which they are familiar, at the same time that I give the originals, as vouchers for the fidelity of my translation, as far as two idioms so widely different would allow.

However deficient in the powers requisite to so important a task, I may yet be permitted to point out some of the good consequences which might result from it, if it were but performed to my wishes. The productions of our Irish Bards exhibit a glow of cultivated genius, – a spirit of elevated heroism, – sentiments of pure honor, – instances of disinterested patriotism, – and manners of a degree of refinement, totally astonishing, at a period when the rest of Europe was nearly sunk in barbarism: and is not all this very honorable to our countrymen? Will they not be benefited, – will they not be gratified, at the lustre reflected on them by ancestors so very different from what modern prejudice has been studious to represent them? But this is not all.

[1]There are upwards of forty names to express a *Ship* in the Irish language, and nearly an equal number for a *House*, etc.

ANNE HAVERTY

from *Constance Markievicz: An Independent Life*

With characteristic courage, Constance presented a smiling face to her sister and those around her. But a poem she wrote in memory of James Connolly at this time betrays her inner anguish – and also that she was steeling her courage to her 'stern destiny'. That it was written in romantic terms suggests most probably not that she and Connolly were lovers, but that the most vital emotional bond she experienced was for her dead brothers in arms, especially Connolly. She gave the poem to a warden before she was removed to England.

> You died for your country my Hero-love
> In the first grey dawn of spring;
> On your lips was a prayer to God above
> That your death will have helped to bring
> Freedom and peace to the land you love,
> Love above everything.

The weeks in prison and their deaths had not cooled her ardour or killed her hopes, on the contrary:

> For the woman you found so sweet and dear
> Has a sterner destiny –
> She will fight as she fought when you were here
> For freedom I'll live and die . . .

At first, Constance worked in the sewing-room, where night-gowns and underwear were made from hard unbleached calico for the prisoners. It was a posting envied by the other inmates because it was warm and dry in comparison with other areas in the cold, damp, run-down jail. But she soon chafed at the inactivity and asked to be transferred elsewhere. She was sent to the prison kitchens and later described what the work there was like:

> The dinners were served in two-storey cans, used indiscrimi-nately among 200 women and, more, some of the cans were very old and musty. A great many of the women were known to be suffering from venereal disease and at the same time an attempt was made to keep their tins separate. This was dropped after a while. There was no proper accommodation for washing these 400 tins. I used to do 200 with another convict. We did our best to get them clean in a big terra-cotta bowl on the kitchen table and to dry them on two towels. Sometimes the water would not be hot, sometimes there was no soap or soda, and then you could neither dry nor clean the tins. Many of the tins were red with rust inside . . .

[Speaking out against the Treaty in the Dáil] She appealed to the assembly to remain true to their ideals, to walk on:

> the stony road that leads to ultimate freedom and the regeneration of Ireland; the road that so many of our heroes walked . . . I fear dishonour; I don't fear death, and I feel at all events that death is preferable to dishonour . . . I have seen the stars and I am not going to follow a flickering will o' the wisp, and I am not going to follow any person juggling with constitutions and introducing petty tricky ways into

this Republican movement which we built up – you and not I – because I have been in jail.

Her stand was echoed unanimously by the five other women members of the Dail. Because all of them had had menfolk, husbands, brothers or sons who had died in the years since 1916, this stand was categorised by Deputy McCabe of Sligo as a 'craving for vengeance'. They repudiated this charge. But in the unhappy years to come, this image of intransigence and fury was given to all republican women and reached the level of caricature. . . .

In March, the Dail refused to allow the vote to women between 21 and 30; partly because it was thought that Cumann na mBan which had been the first body to overwhelmingly reject the treaty reflected the views of women generally; partly because in the preparation of a new electoral register, the franchise would be also extended to young militant men who were not at present on the register. Constance in her Dail speech described how equality for women was her 'first bite, you may say, at the apple of freedom':

And soon I got on to the other freedom, freedom to the nation, freedom to the workers . . . I would work for it anywhere, as one of the crying wrongs of the world, that women because of their sex, should be debarred from any position or any right that their brains entitle them to hold . . . Today I would appeal . . . to see that justice is done to those young women and young girls who took a man's part in the Terror.

9

Religion

CATHERINE BYRON

Churching

*Her daughter in England is delivered of her first child – Birmingham
1938*

The church clanks empty after late Mass.

Returned from the far country of caring
and giving suck, she walks softly
to the familiar altar rails.

She notes the gew-gaw fleur de lys
her eye grown critical investigating
the pale and curling fronts
of her child's astonishing extremities.

She awaits the priest in an attitude
of humility, mantilla veiling
her amazement at sameness in this place only
amongst a world newmade
by her act of making.
Through the fingers of attempted prayer
she summons the hosanna tree
of the dawn of her delivery,
the sparrows' and starlings' gloria.
She hears the priest hurry
in cassock and crossed stole
from sacristy to sanctuary
and prepares her spirit for the spell
that will pronounce her
clean.

BRIAN MERRIMAN

from *The Midnight Court*

(Eighteenth Century)

TRANSLATED BY DAVID MARCUS

Another thing I'd like to mention
That's beyond my comprehension –
Whatever made the Church create
A clergy that is celibate?
The lack of men is a cruel curse
Just now when things were never worse;
I'd give my eyes to have a lover
The ripest, though, are under cover.
It's such a bitter pill to swallow
For one like me, who hasn't a fellow,
To see them big and strong of stature,
Full of charm and bright good-nature,
Each one seems a fresh young stripling,
Hard of bone and muscles rippling,
Backs as straight as a sergeant-major's,
And desires as keen as razors.
They live in the lap of luxury,
And, what's more, it's all tax-free;
Well-dressed, well-treated, and well-fed,
With warming-pans to heat their bed.
Man for man they'd beat the best,
And they're human like the rest.
I'd skip the ones who don't pass muster,
Raddled ancients who lack lustre,
But I'd soon shake up the one
Who snores while work is left undone!
Perhaps you'd find that quite a share
Would play their part, and those I'd spare,

For, after all, it wouldn't do
To damn the many for the few,
A sturdy ship should not be sunk
Because one sailor has no spunk!
We know that some are tough old terrors
Who would never mend their errors,
Frozen fogeys who believe
God blundered when he fashioned Eve;
But others secretly admit
They think her nature's choicest bit!
There's many a house that didn't begin
To prosper and smile till the priest dropped in,
And many a woman could toss her head
And boast of the time he blessed her bed;
Throughout the land there's ample proof
The Church is anything but aloof,
And many a man doesn't know that he
Has a son with a clerical pedigree.
But it's a shame the strength and time
They waste on women past their prime,
While others miss the best in life
Because a priest can't take a wife;
Just think of the massive population
This rule has cost the Irish nation!

ANNE LE MARQUAND HARTIGAN

In That Garden of Paradise

In that garden once she took down the Apple
Casually because she wanted to know, and then
There was all that fuss, Adam going
Bananas saying that she'd tipped the apple cart
And God.

Oh God was a pain getting all huffed up about
His tree and the serpent splitting its sides
Under the bushes laughing.
To save face after all night discussions behind
Closed gates they decided on a lockout. Adam
Raging that he was implicated because of the odd
Bite he took in case She knew more than he did.

She did of course and now she knew it made no
Difference which side of the gates of paradise
They were; until God took a good look at himself
And saw his own womb, his own breast, and not only
His staff of righteousness.

MARY CONDREN

from *The Serpent and the Goddess*

Needless to say, women could not be bearers of the new 'life'
brought in by Christianity, for whereas in the old religion, the
Goddess could be found in the trees, bushes, and holy wells, now
access to God the Father took place through the meditation of the
male priests. Certainly, one could pray to God the Father, but
nothing that he replied would count – unless it met the approval
of the male clergy.

The First Order of Saints admitted women to their ranks
because 'they feared not the blast of temptation'; by now, blasts of
temptation were running riot. Like the Celtic warriors who, it was
claimed, had met their deaths through the seductiveness and
cunning of women, the 'spiritual warriors', unable to take
responsibility for their own passions, projected their anger onto
women, casting them as 'unclean', 'seductive', and 'weak willed'.
Like the warriors, the Christian priests had to be constantly on
their guard.

As the 'guardian devils' of men, women occupy the negative side of the dualism men have established in the theological world between good and evil, heaven and hell, spirituality and sex, God and the Devil. The tragedy, ambiguity, and cyclical regeneration of early Irish religion have been replaced by a harsh code of ethics and one in which women are the constant reminders to men of the depths to which their precariously established 'souls' can fall.

The rape of the abbess of Kildare, begun by one of Dermot MacMurrough's soldiers, was effectively completed by the ecclesiastical machinery of the twelfth-century reform movement. Her rape symbolized the end of an era for women and religion in Ireland. From now on, any power they had would be derivative; that is to say, it would be given or sanctioned by the local male ecclesiastics. No matter how brilliant, holy, or otherwise gifted any woman might be, her religious authority could be overruled by any male cleric, no matter how inept, power hungry, or degenerate.

Women in early Ireland have travelled an ominous path: once revered symbols of creativity, they have become signs of danger and pollution; transformed into virgins, they now need to be 'protected'. The church may well have begun by protecting women from the power of the male warriors, but who would now protect women from the power of the male church?

ANON

Litany to Our Lady

(Eighth Century)

TRANSLATED BY EUGENE O'CURRY

O Great Mary.
O Mary, greatest of Maries.
O Greatest of Women.
O Queen of Angels.

O Mistress of the Heavens.

O Woman full and replete with the grace of the Holy Ghost.

O Blessed and Most Blessed.

O Mother of Eternal Glory.

O Mother of the heavenly and earthly Church.

O Mother of Love and Indulgence.

O Mother of the Golden Heights.

O Honour of the Sky.

O Sign of Tranquillity.

O Gate of Heaven.

O Golden Casket.

O Couch of Love and Mercy.

O Temple of Divinity.

O Beauty of Virgins.

O Mistress of the Tribes.

O Fountain of the Parterres.

O Cleansing of the Sins.

O Purifying of Souls.

O Mother of Orphans.

O Breast of the Infants.

O Solace of the Wretched.

O Star of the Sea.

O Handmaid of the Lord.

O Mother of Christ.

O Resort of the Lord.

O Graceful like the Dove.

O Serene like the Moon.

O Resplendent like the Sun.

O Cancelling Eve's disgrace.

O Regeneration of Life.

O Beauty of Women.

O Leader of the Virgins.

O Enclosed Garden.

O Closely Locked Fountain.

O Mother of God.

O Perpetual Virgin.

O Holy Virgin.

O Serene Virgin.
O Chaste Virgin.
O Temple of the Living God.
O Royal Throne of the Eternal King.
O Sanctuary of the Holy Ghost.
O Virgin of the Root of Jesse.
O Cedar of Mount Lebanon.
O Cypress of Mount Sion.
O Crimson Rose of the Land of Jacob.
O Blooming like the Palm Tree.
O Fruitful like the Olive Tree.
O Glorious Son-Bearer.
O Light of Nazareth.
O Glory of Jerusalem.
O Beauty of the World.
O Noblest-Born of the Christian Flock.
O Queen of Life.
O Ladder of Heaven.

ATTRIBUTED TO ST COLUMCHILLE

Prayer to the Virgin

(Tenth Century)

TRANSLATED BY KUNO MEYER AND JOHN STRACHAN

Gentle Mary, noble maiden, give us help!
Shrine of our Lord's body, casket of the mysteries!

Queen of queens, pure holy maiden,
Pray for us that our wretched transgression be forgiven for thy
sake.

Merciful one, forgiving one, with the grace of the Holy Spirit,
Pray with us to the true-judging King of the goodly ambrosial
clan.

Branch of Jesse's tree in the beauteous hazel-wood,
Pray for me until I obtain forgiveness of my foul sins.

Mary, splendid diadem, thou that hast saved our race,
Glorious torch, orchard of Kings!

Brilliant one, transplendent one, with the deed of pure chastity,
Fair golden illumined ark, holy daughter from Heaven!

Mother of righteousness, Thou that excellest all else,
Pray with me thy first-born to save me on the day of Doom.

Noble rare star, tree under blossom,
Powerful choice lamp, sun that warmeth every one.

Ladder of the great track by which every saint ascends,
Mayest thou be our safeguard towards the glorious Kingdom.

Fair fragrant seat chosen by the King,
The noble guest who was in thy womb three times three months.

Glorious royal porch through which He was incarnated,
The splendid chosen sun, Jesus, Son of the living God.

For the sake of the fair babe that was conceived in thy womb,
For the sake of the holy child that is High-King in every place,

For the sake of His cross that is higher than any cross,
For the sake of His burial when He was buried in the stone tomb,

For the sake of His resurrection when He arose before everyone,
For the sake of the holy household from every place to Doom,

Be thou our safeguard in the Kingdom of the good Lord,
That we may meet with dear Jesus – that is our prayer – hail!

Eva Gore-Booth

A Heretic's Pilgrimage

Here, all star-paven at our Lady's well,
A milky way of white anemones
Leads to her simple shrine among the trees,
The silver willow woods of Lissadel.
Grey winds pass sighing and strange forces thrill
The holy water, sheltered from the breeze,
Fresh from the spring of earth's lost mysteries
Beneath the shadow of the haunted hill.
Madonna of the way-side thronèd here!
We bring thee poppies grown amongst the wheat,
Frail blue-bells and the silver marguerite,
And all the golden tribute of the year,
We lay our dreams and flowers at thy feet,
Because the country people hold thee dear.

Above her head full seven cold glories shine,
Before the mighty Virgin Gabriel stands –
His feet are flame, and in his claspèd hands
He holds a tall white lily for a sign.
This is the mortal angels call divine,
The winds of heaven obey her high commands,
Her's is the secret of all times and lands,
The glory of the temple's inmost shrine.
Ah, Mary Mother, thine it was alone
For all the majesty of youth to find
The spirit's glory out of darkness grown,
To leave the soilèd joys of earth behind,
And seek the splendour of the white unknown,
The sacred loneliness of star and wind.

Hail Virgin spirit of the world's desire,
Have pity on us, who, like thee of late
Saw the great angel at life's outer gate,
And paused to greet him with our hearts on fire,
Yet, went away and sold our souls for hire,
And wandered far in the wild ways of fate
And learned the hunger naught can satiate,
And dragged the angel's lily through the mire.
Ah, pray for us, poor children of blind chance,
Who have lost Hope beneath the world's control,
Forgot the glory of the angel's glance,
The dim light of the half-deciphered scroll,
Our one strange glimpse of God's unknown Romance,
Life's salutation to the virgin soul.

RUTH HOOLEY

Cut the Cake

Our Lady, dispossessed
on some alpen ice-cap
would not look out of place
in ski-pants, zipping
down virgin slopes
to the sound of music.

But wait for her second
coming round the mountain –
the icon-shattering thaw.
Our immaculate image, white-iced
and frosted for two thousand years,
might melt to nothing more divine
than a seething woman, cheated
out of sex and a son in his prime.

Austin Clarke

Unmarried Mothers

In the Convent of the Secret Heart,
The Long Room has been decorated
Where a Bishop can dine off golden plate:
As Oriental Potentate.
Girls, who will never wheel a go-cart,
Cook, sew, wash, dig, milk cows, clean stables
And, twice a day, giving their babes
The teat, herdlike, yield milk that cost
Them dearly, when their skirts were tossed up
Above their haunches. Hook or zip
Has warded them at Castlepollard.
Luckier girls, on board a ship,
Watch new hope spraying from the bollard.

Anon

from *The Land of Cockaigne*

(Fourteenth Century)

The young monks each day
After meat, go out to play:
Despite their sleeves and cowl
There is no hawk or swift fowl
Faster flying through the sky
Than these monks when feeling high.
When the abbot sees them flee,
He follows them with glee,
But nevertheless bids the throng
To alight for evensong.

When the monks don't come down,
But further flee, at random,
He takes a maiden, from the mass,
And turning up her plump white ass,
Beats the tabours with his hand,
To make his monks alight to land.
The monks, all seeing that,
Drop from the sky, upon the dot,
And ring the wench all about
To thwack her white toute,
And after this pleasant work
Wend meekly home to drink
Going to their collation
In a goodly fair procession.

Another abbey is thereby –
Forsooth, a great fair nunnery,
Up a river of sweet milk,
Where there is surplus of silk.
When the summer sun is hot,
The young nuns take a boat
And sail upon that river,
Both with oars and rudder.

When they are far from the abbey
They strip themselves naked to play,
And leaping down into the brim
Set themselves skilfully to swim.
The monks, when they this espy,
Rise up, and forthwith fly
And coming to the nuns anon
Each monk grabs him one
And quickly bears forth his prey
To the great, grey abbey,
And teaches the nuns an orison
With jigging up and down.

He that would be a stallion good
And can set straight his hood,
That monk shall have, without fear,
Twelve new wives each year,
While the monk who sleeps the best
And above all, likes his rest,
There is hope for him, Got wot,
Soon to be a father abbot.

from THE IRISH SISTERS OF CHARITY
CENTENARY BROCHURE (1959)

No local help was forthcoming. There was episcopal approval of course, but no more. The only building the Sisters could acquire was a dilapidated little house. The contractor dismissed it as wholly unsuitable, because he said that no cobbling could turn it into a decent habitation. It was only with great coaxing he was persuaded into drawing up a modest plan of rehabilitation. Unlike Ballaghaderreen, no public welcome awaited the Sisters in Foxford. When Mother Arsenius called on the parish priest, he was out, and the woman who answered the door cautiously kept the chain on while she talked. Next day, the parish priest spoke to the contractor and his acid comment on the new foundation was: 'What do the nuns want here? There is no money to support them.' . . .

Mother Arsenius now became the voice of the people whom defeat had made quite dumb. On their behalf she tackled the Congested Districts Board, then recently instituted, for grants to enable the tenants to buy vegetable and flower seeds, new breeds of fowl, incubators, seed potatoes, oats, fruit trees, so as to break down once and for all their dependence on the potato. She secured the planting of six hundred apple trees around the homes. Later

on, the Sisters expended the same energy in finding a market for
the local produce. . . .

But the plain truth was that the land was so poor, a living could
not be got out of it. Mother Arsenius saw that the supreme need
was remunerative employment which would give the people the
habit of work and restore their self-respect. This inspired her to
found the Providence Woollen Mills in Foxford.

It was a daring plan, immediately condemned on all sides for its
rashness. A nun in business! As if the very terms of her religious
life did not make such an idea impossible! There was one factor,
however, which the scoffers overlooked – her genius for organisation. None knew better than she did how to make a levy on the
knowledge she herself lacked. It was not long before she had found
the ideal helper, Mr J. C. Smith, proprietor of the Caledon
Woollen Mills in County Tyrone. He was a Protestant Freemason,
but he, too, succumbed to her force of character and devoted a
considerable amount of his time to giving her the benefit of his
long experience.

The story is told how, on one occasion, when they had covered
all the ground of the new project, they came at last to the question
of finance. Up to this point, Mr Smith had taken it for granted
that Mother Arsenius was in a position to get hold of the necessary
capital. He hazarded a sum of between four and five thousand
pounds for a beginning. Mother Rectress undeceived him. She was
the possessor of fifty pounds. The businessman turned away as if
stung: 'I am sorry,' he muttered, horrified. 'It is absolutely out of
the question . . . ' He prepared to take his leave with an air of
finality and said goodbye. 'All the same,' said Mother Arsenius
meekly, 'I'm going on with it.'

Mr Smith rallied again from this shock. He had never before
been associated with such a scheme, mainly built on the airy, and
to his mind, insecure foundation of hope. Nevertheless, he
continued to give his advice. He superintended the preparation of
the original buildings, and the choice of the first machines, he
selected from his own factory a skilled man capable of managing
the new industry. The Foxford Mill was opened on 2nd May 1894.

Mother Arsenius soon proved that she was justified in her

confidence. The Congested Districts Board approved her scheme and gave her a loan of £7,000 at a modest rate of interest. They also gave her a free grant of £1,500 for the training of the first operatives.

ROZ COWMAN

Taking the Veil

Zip into the honeycomb,
sister; lie jelly coddled
in your hexagon; listen to bees
drilling bee-paths in oxygen, outside,
and the hush of hatchery.

See sun filtered
in mica flakes through wax;
mote-pollened stamens
of light piercing
cracks of the wall.

Lie fallow; few
are chosen for the flight
into the sun's eye,
the disembowelling,
the fall.

Saint Brigid's Prayer

(Tenth Century)

TRANSLATED BY BRENDAN KENNELLY

I'd like to give a lake of beer to God.
   I'd love the Heavenly
Host to be tippling there
   For all eternity.

I'd love the men of Heaven to live with me,
   To dance and sing.
If they wanted, I'd put at their disposal
   Vats of suffering.

White cups of love I'd give them
   With a heart and a half;
Sweet pitchers of mercy I'd offer
   To every man.

I'd make Heaven a cheerful spot
   Because the happy heart is true.
I'd make the men contented for their own sake.
   I'd like Jesus to love me too.

I'd like the people of Heaven to gather
   From all the parishes around.
I'd give a special welcome to the women,
   The three Marys of great renown.

I'd sit with the men, the women and God
   There by the lake of beer.
We'd be drinking good health forever
   And every drop would be a prayer.

ROSITA SWEETMAN

from *On Our Backs: Sexual Attitudes in a Changing Ireland*

M CRIBBINS. Mná na h-Eireann was founded in 1970. We saw family life in Ireland being attacked. Our aim is to keep traditional Irish family life and we haven't qualified that aim.

What would you regard as traditional Irish family life?
M CRIBBINS. The kind of life I grew up in where the man of the house worked, the women brought children into the world, fed them, looked after them, and was always there. The traditional Catholic values were the values of the household. Catholic and Irish, in that order.

Who led the attack on family life, and why?
M CRIBBINS. There's no doubt at all in our minds that this whole campaign was planned internationally, money was poured in from abroad and the family planning clinics are the main agents of it. Their first attack was on the Irish language, they had to get rid of the language because that's the basis of any country; then they set up a group to remove corporal punishment from schools, they had to rear a generation that would know no control; then they were ready; their next step was contraception.

How does Mná na h-Eireann work?
M CRIBBINS. Well we're not a big organization, not because a lot of people aren't with us but because we haven't bothered to enrol a lot. We count 1,000 members but we know we speak for tens of thousands. We meet once a month just to make decisions.

We campaign by writing to the newspapers, appearing on television. In the last election we circularized thousands of houses telling people not to vote for a certain politician who was in favour of contraception. He didn't get in either. Another campaign is against Mr Haughey's Bill [for the legalization of contraception], we want to make sure this evil is never made legal. We've picketed the contraceptive clinics too. But our biggest sore point at the moment is the Equal Pay Bill. We never at all, at all, agreed with women working. Traditional Irish family life depends on a man who is allowed his own manhood, which is to earn enough money to keep his wife and children. The whole idea of women at work is repugnant to us. We've said, 'Okay, if you're going to punish the one income family we're going to demand that you give an allowance to the wife who stays at home.'

How do you think Ireland is changing?
M CRIBBINS. Your generation thinks in my day that we were terribly inhibited, that we got no education; there's not a grain of truth in that. My age group here is one of the best educated in the world. But obviously there was no trade in the lives we live, no big business. We don't drink, don't smoke, don't need drugs, so big business decided they had to get customers for their goods.

Take the ordinary married women in Dublin today with three or four children. She gets a bit anaemic, or some tummy trouble, she goes to the health centre and the doctor gives her the Pill. If she won't take it he says well there's nothing else. It's dreadful, they've just foisted it on Irish women. I've seen sound healthy women turned into nervous wrecks.

But isn't it true people want smaller families?
M CRIBBINS. Why should people want smaller families when they've better housing, better conditions, than we ever had? Usually it's for selfish reasons. But, if a couple want to have lesser families than God Almighty would send them, there are plenty of natural methods. The natural system is 100 per cent safe, which no other system is. It costs nothing, it doesn't damage your health, it fosters married life. But, there's no money in it so they just crushed it. With Billings method we just don't know the meaning of failure.

What then of the 5,000 Irish women who got pregnant last year outside of marriage? Many of them were using the so-called 'safe period'.

M CRIBBINS. Well first of all it's a sin, and it offends God. Obviously these women have lost their faith. Number two is, they were assured by these contraceptive people these artificial methods were safe. We know they're not safe. The latest reports from America would lift the hair on your head. IUDs, and other methods, can't work under the age of about sixteen, but the whole purpose of feeding the kids on this and that, so that they have these fittings and these pills, is *in order* to get them pregnant so they can have the money for abortions. The whole thing is absolutely vile.

Would you not accept that it's a fact that young people are having sex and therefore it would be better for them to use contraceptives, than have unwanted pregnancies?
M CRIBBINS. To have sex outside of marriage is a mortal sin and Catholic traditional families tell their children that, so, if they go and commit sin, well, well then they have to work that out in their own conscience. Mortal sin kills the soul. But to tell me because they're committing sin I have to provide for them – no way. Mná na h-Eireann says, 'Don't do it because it's sin.'

NUALA O FAOLAIN

Bishop Casey and the Conflict of Public and Private Lives

I was in Galway on Saturday morning, as it happens, and I went to early Mass in the Cathedral. Maybe 30 of us were there, more than 20 with grey or white hair. There was a stone plaque on the wall of the chapel, with the names and dates of birth and death of the four Bishops of Galway there since the diocese was established in 1888. Bishop Casey's name will be there, though the date won't be that of his death. There's lots of space underneath for the next name, and the next, and the next. The Roman Catholic Church persists. Worship persists. And there's a way around everything: Bishop Casey's name wasn't, of course, mentioned in the prayer after the consecration, when you pray first for the Pope, then for the Bishop. But the priest did lead us in saying a Hail Mary for him. 'And Blessed is the fruit of thy womb . . . '

Further up the Cathedral is the chapel commemorating John F. Kennedy, a place I haven't visited since I learnt that he was a man who used women like waste-disposal units. A man who lived with the same disjunctions Bishop Casey seems to have lived with – loving people, but not the person. Impeccable with the general – lost with the particular. There are no heroes.

I cried tears of sympathy, driving out of Dublin the day of the revelations, at the painful bewilderment of a man who rang in to the 'Gay Byrne Show'. He had brought his children up, he said, by showing them examples. Bishop Casey had been one of the examples. What was he to do now? There's a little smile playing around my daughter's lips. He said, That man himself, in his love for his children, is the only example anyone needs. I hope he'll come to see that the death of reverence, hero-worship, and the attribution of moral superiority to remote men, is an opportunity, not a loss.

There is a real sense of opportunity in the air. We are being called to the real. The Maastricht referendum is asking us what we really believe about ideals of self-sufficiency and neutrality. The Supreme Court decision has superimposed the reality of Irish abortions on the ideal of the Eighth Amendment. What we know of Bishop Casey's story most powerfully reclaims real life, in all its sensational accident, from ideal formulations. Many clerics, I presume, are asking themselves what they really mean by celibacy.

There was even an opportunity last week, for the few who might take it, to really think about patriarchy. The 'Today Tonight' programme wonderfully coincided with the story of the Bishop and Annie Murphy which – if what we have heard is true – is about patriarchy. It is about the relative claims of the public and the private life. Most men don't enjoy or very much value the rearing of children. When it comes to the choice then, having fathered a child, between continuing a dynamic and useful and rewarding and self-affirming public life, or setting up a simple private household in which to nurture that child, there wouldn't be much of a conflict. Many, many men avoid as best they can the *ennui* of caring for their children. They work 20 hours a day and then blandly say, when they're rich, that the one thing they regret is having missed their children growing up. They train football teams five nights a week. They discover that such and such a politics is what really matters to them, and that their political vocation unfortunately means that they must leave home and children (usually accompanied by a young, female fellow-ideologue).

Not only men but women have absorbed the values of patriarchy. If I were a Bishop and believed my work to be terribly important and was loved and respected and acclaimed and constantly praised, I wouldn't want to leave all that just to rear my child. I don't value the task enough. I'm not open enough to its beauty or its importance, or to the responsibility entailed in using my body to make a child. If we all did think that the raising of children is the most important task on earth then women, because they do it, would be valued. We do not think that. We do not value the domestic. There is a huge struggle about to take place, mainly between men and women, about the re-valuing of child-rearing. The story of Bishop Casey and Annie Murphy is a lurid and exceptional one, but basically it is about that question: if a man and a woman equally make a child, should they not equally bring that child through to adulthood?

It may seem callous to stress the opportunity for thinking and perhaps for change that Bishop Casey's resignation provides. There is undoubtedly personal suffering involved. And terrible human waste. I heard Peter Murphy on the radio and he sounded such a pleasant, intelligent young man. How terrible that he had no father. How terrible that nobody had the pleasure of being his father. But things do progress, sometimes, through the suffering of individuals. There has been so much silent suffering in Ireland – so much that has counted for nothing – has affected nothing. All the lonely furtive silent women – made such by the teachings of the

Roman Catholic Church. I went to the Good Friday liturgy a few weeks ago and as the great account of the Passion of Christ was built up the congregation became solemn with identification and compassion. It occurred to me that there would be more women than usual going over to England for abortions that night, because Easter's the kind of time you can cover up a few days' absence. We must learn to ground compassion in the real. For this we must both deconstruct the ideal and acknowledge the real. The story of Annie Murphy and her son and Bishop Casey is helpful to both endeavours. Untold stories are not.

I know that it is too much to ask – there are no heroes, as I've said – but I wish that Bishop Casey had stayed. I think his being here would have prevented some of the ugliness which has rushed to fill the vacuum in the overall account. There's the vicious misogyny, especially on the part of older, 'Catholic' women. 'The bloody bitch,' I've heard Annie Murphy called. Villain. Money-grabber. Whore. There's the crazy legalism, whereby a complex human situation is scanned to Spot the Sin. He didn't use a condom, so he didn't sin. He didn't use Trocaire funds, so he didn't sin. As if God is not other people, and as if sin is anything other but what we do to God in them.

Then there's the very understandable *schadenfreude* on the part of those, mainly women, who have been hurt and insulted by the Catholic Church. They are full of glee at its present discomfiture. They even – wildly – hope that this episode will damage its authority in socio-sexual matters. 'They shoved us around long enough,' a woman said to me. 'Now we can shove them around.' But we can't, really, even if what we wanted was to behave like them. There are quite a few people in this country, and not just Catholics, who are deeply, deeply hurt and shaken by these events. The older people, in particular, were formed in a world of flocks and their good shepherds. The least one can do is pause to respect their bewilderment.

But also, in a way this whole thing is old-fashioned, and its terms are antique. It could be a melodrama, all the way from the 'Thorn Birds' scenario of the relationship to the notion that Irish society is rocked by its revelation. Of course it's not rocked. This isn't the 19th century. Over the last few days I've been driving around the west and south, giving lifts, talking to people here and there. Of course, we talked about little else. What a story, after all. 'But – do you care?' I'd ask. 'Does it matter to you?' The practising Catholics said that of course it didn't affect them and God. It was only about the Church, and about God. And the others – and hitch-hikers, because they're poor, usually are the others – said of course it didn't affect them. It was only about the Church, which doesn't matter to them. Maybe that phase will pass, and there will be a realisation that it is about men, women and the claims of their babies, everywhere. But we have to work through the surface sensation of the story to get to that, especially the mock sensation that under the purple and the mitres there are poor, bare-forked animals, like any other.

MARY LAVIN

from *Sunday Brings Sunday*

Jimmy said it was all right. He said every fellow did it, some time or another. That's what he said. And Jimmy never told a lie. That was one thing certain. Jimmy wore a medal too pinned on the inside of his trouser pocket. And one day in the graveyard when he stood on a wreath and broke the glass he took a shilling and he buried it in the grave. Jimmy was good. He said what they did was all right. But when he said it his voice was caught up with phlegm and when he put his head down in the hay she could hear him snuffling.

Maybe they oughtn't to have done it? But they didn't do it on purpose. They were only pushing and shoving and having fun.

Again a scatter of rain struck the window-panes and the cold voice of the curate struck through her stifling thoughts.

'It is the duty of parents and teachers to instruct children and servants and all those entrusted to their care.'

In the pew behind her she could hear the wintry moaning of the hag, who had come in out of the rain.

'Sunday brings Sunday.'

Mona felt a great fear growing in her heart when she thought of the way the priest's voice every Sunday, and the voice of the hag, and the voices of the fellows calling 'How' you' from the wall were lashing on the year till it galloped, taking seven steps at a time. If she kept on feeling this queer way she would have no choice but to get up and go down the aisle and out of the chapel. And outside it would be colder. What would she do outside? If she cycled home to her own house she mightn't get back in time before the Mass ended and she might miss the doctor's car. And anyway there was next Sunday to face. If she felt worse today than she did last Sunday she might be worse again next week. And at home there'd be so many questions; she'd sooner die than face them. And Jimmy across the aisle in the men's side of the chapel would be sweating and wetting his lips if he saw her go out. He'd be scared. And people would see him. And it would all be talked over later on, in the chapel yard, when the people were straggling out from Mass. The old hag might have something to say, in a cracked voice for all to hear. She couldn't go out. That was all there was to it. She'd have to bear it.

Mona clenched her hands together. She'd bear it. And she'd pray as hard as she could that nothing would happen to her. She'd light as many candles as she could out of what was left of her pay after some was sent home to her father. She might, maybe, skip a week of sending money home and put such a blaze of candles all over the candelabra that the smoke of them would go up like the souls of the dead went up out of the tombstones. Prayer was an efficacious thing, the priest said. By prayer we avoid sin. She always did what the priest said. Her mother often told people that her Mona would cut off her right hand if the priest told her to do it. That was right. She'd cut off her right hand. She'd do it that minute, if it was any good. She'd do anything if only it would be that there was nothing the matter with her. She'd pray and pray and pray that in the lovely summertime she'd have red cheeks again.

'Sunday brings Sunday.' If there was anything the matter she'd soon find out. The priest was still talking and the light was still glinting off his glasses. It wasn't his fault that Jimmy didn't know anything about anything any more than she did. It wasn't. Sure it wasn't? And anyway, it wasn't right to blame anyone for anything they didn't mean to do, least of all a priest. He didn't know how easy things could happen. He didn't know anything about the like of her or Jimmy, only seeing them in school and giving them pictures to put in their prayer books.

PATRICK KAVANAGH

from *The Great Hunger*

'Now go to Mass and pray and confess your sins
And you'll have all the luck,' his mother said.
He listened to the lie that is a woman's screen
Around a conscience when soft thighs are spread.
And all the while she was setting up the lie
She trusted in Nature that never deceives.
But her son took it as literal truth.
Religion's walls expand to the push of nature. Morality yields
To sense – but not in little tillage fields.

Life went on like that. One summer morning
Again through a hay-field on her way to the shop –
The grass was wet and over-leaned the path –
And Agnes held her skirts sensationally up,
And not because the grass was wet either.
A man was watching her, Patrick Maguire.
She was in love with passion and its weakness
And the wet grass could never cool the fire
That radiated from her unwanted womb
In that country, in that metaphysical land
Where flesh was a thought more spiritual than music
Among the stars – out of reach of the peasant's hand.

Ah, but the priest was one of the people too —
A farmer's son — and surely he knew
The needs of a brother and sister.
Religion could not be a counter-irritant like a blister,
But the certain standard measured and known
By which man might re-make his soul though all walls were down
And all earth's pedestalled gods thrown.

ART BYRNE AND SEAN MCMAHON

Mother Mary Martin

The International Missionary Training Hospital at Drogheda was
en fête in 1962; among the distinguished guests were the patriarch
of Armenia and Cardinal Montini (later Paul VI). A great army of
white-habited doctors and nurses were celebrating the twenty-
fifth anniversary of the founding of their order, the Medical
Missionaries of Mary. The visitors from Rome were being guided
around the gathering by the diminutive figure of Mary Martin, the
Mother-general. Born the eldest of twelve children of a wealthy
Dublin timber-merchant, she was educated by the Sacred Heart
nuns in Leeson Street and was later a boarder at Harrogate in
England. During the 1914–18 war she worked as a nurse in
France, afterwards returning to Dublin to do midwifery at Holles
Street hospital. She had decided to devote her life to the sick, and
so set out for Nigeria to work for the Bishop of Calabar, Joseph
Shanahan. She came to believe that dedicated medical missionaries
could do enormous good among the poor and the sick. Shanahan,
who had just helped found the Missionary Sisters of the Holy
Rosary, sent her to them at Killeshandra. After two years she left,
and there followed a period of ill-health. But she never lost faith in
her idea, which she continually pressed on the Papal Nuncio,
Paschal Robinson. In 1936 Pius XI announced that nuns could
become doctors, and within a year Mary Martin had set up the

Medical Missionaries of Mary (MMM) in Nigeria. Unable to remain in Africa because of her health, she returned to Ireland, there to establish a student house at Booterstown, a novitiate at Collon, and finally the maternity hospital at Drogheda which became the order's headquarters. By the time of the twenty-fifth anniversary, the MMM had hospitals in Africa, USA, Italy and Spain. Mary Martin's greatest achievement was to get the Church to recognise the unique work which could be done by women religious as doctors. For this she was decorated both by the International Red Cross and the Royal College of Surgeons of Ireland before her death at Drogheda (27 January 1975).

A Prayer

(Thirteenth Century)

TRANSLATED BY GIOLLA BRIGHDE MACNAMEE

Get for me, O Mother Mary,
A son before I go from this world.
Do not delay to put his seed into my blood,
O Womb in which the humanity of God was formed.

FRANCES MOLLOY

from *No Mate for the Magpie*

A toul me ma an' da that they had no need te keep me for a had decided te lave home. They said, ye'll do no such thing, me lady, ye'r too young te be lavin' home, ye'll stay in this house way us till the day an' hour ye get married. A allowed that at that rate of goin'

a would be at home for a quare long time because a had no
intention of iver gettin' married.

If me ma had of went te any hops hirsel' an' seen the kine of boys
that were at them she mightn't have been so keen on talkin' about
me marryin'. They were no Beatles them, oh no, they didn't want
te hold yer hand or love ye, yeah, yeah, yeah. All they wanted te
do was ate big pieces outa the side of yer neck or shove their slevery
oul tongues down yer throat till ye were damn near choked, or
grope aroun' way their dirty hacked oul han's inside yer knickers
when they had ye pasted to the nearest wall without even askin' ye
yer name.

A could see that me ma an' da had their plans laid, for me te
carry on workin' in the factory till a married wan of these boyos,
an' a wanted none of it. A decided then an' there that a might as
well do some good in the worl' instead, but a must of been headin'
in the wrong direction, for a ended up in a convent.

Wheniver a toul me ma an' da that a wanted te be a nun, me da
tried to get me te change me mine be gowling' an' shoutin' an'
sayin' that a would go away te be a bloody nun over hes dead body,
me lady. A toul me da that a thought it a cryin' shame that he
planned to die so young an' lave me poor ma a lonely widda
woman. When a said that me da took a swipe at me an' missed for
he wasn't a very good shot.

He kept on gowlin' at me ivery day till the very day the nuns
landed at our house te interview me. Then me da got feared that a
was maybe goin' te go away after all an' that he would niver see me
again so he started te be wile nice te me allthegether instead.

A wheen of weeks before a was due te go inte the convent, a took
a wile yearnin' for life an' got it inte me head that if a didn't get te
see Brendan Boyer doin' the Hucklebuck just wan time before a
went away a would probably die. When a made this announcement te me family they were highly delighted.

The Royal Showband was makin' a tour of the north of Ireland
at the time, an' weren't they comin' te our town just two nights
before a was due to go away. Me ma an' da took this as a blessin' in
disguise an' a fair enough indication of how the Lord could be seen
te act in strange an' mysterious ways. Me da put himsel' inte debt

be buyin' me a gran' new frock, me big brother bought me a pair of red shoes way heels on them seven inches high, an' me ma surpassed hirsel' completely be gettin' me lipstick an' powder te put on me face, a thing she'd forbid me te do in the past.

On the night of the dance when a landed at the hall way me big brother, there were two thousand other people standin' waitin' te get in an' we were nearly kilt in the crush as soon as the doors opened. In the first half of the night, some wee band from the back of beyond come on te play for us, but the two thousand people threw pennies at them an' shouted at them te get aff. (In them days pennies were fairly big things.)

Be the time Brendan Boyer an' the Royal Showband got up on the stage te play, a had managed te fight me way forward te the front of the hall an' get mesel' inte a quare good position te view the Hucklebuck. It was ivery thing a had iver imagined it te be an' a was so delighted that be the time the dance was over a had plucked up courage te go an' ask Brendan Boyer for hes autograph. A toul him that a was goin' away te a convent an' a would niver see him again so he wrote his name on me arm an' asked me to pray for him. A toul him a would, ivery day, an' a would niver wash me arm again for the rest of me life. Well, a prayed for him ivery day all right but a had to wash me arm a lot sooner than a thought.

GEORGE BERNARD SHAW

from *The Adventures of the Black Girl in her Search for God*

'How many wives have you?' said the black girl.

'I have long since ceased to count them' replied the Arab; 'but there are enough to shew you that I am an experienced husband and know how to make women as happy as Allah permits.'

'I do not seek happiness: I seek God,' said the black girl.

'Have you not found Him yet?' said the conjurer.

'I have found many gods,' said the black girl. 'Everyone I meet has one to offer me; and this image maker here has a whole shopful of them. But to me they are all half dead, except the ones that are half animals like this one on the top shelf, playing a mouth organ, who is half a goat and half a man. That is very true to nature; for I myself am half a goat and half a woman, though I should like to be a Goddess. But even these gods who are half goats are half men. Why are they never half women?'

'What about this one?' said the image maker, pointing to Venus.

'Why is her lower half hidden in a sack?' said the black girl. 'She is neither a goddess nor a woman: she is ashamed of half her body, and the other half of her is what the white people call a lady. She is ladylike and beautiful; and a white Governor General would be glad to have her at the head of his house; but to my mind she has no conscience; and that makes her inhuman without making her godlike. I have no use for her.'

'The Word shall be made flesh, not marble' said the conjurer. 'You must not complain because these gods have the bodies of men. If they did not put on humanity for you, how could you, who are human, enter into any communion with them? To make a link between Godhood and Manhood, some god must become man.'

'Or some woman become God' said the black girl. 'That would be far better, because the god who condescends to be human degrades himself; but the woman who becomes God exalts herself.'

'Allah be my refuge from all troublesome women' said the Arab. 'This is the most troublesome woman I have ever met. It is one of the mysterious ways of Allah to make women troublesome when he makes them beautiful. The more reason he gives them to be content, the more dissatisfied they are. This one is dissatisfied even with Allah Himself, in whom is all majesty and all might. Well, maiden, since Allah the glorious and great cannot please you, what god or goddess can?'

'There is a goddess of whom I have heard, and of whom I would know more' said the black girl. 'She is named Myna; and I feel there is something about her that none of the other gods can give.'

'There is no such goddess' said the image maker. 'There are no other gods or goddesses except those I make; and I have never made a goddess named Myna.'

'She most surely exists,' said the black girl; 'for the white missy spoke of her with reverence, and said that the key to the universe was the root of her womanhood and that it was bodiless like a number, and that it was before the beginning instead of after it, just as God was before creation.' . . .

'I take refuge with Allah against this black daughter of Satan' cried the Arab vehemently. 'Learn to hold your peace, woman, when men are talking and wisdom is their topic. God made Man before he made Woman.'

'Second thoughts are best' said the black girl. 'If it is as you say, God must have created Woman because he found Man insufficient. By what right do you demand fifty wives and condemn each of them to one husband?'

KATIE DONOVAN

Underneath Our Skirts

Although a temple
to honour one man's voluntary death,
his ceaseless weep of blood,
the women cannot enter
if they bleed –
an old law.

As the bridal couple glides
down the aisle,
her white veil twitching,
I feel my pains.
A woman
bleeding in church,
I pray for time,
for slow motion.

Unprotected, I bleed,
I have no bandage,
my ache finds no relief.
My thorns
are high heels
and itchy stockings.
He, the imitator, bleeds on
in numb eternal effigy,
his lugubrious journey of martyrdom
rewarded with worship.

Tonight custom demands more blood:
sheets must be stained
with the crimson flowers
of a bride's ruptured garden.
Her martyrdom
will be silent knowledge
suffered in solitude.

As we leave the house
of the male bleeder,
I feel myself wet and seeping,
a shameful besmircher of this ceremony
of white linen
and creamy-petalled roses,

yet underneath our skirts
we are all bleeding,
silent and in pain,
we, the original
shedders of ourselves,
leak the guilt of knowledge
of the surfeit
of our embarrassing fertility
and power.

Clairr O'Connor

from *For the Time Being*

To break the bind of catholic orthodoxy my parents embraced, I resolved on several things. The first being, to eat meat only on Fridays. Big steaks preferably. Friday had always been a fish day in my childhood home. Next, I decided to go to mass when I felt like it, but never on a Sunday. I resolved absolutely, not to attend funerals except those of close friends. Should be safe on that one for a few years anyway.

These resolutions worked in their own way, at least for a while. But the day came when I realised that the deritualisation of my parents' rituals had, in themselves become rituals. Their observation pushed me in the opposite direction merely. New lists were necessary. I understood this when my local butcher didn't have any steak left on Friday night and I left his shop redfaced and crying. My misery at that present moment was rooted in fish Fridays.

But it was when I was gorging boxes of chocolates during Lent just for the hell of it, that I knew things were far gone. The present is a natural sequence to the past for most people. They don't have to use reverse ritual to try and convince themselves of their adulthood. After the gorge came austerity. To outdo the ascetics became a new goal. Frugality and restraint mastered me for a time. I lost two stone and played Peter Pan in panto on a three month run. I felt I was a child for the first time in my life, the eternal child, in fact.

After the show, when others were tucked into pizzas, I sipped my coffee and munched salad, crunching my carrots with happiness. I made personal appearances opening toyshops, children's clothes shops and loved it all. The family came to see me fly through air. Daddy said, 'A bit dangerous, isn't it? I hope you've got proper insurance.'

Tim came backstage on one of his trips home. He thought I was terrific and slipped me a hefty cheque to prove it. His business was expanding. He was excited about the possibilities of a dry-freeze method of storing the bodies of pets and humans at the precise moment of death. At some future date, when scientific research caught up, the bodies could be brought back to life. So, it had finally happened. In a little while, death would be cancelled altogether. The future would stretch out indefinitely. As well as the family mortgage, all the average young couple had to do was to take out financial cover for a family freeze compartment to secure togetherness beyond the last breath. I couldn't eat for several days, not even a carrot.

Not even a carrot! Tim had surpassed himself. While he'd been beating the future, I remained mired in doubt. I'd run the gamut from gorge to abstinence on the see-saw between past and future, the present somehow escaping. Then I saw my mistake. I had assumed the present was happening to other people elsewhere while the memories of shattered glass, spewed chocolate and final rites speared me to the past. But maybe they were precisely the things that catapulted me forward? Not a fast forward, but forward nevertheless. Just then, the telephone rang. It was Richard. He was ringing to say it was our tenth anniversary. I said, how could that be if I'd fled the marital tomb seven years ago? I hung up and decided to get an answering machine as an early birthday present.

BRENDAN KENNELLY

The Twelve Apostlettes

'How is it?' I asked Jesus, 'You haven't even
A single woman among your twelve apostles?
I mean, aren't you a prejudiced son-of-a-bitch?
Bit of a male chauvinist pig? I'd like to suggest

A dozen women – to be known as the Twelve Apostlettes
Who will constitute an alternative to your men,

Introduce another notion of salvation,
An alternative hell and heaven.

I wish to nominate Sally Noggin, Dolly Mount, Nell Flynn,
Biddy Mulligan, Valerie Valera, myself, Tosser Conner,
Molly Malone, Bonny Bell, Paula Foll, Vinnie Greene

And bearing in mind inevitable sin
As well as necessary concepts of virtue and honour
I nominate, lastly, Mary Magdalene.'

'Thank you,' Jesus smiled (the smile was fleeting)
'I'll bring the matter up at our next meeting.'

W. R. RODGERS

Lent

Mary Magdalene, that easy woman,
Saw, from the shore, the seas
Beat against the hard stone of Lent,
Crying, 'Weep, seas, weep
For yourselves that cannot dent me more.

O more than all these, more crabbed than all stones,
And cold, make me, who once
Could leap like water, Lord. Take me
As one who owes
Nothing to what she was. Ah, naked.

My waves of scent, my petticoats of foam
Put from me and rebut;
Disown. And that salt lust stave off
That slavered me – O
Let it whiten in grief against the stones

And outer reefs of me. Utterly doff,
Nor leave the lightest veil
Of feeling to heave or soften.
Nothing cares this heart
What hardness erates it now or coffins.

Over the balconies of these curved breasts
I'll no more peep to see
The light procession of my loves
Surf-riding in to me
Who now have eyes and alcove, Lord, for Thee.'

'Room, Mary,' said He, 'ah make room for me
Who am come so cold now
To my tomb.' So, on Good Friday,
Under a frosty moon
They carried Him and laid Him in her womb.

A grave and icy mask her heart wore twice,
But on the third day it thawed,
And only a stone's-flow away
Mary saw her God.
Did you hear me? Mary saw her God!

Dance, Mary Magdalene, dance, dance and sing,
For unto you is born
This day a King. 'Lady', said He,
'To you who relent
I bring back the petticoat and the bottle of scent.'

ANON

The Irish Dancer

(Fourteenth Century)

I am of Ireland,
And of the holy land
    Of Ireland.
Good sir, pray I thee,
For of saint charity,
Come and dance with me
    In Ireland.

10

Women Alone

EAVAN BOLAND

Mise Eire

I won't go back to it –

my nation displaced
into old dactyls,
oaths made
by the animal tallows
of the candle –

land of the Gulf Stream,
the small farm,
the scalded memory,
the songs
that bandage up the history,
the words
that make a rhythm of the crime

where time is time past.
A palsy of regrets.
No. I won't go back.
My roots are brutal:

I am the woman –
a sloven's mix
of silk at the wrists,
a sort of dove-strut
in the precincts of the garrison –

who practises
the quick frictions,
the rictus of delight
and gets cambric for it,
rice-coloured silks.

I am the woman
in the gansy-coat
on board the 'Mary Belle',
in the huddling cold,

holding her half-dead baby to her
as the wind shifts East
and North over the dirty
water of the wharf

mingling the immigrant
guttural with the vowels
of homesickness who neither
knows nor cares that

a new language
is a kind of a scar
and heals after a while
into a passable imitation
of what went before.

BRIAN MOORE

from *The Lonely Passion of Judith Hearne*

Miss Hearne lifted her teary face from the shelter of her elbows. Her rouge was smudged into two blurred scars across the paleness of her cheeks.

'Moira. I've lost my faith. And I've left Camden Street and I'm living in the Plaza Hotel and everything's finished, Moira, everything.'

'But why, Judy, why?'

'What am I doing with my life? I ask you,' Miss Hearne cried loudly, leaning across the table and catching hold of Moira's bare arm. 'A single girl with no kin, what am I doing? O Moira, you always were the lucky one, a husband and children around you, you'll never know what it's like to be me.'

'Judy dear, I know it must be hard at times. But just a little bit quieter, please, Judy! The children.'

'But I have to say it, I have to tell somebody and you've always been kind to me, inviting me over here on Sundays, you'll never know what it meant to me, Moira, to come here and sit with a family and feel that I belonged here, that I was welcome. Do you know what I mean, Moira, do you know what I mean?'

Only you didn't belong, you poor thing, Mrs O'Neill thought sadly. 'Yes, Judy, I think I know.'

'And then, just a few weeks ago, I might have got married. Do you know how long I've waited to be married, Moira? Do you know how many long years, every one of them twelve long months? Well, I'll tell you, it's twenty odd years, Moira, if you count from the time I was twenty. O, I know I didn't think about it all that time – when my aunt was ill, I gave up thinking about it for a while. But a woman never gives up, Moira, does she? Even when she's like me and knows it's impossible, she never gives up. There's always Mr Right, Moira, only he changes as the years go by. At first he's tall, dark and handsome, a young man, Moira, and then you're not so young and he's middle-aged, but still tall and handsome. And then there's moments when he's anybody, anybody who might be eligible. O, I've looked at all sorts of men, men I didn't even like. But that's not the end, that's not the worst of it.'

Her fingernails dug into the flesh of Moira's arm. She leaned forward, across the table, her dark nervous eyes filled with confessional zeal.

'No, no, I'm going to tell you the whole thing, Moira, the whole thing. Because I have to tell it to somebody, somebody must listen. That's not the worst when he's just anybody who might be eligible. You might as well forget about eligible men. Because you're too late, you've missed your market. Then you're up for any offers. Marked down goods. You're up for auction, a country auction, where the auctioneer stands up and says what am

I bid? And he starts at a high price, saying what he'd like best. No offers. Then second best. No offers. Third? No offers. What am I bid, Moira? and somebody comes along, laughable, and you take him. If you can get him. Because it's either that or back on the shelf for you. Back to your furnished room and your prayers. And your hopes.'

Mrs O'Neill began to weep. 'O Judy,' she said. 'Don't.'

'Your hopes,' Miss Hearne repeated, her dark eyes clouded and strange. 'Only you've got no hopes left, Moira. Then you're like me. You've got daydreams instead and you want to hold on to them. And you can't. So you take a drink to help them along, to cheer them up. And anybody, Moira, who so much as gives you a kind word is a prince. A prince. Even if he's old and ugly and common as mud. Even if the best he can say for himself is that he was a hotel doorman in New York. Would you believe that now, would you believe it?'

The American. The one she was talking about. A doorman. O, the poor soul!

'That would be bad enough, wouldn't it?' Miss Hearne cried. 'Bad enough, yes, you'd be ashamed of yourself. And rightly so. But there's worse yet. What if that doorman turned you down? TURNED YOU DOWN!'

Miss Hearne stopped open-mouthed, her face quivering. 'Have you got a drink, Moira?' she said. 'I need a drink.'

SOMERVILLE AND ROSS

from *The Real Charlotte*

'Leave me alone! What is it to you who I marry?' she cried passionately; 'I'll marry who I like, and no thanks to you!'

'Oh, indeed,' said Charlotte, breathing hard and loud between the words; 'it's nothing to me, I suppose, that I've kept the roof

over your head and put the bit into your mouth, while ye're
carrying on with every man that ye can get to look at ye!'

'I'm not asking you to keep me,' said Francie, starting up in her
turn and standing in the window facing her cousin; 'I'm able to
keep myself, and to wait as long as I choose till I get married; *I'm*
not afraid of being an old maid!'

They glared at each other, the fire of anger smiting on both their
faces, lighting Francie's cheek with a malign brilliance, and
burning in ugly purple-red on Charlotte's leathery skin. The girl's
aggressive beauty was to Charlotte a keener taunt than the
rudimentary insult of her words; it brought with it a swarm of
thoughts that buzzed and stung in her soul like poisonous flies.

'And might one be permitted to ask how long you're going to
wait?' she said, with quivering lips drawn back; 'will six months
be enough for you, or do you consider the orthodox widower's year
too long to wait? I daresay you'll have found out what spending
there is in twenty-five pounds before that, and ye'll go whimper-
ing to Roddy Lambert, and asking him to make ye Number Two,
and to pay your debts and patch up your character!'

'Roddy Lambert!' cried Francie, bursting out into shrill unpleasant laughter; 'I think I'll try and do better than that, thank ye,
though you're so kind in making him a present to me!' Then,
firing a random shot, 'I'll not deprive you of him, Charlotte; you
may keep him all to yourself!'

It is quite within the bounds of possibility that Charlotte might
at this juncture have struck Francie, and thereby have put herself
for ever into a false position, but her guardian angel, in the shape
of Susan, the grey tomcat, intervened. He had jumped in at the
window during the discussion, and having rubbed himself
unnoticed against Charlotte's legs with stiff, twitching tail, and
cold eyes fixed on her face, he, at this critical instant, sprang
upwards at her, and clawed on to the bosom of her dress, hanging
there in expectation of the hand that should help him to the
accustomed perch on his mistress's shoulder. The blow that was so
near being Francie's descended upon the cat's broad confident face
and hurled him to the ground. He bolted out of the window again,

and when he was safely on the gravel walk, turned and looked back with an expression of human anger and astonishment.

When Charlotte spoke her voice was caught away from her as Christopher Dysart's had been the day before. All the passions have but one instrument to play on when they wish to make themselves heard, and it will yield but a broken sound when it is too hardly pressed.

'Dare to open your mouth to me again, and I'll throw you out of the window after the cat!' was what she said in that choking whisper. 'Ye can go out of this house tomorrow and see which of your lovers will keep ye the longest, and by the time that they're tired of ye, maybe ye'll regret that your impudence got ye turned out of a respectable house!' She turned at the last word, and, like a madman who is just sane enough to fear his own madness, flung out of the room without another glance at her cousin.

Susan sat on the gravel path, and in the intervals of licking his paws in every crevice and cranny, surveyed his mistress's guest with a stony watchfulness as she leaned her head against the window sash and shook in a paroxysm of sobs.

Ronit Lentin

from *Tea with Mrs Klein*

'And that's that.' Barbara's voice hardens up. 'Your mother's fate is sealed. The house is sold for her. She is given a small room, with a separate entrance mind you, plus permission to sit in the living-room. And the money from the sale of the house? Dividing the goodies while she is still alive? And you have the cheek to say that your mother is perfectly happy to live on her own? If she is so happy alone, why change the status quo? All because of a few grand?'

'You're wrong as usual, Barbara,' Joan says. 'No one will take the money away from her. Apart from the expenses Doris and

David will incur. That's all. The rest she can leave in her bank, or invest, whatever she wants.'

'As long,' Barbara's sarcasm erases her former naiveté, 'as this priest disappears. From now on we shall guard both mother and her small fortune and mother and her little soul. A perfect plan.'

'I don't understand,' Doris says, groping, but aggressive, 'the objection. You're the one who claims she is always alone, that it's dangerous for her to remain alone, in case she faints again, God forbid, or falls ill suddenly. I think it's a very sound plan.'

'Your mother, have you asked her already?' Barbara asks.

'I suggested it to her a long time ago,' Doris says, 'and she refused. But one can pressure her, we shall all be here next week and if everyone talks to her she is sure to be persuaded.'

'In other words,' Barbara says, 'we shall brainwash her to death, we'll scare her about the unknown future, including conversion by Father Daly, faintings, death in the bathroom, arteriosclerosis, or loneliness. What a perfect scenario for a woman's magazine. Mother in danger of losing her religion, or in danger of death. What could be more convincing, more powerful? And she will, of course, be convinced. Because we shall all work on her for a whole week, which is supposed to be the most wonderful week of her life, her seventy-fifth birthday, mass celebrations and queenly feeling. All this, Doris and Joan, is simply touching! Your worry and consideration, your care. Only don't count on me, sisters. Or on Alex. I shall do for your mother what she wants, not what you want.' . . . 'I won't take part in brainwashing her and I won't have you spoil her last few years only because you need the money or because you are scared, in a real ghetto-mentality way, of one little man who made friends with your mother, scared just because he happens to be a priest.'

'Barbara,' Joan says, her voice calm and deliberate, 'I am sorry to say you don't seem to understand the problem. It's dangerous to let mother go on living on her own, but it's also dangerous to let her continue her friendship with this Daly. He has a bad influence on her. Her faints started since she has been seeing him. She . . .'

'She can tell him things she could never tell anybody else, that she never dreamt she'd be able to tell anyone,' Barbara interrupts,

'she can, suddenly, after all those years, talk.' . . . Barbara has
sensed a change in Gertrude during the past few months. The old
woman is more open, laughs more, sings to herself. She doesn't
look at herself much, doesn't talk as much about shopping. Once
she even said to Barbara, out of the blue, 'You know, Barbara, I
am happy. As if I have just grown old, just become a grandmother. Everything is peaceful suddenly, everything is bright.'
Barbara understands the cause of the change and says to Alex that
these are the happiest months in Gertrude's life. After years of
suppression, of mental masturbation, of bitterness, she suddenly
has someone, someone who comes to see just her, to listen to her
alone. . . .

Alex asks her if she is lonely on her own.

'But I am not lonely. I have friends. Father Daly comes here
quite often.'

No one interferes in the conversation so far, but on hearing the
father's name Doris cannot help saying, 'What does he want from
you, Father Daly? Why does he come here, Mother? Why doesn't
he leave you in peace?'

Gertrude looks Doris straight in the eye. Doris looks
frightened.

'I have something which is mine. Mine only. Never, all my life,
even when I was a young girl, did I have something which was
only mine. Apart from my singing. Perhaps. And even this your
father had to take away. Now I have something which nobody can
take away from me. Not one of you can take away from me.' She
recoils suddenly and stops. There is a thick, heavy silence in the
air.

Barbara breaks the silence and says, 'It's wonderful, Gertrude.
It's wonderful you have such a friend. I am sure you're happier now
than ever before. You would like to stay in your own home, to
leave things as they are, wouldn't you?' Ignoring Joan and Doris's
hostile glances, she carries on, 'We would like to hear your views
on moving in with Doris or staying here. What do you think?'

But Gertrude retreats into herself. She can't say more than what
she has already said. They all talk at the same time, the room is

full of voices, murkily filling her head with a low humming noise. Everything seems vague, far away, unreal.

Alex pressurises her, says he has to know, once and for all, what she thinks about the plans others have made for her. He talks and talks, crowding his mother.

She suddenly bursts out, 'Take everything. Take it all. The house. The furniture. The linen and the crockery. I don't need a thing. Take it. Take it all.'

'Nonsense,' says Alex, 'this is not what we're saying. We simply would like to hear what you think of Doris's plans. To hear what you really think.'

'Take it all,' she says again. 'All. The last six months you cannot take away from me. The rest, I don't mind. Take it.'

After this outburst they drop the subject.

DERVLA MURPHY

from *Wheels Within Wheels*

From Flanders I cycled to Bruges, Antwerp, Brussels, Luxemburg, Maastricht, Aachen, Bonn and so up the Rhine – which greatly disappointed me – to Mainz. There I spent a week-end with the Hilckmanns, whom we were to have visited in August 1939. Then on to Heidelberg, Rothenburg, Biberach, Regensburg, Creglingen (where Riemenschneider's Marienaltar excited me more than anything else on this trip), Munich, the Black Forest, Strasbourg and across central France. In Paris I spent four days feeling euphoric, except when I was kidnapped one night by White Slavers in the Place de la Concorde on my way back from the Opera to my left-bank doss-house.

It was midnight as I crossed the Place de la Concorde and when a large car pulled up just ahead of me I ignored it, assuming that some lustful male was in search of willing prey. Then a pleasant-looking woman beckoned me and, speaking in English with only a slight accent, warned me that it is very dangerous for girls to walk alone in Paris after midnight. 'Where are you staying?' she asked. 'You are taking a terrible risk. My husband and I would like to take you to your hotel.' I was too touched by this solicitude to point out that I *enjoyed* walking around Paris in the middle of the night. And because it would have seemed churlish to refuse such a kind offer I slipped into the back seat, explaining that I was lodging just off the rue St Jacques.

It struck me as rather odd that my protectress left the front seat to sit beside me, but I became suspicious only as we passed Notre Dame. As I began to protest that we had missed our turning my companion switched on an electric torch and opened a large photograph album which she laid on my knee. 'Look at those, my dear,' she said. 'We're just going to take you home for a little fun and a drink – some champagne, you would like? And then within an hour you shall be safely home in bed.'

While she was speaking I had been staring at the album with a mixture of horror, terror and nausea. I had never before seen pornographic photographs – or, indeed, even heard of them. Noticing my expression, the woman's voice changed. 'Look at me!' she said sharply. I looked up at her and she ordered, 'Keep on looking – don't move!' Terrified, I kept on looking; she was pointing one finger directly at my eyes and gazing fixedly at me by torchlight. When I realised that she was trying to hypnotise me I swung away and groped for the door-handle – though we had crossed the river and were travelling at some 40 mph up the Boulevard de la Bastille. Her voice changed again. 'You mustn't be afraid,' she soothed. 'We are going to have a nice party for only a little while. We are so fond of young people and we have no children for ourselves.'

I sat for a moment, calculating fast. If I tried to escape at this speed I would probably be killed. If I waited for the car to stop at its destination I would certainly be overpowered by both my captors. How often had I put the hero of an adventure story into just such a dilemma! But always I provided someone to rescue him – or at least staged an earthquake for the purpose – and there was no one to rescue me, nor any likelihood of an earthquake in Paris.

There were, however, two policemen standing in the Place de la République refereeing an argument between a taximan and his fare. As I reached again for the door-handle my 'protectress' grabbed me by the wrists. But at that age I had the strength of a young ox and very few women could have restrained me. Here we had to slow down almost to walking pace – traffic was streaming from the nearby railway stations – and when I had made it clear that I intended to escape the car stopped. As I scrambled out it half-turned and raced away down the Avenue de la République.

Had I been able to afford it I would have taken a taxi back to the rue St Jacques because my legs felt extraordinarily wobbly. But I had just enough money left to keep me in food until I got home. So I walked, only pausing to buy a bottle of plonk for my nerves in an all-night lorry-drivers' restaurant.

My landlady – whose mother had been for three years my father's landlady – did not believe that the kidnappers were professional White Slavers. Had they been, she said, they would not have shown me 'dirty pix' – at least at that stage – and would have drugged me as soon as I entered the car. In her view they were one of the amateur gangs who had recently begun to operate to supply brothels in – of all places – Soviet Central Asia.

This was the first time I became aware of a curious personal inhibition which I have never been able to overcome. When we reached the Place de la République and I saw the policemen it would have been simpler to yell for help than to struggle to open the car door. But even had my situation been much more desperate I could not have done so. And in various other awkward situations I have experienced the same difficulty. Something very deeply rooted and stupid – I have no idea what it is – prevents me from calling out for help.

RHODA COGHILL

Runaway

Somebody has got to tell me something real
and that very quickly.
Someone must show me a thing
that will not disappear when I touch it,
or fade into a cloud to walk through
when I have looked at it and
thought about it long enough.

You are not final:
you will be bones.
The feet I see marking the pavements
will walk too long
and not long enough,
and I will see the streets
clean in the morning, (tomorrow morning) after rain;
but the feet that marked the footpaths
will have stepped into the grave,
stepped into the grave,
before I have done with them.

Who is going to tell me where the dark horses of the spirit go?
Have I come into this room now?
Or was I always in this place?
And could you in your speech
have an inference different from mine?
Do you signify, proud other people,
what you appear to be,
or imply quite another meaning in your existence?

Place me on the edge of a cliff
and tell me now where to leap,
for the horses are pulling on the reins –
I have no wish to hold them.

THOMAS MOORE

She Is Far From the Land

Emmet would certainly have escaped to France, where he would again have been made welcome, had it not been for his consistent romanticism in visiting his sweetheart, Sarah Curran, at her house at Harold's Cross. Here he was captured by the efficient Major Sirr who earlier had taken Lord Edward Fitzgerald. Moore wrote the song in honour of Sarah Curran but the tune to which it is now customarily sung was not one of Moore's original *Melodies*.

She is far from the land where her young hero sleeps,
    And lovers are round her sighing;
But coldly she turns from their gaze and weeps,
    For her heart in his grave is lying!

She sings the wild song of her dear native plains,
    Every note which he loved awaking;
Ah! little they think, who delight in her strains,
    How the heart of the minstrel is breaking!

He had lived for his love, for his country he died;
    They were all that to life had entwined him;
Nor soon shall the tears of his country be dried,
    Nor long will his love stay behind him!

Oh! make her a grave where the sunbeams rest
    When they promise a glorious morrow;
They'll shine o'er her sleep, like a smile from the west,
    From her own loved island of sorrow.

LOUISE C. CALLAGHAN

The Palatine Daughter Marries a Catholic

1

I act as a stranger in your country.
It is my hair,
quite unlike anyone else's.
You say it is the wrong kind of water
to wash brass-coloured hair.
Rain water I suppose!

I was taken from my own Rhine-watered land
washed up on someone else's tide: A pale corpse
      cordially hated by the natives.
                           You said
I was a lily, my skin reminded you of beeswax.

But I have not the least sense of place,
never wear the same colour twice –
work wherever I find myself. Read
as if I don't exist. Make the land ripen,
the timeless hill-side a furze of apple-blossom,
the compost dark and smell-less
by constant turning – till I'm summoned
by marriage like a piece of furniture
to the nearby barony
the other side of Seefin.

2

Our bibles are all buried now.
My back is against the light of Glenosheen.
I have not given birth in this land.

And when you say you love me
I wonder what it is you think you love;
the land of no return,
the river of the Morningstar,
the warm-walled kitchen gardens, the flax-
patches of blue haze? Or is it
the grey canvas shoes
placed beneath my strange Palatine bed?

And yes, I will let you come to me –
(on someone else's tide). I am all yours.
Don't expect me to talk of love,
even in my sleep or honour your people's
oppositions. Here is no safe haven –
'an ordinary hope' – for settler or dispossessed.

Áine Ní Ghlinn

The Broken Step

I hear you coming up the stairs. You walk on the
broken step. Everyone avoids it but you walk on
it always.

You asked me my name. We were together and you
said I had blue eyes.

If you see the sunlight at the end of the day
and it awakens a poem in you . . .
> That is my name.

If you come to visit me and I know it is you
because I hear your footstep on the stairs . . .
> That is my name.

You said you understood and that my eyes were
blue. You walked on it again when you were leaving
in the morning.

You come into the room and I see in your eyes that
you were with her. You don't speak and you don't
look at my eyes. Her perfume flows from you.

The perfume is tall slender and well-formed and her
hair is long and curling. I hear you tell her that her
eyes are blue and that you love her.

I open the door and you walk out.

You can explain you say. I close the door.

You don't walk on it. You avoid the broken step.
Nobody walks on the broken step. They avoid it always.

JEAN O'BRIEN

Celebrating the Light of the Moon

Rita Ann asked, was it the moon
that brought her to the maternity;
and glad I was to hear her answer.
I had thought it was the 14A bus:
reared on stories of frantic journeys
at midnight, petrol running low
and the woman with not long to go,
pleading 'hurry, please hurry'.

Me constantly asking, 'but how will
I know?', brusque answers, 'Oh you will
know when the time is right.'
Me knowing damn well I wouldn't
and didn't.
The designated date long past,
at last bored I picked up my case
and boarded the 14A bus.
So glad I was for Rita Ann
that she had a bit of excitement,
all I saw was the low tide of the Liffey
as I paid the conductor, one fare
with defiance. Damned if I'd pay
a double yet, it still being daylight
and me on my own.

DAVID MARCUS

from *A Land Not Theirs*

Soon afterwards, when the time came for him to commence his secondary education, he had to face the ordeal that followed his mother's refusal to enrol him in the local St Dominic's which the other Jewish boys attended. Was it the best school in Cork? Bertha Cohen asked, in a tone that clearly dared any of her family to say it was. Of course, they couldn't. St Dominic's was average, at best adequate. They agreed that there were far better schools in the city. But she knew, didn't she, that they refused to take Jewish students?

'I shall go to Max Klein,' she declared. 'He's the President. Let *him* do something about it. Let him go to the Lord Mayor. Let him go to the Government. That's his duty. What does he think he's President for? Just for the *yichas*? Just for the honour?'

Jacob had recognised the familiar signs of battle in his mother's gestures – the way she flicked a wisp of black hair from her eyes as if to see the enemy more clearly, the way she rubbed her hands up and down her apron like a wrestler positioning for an opening. He wished she wouldn't get such ideas into her head. St Dominic's would have suited him. It was used to Jewish students; he would have companions there, boys he already knew. Joshua, too, was upset, and had thrown his eyes up to heaven in despair at his wife's obstinacy. He was heart-sore in advance for the defeat she was going to suffer, for the bitterness of soul that would be visited on her. She was not one to lose easily. When did she ever give best before? But this time . . . If Max Klein couldn't get his own sons into a better school – and everyone knew that Dora had insisted he try – then what chance had he of getting someone else's son in?

'You're wasting your time,' Joshua told his wife.

'We'll see,' was all Bertha Cohen replied.

'You're wasting your time, Mrs Cohen,' the President echoed after all his arguments had failed to move her.

His words only roused her to anger. Why were men such sheep?

'What do you mean? Why should my son not have the best? Isn't our money as good as the Christians'?'

In his impatience Max Klein almost made to grasp the lapel of Bertha Cohen's coat the better to persuade her of her wrongheadedness. But remembering that she was a woman, and a *baaleboosta* into the bargain, he continued to plead.

'Mrs Cohen, I can't help you. *Hub a bissl sechel* – have some sense. Send Jacob to St Dominic's. That's where all the *Yiddisheh* boys go. Why shouldn't he go there like all the others?' Like his own sons, he would have added, if he had thought his visitor wouldn't know of his own unsuccessful efforts to place them elsewhere.

Bertha Cohen gave him a cold look that said *her* son wasn't like all the others. The others' parents might be content with St Dominic's – she refrained from adding that in her opinion the President was a weakling to settle for it – but she had made her mind up. All she wanted was the best for her son, and St Dominic's was not the best.

'Of course it's not,' Max Klein agreed. 'But it's not the worst, either. Take my word for it.'

'The best. Only the best.' Her voice was firm. 'You tell me: *vos iz* the best?'

Max Klein sighed. What could he do with such a blockhead of a woman?

'I don't know which is the best, Mrs Cohen. There are two or three supposed to be very good. They're all run by *galuchim* or religious Orders. But I told you: you're wasting your time. They just don't take Jews!'

'Two or three! And none of them takes Jews. A *skandale*! What are their names, Mr Klein?'

'Well, there's Presentation Brothers College on the Western Road —'

'Thank you. That will do. Jacob shall go there.'

And there Jacob went.

ELIZABETH BOWEN

Her Table Spread

Miss Cuffe was an heiress to whom the Castle belonged and whose guests they all were. But she carefully followed the movements of her aunt, Mrs Treye; her ox-eyes moved from face to face in happy submission rather than expectancy. She was continually preoccupied with attempts at gravity, as though holding down her skirts in a high wind. Mrs Treye and Miss Carbin combined to cover her excitement; still, their looks frequently stole from the company to the windows, of which there were too many. He received a strong impression someone outside was waiting to come in. At last, with a sigh they got up: dinner had been announced.

The Castle was built on high ground, commanding the estuary; a steep hill, with trees, continued above it. On fine days the view was remarkable, of almost Italian brilliance, with that constant reflection up from the water that even now prolonged the too-long day. Now, in continuous evening rain, the winding wooded line of the further shore could be seen and, nearer the windows, a smothered island with the stump of a watch-tower. Where the Castle stood, a higher tower had answered the island's. Later a keep, then wings, had been added: now the fine peaceful residence had French windows opening on to the terrace. Invasions from the water would henceforth be social, perhaps amorous. On the slope down from the terrace, trees began again; almost, but not quite concealing the destroyer. Alban, who knew nothing, had not yet looked down.

It was Mr Rossiter who first spoke of the destroyer – Alban meanwhile glancing along the table; the preparations had been stupendous. The destroyer had come today. The ladies all turned to Alban: the beads on their bosoms sparkled. So this was what they had here, under their trees. Engulfed by their pleasure, from now on he disappeared personally. Mr Rossiter, rising a note, continued. The estuary, it appeared, was deep, with a channel buoyed up it. By a term of the Treaty, English ships were permitted to anchor in these waters.

'But they've been afraid of the rain!' chimed in Valeria Cuffe.

'Hush,' said her aunt, 'that's silly. Sailors would be accustomed to getting wet.'

But, Miss Carbin reported, that spring there *had* already been one destroyer. Two of the officers had been seen dancing at the hotel at the head of the estuary.

'So,' said Alban, 'you are quite in the world.' He adjusted his glasses in her direction.

Miss Carbin – blonde, not forty, and an attachment of Mrs Treye's – shook her head despondently. 'We were all away at Easter. Wasn't it curious they should have come then? The sailors walked in the demesne but never touched the daffodils.'

'As though I should have cared!' exclaimed Valeria passionately.

'Morale too good,' stated Mr Rossiter.

'But next evening,' continued Miss Carbin, 'the officers did not go to the hotel. They climbed up here through the trees to the terrace – you see, they had no idea. Friends of ours were staying

here at the Castle, and they apologised. Our friends invited them
in to supper . . . '

'Did they accept?'

The three ladies said in a breath: 'Yes, they came.'

Valeria added urgently, 'So don't you *think* –'

'So tonight we have a destroyer to greet you,' Mrs Treye said
quickly to Alban. 'It is quite an event; the country people are
coming down from the mountains. These waters are very lonely;
the steamers have given up since the bad times; there is hardly a
pleasure boat. The weather this year has driven visitors right
away.'

'You are beautifully remote.'

'Yes,' agreed Miss Carbin. 'Do you know much about the Navy?
Do you think, for instance, that this is likely to be the same
destroyer?'

'*Will they remember?*' Valeria's bust was almost on the table. But
with a rustle Mrs Treye pressed Valeria's toe. For the diningroom
also looked out across the estuary, and the great girl had not once
taken her eyes from the window.

Grania

TRANSLATED BY FRANK O'CONNOR

Grania is the original Iseult of the Tristan legend. Married to the
elderly Fionn, she drugged the watchmen's drink and eloped with
her lover Diarmuid. In the Lullaby we are to understand that they
are being followed by Fionn and the Fianna, whose quest has set all
nature in a tumult, but she sings Diarmuid to sleep with
memories of the great lovers of Irish history.

This was the basis of Yeats's beautiful 'Lullaby', which he wrote
after reading my first version of the poem. But I was never satisfied
with that; nor am I particularly satisfied with this, except that it is
closer in spirit to the original.

Stag does not lay his side to sleep;
    He bellows from the mountainside,
And tramples through the woods, and yet
    In no green thicket can he hide.

Not even the birds within their house —
    From bough to bough all night they leap,
And stir the air with startled cries.
    Among the leaves they will not sleep.

The duck that bears her brood tonight
    By many a sheltering bank must creep,
And furrow the wild waters bright;
    Among the reeds she will not sleep.

The curlew cannot sleep at all
    His voice is shrill above the deep
Reverberations of the storm;
    Between the streams he will not sleep.

But you must sleep as in the south
    He who from Conall long ago
With all the arts of speech and song
    Made Morann's daughter rise and go.

Or sleep the sleep that Fionncha found
    In Ulster with his stolen bride,
When Slaney ran from home with him
    And slept no more at Falvey's side.

Or sleep the sleep that Aunya slept
    When with the torchlight round her head,
From Garnish and her father's house
    To her beloved's arms she fled.

Or Dedaid's sleep who in the east
    Did not think for one sweet night,
His head upon his lover's breast
    Of the terrors of the flight.

SUSAN CONNOLLY

Lily

Into this world I came
and my mother wrote
my name
in the blood-sunrise
which tore us apart.

I found intimacy
with a woman
hired to look after
children.
    Aged six,
my only wish
'to sleep with you'
made her laugh,
so she carried me
far away.

Twelve years old
I shivered in a heatwave.
She was leaving,
returning home.
    Within,
I held her gently;
but there, I hugged her
fiercely: 'Don't Go.'

Now each goodbye
brings back
her name till
like a caged
animal
I bellow out
my pain.

OLIVER GOLDSMITH

Stanzas on Woman

When lovely Woman stoops to folly,
  And finds too late that men betray,
What charm can soothe her melancholy,
  What art can wash her guilt away?

· The only art her guilt to cover,
  To hide her shame from every eye,
To give repentance to her lover,
  And wring his bosom – is, to die.

SEAN O'CASEY

from *The Plough and the Stars*

CLITHEROE. I don't understand this. Why does General Connolly call me Commandant?
CAPT. BRENNAN. Th' Staff appointed you Commandant, and th' General agreed with their selection.
CLITHEROE. When did this happen?

CAPT. BRENNAN. A fortnight ago.

CLITHEROE. How is it word was never sent to me?

CAPT. BRENNAN. Word was sent to you . . . I meself brought it.

CLITHEROE. Who did you give it to, then?

CAPT. BRENNAN (*after a pause*). I think I gave it to Mrs Clitheroe, there.

CLITHEROE. Nora, d'ye hear that? (*Nora makes no answer.*)

CLITHEROE (*there is a note of hardness in his voice*). Nora . . . Captain Brennan says he brought a letter to me from General Connolly, and that he gave it to you . . . Where is it? What did you do with it?

NORA (*running over to him, and pleadingly putting her arms around him*). Jack, please, Jack, don't go out to-night an' I'll tell you; I'll explain everything . . . Send him away, an' stay with your own little red-lipp'd Nora.

CLITHEROE (*removing her arms from around him*). None o' this nonsense, now; I want to know what you did with th' letter? (*Nora goes slowly to the lounge and sits down.*)

CLITHEROE (*angrily*). Why didn't you give me th' letter? What did you do with it? . . . (*He shakes her by the shoulder.*) What did you do with th' letter?

NORA (*flaming up*). I burned it, I burned it! That's what I did with it! Is General Connolly an' th' Citizen Army goin' to be your only care? Is your home goin' to be only a place to rest in? Am I goin' to be only somethin' to provide merry-makin' at night for you? Your vanity'll be th' ruin of you an' me yet . . . That's what's movin' you: because they've made an officer of you, you'll make a glorious cause of what you're doin', while your little red-lipp'd Nora can go on sittin' here, makin' a companion of th' loneliness of th' night!

CLITHEROE (*fiercely*). You burned it, did you? (*He grips her arm.*) Well, me good lady —

NORA. Let go — you're hurtin' me!

CLITHEROE. You deserve to be hurt . . . Any letter that comes to me for th' future, take care that I get it. . . . D'ye hear — take care that I get it!

(*He goes to the chest of drawers and takes out a Sam Browne belt, which he puts on, and then puts a revolver in the holster. He puts on his hat, and*

*looks towards Nora. While this dialogue is proceeding, and while
Clitheroe prepares himself, Brennan softly whistles 'The Soldiers' Song'.)*
CLITHEROE (*at door, about to go out*). You needn't wait up for me; if
I'm in at all, it won't be before six in th' morning.
NORA (*bitterly*). I don't care if you never come back.

ANON

Let Him Go, Let Him Tarry

Farewell to cold winter, summer's come at last,
Nothing have I gained, but my true love I have lost.
I'll sing and I'll be happy like the birds upon the tree,
But since he deceived me I care no more for he.

Chorus

Let him go, let him tarry,
Let him sink or let him swim,
He doesn't care for me nor I don't care for him,
He can go and get another, that I hope he will enjoy,
For I'm going to marry a far nicer boy.

He wrote me a letter saying he was very bad,
I sent him back an answer saying I was awful glad.
He wrote to me another saying he was well and strong,
But I care no more about him than the ground he walks upon.

Chorus

Some of his friends they had a very good kind wish for me,
Other of his friends, they could hang me on a tree;
But soon I'll let them see my love and soon I'll let them know
That I can get a new sweetheart on any ground I go.

Chorus

He can go to his old mother now, and set her mind at ease,
I hear she is an old, old woman, very hard to please.
It's slighting me and talking ill is what she's always done.
Because that I was courting her great big ugly son.

Chorus

LINDA ANDERSON

Blinding – Lucy

I put out my eyes. Because I must be invisible. Out of your sight.
Now you dare not see me. I am what you cannot countenance.
Rape of the head. Bulges around the weeping slits. The slimy
severed stalks of my eyes.

I am a honeycomb of holes. A holey woman. Pores, sense
organs, orifices. The gape between the legs. The cavity of the
womb. Multitude of entrances. Entrancements. Honeycomb.

There is a man who loves me. He compared me to milk and
honey. He steals milk from the goats, plunders honey from the
bees. He thought I was a flow of nurture and sweetness.

I am fire and gall. He called my hair a redgold flame and said
my eyes burned as if from caverns. But he imagined a tame
fireside, not a blazing forest.

He loves me so much, my devoted suitor! He loves me to death.
'I have eyes only for you,' he said, blocking out the sun. Love! He
is an old man, lonely and afraid. He wants to hide from death by
draping my flesh over his.

I refused to marry. I would not lie impaled beneath him,
inhaling his dirty breath. I did not want to wake up with him
thick upon me. I would not bear a flock of children. Tiny hands to
scatter me. I am I. Sole. Unwon.

I was happy before his glance felled me. When I was a child I visited the shrine of Saint Bridget and I heard her speak to me. She whispered: 'Lucy, you will be a light unto the world!'

A light unto the world! Not one old man's delight!

O little, little man! Love made him spiteful. He denounced me to the persecuting authority. The judge ordered me to be violated in a brothel. Tortured. Hot lead poured into my eyes. My breasts slashed. Love broke me to bits. Cracked my I. Turned my aye into Please No Please No Please No . . .

I gutted my eyes. I wanted to tear out the tear ducts forever! I sent the mess to my lover. Titbits on a dish. Two glistening globes. Yes, feast your gaze on that! You will never be rid of my terrible stare.

But why has no one ever seen *me*? I live in my body, not his mind! Nor yours! Do not cast me as a saint. Some scrawny icon with neat wounds and no breasts. Don't invent a serene uplifted face. Don't add a golden nimbus nor any downpour of heavenly balm to cancel my pain. Forget miracles! No missing eye grows back.

And do not tell yourself that I was passionless! There was a man who could make me howl and claw the ground. I was true to him though we never met.

I lie here quietly on my bier. The fragrance of flowers penetrates my chamber although the door is sealed. I thought I would be free. That they would let me rot on this border between life and death. But my punishment is not over. The judge has ordered me to be burnt. 'Better to marry than to burn' the churchmen say. Now I know what they mean.

Eibhlín Dubh Ní Chonaill

A Cry for Art O'Leary

TRANSLATED BY Brendan Kennelly

White rider of love!

I love your silver-hilted sword
How your beaver hat became you
With its band of gold
Your friendly homespun suit
Revealed your body
Your pin of glinting silver
Glittered in your shirt

On your horse in style
You were sensitive pale-faced
Having journeyed overseas
The English respected you
Bowing to the ground
Not because they loved you
But true to their hearts' hate

They're the ones who killed you
Darling of my heart

My lover
My love's creature
Pride of Immokelly
To me you were not dead
Till your great mare came to me
Her bridle dragging ground
Her head with your startling blood
Your blood upon the saddle
You rode in your prime

I didn't wait to clean it
I leaped across my bed
I leaped then to the gate
I leaped upon your mare
I clapped my hands in frenzy
I followed every sign
With all the skill I knew
Until I found you lying
Dead near a furze bush
Without pope or bishop
Or cleric or priest
To say a prayer for you

Only a crooked wasted hag
Throwing her cloak across you

I could do nothing then
In the sight of God
But go on my knees
And kiss your face
And drink your free blood

My man!
Going out the gate
You turned back again
Kissed the two children
Threw a kiss at me
Saying 'Eileen, woman, try
To get this house in order
Do your best for us
I must be going now
I'll not be home again'
I thought that you were joking
You my laughing man

My man!
My Art O'Leary!
Up on your horse now
Ride out to Macroom
And then to Inchigeela
Take a bottle of wine
Like your people before you
Rise up
My Art O'Leary
Of the sword of love

Put on your clothes
Your black beaver
Your black gloves
Take down your whip
Your mare is waiting
Go east by the thin road
Every bush will salute you
Every stream will speak to you
Men and women acknowledge you

They know a great man
When they set eyes on him
God's curse on you, Morris,
God's curse on your treachery
You swept my man from me
The man of my children
Two children play in the house
A third lives in me

He won't come alive from me

My heart's wound
Why was I not with you
When you were shot
That I might take the bullet
In my own body?

Then you'd have gone free
Rider of the grey eye
And followed them
Who'd murdered me

My man!
I look at you now
All I know of a hero
True man with true heart
Stuck in a coffin
You fished the clean streams
Drank nightlong in halls
Among frank-breasted women

I miss you

My man!

DERMOT BOLGER

The Lament for Arthur Cleary

My lament for you Arthur Cleary
As you lay down that crooked back lane
Under the stern wall of a factory
Where moss and crippled flowers cling

To stone crested by glass and wire
With a runlet of blood over your chest
When I raced screaming towards you
Hearing their cluster of boots retreat

I cupped your face in my palms
To taste life draining from your lips
And you died attempting to smile
As defiant and proud as you had lived

Behind me I could hear the cry
Of an engine kick-starting to life
And vanishing through laneways
Where we had rode on autumn nights

May it have led them mesmerised
Beneath railway bridges to the river
And skidded over oily cobbles
To drown those who killed its master

You were the only man I knew
The rest were all dancing clones
Lions swaggering in packs
Kittens petrified on their own

Unable to glance at a girl
Unless cocky with drink or stoned
But you stared into my face
Caught in the strobe lights alone

Not leering or smart-assed
Nor mumbling like a blushing bride
Leading me onto that floor
Where firm hands brushed my thighs

Gormlaith

Poem IX

(Fifteenth Century)

Translated by Osborn Bergin

Heavy to-night is my sighing, O God! It is heavier to-day than yesterday. Through grief for the son of bright Niall Glúndubh I desire to go alive into the earth.

My friends grow fewer and fewer, since I no more have sight of Niall: my fair bright ear hears nothing at which I laugh.

Dead is my father, dead my mother, dead are my two brothers, dead my fosterer, honoured and revered, dead my two fosterbrothers.

Dead alas! is Dubh Chabhlaigh the just, who would set me upon a golden vat, and would give me no morsel without honey, Dubh Chabhlaigh of fair bright skin.

Dead the son of the king of Innsi Gall, he the son of Amhlaeibh of Arann; Amhlaeibh's son used to be on . . . of my fair knee like a beloved son.

Though all these have gone from the glorious yellow-topped earth, sorer to me is it that dear Domhnall should be one night under the earth.

Though bitter every sickness and strife that is given to living man, the child that is born of one's fair body, that is what lives in one's mind.

Had I sent my darling to the men of Meath, the race of upright Colmán would have guarded and kept my lad.

Alas for her who entrusts to a foolish woman the keeping of her tender child, since the protection of life should be enjoined upon a king's son or a royal heir.

Woe to her who allowed the gentle sweet-voiced lad to go into Uí Fiachrach, a land where water is plentiful, and men are unruly.

Domhnall son of Niall Glúndubh the bright, son of Aed Finnliath of Febhal, son of Niall Caille — motionless! — son of noble Aed Oirdnide.

Son of Niall Frasach from Ráith Mór, who bestowed honour upon poets, son of Fergal who was prince of Femen, son of hospitable Mael Dúin.

Son of Mael Fithrigh, son of Aed, son of Domhnall the generous and comely, son of Muirchertach the Great from the plain, son of Muiredach, son of Eogan.

Son of Niall of the Nine Hostages, the festive, son of Eochaidh Muighmheadhón: the grandmother of dear Domhnall was daughter of Alpin from Scotland.

There is the pedigree of my own son, whose death darkens the sun. White was his neck, white his foot. My heart has found nought so heavy.

EMILY LAWLESS

After Aughrim

She said, 'They gave me of their best,
They lived, they gave their lives for me;
I tossed them to the howling waste,
And flung them to the foaming sea.'

She said, 'I never gave them aught,
Not mine the power, if mine the will;
I let them starve, I let them bleed, –
They bled and starved, and loved me still.'

She said, 'Ten times they fought for me,
Ten times they strove with might and main,
Ten times I saw them beaten down,
Ten times they rose, and fought again.'

She said, 'I stayed alone at home,
A dreary woman, grey and cold;
I never asked them how they fared,
Yet still they loved me as of old.'

She said, 'I never called them sons,
I almost ceased to breathe their name,
Then caught it echoing down the wind,
Blown backwards from the lips of Fame.'

She said, 'Not mine, not mine that fame;
Far over sea, far over land,
Cast forth like rubbish from my shores,
They won it yonder, sword in hand.'

She said, 'God knows they owe me nought,
I tossed them to the foaming sea,
I tossed them to the foaming waste,
Yet still their love comes home to me.'

CHRISTY MOORE AND NIGEL ROLFE

Middle of the Island

Everybody knew and nobody said,
A week ago last Tuesday,
She was just fifteen years,
When she reached full bloom,
She went to a grotto,
In a field,
In the middle of the island,
To deliver herself,
She died,
Her baby died,
A week ago last Tuesday.
It was a sad, slow, stupid death for them both,
Everybody knew,
Nobody said,
A week ago last Tuesday.
At a grotto,
In a field,
In the middle of the island.

RUTH RIDDICK

from *Towards a Feminist Morality of Choice*

A common theme running through women's decision-making process concerning crisis pregnancy is worry about how the pregnancy brought to term, would affect others, principally parents and existing children. Summarising the reasons given for considering abortion, Open Line Counselling reported as follows:

Many younger women feel unprepared for a child, particularly where family and social support is unlikely or insufficient. Many women are also anxious to avoid causing hurt to their parents, especially where a parent has health problems. Older women are worried about the effects of another pregnancy on a grown family, and also about the possibility of a sub-normal child. Instability in the relationship with the putative father, whether casual acquaintance, ex-boyfriend, or where a marriage is under stress, is another common factor.

Separated women with an extra-marital pregnancy are concerned about the irregular status of their relationship with the putative father and also about the threat to their separation agreements if the husband is unsympathetic to the pregnancy. Professional women are increasingly concerned about their future training and employment prospects, particularly in nursing and teaching. Most women decide to seek termination of pregnancy because of a multiplicity of these pressures. (October 1983)

While children born out of wedlock are no longer stigmatised in law as 'illegitimate', post-referendum Ireland has not been notable for its regard for its mothers. A number of tragic cases, from the death in childbirth of a fifteen-year-old girl to the sacking of a teacher for giving birth to the child of a separated man, have come to light since the Human Life amendment of 1983. The lessons of these cases, and the social attitudes they reveal, are not lost on other women with unplanned pregnancies.

Although not all of these considerations will be foremost in a woman's mind when she is exploring her options in a crisis pregnancy, they help form the context in which her decisions must be made. Furthermore, in a patriarchal society, there is the problem of the role of men in women's lives which is at best ambiguous, at worst, fatal. In the social arena and mirroring women's domestic responsibilities, the so-called 'caring' professions are, at the helping level, almost exclusively staffed by women. Primary care is given by women; status and authority is male.

On a more sinister level, the European witchcraze of 1450–1750, described by Matilda Joslyn Gage in 1893 as 'the age of supreme despair for women', saw the slaughter by men of a minimum of 200,000 women. In the 1970s a new genre of pornography, depicting the real-life murder of women by men, 'snuff movies', brought the witchcraze to the domestic video screen. Men rape, murder, abandon, dominate, disenfranchise women.

Successful women, riding on the achievements of feminism, boast that they are 'just one of the boys', that women 'make dreadful bosses', that as a woman you have to be twice as good but so what? When was the last time a patently high achieving male boasted that he was 'just one of the girls'? For all our delirious need to believe that men like us, respect us, treasure us, the evidence suggests to the contrary. 'He's just a woman' is a term of abuse, not of respect. And where there is no liking, no respect, there is instead fear and loathing; there is unlikely to be any acknowledgement of rights, of agency, certainly no espousal, no guarantee.

Julie O'Callaghan

Yuppie Considering Life in her Loft Apartment

Jeff is such a bastard.
Like I can't handle it.
All I did was throw the silver fork
he'd left stuck for a week
in the mud at the base
of my weeping willow tree
in the general direction of his chest
and while it was en route added
'What am I, your maid, lunkhead?'

He, as usual, moved *before* the fork
crash landed on his bicep and said,
'No prob, no prob', and those were
his last words to me on his way
out of my orbit and into the
gravitational pull of some dumb broad.
Advice has been pouring in:
'One look and I told you –
he's a no-goodnik, but you said you
liked his shoes, so there's no point
talking to you is there?';
and, 'Cancel him offa yer floppy disk,
revise your memory bank
and write a new programme –
who needs the louse anyway?';
and, 'Join the club. Ya wanna
come with me for a facial? –
Elizabeth Arden have a special offer.'
The part that really gets to me
is that I forget everything I learned
in that Psychology course I took last year:
'The Male Ego and How to Cope With It'.

SINÉAD MORRISSEY

Ciara

We wandered in one Christmas afternoon
On our way to the lakes to ask for her company
But she was crying over potatoes.
My parents stayed with her till they took her away.
There would be no walk.

I noticed a fishtank, her old blue slippers,
The bewildered mother and the silent child,
Formed an image in my head of boiling potatoes
And I wondered about their powers of catastrophe.

Then, bored, I walked the outside wall,
Under the beginnings of stars,
Until a white van pulled in along the gutter.
She was shuttered off from view.
Ruined Christmas.

The potatoes stuck in my mind.
Something easier for her to articulate
Than the mess of love and various motherhood,
Than the son who had his knees blown somewhere else.

A frightening rain, pouring out of the Armagh sky,
Had filled the lives of Ciara's household.
One shattered woman a fraying edge of the legacy.

HEATHER BRETT

No Vacancies

There is only one chair by the fire,
my chair; the children sprawl on the sofa
or the floor, soles upwards and there is
a lack of family portraits.
There is no man in this scene.

This morning I opened the windows wide
to let your scent go, but all day I could
smell you, could feel your skin on mine like
a pressure, like the imprint of fingers
after the grasp is removed.

Tonight I sit in my chair, in my house
The children draw and chat about the
coming communion. There is an audible silence
when they are quiet and I wonder it is me
who wedge open these small spaces – and for what?

I did not give you my chair last night.
There are boundaries everywhere that you
cannot cross and I am quick to mention them
too quick, perhaps, to put you in your place
too quick, also, to assume mine.

But alone I look fondly on the things I
have here, the bits and pieces that we have
accumulated and collectively call mine.
The walls are missing nothing, the house
is furnished, we call it Home.

All the rooms are taken and each bed spoken for
any cracks have long since been papered over or
filled in. We have no space left, no empty drawers
or anywhere where another might make himself at home:
There are no candles burning in the window.

ROSITA BOLAND

from *Sea Legs: Hitch-Hiking Around the Coast of Ireland Alone*

I had been hitching for perhaps fifteen minutes when a car flashed
its lights at me and the driver gestured in front of him. When I
turned to see what it was that he was pointing out to me, I saw
that a red car had pulled into the kerb some yards down the road

and was waiting for me. Usually, when drivers wish to give you a lift, they signal to you that they will pull in by putting their indicators on. I thought it somewhat odd that this driver had not done so, nor, as a second sign, had he sounded his horn after pulling in.

I went up to the car, opened the door and looked across at the driver. Some purely animal instinct of warning jolted through me, sensing something peculiar. It was nothing that would hold any credibility or that I could explain logically, but all I knew was that I instantly felt frightened and unnerved.

'Where are you going?' he asked.

Almost always, I managed to be the one to ask this question first. It allowed me an opportunity to size up the driver and to decide whether or not I wanted this lift, without giving away any information about my destination. But I had been so rattled in this instance that I hadn't been able to say a word and now found myself automatically answering 'Ballycastle', although it was the last thing I actually wanted to say.

'Get in and I'll bring you part of the way.'

The driver's eyes were unfocused and he looked somewhat drunk, although I could get no smell of drink. Other than that, he looked perfectly ordinary, but something made me absolutely determined not to get into the car. 'Where *exactly* are you going?' I asked, playing for time.

He sighed. 'Look, I'll bring you all the way to Ballycastle if that's what you want. I'm on a day off and I'm just driving around, so I've plenty of time. Just get in and I'll bring you all the way.'

I stared at him. 'No,' I said. 'No thanks,' and I shut the door and walked back up the road again towards Coleraine.

When I glanced around a few minutes later, he was still there, watching me. As soon as he saw me looking back, he reversed the car until it was level with me, and beckoned. I shook my head, noted the number plate and make of the car, and kept walking. I found that I was shaking. When I looked around again, the car had disappeared and its driver now knew where I was trying to hitch to. Ballycastle suddenly seemed a very long seventeen miles away.

Nothing had actually happened to me. I had not been threatened or physically forced in any way. But despite this, I felt the
vital confidence and nerve which a hitch-hiker has got to possess in
order to hitch in safety and enjoyment, just draining away.

Hitching, you set out to arrogantly cross uncertain distances by
placing your faith in your ability to swim: to choose the right lifts.
But I had floundered and taken in water and was now aware that
there was the possibility of not always making it safely to the other
side. But with a good half of the Irish coastline still to see, the only
thing to do was to keep hitching. So I hauled myself onto the
floating driftwood of the roadside and struck out again, but this
time with less confidence and more fear. I hitched nervously, but
not the red cars, and am quite certain my face was set in such a
grim expression that people gave me one look and kept going,
since it took a very long time to get a lift. By this time, I was
beginning to consider the unhappy possibility of having to get a
bus.

The car that stopped had a woman driver and I was so relieved
that I found myself telling her about the other car.

'Oh, but you must report him!' she exclaimed. 'Haven't you
heard about that German girl who was raped and murdered in
1988? She came off the ferry at Larne and was hitching up north.
They found her body in the back of Ballypatrick Wood, just south
of Ballycastle. They never found who did it. I wouldn't hitch
round here for *anything*!'

REPORT OF THE TRIBUNAL OF ENQUIRY INTO THE KERRY BABIES CASE

Bridie Fuller assisted at the birth of the baby in Joanne Hayes'
bedroom in the farmhouse, which took place between midnight
on Thursday, the 12th April 1984 and 2:30am on Friday, the
13th April 1984 (5/44: 22/119). The placenta, or afterbirth, came
within ten minutes or so of the birth of the baby and before the
umbilical cord had been cut (10/365). Bridie Fuller cut the

umbilical cord with scissors after some further delay (22/95 and 96: Appendix K, No. 3) because the baby when born appeared in her own words to be 'chesty' (22/100).

The baby was not well at all. It had great difficulty in breathing and although it cried it never succeeded in establishing its breathing properly (22/501 and 662: 24/168 to 172 and 356 and 364). Bridie Fuller cut the umbilical cord exceptionally long, partly because she was not experienced as a maternity nurse and also because the baby was chesty and was doing badly and hence she cut it fairly far away from the body of the baby (24/121 and 122 and 372 to 375 and 391 and 456 and 461 to 474). She did not in fact remember to tie the umbilical cord before cutting it, but as there had been some delay between the delivery of the afterbirth and the cutting of the cord, this did not make much difference to the baby.

Bridie Fuller would have liked to have had available to her a suction tube to try to clear the baby's lungs, but there was none available (22/105 and 106). The baby itself seemed unable to clear its lungs and no effort was made by any of the family to get any form of medical assistance, or more skilled maternity assistance for the baby. Bridie Fuller thought that the baby may have survived for many hours, but in fact it survived at most a couple of hours and more probably no more than half an hour to one hour.

Joanne Hayes' mother, Mrs Mary Hayes, was very annoyed with Joanne Hayes and expressed her annoyance at the prospect of having to rear another child for Jeremiah Locke, especially when the child did not appear to be strong. Bridie Fuller and Kathleen Hayes also showed their displeasure to Joanne Hayes at her having another baby by Jeremiah Locke. Bridie Fuller left the room and went either to her own bedroom or to the kitchen (Appendix K, No. 6, No. 7, No. 10 and No. 11).

Joanne Hayes got into a panic and as the baby cried again she put her hands around its neck and stopped it crying by choking it (22/662 to 665) and the baby did not breathe again (40/144 to 156). At some stage during the course of these events, Joanne Hayes used the bath brush from the bathroom to hit the baby to make sure that it was dead. None of the family tried to stop Joanne

Hayes from either choking or hitting the baby (Appendix K, No. 6 and No. 10).

The whole family now got into a panic. Bridie Fuller had already left the room before the baby died. Ned Hayes was still sleeping below in the cottage and it was decided that he should be sent for, as the eldest son and person of considerable intelligence and imagination. Accordingly, Kathleen Hayes and perhaps also Mrs Mary Hayes, despite the 'flu, or perhaps Michael Hayes, went from the farmhouse down to the cottage to call Ned Hayes and to tell him that Joanne Hayes had had a baby and had killed it. The time was then between 2:30am and 3am on Friday, the 13th April, 1984.

Ned Hayes got up and went from the cottage to the farmhouse and into Joanne Hayes' bedroom where he saw the dead baby. On seeing the dead baby, Ned Hayes said:

'Why in fuck's name did you do a thing like that, we could have reared it?' . . .

Although Joanne Hayes is not the mother of the Cahirciveen Baby and had nothing to do with it, she was nevertheless persuaded into believing that she was its mother and had killed it. She was very vulnerable to persuasion into this belief in view of what she had done to her own baby, the Tralee Baby. Moreover, the fact that it had been firmly agreed between Joanne Hayes and the other members of the Hayes family and Bridie Fuller that Joanne Hayes would say that she had had the baby out in the field and that no one else knew anything about it and that each of the others would say they knew nothing at all about it, rebounded against Joanne Hayes when she heard that her brother Ned Hayes and her mother Mrs Mary Hayes had abandoned this agreed story and were talking about the baby being born in the house and killed in the house. The abandonment by other members of the family of what was supposed to be the firm, agreed story, left Joanne Hayes vulnerable and confused not merely as to what she should say to the Gardaí but as to what had actually happened. She was very suggestible (42/364: 54/219: 55/48) and she understood full well what the Detectives believed she had done and were saying or hinting to her that she had done . . .

The findings in this Report mean that the death of the Cahirciveen Baby remains unsolved. Some people may think that it is too much of a coincidence that two women in County Kerry should have had babies and should have done away with their babies about the same time. But is it all that much of a coincidence?

The most recent available public statistical records show that in the year 1981, there were 2,403 registered births in County Kerry, of which 81 were illegitimate. The number of illegitimate births at 81 represents 3.37% of the total number of registered births at 2,403.

In the year 1981 the illegitimacy rate of registered births for the Republic of Ireland as a whole was 5.24%. In the year 1984 the illegitimacy rate of registered births for the Republic of Ireland as a whole rose to 7.8%. The increase from 5.24% in 1981 to 7.8% in 1984 in itself represents an increase of 44% on the rate of 5.24%. If, therefore, one takes the illegitimacy rate in County Kerry for 1981, namely 3.37% and increases it by 44%, one arrives at an illegitimacy birth rate for County Kerry for the year 1984 of 4.85%.

In the year 1984, there were 2,129 registered births in County Kerry, but the number of illegitimate births for County Kerry is not yet known. If, however, one assumes that the illegitimacy rate of registered births for County Kerry in 1984 was 4.85%, this would give 103 illegitimate registered births in County Kerry in the year 1984, or in other words, two illegitimate registered births per week.

Neither the birth of the Cahirciveen Baby, nor the birth of the Tralee Baby was registered. In fact, there is no evidence to show whether the Cahirciveen Baby was legitimate or illegitimate, or indeed, where it was born. It is, however, probable that it was born in County Kerry and was illegitimate. On average therefore, there were probably at least two illegitimate births per week in County Kerry in the year 1984. What is so unbelievably extraordinary about two women in County Kerry in one of the weeks in 1984 both deciding to do away with their babies?

The Tribunal accepts that it is something of a coincidence, but does not accept that there is anything really unbelievable about it.

J. M. SYNGE

from *Riders to the Sea*

CATHLEEN (*begins to keen*): It's destroyed we are from this day. It's destroyed, surely.

NORA: Didn't the young priest say the Almighty God won't leave her destitute with no son living?

MAURYA (*in a low voice but clearly*): It's little the like of him knows of the sea . . . Bartley will be lost now, and let you call in Eamon and make me a good coffin out of the white boards, for I won't live after them. I've had a husband, and a husband's father, and six sons in this house – six fine men, though it was a hard birth I had with every one of them and they coming into the world – and some of them were found and some of them were not found, but they're gone now the lot of them . . . There were Stephen and Shawn were lost in the great wind, and found after in the Bay of Gregory of the Golden Mouth, and carried up the two of them on one plank, and in by that door.

(*She pauses for a moment; the girls start as if they heard something through the door that is half open behind them.*)

NORA (*in a whisper*): Did you hear that, Cathleen? Did you hear a noise in the north-east?

CATHLEEN (*in a whisper*): There's someone after crying out by the seashore.

MAURYA (*continues without hearing anything*): There was Sheamus and his father, and his own father again, were lost in a dark night, and not a stick or sign was seen of them when the sun went up. There was Patch after was drowned out of a curragh that turned over. I was sitting here with Bartley, and he a baby, lying on my two knees, and I seen two women, and three women, and four women coming in, and they crossing themselves and not saying a word. I looked out then, and there were men coming after them, and they holding a thing in the half of a red sail, and water dripping out of it – it was a dry day, Nora – and leaving a track to the door.

(She pauses again with her hand stretched out towards the door. It opens softly and old women begin to come in, crossing themselves on the threshold, and kneeling down in front of the stage with red petticoats over their heads.)

Half in a dream, to Cathleen. Is it Patch, or Michael, or what is it at all?

CATHLEEN: Michael is after being found in the far north, and when he is found there how could he be here in this place?

MAURYA: There does be a power of young men floating round in the sea, and what way would they know if it was Michael they had, or another man like him, for when a man is nine days in the sea, and the wind blowing, it's hard set his own mother would be to say what man was in it.

CATHLEEN: It's Michael, God spare him, for they're after sending us a bit of his clothes from the far north.

(She reaches out and hands Maurya the clothes that belonged to Michael. Maurya stands up slowly, and takes them in her hands. Nora looks out.)

NORA: They're carrying a thing among them, and there's water dripping out of it and leaving a track by the big stones.

CATHLEEN (*in a whisper to the women who have come in*): Is it Bartley it is?

ONE OF THE WOMEN. It is, surely, God rest his soul.

(Two younger women come in and pull out the table. Then men carry in the body of Bartley, laid on a plank, with a bit of a sail over it, and lay it on the table.)

CATHLEEN (*to the women as they are doing so*): What way was he drowned?

ONE OF THE WOMEN: The grey pony knocked him over into the sea, and he was washed out where there is a great surf on the white rocks.

(*Maurya has gone over and knelt down at the head of the table. The women are keening softly and swaying themselves with a slow movement. Cathleen and Nora kneel at the other side of the table. The men kneel near the door.*)

MAURYA (*raising her head and speaking as if she did not see the people around her*): They're all gone now, and there isn't anything more the sea can do to me . . . I'll have no call now to be up crying and praying when the wind breaks from the south, and you can hear the surf is in the east, and the surf is in the west, making a great stir with the two noises, and they hitting one on the other. I'll have no call now to be going down and getting Holy Water in the dark nights after Samhain, and I won't care what way the sea is when the other women will be keening. (*To Nora.*) Give me the Holy Water, Nora; there's a small sup still on the dresser.

(*Nora gives it to her.*)

(*Drops Michael's clothes across Bartley's feet, and sprinkles the Holy Water over him.*)
It isn't that I haven't prayed for you, Bartley, to the Almighty God. It isn't that I haven't said prayers in the dark night till you wouldn't know what I'd be saying; but it's a great rest I'll have now, and it's time, surely. It's a great rest I'll have now, and great sleeping in the long nights after Samhain, if it's only a bit of wet flour we do have to eat, and maybe a fish that would be stinking. (*She kneels down again, crossing herself, and saying prayers under her breath.*)
CATHLEEN (*to an old man*): Maybe yourself and Eamon would make a coffin when the sun rises. We have fine white boards herself bought, God help her, thinking Michael would be found, and I have a new cake you can eat while you'll be working.
THE OLD MAN (*looking at the boards*): Are there nails with them?
CATHLEEN. There are not, Colum; we didn't think of the nails.
ANOTHER MAN. It's a great wonder she wouldn't think of the nails, and all the coffins she's seen made already.
CATHLEEN. It's getting old she is, and broken.

(*Maurya stands up again very slowly and spreads out the pieces of Michael's clothes beside the body, sprinkling them with the last of the Holy Water.*)

NORA (*in a whisper to Cathleen*): She's quiet now and easy; but the day Michael was drowned you could hear her crying out from this to the spring well. It's fonder she was of Michael, and would any one have thought that?

CATHLEEN (*slowly and clearly*): An old woman will be soon tired with anything she will do, and isn't it nine days herself is after crying and keening, and making great sorrow in the house?

MAURYA (*puts the empty cup mouth downwards on the table, and lays her hands together on Bartley's feet*): They're all together this time, and the end is come. May the Almighty God have mercy on Bartley's soul, and on Michael's soul, and on the souls of Sheamus and Patch, and Stephen and Shawn (*bending her head*); and may He have mercy on my soul, Nora, and on the soul of every one is left living in the world.

(*She pauses, and the keen rises a little more loudly from the women, then sinks away.*)

(*Continuing*) Michael has a clean burial in the far north, by the grace of the Almighty God. Bartley will have a fine coffin out of the white boards, and a deep grave surely. What more can we want than that? No man at all can be living for ever and we must be satisfied.

(*She kneels down again and the curtain falls slowly.*)

11

Talk

ANNE CHAMBERS

from *Granuaile*

The details of the meeting of these two women, each outstanding and unique in her own special role as ruler and leader and alike in their personal characteristics, must unfortunately remain the realm of fantasy and legend. Curiosity must have been a motivation for them both, curiosity about each other. Elizabeth, as a rule in a male-dominated preserve, must have marvelled at how Grace, without the supporting facilities of state that she herself enjoyed, could successfully lead and govern so effectively and perform all the exploits for forty years credited to her by Elizabeth's own Irish deputies and governors. Grace in turn must have been anxious to see this paragon of English power whose orders and plans had affected and altered her very lifestyle so completely. The palace of Elizabeth was far removed from the stone castles of the west of Ireland, fortresses which were built with comfort as the minimum and security the maximum consideration; whose bare walls were constantly exposed to the Atlantic; the luxury of the Elizabethan court must have been over-powering. We can picture the stately Tudor court of the Virgin Queen with its luxury, colour, culture and refinements. Tapestry-covered walls, carved oak wainscots and furniture, ceilings ornate with intricate plaster-work; the long corridors leading to the royal apartments humming with the subdued and modulated tones of courtiers, emissaries, petitioners and many fair and fragile court ladies in exquisite dress and shining jewels, powdered and coiffed like tropical birds, flitting hither and thither trading the latest court gossip. And among this gathering, Grace O'Malley, leader of men, seawoman without equal, pirate, trader, self-appointed ruler contrary to law and tradition but too powerful to be dethroned, an elderly woman whose lined and weather-beaten face proclaimed the harsh conditions of her trade. . . .

Tradition states that at the introduction of these two remarkable women, Elizabeth held her hand high, but Grace was the taller of the two and the English queen had to raise her hand to that of the Irish woman. A portrait of the meeting is from an old engraving made two centuries later and professes to show the dress and attitude of Grace on that occasion. It is said that during her conversation with Elizabeth, which was conducted in Latin, one of the ladies-in-waiting perceived that Grace required a handker- chief. A minute cambric and lace one was handed to her. After using it she threw it into the fire but Elizabeth informed her that it was meant to be put in her pocket. Amazed, Grace declared that in her country they had a higher standard of cleanliness than to pocket a soiled article.

Elizabeth was in her declining years yet the chalk-like features, piercing eyes and haughty demeanour had made many, more powerful figures tremble; yet Grace, knowing her own long record of unloyal activities had preceded her to Elizabeth's court, dared to ask not necessarily for forgiveness but for special favours and protection from Elizabeth's own administrators in Ireland. . . . The favours won by Grace from Elizabeth reflected on the one hand the courage and ability of Grace and on the other the admiration and compassion Elizabeth entertained for Grace. . . .

Grace was in fact granted all her requests by the Queen in spite of the opinions and recommendations of her governor, Bingham. Grace's son, although strongly suspected of collusion with O'Rourke, was to be freed, as was her brother Donal. The compassion shown by Elizabeth for Grace's personal plight is evidenced by the provision for her maintenance for the remainder of her life from her sons' estates and that the amount be deductible from their taxes payable to the state. It was an unprecedented act of clemency and understanding of a woman's plight on Elizabeth's part and Grace must have departed from the royal presence with her 'burden' much lightened.

EITHNE STRONG

Juxtaposition

Now dear professor I have sat an hour
in your class: I do not know what
you are at. I look at you and wish
I knew the man behind the man I see,
and what moves you to such emphasis
on movements in the history of words
long obsolete. Everyone so keen and
scribbling taking notes most relevant.
I barely get the merest air of your
rare incredible vocabulary, me, the
mute moronic sitting stupefied. I'd
wish to be a sponge to sop it briskly
as it comes, and later squeeze it
out again to inspect and re-assimilate.
I'd wish that you would start once more
and go it very slow, that I might
question here and there without the fear
of O (despite your erudition) that
bloody eejit woman!

ETHNA CARBERY

The Love-Talker

I met the Love-Talker one eve in the glen,
He was handsomer than any of our handsome young men,
His eyes were blacker than the sloe, his voice sweeter far
Than the crooning of old Kevin's pipes beyond in Coolnagar.

I was bound for the milking with a heart fair and free –
My grief! my grief! that bitter hour drained the life from me;
I thought him human lover, though his lips on mine were cold,
And the breath of death blew keen on me within his hold.

I know not what way he came, no shadow fell behind,
But all the sighing rushes swayed beneath a fairy wind;
The thrush ceased its singing, a mist crept about,
We two clung together – with the world shut out.

Beyond the ghostly mist I could hear my cattle low,
The little cow from Ballina, clean as driven snow,
The dun cow from Kerry, the roan from Inisheer,
Oh, pitiful their calling – and his whispers in my ear!

His eyes were a fire; his words were a snare;
I cried my mother's name, but no help was there;
I made the blessed Sign – then he gave a dreary moan,
A wisp of cloud went floating by, and I stood alone.

Running ever thro' my head is an old-time rune –
'Who meets the Love-Talker must weave her shroud soon.'
My mother's face is furrowed with the salt tears that fall,
But the kind eyes of my father are the saddest sight of all.

I have spun the fleecy lint and now my wheel is still,
The linen length is woven for my shroud fine and chill.
I shall stretch on the bed where a happy maid I lay –
Pray for the soul of Maire Og at dawning of the day!

J.M. Synge

The Curse

To a sister of an enemy of the author's who disapproved of 'The Playboy'

Lord, confound this surly sister,
Blight her brow with blotch and blister,
Cramp her larynx, lung, and liver,
In her guts a galling give her.

Let her live to earn her dinners
In Mountjoy with seedy sinners:
Lord, this judgment quickly bring,
And I'm Your servant, J. M. Synge.

George Bernard Shaw

Aphorism

Talk to him about himself: then he will love you – to your great alarm.

Anon

Killyburn Brae

There was an ould man down by Killyburn brae,
   Right fol, right fol, titty fol lay.
There was an ould man down by Killyburn brae,
Had a scolding ould wife for the most of his day,
   With a right fol da dol, titty fol lol,
     Fol da-da dol, da dol da-da day.

One day as this man he walk'd out in the glen,
   Right fol, right fol, titty fol lay.
One day as this man he walk'd out in the glen,
Sure he met with the divil, says, 'How are you then?'
   With a right fol da dol, titty fol lol,
     Fol da-da dol, da dol da-da day.

Says he, me ould man I have come for yer wife,
For I hear she's the plague an' torment of yer life,

So the divil he hoisted her up on his back,
An' hot-fut for hell with her then he did pack,

An' when at the finish they got to hell's gate,
Sure he threw her right down with a thump on her pate,

There were two little divils there playing at ball,
Whilst the one he was wee sure the other was small,

There were two other divils there tied up in chains,
An' she lifted her stick an' she scattered their brains,

So the divil he hoisted her up on his back,
They were seven years goin' – nine *days* comin' back,

Says he, me ould man here's yer wife safe an' well,
For the likes of herself we would not have in hell,

Now I've been a divil the most of me life,
But I ne'er was in hell till I met with yer wife,

So it's true that the women is worse than the men,
When they go down to hell they are thrown out again.

MADDEN

How O'Connell Won the Championship of Billingsgate

There was at that time in Dublin, a certain woman, Biddy Moriarty, who had a huckster's stall on one of the quays nearly opposite the Four Courts. She was a virago of the first order, very able with her fist, and still more formidable with her tongue. From one end of Dublin to the other, she was notorious for her powers of abuse, and even in the provinces Mrs Moriarty's language had passed into currency. The dictionary of Dublin slang had been considerably enlarged by her, and her voluble impudence had almost become proverbial. Some of O'Connell's friends, however, thought that he could beat her at the use of her own weapons. Of this, however, he had some doubts himself, when he listened once or twice to some minor specimens of her Billingsgate. It was mooted once where the young Kerry barrister could encounter her, and some one of the company rather too freely ridiculed the idea of his being able to meet the famous Madame Moriarty. O'Connell never liked the idea of being put down, and he professed his readiness to encounter her, and even backed himself for the match. Bets were offered and taken and it was decided that the matter should come off at once.

The party adjourned to the huckster's stall, and there was the owner herself, superintending the sale of her small wares — a few loungers and ragged idlers were hanging around her stall, for Biddy was a character and in her way was one of the sights of Dublin. O'Connell commenced the attack.

'What's the price of this walking-stick, Mrs What's-your-name?'

'Moriarty, sir, is my name, and a good one it is; and what have you to say agen it? One-and-sixpence's the price of the stick. Troth, it's chape as dirt, so it is.'

'One-and-sixpence for a walking stick; whew! why, you are not better than an imposter, to ask eighteen pence for what cost you two pence.'

'Two pence, your grandmother! Do you mane to say it's chating the people, I am? Imposter, indeed!'

'I protest as I am a gentleman . . . '

'Jintleman! Jintleman! The likes of you a jintleman! Wisha, by gor, that bangs Banagher. Why, you potato-faced pippin-sneezer, when did a Madagascar monkey like you pick up enough of common Christian dacency to hide your Kerry brogue?'

'Easy now, easy now,' said O'Connell with imperturbable good humour, 'don't choke yourself with fine language, you whiskey-drinking parallelogram.'

'What's that you call me, you murderin' villain?' roared Mrs Moriarty.

'I call you,' answered O'Connell, 'a parallelogram; and a Dublin judge and jury will say it's no libel to call you so.'

'Oh, tare-an'-ouns! Oh, Holy Saint Bridget! that an honest woman like me should be called a parrybellygrum to her face. I'm none of your parrybellygrums, you rascally gallows-bird; you cowardly, sneakin', plate-lickin' blaguard!'

'Oh, not you, indeed! Why, I suppose you'll deny that you keep a hypotenuse in your house.'

'It's a lie for you. I never had such a thing . . . '

'Why, sure all your neighbours know very well that you keep not only a hypotenuse, but that you have two diameters locked up in your garret, and that you go out to walk with them every Sunday, you heartless old heptagon.'

'Oh, hear that, ye saints in glory! Oh, there's bad language from a fellow that wants to pass for a jintleman. May the divil fly away with you, you micher from Munster, and make celery-sauce of your rotten limbs, you mealy-mouthed tub of guts.'

'Ah, you can't deny the charge, you miserable sub-multiple of a duplicate ratio.'

'Go, rinse your mouth in the Liffey, you nasty tickle-pincher; after all the bad words you speak, it ought to be dirtier than your face, you dirty chicken of Beelzebub.'

'Rinse your own mouth, you wicked-minded old polygon – to

the deuce I pitch you, you blustering intersection of a superficies!'

'You saucy tinker's apprentice, if you don't cease your jaw, I'll . . . ' But here she gasped for breath, unable to hawk up more words.

'While I have a tongue, I'll abuse you, you most inimitable periphery. Look at her, boys! There she stands — a convicted perpendicular in petticoats! There's contamination in her circumference, and she trembles with guilt down to the extremities of her corollaries. Ah, you're found out, you rectilinealantecedent, and equiangular old hag! 'Tis with the devil you will fly away, you porter-swiping similitude of the bisection of a vortex!'

Overwhelmed with this torrent of language, Mrs Moriarty was silenced. Catching up a saucepan, she was aiming at O'Connell's head, when he made a timely retreat.

'You've won your wager, O'Connell, here's your bet,' said the ones who proposed the contest.

RICHARD KELL

The Gentleman Who Sneaked In

Women! Persons! *Please!* Allow me to speak
just for a moment . . . Thank you . . . What I wanted
to say was this. To begin with, I understand.
No, I mean it: I do understand, and even
sympathize. In fact I'd go so far
as to call myself, with your permission of course,
a feminist. But there are, if I may say so,
feminists and feminists. Most of you here,
judging by what I've heard, would like to treat
men as they've treated women. I'm not surprised.
Age after grisly age of patriarchal
pride, insensitivity, exploitation —
no wonder you are militant! But consider:

has anything of enduring value ever
been gained by retaliation? Think, my friends!
Why would you take for model the sex you scorn?
Doing as they did, how would you help the world?
Cry out in protest, not in revenge and malice.
Firmly resist, but only in the name
of co-operation, sharing, mutual care,
equality, gentleness, all the lovely ways
that you can teach us now. We want to learn,
believe me. We *need* to learn if the human race
is not to . . . Thank you, ladies. Thanks for listening.
You're very kind . . . Thank you. I wish you well.

AILBHE SMYTH

Women and Abortion in the Republic of Ireland, 1992

In February 1992, a fourteen-year-old Irish rape victim was prevented by a High Court injunction from leaving the jurisdiction of Ireland to obtain an abortion in Britain. Early in March, following an appeal to the Supreme Court lodged by her family on her behalf, the girl was permitted to leave the jurisdiction. It is understood that she then went to Britain where her pregnancy was terminated.

Put as baldly as this, what has come to be known as the X case seems straightforward, although shocking. In point of fact, it is an extremely complicated case with the most serious consequences for the reproductive freedoms of Irish women and disturbing implications for their rights as citizens of Ireland and of Europe. The case derives directly from the anti-abortion amendment to the Constitution (the Eighth Amendment), inserted by a bitterly divisive referendum in 1983. Further, the case rapidly became entangled with Ireland's imminent ratification of the Maastricht Treaty on European Union . . .

It has been exceptionally difficult to make sense of a situation which has consistently been framed in highly technical legal language, and further obscured by layers of 'Euro-speak' and political whitewash. For much of the time over the past several months, it has seemed as though we are living in a nightmare version of Alice's Wonderland where words can mean whatever lawyers and politicians want them to mean – without any reference to the material realities they supposedly signify. Women's bodies, women's right to bodily integrity, women's freedom to control our reproductive processes are caught in an impenetrable, materially meaningless web of male-generated words.

For of course, women have been signally absent from a debate which concerns them in the most immediate, intimate and serious ways possible. Just two weeks after the case of the fourteen-year-old girl came to light, the Dáil (*Irish Parliament*) belatedly decided to allot limited time to a discussion of the issue. During the course of the debate, Deputy Monica Barnes requested 'one minute of the House's time on behalf of the women of Ireland', only to be ruled out of order by the Chair and invited to show 'respect' for the rules of the House. A woman journalist present in the House commented as follows:

If ever there was a metaphor for a society in which men control the structures of power and are determined to keep it that way, it was the Dáil yesterday afternoon. There were nine women deputies in the chamber and row upon row of middle-aged men in suits . . . This week, at least 100 women will travel to England for abortions. It will be an even more desolate journey than usual because of what has happened in recent days. It is shameful but not, alas, surprising that no woman was allowed to speak for them in what a former Taoiseach (Prime Minister) once described as the 'democratic forum of the nation'. (Mary Holland, *The Irish Times*, 19/02/92)

What women are experiencing in Ireland at present is the literal and literally frightening power of language to constitute social reality. Language is used, in quite explicit and transparent ways, to construct or to deny the contours and material substance of women's lives. Control through discourse is almost naïvely exposed in the present Irish controversy. Women's sexuality and reproduction are confined by politico-legal linguistic formulae (i.e. by being referred to in restrictive or reductive ways in Constitutional amendments, protocols and solemn declarations), or paradoxically defined as non-existent (i.e. by not being spoken at all) . . .

The language of the self-styled 'Pro-Life' movement consciously plays with ethical and biological meanings of 'life' (Pre-life/Pro-Life), re-investing 'Life' with a new (capitalised) foetocentric meaning. Words conjure up a new hierarchy of 'life' values in which the foetus is promoted to the status of 'baby', while women are 'demoted' to the materially undervalued condition of 'mother'. In Pro-Life discourse, women lose their independent lives and are deprived of their civil status: women are represented consistently and exclusively as 'mothers'. As the foetus plays an increasingly visible role in Pro-Life discourse, women become decreasingly visible: for women, the 'law' is one of diminishing returns.

A woman letter-writer to *The Irish Times* identified both the absurdity and the danger of this word 'play' perfectly: since, she mused, the 'unborn' have special Constitutional protections (including exemption from payment of taxes), could these protections not also be extended to the 'undead' (including non-payment of taxes)? But it is one thing to play with words, and quite another to play with lives. Or is it? In nuclear physics, the half-life of a substance is the length of time it takes for a unit of that substance to reduce to half of its original value. How long would it take to reduce women to no value at all?

LAURENCE STERNE

from *Tristram Shandy*

My Dear Brother Toby,

What I am going to say to thee is upon the nature of women, and of love-making to them; and perhaps it is as well for thee – tho' not so well for me – that thou hast occasion for a letter of instructions upon that head, and that I am able to write it to thee.

In the first place, with regard to all which concerns religion in the affair – though I perceive from a glow in my cheek, that I blush as I begin to speak to thee upon the subject, as well knowing, notwithstanding thy unaffected secrecy, how few of its offices thou neglectest – yet I would remind thee of one (during the continuance of thy courtship) in a particular manner, which I would not have omitted; and that is, never to go forth upon the enterprize, whether it be in the morning or the afternoon, without first recommending thyself to the protection of Almighty God, that he may defend thee from the evil one.

Shave the whole top of thy crown clean once at least every four or five days, but oftener if convenient; lest in taking off thy wig before her, thro' absence of mind, she should be able to discover how much has been cut away by Time – how much by *Trim*.

– 'Twere better to keep ideas of baldness out of her fancy.

Always carry it in thy mind, and act upon it as a sure maxim, Toby –

'*That women are timid.*' And 'tis well they are – else there would be no dealing with them.

Whatever thou hast to say, be it more or less, forget not to utter it in a low soft tone of voice. Silence, and whatever approaches it, weaves dreams of midnight secrecy into the brain: For this cause, if thou canst help it, never throw down the tongs and poker.

Avoid all kinds of pleasantry and facetiousness in thy discourse with her, and do whatever lies in thy power at the same time, to keep from her all books and writings which tend thereto: there are some devotional tracts, which if thou canst entice her to read over

— it will be well: but suffer her not to look into *Rabelais*, or *Scarron*, or *Don Quixote* —

— They are all books which excite laughter; and thou knowest, dear Toby, that there is no passion so serious as lust.

Stick a pin in the bosom of thy shirt, before thou enterest her parlour.

And if thou art permitted to sit upon the same sopha with her, and she gives thee occasion to lay thy hand upon hers — beware of taking it — thou canst not lay thy hand upon hers, but she will feel the temper of thine. Leave that and as many other things as thou canst, quite undetermined; by so doing, thou wilt have her curiosity on thy side; and if she is not conquered by that, and thy ASSE continues still kicking, which there is great reason to suppose — Thou must begin, with first losing a few ounces of blood below the ears, according to the practice of the ancient Scythians, who cured the most intemperate fits of the appetite by that means.

Avicenna, after this, is for having the part anointed with the syrup of hellebore, using proper evacuations and purges — and I believe rightly. But thou must eat little or no goat's flesh, nor red deer — nor even foal's flesh by any means; and carefully abstain — that is, as much as thou canst, from peacocks, cranes, coots, didappers, and water-hens —

As for thy drink — I need not tell thee, it must be the infusion of VERVAIN and the herb HANEA, of which Aelian relates such effects — but if thy stomach palls with it — discontinue it from time to time, taking cucumbers, melons, purslane, water-lilies, woodbine, and lettice, in the stead of them.

There is nothing further for thee, which occurs to me at present —

— Unless the breaking out of a fresh war — So wishing everything dear *Toby*, for the best,

> I rest thy affectionate brother,
> Walter Shandy

ANON

Dicey Reilly

One of several national songs of the independent republic near Ireland that Dublin in fact is. Not fully understood by ex-urbanites, it is learned and vigorously sung by 'culchies' newly come to the Smoke in a vain attempt to establish their metropolitan credentials.

Ah poor oul Dicey Reilly, she has taken to the sup,
And poor oul Dicey Reilly she will never give it up,
It's off each morning to the pop that she goes in for another little drop,
But the heart of the rowl is Dicey Reilly.

She will walk along Fitzgibbon Street with an independent air
And then it's down by Summerhill, and as the people stare
She'll say 'It's nearly half past one, time I went in for another little one.'
But the heart of the rowl is Dicey Reilly.

Now at two, pubs close and out she goes as happy as a lark
She'll find a bench to sleep it off down in St Patrick's Park.
She'll wake at five feeling in the pink and say ''Tis time for another drink.'
But the heart of the rowl is Dicey Reilly.

Now she'll travel far to a dockside bar to have another round
And after one or two or three she doesn't feel quite sound
And after four she's a bit unstable, after five underneath the table
The heart of the rowl is Dicey Reilly.

Oh they carry her home at twelve o'clock as they do every night
Bring her inside, put her on the bed and then turn out the light.
Next morning she'll get out of bed and look for a curer for her head
But the heart of the rowl is Dicey Reilly.

Ah poor oul Dicey Reilly she has taken to the sup
And poor oul Dicey Reilly she will never give it up
It's off each morning to the pop then she goes in for another little
	drop
But the heart of the rowl is Dicey Reilly.

JONATHAN SWIFT

Dialogue III: The Ladies at their Tea

LADY SMART. Well, Ladies; now let us have a Cup of Discourse to ourselves.

LADY ANSW[ERALL]. What do you think of your Friend, Sir *John Spendall?*

LADY SMART. Why, Madam, 'tis happy for him, that his Father was born before him.

MISS [NOTABLE]. They say, he makes a very ill Husband to my Lady.

LADY ANSW. But he must be allow'd to be the fondest Father in the World.

LADY SMART. Ay, Madam, that's true; for they say, the Devil is kind to his own.

MISS. I am told, my Lady manages him to Admiration.

LADY SMART. That I believe; for she's as cunning as a dead Pig; but not half so honest.

LADY ANSW. They say, she's quite a Stranger to all his Gallantries.

LADY SMART. Not at all; but, you know, there's none so blind as they that won't see.

MISS. O Madam, I am told, she watches him, as a Cat would watch a Mouse.

LADY ANSW. Well, if she ben't foully belied, she pays him in his own Coin.

LADY SMART. Madam, I fancy I know your Thoughts, as well as if I were within you.

LADY ANSW. Madam, I was t'other Day in Company with Mrs *Clatter*; I find she gives herself Airs of being acquainted with your Ladyship.

MISS. Oh, the hideous Creature! did you observe her Nails? they were long enough to scratch her Granum out of her Grave.

LADY SMART. Well, She and *Tom Gosling* were banging Compliments backwards and forwards; it look'd like Two Asses scrubbing one another.

MISS. Ay, claw me, and I'll claw thou: But, pray, Madam, who were the Company?

LADY SMART. Why, there was all the World, and his Wife; there was Mrs *Clatter*, Lady *Singular*, the Countess of *Talkham*, (I should have named her first;) *Tom Gosling*, and some others, whom I have forgot.

LADY ANSW. I think the Countess is very sickly.

LADY SMART. Yes, Madam; she'll never scratch a grey head, I promise her.

MISS. And, pray, what was your Conversation?

LADY SMART. Why, Mrs *Clatter* had all the Talk to herself, and was perpetually complaining of her Misfortunes.

LADY ANSW. She brought her Husband Ten thousand Pounds; she has a Town-House and Country-House: Would the Woman have her A— hung with Points?

LADY SMART. She would fain be at the Top of the House before the Stairs are built.

MISS. Well, Comparisons are odious; but she's as like her Husband, as if she were spit out of his Mouth; as like as one Egg is to another; Pray, how was she drest?

LADY SMART. Why, she was as fine as Fi'pence; but, truly, I thought, there was more Cost than Worship.

LADY ANSW. I don't know her Husband: Pray, what is he?

LADY SMART. Why, he's a Concealer of the Law; you must know, he came to us as drunk as *David*'s Sow.

MISS. What kind of Creature is he?

LADY SMART. You must know, the Man and his Wife are coupled

like Rabbits, a fat and a lean; he's as fat as a Porpus, and she's one
of *Pharaoh*'s lean Kine: The Ladies and *Tom Gosling* were proposing
a Party at Quadrille, but he refus'd to make one: Damn your
Cards, said he, they are the Devil's Books.

LADY ANSW. A dull unmannerly Brute! Well, God send him
more Wit, and me more Money.

MISS. Lord! Madam, I would not keep such Company for the
World.

LADY SMART. O Miss, 'tis nothing when you are used to it:
Besides, you know, for Want of Company, welcome Trumpery.

MISS. Did your Ladyship play?

LADY SMART. Yes, and won; so I came off with Fidlers Fare,
Meat, Drink and Money.

LADY ANSW. Ay; what says *Pluck*?

MISS. Well, my Elbow itches; I shall change Bed-fellows.

LADY SMART. And my Right Hand itches; I shall receive Money.

LADY ANSW. And my Right Eye itches; I shall cry.

KITTY KIERNAN

Letter to Michael Collins, 1921

I gave you so many chances just because I liked you. Otherwise I
wouldn't have worried and I assure you it would have been all the
same to me – as all men were alike more or less, I believed – and I
could have made it easy by not saying anything, almost taking it
all for granted as so many do, only you were so sincere and
straight. I wanted to be the same and give you every chance. In the
beginning in Dublin those ideas never entered my head seriously,
although I used to talk. It was later when I realised. I fought it
successfully for a short time, then I decided, if it is a question of
marriage (two nights before Helen's wedding on the stairs and the
night following it, when you really wanted me) why not marry the

one I really love, and what a cowardly thing of me to be afraid to marry the one I really want, and who loves me just as well as any of the others I had thought of marrying.

Then London came. I should not have gone. It gave rise to such talk. People got to know about it, and I thought it better from a girl's very conventional and narrow point of view that we better have something definite, and so we have drifted. *Please*, sweetheart, *don't* misunderstand me now. I can't explain. It is only I felt, if we were ever to part, it would be easier for us both, especially for me, to do it soon, because later it would be bitter for me. But I'd love you just the same, even if we both *or you* decided on it.

Now don't think by this that I want a row or want you to end it. Not likely. I want you only not to think bad of me when we had those scenes. Testing you! With the feeling as a girl — 'better have it now than later.' If you were *me* you would see it clearly too. Don't think I want you to decide definitely now. I am happy to drift and drift as long as I know you love me and we will be one day together. I fancy sometimes — as girls do — a little nest, you and I, two comfy chairs, a fire, and two books (now I'm not too ambitious) and no worries. You feeling perfectly free, as if not married, and I likewise. I do believe, as you *used* to say 'it will be a great arrangement'. I will promise you when we feel perfectly confident — as I have done for ages — I'll have no more rows. Truly if I didn't love you so well I wouldn't want your love so badly. I always picture — do you like my picture? — myself sitting on your knee — not the two big chairs so often — until I tire you. Cruel isn't it? We will, won't we, be real lovers? Say we will. You don't trust me or answer my important questions. And as the one I have a dim recollection of, if you liked me to love you so much or if it was a nonsense, can't you tell me all your worries? If you can't have me as a friend {who is} ready to do anything for you (almost?), who could you trust?

This must finish now and it's some letter. You couldn't bring yourself to write this sort of thing, the famous M.C. All I wish now is that it pleases you, gives you some sunshine, and helps to make the day easy for you. That will always be my ambition. With that we should have no worry.

Believe me, your own little pet, friend and everything,
Kit.

MICHAEL HARDING

Misogynist

He calms himself. As therapy he plays with a dictaphone or the video camera which relays images to the screen.

Hello. Hello. Hello. Hello.

You see to be really honest, this . . .
woman . . .
worries me more than I care to admit.
Oh she can go round being kind to all the people she likes.
I can tolerate that.
But it's when she starts talking that the trouble starts.
Opening her big mouth.
You see,
people are very tricky.
They can be . . . persuaded.
Once she places things in a certain
context
they find nothing unacceptable in what she
says.
That's how slithery she is.
Of course, if she were to challenge me
openly. Ha.
Fairly and squarely.
Well, there'd be no contest.
I mean
I'd leave her blood on the wall.

Ha.
But you'll find she won't do that
No sir.
She knows not to stroke the tiger's whiskers too
directly.
No.
Instead she weaves her little web.
And draws people into it.
Yes.
And she's succeeding.
All the fools are mesmerized.

Do you not see what she's doing, I said.
Do you not see what she's doing, I said.
But they would not listen to me.
Fuck them.

He finishes with the camera (or dictaphone).

My brothers,
we have fought many battles,
many adversaries,
over the years.
But this little lizard in the grass is the worst of them all. In the
sweet fragrance of the grass with her kind words, gently
cloaking the fangs of poison.
This is the most deadly enemy of all.
Yes?

That sounds right.

George Farquhar

from *The Recruiting Officer*

MELINDA. Welcome to Town, Cosin *Silvia*. (*Salute*). I envy'd you
your Retreat in the Country; for *Shrewsbury*, methinks, and all
your Heads of Shires, are the most irregular Places for living, here
we have Smoak, Noise, Scandal, Affectation, and Pretension; in
short, every thing to give the Spleen, and nothing to divert it —
Then the Air is intolerable.

SILVIA. Oh! Madam, I have heard the Town commended for its
Air.

MELINDA. But you don't consider, *Silvia*, how long I have liv'd in
it; for I can assure you, that to a Lady the least nice in her
Constitution, no Air can be good above half a Year; Change of Air
I take to be the most agreeable of any Variety in Life.

SILVIA. As you say, Cosin *Melinda*, there are several sorts of Airs,
Airs in Conversation, Airs in Behaviour, Airs in Dress; then we
have our Quality Airs, our sickly Airs, our reserv'd Airs, and
sometimes our impudent Airs.

MELINDA. Pshaw — I talk only of the Air we breath, or more
properly of that we taste — Have you not, *Silvia*, found a vast
Difference in the Taste of Airs?

SILVIA. Pray Cosin, are not Vapours a sort of Air? Taste Air! You
may as well tell me I might feed upon Air; but prithee, my dear
Melinda, don't put on such Airs to me, your Education and mine
were just the same, and I remember the time when we never
troubled our Heads about Air, but when the sharp Air from the
Welsh Mountains made our Noses drop in a cold Morning at the
Boarding-School.

MELINDA. Our Education, Cosin, was the same, but our Temper-
aments had nothing alike; you have the Constitution of a
Horse —

SILVIA. So far as to be troubled with neither Spleen, Cholick, nor
Vapours, I need no Salt for my Stomach, no Hart's-horn for my
Head, nor Wash for my Complexion; I can gallop all the Morning

after the Hunting Horn, and all the Evening after a Fiddle: In short, I can do every thing with my Father but drink and shoot flying; and I'm sure I can do every thing my Mother cou'd, were I put to the Tryal.

MELINDA. You're in a fair way of being put to't; for I'm told, your Captain is come to Town.

SILVIA. Ay, *Melinda*, he is come, and I'll take care he shan't go without a Companion.

MELINDA. You're certainly mad, Cosin.

SILVIA. *And there's a Pleasure sure, in being mad,*
Which none but Mad-men know.

MELINDA. Thou poor Romantick *Quixote*, hast thou the Vanity to imagine that a young sprightly Officer that rambles over half the Globe in half a Year, can confine his Thoughts to the little Daughter of a Country Justice in an obscure corner of the World?

SILVIA. Pshaw! What care I for his Thoughts? I shou'd not like a Man with confin'd Thoughts, it shows a Narrowness of Soul. Constancy is but a dull, sleepy Quality at best; they will hardly admit it among the Manly Vertues, nor do I think it deserves a Place with Bravery, Knowledge, Policy, Justice, and some other Qualities that are proper to that noble Sex. In short, *Melinda*, I think a Petticoat a mighty simple thing, and I'm heartily tir'd of my Sex.

MELINDA. That is, you are tir'd of an Appendix to our Sex, that you can't so handsomly get rid of in Petticoats as if you were in Breeches – O'my Conscience, *Silvia*, hadst thou been a Man, thou hadst been the greatest Rake in *Christendom*.

SILVIA. I shou'd endeavour to know the World, which a Man can never do thoroughly without half a hundred Friendships, and as many Amours. But now I think on't, how stands your Affair with Mr *Worthy*?

MELINDA. He's my Aversion.

SILVIA. Vapours.

MELINDA. What do you say, Madam?

SILVIA. I say, that you shou'd not use that honest Fellow so inhumanely, he's a Gentleman of Parts and Fortune, and beside that he's my *Plume*'s Friend; and by all that's sacred, if you don't use him better, I shall expect Satisfaction.

MELINDA. Satisfaction! You begin to fancy your self in Breeches in good earnest — But to be plain with you, I like *Worthy* the worse for being so intimate with your Captain; for I take him to be a loose, idle, unmannerly Coxcomb.

SILVIA. Oh! Madam — You never saw him, perhaps, since you were Mistress of twenty thousand Pound; you only knew him when you were capitulating with *Worthy* for a Settlement, which perhaps might incourage him to be a little loose and unmannerly with you.

MELINDA. What do you mean, Madam?

SILVIA. My meaning needs no Interpretation, Madam.

MELINDA. Better it had, Madam — for methinks you're too plain.

SILVIA. If you mean the Plainness of my Person, I think your Ladyship as plain as me to the full.

MELINDA. Were I assur'd of that, I shou'd be glad to take up with a Rakely Officer as you do.

SILVIA. Again! Look'e, Madam — You're in your own House.

MELINDA. And if you had kept in yours, I shou'd have excus'd you.

SILVIA. Don't be troubl'd, Madam — I shan't desire to have my visit return'd.

MELINDA. The sooner therefore you make an end of this, the better.

SILVIA. I'm easily advis'd to follow my Inclinations — So Madam — Your humble Servant.

(*Exit.*)

MELINDA. Saucy thing!

(*Enter* Lucy.)

LUCY. What's the matter, Madam?

MELINDA. Did you not see the proud Nothing, how she swells upon the Arrival of her Fellow?

LUCY. Her Fellow has not been long enough arriv'd to occasion any great swelling, Madam — I don't believe she has seen him yet.

Roddy Doyle

from *The Commitments*

The three backing vocalists, The Commitmentettes listened to
The Supremes, Martha and the Vandellas, The Ronettes, The
Crystals and the The Shangri-Las. The Commitmentettes were
Imelda Quirk and her friends Natalie Murphy and Bernie
McLoughlin.

— How yis move, yeh know — is more important than how yis
sing, Jimmy told them.

— You're a dirty bastard, you are.

Imelda, Natalie and Bernie could sing though. They'd been in
the folk mass choir when they were in school but that, they knew
now, hadn't really been singing. Jimmy said that real music was
sex. They called him a dirty bastard but they were starting to agree
with him. And there wasn't much sex in Morning Has Broken or
The Lord Is My Shepherd.

Now they were singing along to Stop in the Name of Love and
Walking in the Rain and they were enjoying it.

Joined together their voices sounded good, they thought.
Jimmy taped them. They were scarlet. They sounded terrible.

— Yis're usin' your noses instead of your mouths, said Jimmy.

— Fuck off slaggin', said Imelda.

— Yis are, I'm tellin' yeh. An' yis shouldn't be usin' your ordin'y
accents either. It's Walking in the Rain, not Walkin' in Dey
Rayen.

— Snobby!

They taped themselves and listened. They got better, clearer,
sweeter. Natalie could roar and squeal too. They took down the
words and sang by themselves without the records. They only did
this though when one of them had a free house.

They moved together, looking down, making sure their feet
were going the right way. Soon they didn't have to look down.
They wiggled their arses at the dressing table mirror and burst out
laughing. But they kept doing it.

Mairéad Byrne

An Interview with Romulus and Remus

What did you think of the wolves?
Did they excite you?
Make you feel different? More human?
What is it like to be twins?
Did the wolves smell?
Did you find that in any way off-putting?
Did you have trouble expressing affection?
What's wolf's milk like for starters?
What were their names?
Where did they go on their holidays?
Did you find it hard to settle down again in Rome?
We call it Rome now.
I don't mean to cause a fight
but did it ever strike you that *Reme*
might have been an equally good name?
How did you boys get along?
Was it dark out there? And cold?
Are you glad to be home and how
do you get along with women, real women?
I mean, do they compare to the wolves?
Do you think your background will cause problems later in life?
I mean sexually.
Did you ever have it off with a wolf?
You're too young, I guess.
I don't mean to be disrespectful
but, you see, we never heard the full story.
A lot of people wonder about you boys,
being brought up by wolves and all that.
Do you miss them?
Do you know that they're nearly extinct?
Would you let your daughter marry a wolf?
How fast can you run?

Say, what's your favourite food?
Do you eat raw meat and tear it apart with your teeth?
Well, I suppose that was quite common in Rome.
Hey, thanks for your time, boys.
It's been real.
You gotta learn to talk soon, boys.
A lotta people are dying to hear about this.

BRIAN FRIEL

from *Dancing at Lughnasa*

AGNES: Wouldn't it be a good one if we all went?

CHRIS: Went where?

AGNES: To the harvest dance.

CHRIS: Aggie!

AGNES: Just like we used to. All dressed up. I think I'd go.

ROSE: I'd go, too, Aggie! I'd go with you!

KATE: For heaven's sake you're not serious, Agnes – are you?

AGNES: I think I am.

KATE: Hah! There's more than Ballybeg off its head.

AGNES: I think we should all go.

KATE: Have you any idea what it'll be like? – Crawling with cheeky young brats that I taught years ago.

AGNES: I'm game.

CHRIS: We couldn't, Aggie – could we?

KATE: And all the riff-raff of the countryside.

AGNES: I'm game.

CHRIS: Oh God, you know how I loved dancing, Aggie.

AGNES (*To* Kate): What do you say?

KATE (*To* Chris): You have a seven-year-old child – have you forgotten that?

AGNES (*To* Chris): You could wear that blue dress of mine – you have the figure for it and it brings out the colour of your eyes.

CHRIS: Can I have it? God, Aggie, I could dance non-stop all night – all week – all month!

KATE: And who'd look after Father Jack?

AGNES (*To* Kate): And you look great in that cotton dress you got for confirmation last year. You're beautiful in it, Kate.

KATE: What sort of silly talk is –

AGNES (*To* Kate): And you can wear my brown shoes with the crossover straps.

KATE: This is silly talk. We can't, Agnes. How can we?

ROSE: Will Maggie go with us?

CHRIS: Will Maggie what! Try to stop her!

KATE: Oh God, Agnes, what do you think?

AGNES: We're going.

KATE: Are we?

ROSE: We're off! We're away!

KATE: Maybe we're mad – are we mad?

CHRIS: It costs four and six to get in.

AGNES: I've five pounds saved. I'll take you. I'll take us all.

KATE: Hold on now –

AGNES: How many years has it been since we were at the harvest dance? – at any dance? And I don't care how young they are, how drunk and dirty and sweaty they are. I want to dance, Kate. It's the Festival of Lughnasa. I'm only thirty-five. I want to dance.

KATE (*Wretched*): I know, I know, Agnes, I know. All the same – oh my God – I don't know if it's –

AGNES: It's settled. We're going – the Mundy girls – all five of us together.

CHRIS: Like we used to.

AGNES: Like we used to.

ROSE: I love you Aggie! I love you more than chocolate biscuits!

(Rose *kisses* Agnes *impetuously, flings her arms above her head, begins singing 'Abyssinia' and does the first steps of a bizarre and abandoned dance. At this* Kate *panics.*)

KATE: No, no, no! We're going nowhere!

CHRIS: If we all want to go –

KATE: Look at yourselves, will you! Just look at yourselves! Dancing at our time of day? That's for young people with no duties and no responsibilities and nothing in their heads but pleasure.

AGNES: Kate, I think we –

KATE: Do you want the whole countryside to be laughing at us? – women of our years? – mature women, *dancing*? What's come over you all? And this is Father Jack's home – we must never forget that – ever. No, no, we're going to no harvest dance.

ROSE: But you just said –

KATE: And there'll be no more discussion about it. The matter's over. I don't want it mentioned again.

MERVYN WALL

from *Leaves for the Burning*

'Please remain seated, ladies,' said the Senator magnanimously, though neither female had made any effort to arise. 'Now, what can I do for you?'

Miss Attracta Thrumcopple wasted no time: 'You own the New Hibernia Cinema, Senator Trefoil, and the films shown there are sometimes not all that is to be desired. Isn't that so, Mrs Wenn?'

The chapel charwoman nodded bleakly.

'Hm!' said the Senator. 'I understand from your letter that you had only one particular incident to complain of last week in "The Cowboy Pimpernel" when the heroine removed her stocking.'

'We'll speak of that first. Later we'll discuss the setting-up of a Cinema Vigilance Committee. Our society is willing to co-operate.'

The Senator looked at her, but said nothing.

'I have made enquiries,' went on the determined masculine voice, 'and I've been informed that it's quite easy for the renter to cut a film before it's shown. No damage is done to the film, which can be stuck together again afterwards. That is the procedure in every town in which a Vigilance Committee exists.'

'This country,' replied the Senator mildly, 'has already got a State Censorship of Films which is said to be the strictest in Europe.'

'It's not strict enough,' snapped Miss Thrumcopple.

Watching her iron jaws there came to the Senator's mind a picture of a rat trap which he had recently bought, advertised as 'strong enough to cut a badger in two'.

'Last week's film was a disgrace, and your cinema was crowded with children.'

The Senator pulled himself together.

'Come now, Miss Thrumcopple,' he said with affected joviality, 'the children came to see "The Cowboy Pimpernel": they're not interested in a lady taking off her stocking.'

Miss Thrumcopple glared at him: 'You wouldn't know what the children nowadays are interested in. It's our duty to see that nothing bad is put into their minds. "He that shall give scandal to one of these My little ones, it were better that a millstone were tied around his neck, and he drowned in the depths of the sea." '

Senator Trefoil instinctively put up his fingers and eased his collar.

'After all,' he said weakly, 'women have legs, you know,'

'It's not generally admitted,' snapped Miss Thrumcopple.

The Senator sat back in his chair to consider the situation. Then slowly there surged back into him the old fighting spirit which twenty-eight years before had sent him doggedly following two armed British tommies into the blackness of a lane in Moymell, from the shelter of a doorway to shoot them dead, first one, and then the other. The same savage fighting spirit possessed him now, but twenty-five years of party politics had added finesse.

'When I got your letter yesterday requesting an interview,' he said, 'I telephoned every priest in the town. Four of them had seen that film, and not one of them saw anything in it to complain of.'

'Some of the clergy are not all that they should be,' replied Miss Thrumcopple venomously. 'That's why organizations like ours exist. That's why the lay apostolate is necessary, what we call Catholic Action.'

Maura Dooley

Neighbours

We helped each other and lived in the shelter of each other.
Friendship was the fastest root in our hearts.
    Peig Sayers, An Old Woman's Reflections

I'd been looking out for a loop of swallows
to tie up the end of those bitter months, when
you came carrying a litre of Chianti,
a packet of McVities Yoghurt Creams, a shovel
to bite into drifts of snow, a bag of salt to
throw at blue ice or over my shoulder
into the eyes of that devil, Winter.

Months passed, seeing your headlights cross
the valley, a low hum of engine heading home,
your washing line like a brave flag.
Spring was late, you dug through the dregs
of an old year, sawing and sowing. Things grew
and your bonfires sent more signals to me,
we're here, we're in, we're happy, busy.

It's you again today, your hands filled
with the last flowers of summer, asking me
about Yarrow. Achilles used the plant to soothe
battle wounds, daggers through the heart.
Take it, let its green fingers bind
with yours. This valley is full of it.

And know that, like the swallows, when you go
you'll leave a small vibration in the air,
a nest for some cuckoo to fill.

MARINA CARR

from *Low in the Dark*

BENDER. There's plenty where she came from . . . as soon as I get my figure back I'll have another and then another, because I am fertile!

BINDER. I had a dream last night your uterus fell out.

BENDER. I dreamt your ovaries exploded!

BINDER. At least I have ovaries and eggs, lots of eggs, much more than you because I'm young. I'm in my prime.

BENDER. I've had my fair share of eggs. Now give her to me.

BINDER. Take her then! (*Throws the baby*.) But don't expect me to hit her when she starts screaming!

BENDER (*to the baby*). We don't expect anything from her do we?

BINDER. He's a very ugly baby!

BENDER. There's no such thing as an ugly baby. (*To the baby*.) Is there? You're the image of your father, aren't you?

BINDER. Who's his father?

BENDER. None of your business! Isn't it enough that he has a father . . . somewhere . . . here now put him away gently. (*Kisses the baby and gives it to Binder*.)

BINDER (*examining the baby*). I still think it's a she. (*Throws it in the shower*.)

BENDER. I'd better write to him. Get out the pen and paper!

(Curtains *enters, goes straight for the Venetian blinds and examines them*.)

BINDER. Hello, how are you?

BENDER. Oh, there you are!

CURTAINS. I love your blinds, they really keep the light out.

BINDER. And the shower curtain?

CURTAINS (*examines the shower curtain*). Yes it's magnificent! Truly magnificent.

BENDER. I bought it in a sale. Eh where did you get your curtains?

CURTAINS (*outraged*). Don't be so impudent!

BINDER. We told you all about our blinds and our curtains!

CURTAINS (*smugly*). Did I ask you about them! No I didn't!

BENDER. Yeah, well you're always in here touching them up, looking for information about them. I even lent you one of the blinds and it came back filthy!

BINDER. I had to scrub it!

CURTAINS. What about the stories I tell you about the man and the woman?

BINDER. I don't need your stories! I have my own man.

BENDER. So have I.

BINDER. You have not! You've no one, only me!

CURTAINS. So you don't want my stories anymore? (*Goes to walk off.*)

BENDER. No wait! We didn't say that.

CURTAINS. I can always talk to myself you know. I don't need this abuse.

BENDER. Calm down will you . . . was the man very handsome?

CURTAINS (*sitting in state on the toilet*). Yes.

BINDER. And strong?

CURTAINS. Yes.

BENDER. And the woman?

BINDER. She was lovely.

CURTAINS. Yes she was. And the woman said to the man, 'I believe you're born to haunt me'.

BENDER. The woman was right.

BINDER. The woman was wrong.

CURTAINS. The woman was right.

BENDER. And what did the man reply?

CURTAINS. He said nothing.

BINDER. Ah, why didn't he say something?

BENDER. I bet he said something, you're just too mean to tell us!

OSCAR WILDE

from *The Importance of Being Ernest*

CECILY (*rather shy and confidingly*): Dearest Gwendolen, there is no reason why I should make a secret of it to you. Our little county newspaper is sure to chronicle the fact next week. Mr Ernest Worthing and I are engaged to be married.

GWENDOLEN (*quite politely, rising*): My darling Cecily, I think there must be some slight error. Mr Ernest Worthing is engaged to me. The announcement will appear in the 'Morning Post' on Saturday at the very latest.

CECILY (*very politely, rising*): I am afraid you must be under some misconception. Ernest proposed to me exactly ten minutes ago. (*Shows diary.*)

GWENDOLEN (*examines diary through her lorgnette carefully*): It is certainly very curious, for he asked me to be his wife yesterday afternoon at 3:30. If you would care to verify the incident, pray do so. (*Produces diary of her own.*) I never travel without my diary. One should always have something sensational to read in the train. I am so sorry, dear Cecily, if it is any disappointment to you, but I am afraid I have the prior claim.

CECILY: It would distress me more than I can tell you, dear Gwendolen, if it caused you any mental or physical anguish, but I am bound to point out that since Ernest proposed to you he clearly has changed his mind.

GWENDOLEN (*meditatively*): If the poor fellow has been entrapped into any foolish promise I shall consider it my duty to rescue him at once, and with a firm hand.

CECILY (*thoughtfully and sadly*): Whatever unfortunate entanglement my dear boy may have got into, I will never reproach him with it after we are married.

GWENDOLEN: Do you allude to me, Miss Cardew, as an entanglement? You are presumptuous. On an occasion of this kind it becomes more than a moral duty to speak one's mind. It becomes a pleasure.

CECILY: Do you suggest, Miss Fairfax, that I entrapped Ernest into an engagement? How dare you? This is no time for wearing the shallow mask of manners. When I see a spade I call it a spade.

GWENDOLEN (*satirically*): I am glad to say that I have never seen a spade. It is obvious that our social spheres have been widely different.

J. M. SYNGE

from *The Playboy of the Western World*

WIDOW QUIN (*Peaceably*). We'll be walking surely when this supper's done, and you'll find we're great company, young fellow, when it's of the like of you and me you'd hear the penny poets singing in an August Fair.

CHRISTY (*Innocently*). Did you kill your father?

PEGEEN (*Contemptuously*). She did not. She hit himself with a worn pick, and the rusted poison did corrode his blood the way he never overed it, and died after. That was a sneaky kind of murder did win small glory with the boys itself.

(*She crosses to Christy's left.*)

WIDOW QUIN (*With good humour*). If it didn't, maybe all knows a widow woman has buried her children and destroyed her man is a wiser comrade for a young lad than a girl, the like of you, who'd go helter-skeltering after any man would let you a wink upon the road.

PEGEEN (*Breaking out into wild rage*). And you'll say that, Widow Quin, and you gasping with the rage you had racing the hill beyond to look on his face.

WIDOW QUIN (*Laughing derisively*). Me, is it? Well, Father Reilly has cuteness to divide you now. (*She pulls Christy up.*) There's great temptation in a man did slay his da, and we'd best be going, young fellow; so rise up and come with me.

PEGEEN (*Seizing his arm*). He'll not stir. He's pot-boy in this place, and I'll not have him stolen off, and kidnapped while himself's abroad.

WIDOW QUIN. It'd be a crazy pot-boy'd lodge him in the shebeen where he works by day, so you'd have a right to come on, young fellow, till you see my little houseen, a perch off on the rising hill.

PEGEEN. Wait till morning, Christy Mahon. Wait till you lay eyes on her leaky thatch is growing more pasture for her buck goat than her square of fields, and she without a tramp itself to keep in order her place at all.

WIDOW QUIN. When you see me contriving in my little gardens, Christy Mahon, you'll swear the Lord God formed me to be living lone, and that there isn't my match in Mayo for thatching, or mowing, or shearing a sheep.

PEGEEN (*With noisy scorn*). It's true the Lord God formed you to contrive indeed. Doesn't the world know you reared a black ram at your own breast, so that the Lord Bishop of Connaught felt the elements of a Christian and he eating it after in a kidney stew? Doesn't the world know you've been seen shaving the foxy skipper from France for a three-penny bit and a sop of grass tobacco would wring the liver from a mountain goat you'd meet leaping the hills?

WIDOW QUIN (*With amusement*). Do you hear her now, young fellow? Do you hear the way she'll be rating at your own self when a week is by?

PEGEEN (*To Christy*). Don't heed her. Tell her to go on into her pigsty and not plague us here.

WIDOW QUIN. I'm going; but he'll come with me.

PEGEEN (*Shaking him*). Are you dumb, young fellow?

MAUD GONNE

Two Letters to W. B. Yeats

15 September 1911
As the great poet of our nation if you lecture in America it should be on literature itself & its bearing on Ireland not on the theatre

Co. which is but an incident, a beautiful incident, but still an incident.

It sounds so obvious & I am afraid to write it, but being as near things as you are to that theatre Co. makes one lose one's sense of proportion, it may not appear so to you – one of your beautiful poems enriches Ireland, indeed the world a hundred times more than the most successful theatre Co. that ever was organised & yet the Abbey theatre Co. has prevented you writing many beautiful poems, this thought has come to me out of my ill humour about your journey to America for the theatre, it may amuse you (to know) to its truth & strangeness.

Our children were your poems of which I was the Father sowing the unrest & storm which made them possible & you the mother who brought them forth in suffering & in the highest beauty & our children had wings –

You & Lady Gregory have a child also *the theatre company* and Lady Gregory is the Father who holds you to your duty of motherhood in true marriage style. That child requires much feeding & looking after. I am sometimes jealous for my children.

26 August 1914

This war is an inconceivable madness which has taken hold of Europe – It is unlike any other war that has ever been. It has no great idea behind it. Even the leaders hardly know why they have entered into it, & certainly the people do not – (I except England from this, she, as usual, is following her commercial selfishness getting others to fight so her commerce of existence shall be ensured by the weakening of Germany).

Is it the slave & Germanic race trouble? If so, what logically has France to do with it?

If it goes on, it is race suicide for all the countries engaged in it who have conscription, only the weaklings will be left to carry on the race; & their whole intellectual and industrial life is already at a standstill. The victor will be nearly as enfeebled as the vanquished. And who is to end it? In France, in Germany, in Austria only the old men & children & women are left, these are not necessary elements for a revolution which might bring peace.

Could the women, who are after all the guardians of the race, end it? Soon they will be in a terrible majority, unless famine destroys them too. I always felt the wave of the woman's power was rising, the men are destroying themselves & we are looking on – Will it be in our power to end this war before European civilisation is swept away.

MICHÉAL O SIADHAIL

While You Are Talking

While you are talking, though I seem all ears,
forgive me if you notice a stray see-through
look; on tiptoe behind the eyes' frontiers
I am spying, wondering at this mobile you.
Sometimes nurturer, praise-giver to the male,
caresser of failures, mother earth, breakwater
to my vessel, suddenly you'll appear frail –
in my arms I'll cradle you like a daughter.
Now soul-pilot and I confess redemptress,
turner of new leaves, reshaper of a history;
then the spirit turns flesh – playful temptress
I untie again ribbons of your mystery.
You shift and travel as only a lover can;
one woman and all things to this one man.

Lady Morgan

To Him Who Said, 'You Live Only for the World'

Oh! no I live not for the throng
Thou seest me mingle oft among.
By fashion driven.
Yet one *may* snatch in this same world
of noise and din, where one is hurl'd,
Some glimpse of heaven!

When *gossip* murmurs rise around,
And all is empty shew and sound,
Of *vulgar* folly,
How sweet! to give wild fancy play,
Or bend to thy dissolving sway.
Soft melancholy.

When silly beaux around one flutter,
And silly belles gay nonsense utter,
How sweet to steal
To some lone corner (*quite perdue*)
And with the dear elected *few*
Converse and *feel*!

When forced for tasteless crowds to sing,
Or listless sweep the trembling string,
Say, when we meet
The eye whose beam alone inspires,
And wakes the warm soul's latent fires,
Is it not sweet?

Yes, yes, the dearest bliss of any
Is that which midst the BLISSLESS many
So oft *we* stole:
Thou knowst 'twas midst much cold parade
And idle crowds, we each betray'd
To each — a soul.

EVELYN CONLON

I Deserve a Brandy and Port

I settled myself in a comfortable corner re-enforced now with two
magazines. (There comes a time when all reading material looks
like the prop of a lonely person — nothing else when it's produced
in a pub particularly, but I couldn't very well afford to think about
that.) I made it clear to all patrons that I was on my own and was
here for the duration of the night, or as much of it as I could stand.
The new confidence had come with the drink. The place was
getting busy. People meeting people. All talking to each other.
Human nature as it is I suddenly longed for conversation. Just a
little conversation. I've only myself to blame. I'm the one who
thought it would be a good idea. Right, I'll start a conversation.
I'll talk but I'll be careful. The problem is — the other problem is —
to tell you the truth I'm getting a bit drunk. Say if I start a
conversation with someone really nice, can I trust myself? Will I
be able to control myself? Will I be able to get through it without
making a pass at him. You know what men are like about women
making passes at them. I won't worry. By the looks of things
someone really nice is elsewhere tonight. So I started talking to
this man. I kind of like him. It's now 9.30 and I've had plenty of
pints. I'm beginning to get very clear in my head. I can see why
women are bitter or something like that. I'm thinking how clear-
headed I am. Drink does that you know. You can spend hours
marvelling how clear-headed you are. Mornings you usually

forget. Anyway I'm talking to this man. I think I like him but I'm not absolutely sure. At least he's letting me talk. Unusual. We're talking about marriage now. I hadn't meant to talk about those matters. When I'm drunk I prefer to talk about politics or something like that because it's safe. No one gets randy talking about politics. Next thing I know I hear him saying, 'I haven't got along with my wife for two years.'

I can't bloody believe it.

And I was just beginning to know that I liked him. Does he think that I started drinking yesterday or that I was born with an inbuilt sympathy detector for men or whatever other cliché a man like him would know? 'You must be trying to chat me up. Men always say that when they're trying to chat a woman up. Married men that is.'

He was flabbergasted at my cheek.

'What fascinates me,' I continue, 'is that they always say two years, never one, never three. I wonder why that is. Do you have any ideas?'

He winced.

'I feel sorry for you,' he said in a low menacing voice and then, warming to his own menacing, 'You are so bitter and unreasonable. You must have had some terrible experiences in your life.'

He says that he feels sorry for me. Hah! I give my short sarcastic laugh, the one that worries even me. It makes me feel sometimes that I'm getting too cynical. He's talking again in response to my laugh.

'I feel sorry for you. I feel sorrier for the men that have to meet you. I feel even sorrier for the young men coming in ten or twenty years' time if the girls are going to get even worse with all this lib stuff. And they are going to get worse. Mark my words. Unless there's a stop put to it.'

Maria Edgeworth

Letters from France, 1802

To her aunt Mrs Ruxton   *From Paris*
    'Here, my dear Aunt, I was interrupted in a manner that will
surprise you as much as it surprised me, by the coming in of
Monsieur Edelcrantz, a Swedish gentleman, whom we have mentioned to you, of superior understanding and mild manners; he
came to offer me his hand and heart!!

    'My heart, you may suppose, cannot return his attachment, for I
have seen but very little of him, and have not had time to have
formed any judgment, except that I think nothing could tempt
me to leave my own dear friends and my own country to live in
Sweden.

    'My dearest Aunt, I write to you the first moment, as next to my
father and mother no person in the world feels so much interest in
all that concerns me. I need not tell you that my father,
                "Such in this moment as in all the past,"
is kindness itself; kindness far superior to what I deserve, but I am
grateful for it.'

To Miss Sophy Ruxton   *Paris, December 8th, 1802*
    'I take it for granted, my dear friend, that you have by this
time seen a letter I wrote a few days ago to my aunt. To you, as to
her, every thought of my mind is open. I persist in refusing to
leave my country and friends to live at the Court of Stockholm,
and he tells me (of course) that there is nothing he would not
sacrifice for me except his duty: he has been all his life in the
service of the King of Sweden, has places under him, and is
actually employed in collecting information for a large political
establishment. He thinks himself bound in honour to finish what
he has begun. He says he should not fear the ridicule or blame that
would be thrown upon him by his countrymen for quitting his
country at his age, but that he should despise himself if he
abandoned his duty for any passion. This is all very reasonable, but

reasonable for him only, not for me; and I have never felt anything for him but esteem and gratitude.'

From the *Memoir*.

'Maria was mistaken as to her own feelings. She refused M. Edelcrantz, but she felt much more for him than esteem and admiration, she was exceedingly in love with him. Mr Edgeworth left her to decide for herself; but she saw too plainly what it would be to us to lose her, and what she would feel at parting from us. She decided rightly for her own future happiness and for that of her family, but she suffered much at the time and long afterwards. While we were at Paris, I remember that in a shop where Charlotte and I were making some purchases, Maria sat apart absorbed in thought, and so deep in reverie, that when her father came in and stood opposite to her she did not see him till he spoke to her, when she started and burst into tears. She was grieved by his look of tender anxiety, and she afterwards exerted herself to join in society, and to take advantage of all that was agreeable during our stay in France and on our journey home, but it was often a most painful effort to her. And even after her return to Edgeworthstown, it was long before she recovered the elasticity of her mind. She exerted all her powers of self-command, and turned her attention to everything which her father suggested for her to write. But *Leonora*, which she began immediately after our return home, was written with the hope of pleasing the Chevalier Edelcrantz; it was written in a style which he liked, and the idea of what he would think of it was I believe present to her in every page she wrote. She never heard that he had even read it. From the time they parted at Paris there was no sort of communication between them, and beyond the chance which brought us sometimes into company with travellers who had been in Sweden, or the casual mention of M. Edelcrantz in the newspapers or scientific journals, we never heard more of one who had been of such supreme interest to her, and to us all at Paris, and of whom Maria continued to have all her life the most romantic recollection.

Brendan Kennelly

The Names

'The names he gives me

good thing
fast bit
born whore
tight cunt
snazzy bitch
would-be nun
dirty slut
sizzling witch
great ride
heart o' the home
snowy bride
randy spark.

Throw a bag over our heads

We're all the same in the dark.'

Somerville and Ross

from *The Real Charlotte*

'How do you do, Miss Mullen?' she said in tones of unconcealed gloom. 'Have you ever seen so few men in your life? and there are five and forty women! I cannot imagine where they have all come from, but I know where I wish they would take themselves to, and that is to the bottom of the lake!'

. . . Charlotte understood that nothing personal was intended; she knew that the freedom of Bruff had been given to her . . .

'Well, your ladyship,' she said, in the bluff, hearty voice which she felt accorded best with the theory of herself that she had built up in Lady Dysart's mind, 'I'll head a forlorn hope to the bottom of the lake for you, and welcome; but for the honour of the house you might give me a cup o' tay first!'

Charlotte had many tones of voice, according with the many facets of her character, and when she wished to be playful she affected a vigorous brogue, not perhaps being aware that her own accent scarcely admitted of being strengthened.

This refinement of humour was probably wasted on Lady Dysart. She was an Englishwoman, and, as such, was constitutionally unable to discern perfectly the subtle grades of Irish vulgarity.

RICHARD BRINSLEY SHERIDAN

Let the Toast Pass

Here's to the maiden of bashful fifteen,
Here's to the widow of fifty
Here's to the flaunting extravagant quean
And here's to the housewife that's thrifty.

Chorus

Let the toast pass,
Drink to the lass,
I'll warrant she'll prove an excuse for the glass.

Here's to the charmer, whose dimples we prize,
Now to the maid who has none, sir,
Here's to the girl with a pair of blue eyes,
And here's to the nymph with but one, sir.

Chorus

Here's to the maid with a bosom of snow,
And to her that's as brown as a berry;
Here's to the wife, with a face full of woe,
And now to the girl that is merry.

Chorus

For let 'em be clumsy, or let 'em be slim,
Young or ancient, I care not a feather;
So fill the pint bumper, quite up to the brim,
And let us all toast them together.

Chorus

12

Time

HELEN WADDELL

I Shall Not Go To Heaven

I shall not go to Heaven when I die,
  But if they let me be
I think I'll take the road I used to know
  That goes by Shere-na-garagh and the sea.
And all day breasting me the wind shall blow,
  And I'll hear nothing but the peewits cry
And the waves talking in the sea below.

I think it will be winter when I die
  For no one from the North could die in spring –
And all the heather will be dead and grey
  And the bog-cotton will have blown away,
And there will be no yellow on the whin.

But I shall smell the peat,
  And when it's almost dark I'll set my feet
Where a white track goes glimmering to the hills,
  And see far up a light . . .
Would you think Heaven could be so small a thing
  As a lit window on the hills at night?
And come in stumbling from the gloom,
  Half-blind, into a fire-lit room,
Turn, and see you,
  And there abide.

If it were true
  And if I thought they would let me be
I almost wish it were tonight I died.

Susan Mitchell

Immortality

Age cannot reach me where the veils of God
        Have shut me in,
For me the myriad births of stars and suns
        Do but begin,
And here how fragrantly there blows to me
        The holy breath,
Sweet from the flowers and stars and the hearts of men,
        From life and death.

We are not old, O heart, we are not old,
        The breath that blows
The soul aflame is still a wandering wind
        That come and goes;
And the stirred heart with sudden raptured life
        A moment glows.

A moment here – a bulrush's brown head
        In the grey rain,
A moment there – a child drowned and a heart
        Quickened with pain;
The name of Death, the blue deep heaven, the scent
        Of the salt sea,
The spicy grass, the honey robbed
        From the wild bee.

Awhile we walk the world on its wide roads
        and narrow ways,
And they pass by, the countless shadowy groups
        of nights and days;
We know them not, O happy heart,
        For you and I
Watch where within a slow dawn lightens up
        Another sky.

The Old Woman of Beare

(Ninth Century)

TRANSLATED BY BRENDAN KENNELLY

The sea crawls from the shore
Leaving there
The despicable weed,
A corpse's hair.
In me,
The desolate withdrawing sea.

The Old Woman of Beare am I
Who once was beautiful.
Now all I know is how to die.
I'll do it well.

Look at my skin
Stretched tight on the bone.
Where kings have pressed their lips,
The pain, the pain.

I don't hate the men
Who swore the truth was in their lies.
One thing alone I hate —
Women's eyes.

The young sun
Gives its youth to everyone,
Touching everything with gold.
In me, the cold.

The cold. Yet still a seed
Burns there.
Women love only money now

But when
I loved, I loved
Young men.

Young men whose horses galloped
On many an open plain
Beating lightning from the ground,
I loved such men.

And still the sea
Rears and plunges into me,
Shoving, rolling through my head
Images of the drifting dead.

A soldier cries
Pitifully about his plight;
A king fades
Into the shivering night.

Does not every season prove
That the acorn hits the ground?
Have I not known enough of love
To know it's lost as soon as found?

I drank my fill of wine with kings,
Their eyes fixed on my hair;
Now among the stinking hags
I chew the cud of prayer.

Time was the sea
Brought kings as slaves to me;
Now I near the face of God
And the crab crawls through my blood.

I loved the wine
That thrilled me to my fingertips;
Now the mean wind
Stitches salt into my lips.

The coward sea
Slouches away from me.
Fear brings back the tide
That made me stretch at the side
Of him who'd take me briefly for his bride.

The sea grows smaller, smaller now.
Farther, farther it goes
Leaving me here where the foam dries
On the deserted land,
Dry as my shrunken thighs,
As the tongue that presses my lips,
As the veins that break through my hands.

DEIRDRE MADDEN

from *The Birds of the Innocent Wood*

But where to begin? With her mother? It would be good, she
thinks, looking at him steadily, if she could bring herself to speak
of the time of her mother's death. Would he be shocked or
sympathetic if she told him the truth? The death had been sudden,
and for the first few days Sarah had been grieved and stunned.
Every morning when she awoke the loss of her mother had been
the first thought in her mind, and she now remembers how
incongruous simple things had been: the sound of the wild birds
crying out over the lough; the way the morning light lay dappled
on the pillow and quilt; the sweet intimate smell of the sheets: to
lie quietly in bed and think that these things, and that every other
little thing in a house as familiar to her as her own body had not
changed, but that one great change had been permitted – that her
mother had died and would never be seen in the house again – had
seemed shocking to her. It was an affront to reality.

On those first mornings she lay and felt grief descend like a great weight upon her heart and mind, and she knew that throughout the day ahead that grief, that heaviness would still be there, made worse by the sight of her father's suffering. He could hardly bear the loss of his wife, and it frightened Sarah to see him suffer so much.

And then, amazingly, on the fifth day after the death, she awoke in the morning to the exact converse of these feelings, for she felt relief and a great sense of lightness, as though some terrible constraint had been lifted from her. Rolling over in bed, she had whispered into the pillow, 'Thank God she's dead.'

Throughout the following day she could scarcely hide her happiness, and Catherine was shocked when she found her sister humming pleasantly to herself as she sifted through the letters of sympathy. After that, Sarah had tried to be more discreet, but she found it difficult to contain these feelings, and she tried to explain them to herself. 'I did love Mama,' she thought, 'I did, I did.' But only now when her mother was safely dead could she admit to the knowledge which qualified that; she had been afraid of her too, and had often even hated her for her cold self-possession. She had been quietly scornful of anyone who fell short of her own level of self-sufficiency. Against the sadness of loss Sarah had to set the honest relief of knowing that her mother would never again sit there, pretending to read or knit or do a crossword, while secretly watching every move her daughters made, watching and silently judging. All her life, Sarah now saw, had been an unconscious struggle against her mother, for she had been afraid that she would grow up to be just like her: just as cold, just as calculating, and just as self-contained. Perhaps if she had lived she would have beaten Sarah and made of her what she wanted; but her death was her failure, her death gave victory to her daughter. Sarah could not feel or even imagine her mother's spiritual presence after her death, nor did she want to. She even found it hard at times to take seriously the great grief of her father and sister and often she wanted to say to them, 'Can't you see that this is for the best? We will get over the loss of her, and we'll be much happier without her than we ever were with her.' But she could never bring herself to speak like this until one afternoon when she and Catherine were standing by their mother's grave. Catherine cried while her sister looked indifferently at the fresh dark earth and the fading flowers, and suddenly she heard her own voice say, 'I don't care that she's dead. We're not. We're alive.'

JULIE O'CALLAGHAN

Change

Are you a woman
between the ages of 49 and 51?
I bet you feel like
elbowing the person
beside you at the cucumber display
or making mean faces
at somebody
you don't even know
on your way to work
each morning.
Do you say nasty things
about the couple across the street
and want to belt those kids
making so much noise?
I can sympathise.
Only, ladies, stop it.
That's a bad way to act.
Get a grip on your bio-rhythms.
Hormone Replacement Therapy
can have dramatic results.
Why not ask your doctor about it today?

Jonathan Swift

Stella's Birthday

This Day whate'er the Fates decree,
Shall still be kept with Joy by me:
This Day then let us not be told
That you are sick, and I grown old,
Nor think on our approaching Ills,
And talk of Spectacles and Pills;
Tomorrow will be Time enough
To hear such mortifying Stuff.
Yet since from Reason may be brought
A better and more pleasing Thought,
Which can, in spite of all Decays,
Support a few remaining Days;
From not the gravest of Divines
Accept for once some serious lines

    Although we now can form no more
Long Schemes of Life as heretofore;
Yet you, while Time is running fast
Can look with Joy on what is past.

    Were Future Happiness and Pain,
A mere Contrivance of the Brain,
As Atheists argue, to entice
And fit their Proselytes for Vice;
(The only Comfort they propose
To have Companions in their Woes).
Grant this the Case, yet sure 'tis hard
That Virtue stil'd its own Reward
And by all Sages understood
To be the chief of human Good,
Should acting, die, nor leave behind
Some lasting Pleasure in the Mind,

Which by Remembrance will assuage
Grief, Sickness, Poverty and Age;
And strongly shoot a radiant Dart
To shine through Life's declining Part.

Say, *Stella*, feel you no Content
Reflecting on a Life well spent?
Your skilful Hand employ'd to save
Despairing Wretches from the Grave;
And then supporting with your Store
Those whom you dragg'd from Death before
(So Providence on Mortals waits,
Preserving what it just creates)
Your gen'rous Boldness to defend
An innocent and absent Friend;
That Courage which can make you just
To Merit humbled in the Dust:
The Detestation you express
For Vice in all its glitt'ring Dress:
That Patience under tort'ring Pain,
Where stubborn Stoicks would complain.

Must these like empty Shadows pass,
Or Forms reflected from a Glass?
Or mere Chimaera's in the Mind,
That fly and leave no Marks behind?
Does not the Body thrive and grow
By Food of twenty Years ago?
And, had it not been still supply'd
It must a thousand Times have dy'd:
Then, who with Reason can maintain
That no Effects of Food remain?
And is not Virtue in Mankind
The Nutriment that feeds the Mind?
Upheld by each good Action past,
And still continued by the last:

Then, who with Reason can pretend
That all Effects of Virtue end?

Believe me *Stella*, when you show
That true Contempt for Things below,
Nor prize your Life for other Ends
Than merely to oblige your Friends;
Your former Actions claim their Part,
And join to fortify your Heart.
For Virtue in her daily Race,
Like *Janus*, bears a double Face;
Looks back with Joy where she has gone,
And therefore goes with Courage on.
She at your sickly Couch will wait,
And guide you to a better State.

O then, whatever Heav'n intends,
Take Pity on your pitying Friends;
Nor let your Ills affect your Mind,
To fancy they can be unkind.
Me, surely me, you ought to spare,
Who gladly would your Suff'rings share;
Or give my Scrap of Life to you,
And think it far beneath your Due,
You, to whose Care so oft I owe,
That I'm alive to tell you so.

EITHNE STRONG

Statement to Offspring

Look, I'll never leave you, issue
of my bone: inside
the marrow's marrow tissue
I am true no matter what.

But I must not be your slave
and do not suck my later life.
I, of sweat and pain have
given, and breaking labour.

Let me be. There is much
I am starving for.
No muffler I to scarf your
years. I cannot aye be shield.

Rebellion? Yes. I am but part
grown. We grow till death.
Let me space. I cry for stars
as in my callow years.

But test me and I'm there.
In the meantime, let me burgeon
whatever else may fruit.
I have suckled without stint.

Let my statement grate who will.
I am no easy choice.
I never asked to have you
but having, am entirely true.

Just allow me room.

LYLE DONAGHY

A Leitrim Woman

People of Ireland – I am an old woman; I am near my end;
I have lived, now, for seventy-five years in your midst;
I have grown up among you, toiled among you, suffered with you
    and enjoyed with you;

I have given and received in faith and honour;

what was to be endured I have endured, what was to be fought
    against I have fought against, what was to be done I have
    done;

I have married in my country; I have borne two men-children and
    three women-children

    two sons and three daughters of a Fenian father;

I have brought them up to love and serve Ireland,

    to fight for her to death,

    to work for her at home and abroad,

    to cherish the old glory of Ireland and to strive manfully to
    bring in new light –

    to go forward;

I have brought them up in faith, to know freedom, and love
    justice,

    to take sides with the poor against their spoilers, against the
    leaders who say to a strong class 'Hold all thou hast, take all
    thou canst,'

    to unbind heavy burdens and grievous to be borne from men's
    shoulders,

    to render unto the people what is the people's;

I have brought them up to believe in our Lord's prayer,

    to believe in the coming of His Kingdom upon earth and to
    labour that it come indeed;

The strength of my body has gone into the soil of this land, and
    the strength of my children's bodies;

the strength of my soul and the strength of the children's soul has
    been given in the cause of the people of this land:

I have suffered, I have endured, when they were in exile and in
    danger of death –

now my husband and one son are dead,

    my last son deported without trial, uncharged –

the spoilers and their friends

the strong and their helpers

    have taken him from me;

I am old, now, and near to death;
those who would have supported me and eased my going have
    been taken from me –
I looked for a little peace before the hour of my departure,
  my last son in the house with me, to see me into the grave –
they have driven him forth –
may the curse of heaven, if there be a heaven, light on them;
    the curse of the widow and childless light on them;
    the curse of the poor without advocates,
    the curse of the old without protection,
    the curse of a mother light on them.

Fanny Parnell

After Death

Shall mine eyes behold thy glory, O my country?
    Shall mine eyes behold thy glory?
Or shall the darkness close around them, ere the sunblaze
    Break at last upon thy story?

When the nations ope for thee their queenly circle,
    As a sweet new sister hail thee,
Shall these lips be sealed in callous death and silence,
    That have known but to bewail thee?

Shall the ear be deaf that only loved thy praises,
    When all men their tribute bring thee?
Shall the mouth be clay that sang thee in thy squalor,
    When all poets' mouths shall sing thee?

Ah! the harpings and the salvos and the shoutings
    Of thy exiled sons returning!
I should hear, tho' dead and mouldered, and the grave-damps
    Should not chill my bosom's burning.

Ah! the tramp of feet victorious! I should hear them
  'Mid the shamrocks and the mosses,
And my heart should toss within the shroud and quiver,
  As a captive dreamer tosses.

I should turn and rend the cere-clothes round me,
  Giant sinews I should borrow –
Crying, 'O, my brothers, I have also loved her
  In her loneliness and sorrow!

'Let me join with you the jubilant procession.
  Let me chant with you her story;
Then contented I shall go back to the shamrocks,
  Now mine eyes have seen her glory!'

MAUREEN GAFFNEY

from *Glass Slippers and Tough Bargains: Men, Women and Power*

Waiting for the New Man and helping him find himself as a way of changing sexual politics had a fatal flaw. The issue of power was forgotten. In fact, even the issue of politics was forgotten. What had started as a revolutionary enterprise had become a kind of grand-scale therapy instead. Part of the explanation for this can be found in the broader history of the last two or three decades. The first stage of the Women's Movement happened in the heady 1960s, when politics, struggle and liberation from oppression were still fashionable issues. In the more sober, conservative 1980s we had time to look again at the fall-out from the counterculture. And it became clear that it had often amounted to little more than an extension of privileges for the already powerful. In the second stage of the Women's Movement, the struggle became more specialised. Women in business tried to fight their corner.

Women in politics did their bit. Women academics started women's study groups. Piecemeal progress was made (though generally by those who were already privileged). The basic politics often got lost. Hanging over the whole enterprise was the big, unfinished business: When were men going to change? When were men going to free up women at home and change their way of relating so that women could begin to realize their full potential? Women found themselves, once again, doing what they have always done: playing the waiting game with men.

The problem with a concept like the New Man is that it implied that the problem with men is their personalities. The problem with men is their power. Look at the traditional definition of masculinity: courage, inner direction, aggression, autonomy, mastery, adventure, toughness of mind and spirit. Enough to set a woman's heart on fire? In reality, it has much more to do with being dominant in the power structure than with male personality as such. Just read that list of qualities again – and think of Margaret Thatcher.

Of course, most individual men are not all that powerful. The power structures in our society are organized in hierarchies. Men have to fight their way up these hierarchies – in politics, in business, in the unions, in sport. Even when they do not actually get to the top, their eyes are always on the next step. A lot of their energy goes into maintaining whatever place they already have on the various hierarchies in their lives. Whether he is one-up or one-down is a major motif in male psychology.

Inevitably, men bring all their skill and practice in power dealings into their relationships with women. They don't, by and large, do it consciously or maliciously. They do it automatically. For example, they do it by assuming from their earliest youth that whole families will be organized around their work and careers, freeing them to move house when they need to, and allowing them to work the long and unsociable hours necessary for promotion. More importantly, they assume that their wives' task is to ensure that family life runs smoothly so that they can face the world of work and competition feeling confident and unhindered. Such male assumptions are based on the idea of others' service, and may be supported by traditional ideology or even violence. The idea that other people should service your needs is part of being powerful. And it is women who do most of the servicing of men's needs.

Men, whether of the Old or New variety, cannot and will not liberate women. It is not in their interest to do so. Because it is in the nature of power and privilege that if one group gets more of these scarce commodities there will be less for the rest. Men, true veterans in the pursuit and retention of power, know this. For example, an increase in women's participation at work will mean greater competition for men. More rights for women in family life inevitably means a lessening of privileges for men. It is not that men are instinctively against women in some simple-minded way. They are just determined to hold on to their access to power and privilege. It's a tough old world out there, men say. And you have to keep your eye on the ball. It is women who must do the real struggling. Sexual politics does not mean a moral crusade – promising to be a good girl and to do it better than men. Neither does it mean a crusade to improve men. Nor does it mean waiting for the New Man. The New Man will not be created from the tender, therapeutic rib of woman. Rather, when the fight for sexual equality is well and truly won, it's the New Man who will come to the negotiating table. Men will change, all right. But only when they have to.

BLANAID SALKELD

Optimism

So this is life, the ranger said:
A bald brush for a bald head.
I'd get more comfort with the dead.
Man builds a house, fills a shop,
Rears gentle flower, gallant crop –
To smash up with his thunder-clap.

Self, self, eat her whelp;
Left its fur upon the shelf;
Sits alone, dumb as stone;
All she loved is dead as delph.
Spinning plane and nursery top
Hum a rhythm will not stop.
When will the adult world grow up?
We are too late too long commencing
For flights to be delight-dispensing,
Man to take down his barbed wire fencing,
And make no mischief with his breath –
In stratosphere, on lake or heath,
Whistling his gala tunes of faith
Into the empty ear of death.
I diced my way from coast to coast,
Though every rattled throw I lost.
My luck will turn when I'm a ghost.

TRUDY HAYES

from *Out of My Head*

(*Lisa gets up and sits on a chair.*)

LISA. Hello – my name's —

TIM (*shouts*). Lisa!

LISA. And I'm an alcoholic. This is the first Alcoholics Anonymous meeting I've ever attended. I don't know quite what I'm doing here but – my life's falling apart. Something – happened. You see – there's this man I love. I met him three years ago and we – I suppose we fell in love. At the time I was working in a nightclub. Every night he picked me up after work and brought me home. I was so crazy about him – mad about him. When I wasn't working we drank most nights – I was terribly happy. I'd spend the night with him and in the morning he'd go out and get me a bottle of fizzy orange and we'd lie around in bed for hours.

Then one morning I asked him to get a bottle of cider instead. And it was – still a joke. But then I started waking up shaking every morning, and drinking. One morning I woke up and all I had from the previous evening was a bottle of Guinness. I opened the bottle with a key – my hands were trembling and I cut myself – there was blood all over the sink. I drank it but I was still shaking and terrified. I went in to Tim and asked him had he any drink and he had a bottle of whiskey. We drank it together, sitting up in his room and chatting as though drinking whiskey at nine o'clock in the morning was perfectly normal.

One time I went on a massive binge with Tim and I woke up in the early morning. All I had from the previous evening was some wine and I drank it as slowly as possible waiting for the morning to come so's I could go to the early morning pubs. I walked into town in darkness, passing houses full of sleeping people who would not wake up in the morning groping for a few drops of alcohol under the bed. Sometimes Tim came to the early morning pubs with me and things seemed normal. This – madness seemed normal. But one time I just started to cry. I couldn't stop. I just sat there crying, and Tim didn't say anything, didn't do anything, didn't comfort me.

We started rowing – tearing each other apart. I left his house after a row one morning and went into a pub. I sat in the pub on my own drinking vodka, avoiding the smiles of a woman sitting near-by who was also drinking vodka at 11 o'clock in the morning. I often drank on my own.

I'm drunk all the time. I'm out of my head all the time. I drink at night in bed while my boyfriend lies there, making irritated noises every time I clink a cider can. Sometimes I think I really hate him. I fight with him – constantly. One minute I'm lying in his arms laughing and then . . . I don't know how . . . I don't know how things went so wrong. But I love my boyfriend. I need him as much as I need drink. I desperately need to stop drinking. I can't . . . I can't see how . . . if anyone here can help me. (*Black-out.*)

VAL MULKERNS

from *Very Like a Whale*

'Ben!' She had been caught as he knew she hated to be caught, wearing her oldest denims and a shirt covered in paint stains. It was, after all, March, the time she had always looked around for something to change even if it was only the colour of a room. But her welcome was real enough. She hugged him in the way that used to embarrass him as a schoolboy and that, even now, amused and touched him. 'Ben! Without a word to us, walking in like this out of the world. Come in. But maybe I knew in my bones you were coming all the same. Why else was *this* the day I got dressed in my oldest rags for finishing the job on the spare room? Only one door left to do. Come and let me look at you.'

'Hello Mother!' He examined her carefully too and saw that she'd never look young again as she still did four years ago. Her eyes were the colour of a blue shirt washed too often and her skin, though brown still from last summer, was papery at long last, like the hands holding his face.

She gave him breakfast in a room with yellow curtains whose window had hanging plants and a distant prospect of Howth Head. For him she had cooked eggs and bacon and predictably for herself had assembled a collection of nuts and fruit. As they talked she kept offering him morsels on his plate, as though he were a child still and not twenty-seven. She promised to bake wholemeal bread later that day.

'It seems selfish to go to all the bother baking for oneself, but I'll enjoy doing it today,' she assured him, and then quite suddenly, before he got out his own question, she began to tell him about his father. She might have been talking about a stranger of whom she was quite fond. As she spoke he looked around the room which was now full of filtered sunshine. The old walnut chest used to be in the back hall at home. The hanging book-shelves used to be in the dining-room. A blue pottery jar now filled with daffodils used to be in the small side window through which he would look coming in from school to see if anybody was in. For the first time since his arrival he felt disturbed. The rooms and passages that were his home were now full of other people's furniture. Other people wrote at the head of their letters 34, Victoria Place. It had happened two years ago, but it had seemed quite unreal on paper. Now in this pleasant, strange room were the familiar pieces of furniture that gave reality to the break-up. He rolled a piece of fresh bread between his fingers, feeling it become sticky again like dough. His mother looked as she used to look when she was anxious to make amends after punishment. She had never punished anybody very seriously except his father.

'We don't by agreement see one another too often, Ben. One has to become accustomed to separation.' She paused, and he remembered from a letter of his sister's that she had experienced two separations in two years. The man with whom she had set up this flat had walked out after a year. Back to his wife, Alison had written. And quite suddenly he also wanted to escape from his mother, from this sunny room where she had welcomed him and fed him before starting to tell him about his father.

'When you go to see him, Ben, make sure there's enough food in the flat. I'm sure he must often forget to buy replacements. And check on his elbows for thinning patches, won't you, and tell me if that boggy brown sweater that he likes to live in is on its last legs. I could buy him another one for his birthday. Why are you laughing at me, Ben?' In a second she was laughing at herself, covering her face with both hands in a youthful gesture that he remembered. 'Oh, I know. It's bloody hard for you to understand. It was hard for him too. But I'm not going to try to explain it to you now, except to say that you can't switch off almost thirty years like a light. Ask him, Ben, would he like some cuttings of the Wandering Jew for his inside window-box. He admired that. And say he can have any number of spider plants if he wants them. They grow if you simply show them the soil, they never fail.'

'Have all the telephone lines in Dublin been cut, Mother?'

'I told you, Ben, it's not as simple as all that. Having separated from him, I will *not* crowd him. He must be given the same chance I took to remake his own life for himself — can't you see that?'

'But it's two years ago.'

'He doesn't find change as easy as — as we do.'

That was cunning. She was reminding him that he had walked out of a perfectly good job as a junior maths teacher four years ago. He had reverted to being a footloose student again and packed his rucksack with a suddenness which had shocked everybody.

'I think I'll stay with him if he'll have me,' Ben said suddenly. 'You don't mind?'

'No,' she said quickly, 'not at all.' But he saw the shock in her face and he knew she had probably been planning to finish the remaining door of the spare room before lunchtime with fast-drying paint.

HELEN SELINA BLACKWOOD

The Irish Emigrant

I'm sitting on the stile, Mary,
    Where we sat, side by side,
That bright May morning long ago
    When first you were my bride.
The corn was springing fresh and green,
    The lark sang loud and high,
The red was on your lip, Mary,
    The love-light in your eye.

The place is little changed, Mary,
    The day is bright as then,
The lark's loud song is in my ear,
    The corn is green again;
But I miss the soft clasp of your hand,
    Your breath warm on my cheek,
And I still keep list'ning for the words
    You never more may speak.

'Tis but a step down yonder lane,
   The little Church stands near –
The Church where we were wed, Mary –
   I see the spire from here;
But the graveyard lies between, Mary –
   My step might break your rest –
Where you, my darling, lie asleep
   With your baby on your breast.

I'm very lonely now, Mary –
   The poor make no new friends; –
But, oh! they love the better still
   The few our Father sends.
And you were all I had, Mary,
   My blessing and my pride;
There's nothing left to care for now
   Since my poor Mary died.

Yours was the good brave heart, Mary,
   That still kept hoping on,
When trust in God had left my soul,
   And half my strength was gone.
There was comfort ever on your lip,
   And the kind look on your brow.
I bless you, Mary, for that same,
   Though you can't hear me now.

I thank you for the patient smile
   When your heart was fit to break;
When the hunger pain was gnawing there
   You hid it for my sake.
I bless you for the pleasant word
   When your heart was sad and sore.
Oh! I'm thankful you are gone, Mary,
   Where grief can't reach you more!

I'm bidding you a long farewell,
　　My Mary – kind and true!
But I'll not forget you, darling,
　　In the land I'm going to.
They say there's bread and work for all,
　　And the sun shines always there;
But I'll not forget old Ireland,
　　Were it fifty times as fair.

And when amid those grand old woods
　　I sit and shut my eyes,
My heart will travel back again
　　To where my Mary lies;
I'll think I see the little stile
　　Where we sat, side by side, –
And the springing corn and bright May morn,
　　When first you were my bride.

To Crinog

(Tenth Century)

TRANSLATED BY KUNO MEYER

Crinog belonged to that company of women known in the literature of the early Christian Church as *virgo subintroducta* or *conhospita*, i.e. a nun who lived with a priest, monk or hermit like a sister or 'spiritual wife' (uxor spiritualis). This practice, which was early suppressed and abandoned everywhere else, seems to have survived in the Irish Church until the tenth century.

Crinog, melodious is your song.
Though young no more you are still bashful.
We two grew up together in Niall's northern land,
When we used to sleep together in tranquil slumber.

That was my age when you slept with me,
O peerless lady of pleasant wisdom:
A pure-hearted youth, lovely without a flaw,
A gentle boy of seven sweet years.

We lived in the great world of Banva
Without sullying soul or body,
My flashing eye full of love for you,
Like a poor innocent untempted by evil.

Your just counsel is ever ready,
Wherever we are we seek it:
To love your penetrating wisdom is better
Than glib discourse with a king.

Since then you have slept with four men after me,
Without folly or falling away:
I know, I hear it on all sides,
You are pure, without sin from man.

At last, after weary wondering,
You have come to me again,
Darkness of age has settled on your face:
Sinless your life draws near its end.

You are still dear to me, faultless one,
You shall have welcome from me without stint:
You will not let us be drowned in torment;
We will earnestly practise devotion with you.

The lasting world is full of your fame,
Far and wide you have wandered on every track:
If every day we followed your ways,
We should come safe into the presence of dread God.

You leave an example and a bequest
To every one in this world,
You have taught us by your life:
Earnest prayer to God is no fallacy.

Then may God grant us peace and happiness!
May the countenance of the King
Shine brightly upon us
When we leave behind our withered bodies.

PHILIP CASEY

Into Whiteness

Winter, and green apples still unripe.
A madness even in the seasons.
The sun, like an anaemic orange
throws a watery light on an earth
as cold as the linoed bedrooms
of the poor. The seagulls will never starve
but they clash, illtempered, in the bright,
crackling air. A cat shivers in
an abandoned cul-de-sac, its instinct
to scavenge frozen.

In a musty bed, the body of a woman
cold and stiff with death, its stench
clambering drunkenly onto the solidified morning.
Her only grandchild will visit her in two days time
with flowers to brighten her room a little;
a good, thoughtful girl who will age
within ten seconds into whiteness,
like the century.

Padraic Colum

An Old Woman of the Roads

O, to have a little house!
To own the hearth and stool and all!
The heaped-up sods upon the fire,
The pile of turf against the wall!

To have a clock with weights and chains
And pendulum swinging up and down!
A dresser filled with shining delph,
Speckled and white and blue and brown!

I could be busy all the day
Clearing and sweeping hearth and floor,
And fixing on their shelf again
My white and blue and speckled store!

I could be quiet there at night
Beside the fire and by myself,
Sure of a bed, and loath to leave
The ticking clock and the shining delph!

Och! but I'm weary of mist and dark,
And roads where there's never a house or bush,
And tired I am of bog and road,
And the crying wind and the lonesome hush!

And I am praying to God on high,
And I am praying Him night and day,
For a little house – a house of my own –
Out of the wind's and the rain's way.

MARY ROSE CALLAGHAN

from *The Awkward Girl*

A sales assistant pointed her to a door marked 'Manager'. She knocked and almost immediately a burly young man came out, looking enquiringly at her smart tweed suit.

'I'm Mother Rita Hynes,' she said, walking in.

Maggy May sat in a corner, bent over a hanky.

Briefly their eyes met.

'I was expecting a nun!' He laughed, offering his hand.

'I am a nun.' Rita shook hands limply, taking in the several pairs of frothy panties on the green formica-topped desk. A skimpy bra cascaded down one side.

He pulled out a chair, 'Sister, a seat! Ha! You can't tell who anyone is these days.'

'Thank you, I'd rather stand.' Rita opened her handbag. 'How much do these come to? We have to get back.'

He waved away the uniformed figure appearing in the doorway. As the door shut, he pointed again to a chair. 'A seat, Sister!'

Rita remained standing, eyeing him obstinately.

He smiled back with his mouth.

She put two five pound notes on the desk. 'This should cover it.'

'Ah, I'm afraid it's not so simple.' He held up a pair of panties. 'Sister was apprehended leaving the shop with these items.'

Rita felt herself reddening. 'I'm sure she meant to pay for them.'

He dropped the incriminating garment onto the table. 'Hmm! . . . Well, I'm not so sure. She didn't have the money. And she could hardly wear them.'

Rita ignored his fat smirk.

He planted his palms heavily on the desk and leant towards her. 'In this shop we fight a constant war against shop-lifters. I prefer the word 'thieves'. And when we catch them, we make it hot. Hot!' He gestured towards the old nun. 'Sister here is a *nun*! She should know the difference between right and wrong!'

Maggy May began to sob.

Rita looked over helplessly.

'It's surely not just a case of right and wrong,' she said after a second.

'What did you say?'

'That some things aren't just a case of right and wrong.'

His eyes were an incredulous blue. 'But if *nuns* do it!'

'She's not different because she wears a uniform.'

'Ah! So you admit she's not different from other people.'

'Yes – yes, I do!'

'Well then!' He folded his arms triumphantly. 'Why should she be treated different?'

'I – eh – '

'Take yourself now. You don't want to be treated different.'

'Why do you say that?'

'Well – your clothes.' He glanced appraisingly at her suit.

Rita looked away, flustered.

'Can't you see she's an old woman?' she said after a second.

'Hmm! We have them all ages. All ages!'

Rita groped for the chair and sank into it. He sat down too and, folding his arms, stared at her quizzically. Maggy May wheezed noisily.

A newspaper lay folded on the desk. Headlines flashed into Rita's mind's eye: NUN CAUGHT SHOP-LIFTING! JUDGE CAUTIONS CONVENT! Mutely she fingered the money. It'd be awful. Awful. There'd be courtrooms, clamouring parents, the Bishop. Oh God, she must think of something. Say something! Quickly she caught the manager's cold blue gaze. What was keeping him? Why not call the guards and be done with it?

He sighed, picking up the phone.

She braced herself, looking supportively at Maggy May. I'm behind you, she wanted to say. You're not alone.

There was an awful silence. Awful.

'Send in a bag and a receipt for four pounds fifty pence,' he said at last. He replaced the receiver, sternly eyeing Rita. 'You'll take charge of Sister? You'll guarantee this won't happen again?'

She put five pounds on the table. 'Yes! Of course!'

When the uniformed guard came in with the bag, he told him to bring back the change. Then slowly, carefully, he folded the garments and put them one by one in the bag. 'I wanted you to realise the seriousness of the situation.'

'Yes!' Rita snapped. 'Yes!'

'I know she's a nun, but next time . . . '

'Yes!' Hastily she pulled Maggy May up and steered her out to the white light of the shop. It was closing time, and a cluster of shop assistants stared as they made for the door.

'Sister! Sister, your change!' The guard caught them in the street outside.

Numbly, Rita pocketed the money.

They walked on.

Suddenly the older nun stopped. 'Mother . . . '

Rita pushed her gently onwards. 'You don't have to say anything.'

'I – I just couldn't stop thinking of him . . . A boy I knew. Long, long ago.'

'A *boy* you knew?'

'Ah yes, Mother . . . ' The old eyes hazed over. 'We'd go up the fields together . . . and once . . . '

'What are you saying?'

Maggy May shook her head. 'It was a terrible sin.'

'What?'

'We did it.'

Rita felt hysteria bubbling inside her. In a minute she'd lose control.

'What are you saying?'

'He went away to England afterwards,' Maggy May smiled dreamily. 'There was a big family.'

'Stop it! Do you hear me? Stop it!' Rita shook the old woman's arm. 'You'll never go out alone again! Do you hear me? Do you hear?'

Rita plunged frantically into the crowd with the old nun tottering after. She had to get home. It seemed miles to the parking lot. Miles. At the car she fumbled shakily for her keys and, glancing over the top, saw Maggy May pale and hunched in the rain. Dear God, what was the point of being in a convent? Of slogging for other people's children? If she made an old woman cry?

'What was his name?' she asked when they joined the snake of traffic sliding homewards through the dark.

JAMES STEPHENS

A Woman is a Branchy Tree

A woman is a branchy tree
And man a singing wind;
And from her branches carelessly
He takes what he can find:

Then wind and man go far away,
While winter comes with loneliness;
With cold, and rain, and slow decay,
On woman and on tree, till they

Droop to the earth again, and be
A withered woman, a withered tree;
While wind and man woo in the glade
Another tree, another maid.

MARY BECKETT

from A Belfast Woman

One of the first things I remember in my life was wakening up with my mother screaming downstairs when we were burnt out in 1921. I ran down in my nightgown and my mother was standing in the middle of the kitchen with her hands up to her face screaming and screaming and the curtains were on fire and my father was pulling them down and stamping on them with the flames catching the oilcloth on the floor. Then he shouted: 'Sadie, the children,' and she stopped screaming and said: 'Oh God, Michael, the children,' and she ran upstairs and came down with the baby in one arm and Joey under the other, and my father took Joey in his arms and me by the hand and we ran out along the street. It was a warm summer night and the fires were crackling all over the place and the street was covered with broken glass. It wasn't until we got into my grandmother's house that anybody noticed that I had nothing on but my nightie and nothing on my feet and they were cut. It was all burnt, everything they had. My mother used to say she didn't save as much as a needle and thread. I wasn't able to sleep for weeks, afraid I'd be wakened by that screaming . . .

Then I started having trouble. I looked as if I was expecting again and my stomach was hard and round but I had bleeding and I could feel no life so I was afraid. I went to the doctor and he said, 'No, Mrs Harrison, you're not pregnant. There is something here we shall have to look into.' And I said, 'Is it serious, doctor?' and he said, 'I can't tell you that, can I, until you go into hospital and have it investigated' and I said, 'Do you mean an operation?' and he said, 'I do, Mrs Harrison.' I came home saying to myself it's cancer and who will rear my Eileen and Liam. I remembered hearing it said that once they put the knife into you, you were dead in six months so I made up my mind I'd have no operation and I'd last out as long as I could. Every year I was able to look after them would be a year gained and the bigger they were the better they'd be able to do without me. But oh dear it was terrible hard on everybody. I told William and my mother and Patsy there was nothing at all the matter with me but they knew to look at me it wasn't true. I was a real blay colour and I was so tired I was ready to drop. I'd sit down by the fire at night when the children were in bed and my eyes would close and if I opened them I'd see William staring at me with such a tortured look on his face I'd have to close them again so that I wouldn't go and lean my head against him

and tell him the whole thing. I knew if I did that he'd make me go
back to the doctor and I'd be done for.

MARY DEVENPORT O'NEILL

Scene-Shifter Death

As it is true that I, like all, must die,
I crave that death may take me unawares
At the very end of some transcendent day;
May creep upon me when I least suspect,
And, with slick fingers light as feather tips,
Unfasten every little tenuous bolt
That held me all my years to this illusion
Of flesh and blood and air and land and sea.

I'd have death work meticulously too –
Splitting each moment into tenths of tenths
Replacing each infinitesimal fragment
Of old dream-stuff with new.

So subtly will the old be shed
That I'll dream on and never know I'm dead.

NOTES ON THE WRITERS

AE (short for Aeon, pen name of George Russell, 1867–1935). Born in Lurgan, Co. Armagh, he became a clerk in Dublin, where he studied art in his spare time: in 1899 he joined the Irish Agricultural Organisation Society. He edited its journal the *Irish Homestead* (1905–23), and the *Irish Statesman* (1923–30). A visionary painter and poet, his books included *The Candle of Vision* (1919), *The Interpreters* (1922) and *The Avatars* (1933). His play *Deirdre* (1902) was staged by the Irish Literary Society.

Alexander, Cecil Frances (*née* Humphreys, 1818–95). Born in Co. Wicklow, she married William Alexander, who became Archbishop of Armagh and Primate of all Ireland. Best known as a hymnologist ('There is a green hill far away', 'All things bright and beautiful' and 'Once in Royal David's City') she also wrote poems and songs for children.

Anderson, Linda (*b.* 1949). Born in Belfast, and educated at Queen's University, Belfast, she now lives in London. She has written two novels: *To Stay Alive* (1984) and *Cuckoo* (1986; 1988). *Charmed Lives*, her first play, won a prize at the London Writer's Competition in 1988. Her stories and poetry have appeared in various anthologies.
'Blinding' by Linda Anderson from *Wildish Things: An Anthology of New Irish Women's Writing*. First published by Attic Press, Dublin, 1989. Reproduced by kind permission of the author and Attic Press.

Archer, Nuala (*b.* 1955). Born in New York of Irish parents, she has lived in Ireland, and Latin and Central America, and now teaches at the State University of Oklahoma in Stillwater. She won the Patrick Kavanagh Award in 1980. Her collections of poetry include *Whale on the Line* (1981) and *The Hour of Pan/Ama* (1992). *Two Women, Two Shores* was published as a collaboration with Medbh McGuckian (1989).
'Ordinary Dragonfly Flicks' by Nuala Archer from *Two Women, Two Shores* (Salmon, 1989). Reproduced by kind permission of Salmon Publishing.

Bannister, Ivy (*b.* 1951). Born in New York, she was educated at Smith College, Massachusetts and Trinity College, Dublin. She now lives in Dublin. A playwright and short story writer, her many awards include the Hennessy Award, the O.Z. Whitehead Award for drama and the P.J. O'Connor Award for radio drama.
Extract from *Roz, Danny, Henry and Mum* by Ivy Bannister reproduced by kind permission of the author.

Banville, John (*b.* 1945). Born in Co. Wexford, he now lives in Dublin, where he is literary editor of *The Irish Times*. His novels include *Birchwood*, *The Newton Letter*, *Mefisto* and *Ghost*. *Doctor Copernicus* (1976) won the James Tait Black Memorial Prize and *Kepler* (1981) was awarded the Guardian Fiction Prize. *The Book of Evidence* (1989) won the GPA Book Award.

Extract from *The Newton Letter* by John Banville (Minerva, 1982). Reproduced by kind permission of Sheil Land Associates and Minerva Books.

Bardwell, Leland (*b.* 1928). Born in India and brought up in Co. Kildare, she has lived in London, Paris and Dublin, and now lives in Monaghan. *Dostoevsky's Grave*, her new and selected poems, was published in 1991. Her first collection of short stories was *Different Kinds of Love* (1987) and a recent novel, her fourth, *There We Have Been*, was published in 1989.
'Them's Your Mother's Pills' by Leland Bardwell from *Dostoevsky's Grave* (Dedalus, 1991). Reproduced by kind permission of the Dedalus Press.

Barrington, Sir Jonah (1760–1834). Born at Abbeyleix, he was educated at Trinity College, Dublin. A barrister, he became an MP and an Admiralty Court Judge; he voted against the Union, was deprived of his office in 1830 for misappropriating court funds, and left Ireland. He wrote racy memoirs, *Personal Sketches of His Own Time* (3 vols, 1827–32) and *The Rise and Fall of the Irish Nation* (1833).

Barrington, Margaret (1896–1982). Born in Malin, Co. Donegal, and educated at Dungannon and Trinity College, Dublin, she wrote short stories – *David's Daughter, Tamar* (1982) is a selection of them made by William Trevor – and a novel, *My Cousin Justin* (1939). She married the historian Edmund Curtis in 1922, and, four years later, Liam O'Flaherty. During the Second World War she helped refugees from Nazi Germany, having earlier organised support for the Republicans in the Spanish Civil War.
Extract from *My Cousin Justin* by Margaret Barrington (Blackstaff edition, 1990). Reproduced by kind permission of the Blackstaff Press.

Beckett, Mary (*b.* 1926). Born in Belfast, she now lives in Dublin. After many years of teaching and rearing a family, she had a volume of short stories, *A Belfast Woman*, published in 1980. Of her five subsequent novels *Give Them Stones* appeared in 1987 and *A Literary Woman* in 1990.
Extracts from the short stories 'The Excursion' and 'A Belfast Woman' from *A Belfast Woman* (Poolbeg, 1980). Reproduced by kind permission of the author and Christine Green.

Beckett, Samuel (1906–89). Born in Dublin and educated at Portora Royal School and Trinity College, Dublin, he taught in Belfast, Paris and Dublin before settling in Paris in 1932. He was decorated for his work in the Resistance in the Second World War. Two volumes of verse, a collection of short stories, *More Pricks than Kicks* (1934) and a novel *Murphy* (1938) were published before the war; after it he wrote three novels (in French; he also translated them into English) *Molloy*, *Malone Meurt*, and *L'Innommable*, as well as the play which made his reputation, *En Attendant Godot*, in English *Waiting for Godot* (1956). He subsequently wrote several plays, including *Not I* (1973). He was awarded the Nobel Prize for literature in 1969.
'I would like my love to die' from *Collected Poems 1930–1978* by Samuel Beckett translated from the French by Samuel Beckett. Copyright this translation © Samuel Beckett 1947–1986. Reproduced by kind permission of the Samuel Beckett Estate and The Calder

Educational Trust, London and Grove Press. Extract from *Happy Days* by Samuel Beckett (Faber and Faber Ltd, 1990). By permission of Faber and Faber Ltd and Grove Press.

Behan, Mrs Kathleen (*née* Kearney, 1889–1991). Born in Dublin, she lived there all her life, working for a time with the Whitecross Republican Aid Association and later as a housekeeper to Maud Gonne. A gifted storyteller with a fine singing voice (her brother Peadar Kearney wrote the Irish National Anthem) she made a record *When all the World was Young* in 1981. Her sons Brendan and Dominic both became writers.
Extracts from *Mother of all Behans* by Mrs Kathleen Behan reproduced by kind permission of Mr Brian Behan.

Bell, Sam Hanna (*b.* 1909). Born in Glasgow, he grew up in Co. Down. He held a variety of jobs before becoming a full-time BBC producer. He has written short stories; his works include *December Bride* (1951), *The Hollow Ball* (1961) and *A Man Flourishing* (1973). He is the author of *The Theatre in Ulster* (1973).
Extract from *December Bride* by Sam Hanna Bell (Blackstaff, 1974). Reproduced by kind permission of the Blackstaff Press.

Bergin, Osborn Joseph (1872–1950). Born in Co. Cork, and educated at University College, Cork, and in Germany, he was appointed Professor of Old Irish in University College, Dublin, in 1908. He edited many Old Irish texts, his work including *Maidin i mBearra agus Danta Eile* (1918) and *Tain bo Cuailgne* (1928). He edited the *Book of the Dun Cow* with R.I. Best in 1929.

Berkeley, Sara (*b.* 1967). Born in Dublin and educated at Trinity College, Dublin, she has lived in America and London. Two collections of her poetry *Penn* (1986) and *Home Movie Nights* (1989) have been followed by a volume of short stories *The Swimmer in the Deep Blue Dream* (1991).
'The Beach' by Sara Berkeley from *Penn* (Raven Arts Press, 1986). Reproduced by kind permission of Raven Arts Press.

Binchy, Maeve (*b.* 1940). Born in Dublin, she was educated at Killiney and University College, Dublin. She now lives in Dalkey, Co. Dublin, and London. A school teacher before becoming a journalist in 1968, her novels include *Light a Penny Candle* (1982), *Echoes* (1985), *Firefly Summer* (1987) and *The Copper Beech* (1992). Her short stories are collected in various volumes, *Central Line* (1977), *Victoria Line* (1980) and *Dublin 4* (1982). Her television plays include *Deeply Regretted* (1979), which won two Jacob Awards, and *Ireland of the Welcomes* (1984).
Extract by Maeve Binchy from *A Portrait of the Artist as a Young Girl*, edited by John Quinn (Methuen London, 1986). Reproduced by kind permission of Methuen London.

Blackwood, Helen Selina, Lady Dufferin (1807–87). A grand-daughter of Richard Brinsley Sheridan, she lived in England and Italy. She wrote and illustrated *Lispings from Low Latitudes* (1869). Her *Songs, Poems and Verses* was published posthumously by her son in 1894.

Blessington, Marguerite, Countess of (1789–1849). Born near Clonmel, she was forced into marriage at fourteen, left her husband after three months, and, following his death, married the Earl of Blessington in 1818. They travelled widely, then lived in Paris until his death in 1829. She lived in Kensington until 1849 when debts forced her to flee to Paris with Count Alfred d'Orsay. She wrote a dozen novels; her *Conversations with Lord Byron* appeared in 1834.

Blinco, Anthony (pen name of Anthony Murphy, *b.* 1934). Born in Cork, where he ran a restaurant. His work has appeared in several journals and in *Five Irish Poets* (1970).
'Career Girl' by Anthony Blinco from *Five Irish Poets* (Mercier Press, 1970). Reproduced by kind permission of the Mercier Press Ltd.

Boland, Eavan Aisling (*b.* 1944). Born in Dublin and educated in London, New York and Trinity College, Dublin, her published work includes *New Territory* (1967), *The War Horse* (1975), *In Her Own Image* (1980), and *Night Feed* (1982). She collaborated with Micheál mac Liammóir for *W.B. Yeats and His World* (1971).
'Mise Eire' by Eavan Boland from *Selected Poems* (Carcanet, 1989). Reproduced by kind permission of Carcanet Press Limited and W. W. Norton & Company Inc. 'A Kind of Scar' reproduced by kind permission of Carcanet Press Limited.

Boland, Rosita (*b.* 1965). Born in Co. Clare, and educated at Trinity College, Dublin, she has lived in Australia, London and Dublin. *Muscle Creek* (1991) is her first collection of poetry. *Sea Legs* (1992) recounts her experiences hitch-hiking around the west coast of Ireland.
Extract from *Sea Legs: Hitch-hiking Around the Coast of Ireland Alone* by Rosita Boland (Raven Arts Press, 1992). Reproduced by kind permission of the author and Raven Arts Press.

Bolger, Dermot (*b.* 1959). Born in Finglas, Dublin, he directs Raven Arts Press and New Island Books. He has written plays and poetry; among his collections of the latter are *Finglas Watching the Night* (1977), *The Habit of Flesh* (1980), *No Waiting America* (1982) and *Internal Exiles* (1985). His novels include *Night Shift* (1985).
Extract from *The Woman's Daughter* (first published Raven Arts Press/extended edition published Penguin Books) reprinted by kind permission of the author and A. P. Watt. *The Lament of Arthur Cleary* (first published by Dolmen Press) reprinted by permission of the author and A. P. Watt.

Bourke, Eva. Born in Germany, she now lives in Galway where she works as a teacher and translator. She edits *Writing in the West* in the *Connaught Tribune*. She has published two collections of poetry: *Gonella* (1985) and *Litany for the Pig* (1989).
'For D. W.' by Eva Bourke from *Litany for the Pig* (Salmon, 1989). Reproduced by kind permission of Salmon Publishing.

Bowen, Elizabeth (1859–1973). Born in Dublin, she was brought up in Bowen's Court, Co. Cork and educated at Doune House, Kent. Her novels

include *The Last September* (1929), *The Death of the Heart* (1938) and *The Heat of the Day* (1949). Her *Collected Stories* appeared in 1980; her autobiographical family history, *Bowenscourt*, in 1942.
'The Most Unforgettable Character I've Ever Met' by Elizabeth Bowen from *The Mulberry Tree* (Poolbeg, 1978). Reproduced by kind permission of Poolbeg Press Ltd.

Brennan, Deirdre (*b.* 1934). Born in Dublin, and brought up in Tipperary, she now lives in Carlow where she teaches at St Patrick's College. She writes bilingually, and has published two collections of poetry: *I Reilig Na MBan Rialta* (1974) and *Scoileanna Geala* (1989). The latter was *Poetry Ireland*'s book choice of the year.
'Purgation' by Deirdre Brennan reproduced by kind permission of the author.

Brett, Heather. Born in Newfoundland and brought up in Belfast, she now lives in Co. Cavan. Her first collection of poems, *Abigail Brown*, was published in 1991, and won the Brendan Behan Memorial Prize. She is co-editor of *Windows*, a literary magazine.
'No Vacancies' from *Abigail Brown* by Heather Brett (Salmon, 1991). Reproduced by kind permission of the author.

Brogan, Patricia Burke. Born in Co. Clare, she now lives in Galway. She has supervised penitent women in a Magdalen laundry as a white-veiled novice, and she has worked as a teacher of art at primary and secondary levels, her etching exhibited at various venues. In 1992 *Eclipsed*, her first play, was performed in Galway, in Dublin and in Edinburgh, where it won the *Scotsman* Fringe First Award. Her first book of poems, *Above the Waves Calligraphy* (1994), is accompanied by her etching.
Extract from *Eclipsed* by Patricia Burke Brogan reproduced by kind permission of the author.

Brooke, Charlotte (1740–93). Born in Co. Cavan, one of the twenty-two children of Henry Brooke the novelist, she collected and translated Irish poems, published as the *Reliques of Irish Poetry* (1789).

Butler, Hubert Marshal (1900–90). Born in Kilkenny, and educated at Charterhouse and St John's College, Oxford, he taught English in Alexandria and Leningrad before returning to Kilkenny in 1941. He wrote *Ten Thousand Saints: A Study in Irish and European Origins* (1972). His essays include *Escape from the Anthill* (1985), awarded the American-Irish Foundation Award for Literature, *The Children of Drancy* (1988) and *The Sub-prefect should have held his tongue and other essays* (1990).
'Aunt Harriet' from *The Children of Drancy: Essays by Hubert Butler* (pp.224–5, The Lilliput Press, 1988). Reproduced by kind permission of The Lilliput Press.

Byrne, Mairead (*b.* 1957). Born in Dublin, she now lives in Limerick where she worked briefly as director of the Belltable Arts Centre. She published a tribute to Joyce in 1982, *Joyce – A Clew*, and two of her plays – *The Golden Hair* (1982) and

Safe Home (1985) – were performed at the Project Arts Centre, Dublin. Her poems have been published in various journals.

Byron, Catherine (*b.* 1947). Born in London, her father English, her mother from Co. Galway, she lived in Belfast from 1948–64. Her volumes of poetry include *Settlements* (1987), *Samhain* (broadcast 1986 and published 1987), *Turas* (1988). *Out of Step*, her study of Seamus Heaney's poetry, was published in 1992. She teaches creative writing.
'Churching' by Catherine Byron from *Settlements and Samhain* (Loxwood Stoneleigh, 1993). Reproduced by kind permission of the author.

Callaghan, Louise C. (*b.* 1948). Born in Dublin, she was educated at University College, Dublin. She spent many summers travelling and teaching in Spain and some years as a 'Cambridge wife' before returning to Dublin, qualifying and teaching in a secondary school. She writes poetry, her work published in various journals; her play *Find the Lady: a Life of Kate O'Brien* was commissioned by the Abbey Theatre.
'The Palantine Daughter Marries a Catholic' by Louise C. Callaghan reproduced by kind permission of the author.

Callaghan, Mary Rose (*b.* 1944). Born in Dublin and educated at University College, Dublin, she divides her time between living in Co. Wicklow and in the United States, where she teaches part-time. Her novels include *Mothers* (1982), *Confessions of a Prodigal Daughter* (1985) and *The Awkward Girl* (1990). She has written a biography of Kitty O'Shea and a book for teenagers, *Has Anyone Seen Heather?*.
Extract from *The Awkward Girl* by Mary Rose Callaghan. First published by Attic Press, 1990. Reproduced by kind permission of the author and Attic Press.

Campbell, Siobhan (*b.* 1962). Educated at University College, Dublin, she now lives in Dublin where she is managing editor of Wolfhound Press. Her poetry has appeared in the *Irish Press*, *Cyphers* and *Hard Lines 3* (1987).
'By Design' by Siobhan Campbell reproduced by kind permission of the author.

Cannon, Moya (*b.* 1956). Born in Donegal, and educated at University College, Dublin, and the University of Cambridge, she now lives in Galway, where she teaches in a school for travelling children. *Oar*, her first collection of poetry, was published in 1990 and received a Brendan Behan Award. Some of her poems have been set to music by the Galway-based composer, Jane O'Leary.
'Afterlove' by Moya Cannon from *Oar* (Salmon, 1990). Reproduced by kind permission of Salmon Publishing.

Carbery, Ethna (pseudonym of Anna Isabel Johnson, 1866–1902). Born at Ballycastle, Co. Antrim, she married the poet Seamus MacManus. She founded *The Northern Patriot* with Alice Milligan; it became the *Shan Van Vocht* which she edited from 1896 to 1899. She wrote short stories and songs, and her poetry appeared in *The Nation*, *United Ireland* and other journals and in *The Four Winds of*

Eirinn (1902). Her short stories were collected in *The Passionate Hearts* (1903) and *In the Celtic Past* (1904).

Carlson, Julia (*b.* 1950). Born in the United States, she now lives in the west of Ireland. She received a Ph.D. from the University of North Carolina at Chapel Hill, and is now a tutor at the University of Galway. She edited *Banned in Ireland: Censorship and the Irish Writer* (1990).
Extract from 'Edna O'Brien Interview' by Julia Carlson from *Banned in Ireland: Censorship and the Irish Writer* (Routledge, 1990). Reproduced by kind permission of Routledge Publishers.

Carr, Marina (*b.* 1964). Born in Dublin, and brought up in Co. Offaly, she was educated at University College, Dublin. She has written several plays, including *Low in the Dark* (performed in the Project Theatre, Dublin, in 1989), *This Love Thing* and *Ullaloo* (performed in the Peacock Theatre, Dublin, in 1991).
'Low in the Dark' from *The Crack in the Emerald: New Irish Plays* (Nick Hern Books, 1990). Reproduced by kind permission of Nick Hern Books, 14 Larden Road, London W3 7ST.

Cary, Joyce (Arthur Joyce Lunel Cary 188?–1957). Educated in England, he joined a Red Cross unit in the Balkan War of 1912. In the Nigerian service, he fought in the Cameroons in 1915–16, was invalided out in 1920 and settled in Oxford. His first published novel was *Aissa Saved* (1932): it was followed by, among others, *Herself Surprised* (1941), *To be a Pilgrim* (1942) and *The Horse's Mouth* (1944). *A House of Children* (1941) is based upon his childhood in Donegal. Other novels include *A Fearful Joy* (1949), *Prisoner of Grace* (1952), *Except the Lord* (1953) and *Not Honour More* (1955).
Extract from *To Be A Pilgrim* by Joyce Cary (Penguin, 1957). Reproduced by kind permission of the J. L. A. Cary Estate.

Casey, Philip (*b.* 1950). Born in London and brought up in Co. Wexford, he now lives in Dublin. He has published two collections of poetry: *Those Distant Summers* (1980) and *After Thunder* (1985). *The Year of the Knife, New and Selected Poems*, appeared in 1991. His play, *Cardinal*, was performed in Hamburg in 1991; his first novel is *The Fabulists* (1994).
'Into Whiteness' by Philip Casey reproduced by kind permission of the author and Raven Arts Press.

Chambers, Anne. Born in Co. Mayo, and educated at University College, Cork, she now lives in Dublin. She has written *Granuaile: The Life and Times of Grace O'Malley 1530–1603* (1979); *Chieftain to Knight. Tibbott-ne-Long Bourke 1567–1629, 1st Viscount Mayo* (1983); *As Wicked a Woman: The Biography of Eleanor, Countess of Desmond* (1986); and *La Sheridan, Adoralde Diva. Margaret Burke-Sheridan, Irish Prima Donna 1889–1958* (1989). She has also written documentaries for Radio Telefis Eireann and is co-author of two film scripts.

Claffey, Una (*b.* 1947). Born in Dublin where she now lives, she has worked as a teacher and lived in France and the United States. She joined Radio Telefis

Eireann in 1977 and became its political correspondent in 1991. She has written
The Women Who Won: Women of the 27th Dail (1993).
'Frances Fitzgerald' by Una Claffey from *The Women Who Won: Women of the 27th Dail*. First
published by Attic Press, Dublin, 1993.

Clarke, Austin (Augustine Joseph) (1896–1974). Born in Dublin, he was
educated at University College, Dublin, where he lectured from 1917 to 1921.
After living in London he eventually settled in Templeogue, Co. Dublin. His
work includes *Later Poems* (1961), *Flight to Africa* (1963), *Mnemosyne Lay in Dust*
(1966), *Collected Poems* (1971). His novels include *The Bright Temptation* (1932);
his *Collected Plays* were published in 1963, his autobiographies *Twice Round the
Black Church* and *A Penny in the Clouds* in 1960 and 1968.
'The Redemptorist' and 'Unmarried Mothers' by Austin Clark reproduced by kind
permission of R. Dardis Clarke, 21 Pleasant Street, Dublin 8.

Coghill, Rhoda (*b*. 1903). Born in Dublin, she studied music at Trinity
College, Dublin, became a concert pianist and piano teacher, and, in 1939,
accompanist at the Dublin Broadcasting Station of Radio Eireann. She published
poetry in a variety of literary journals and two collections, *The Bright Hillside*
(1948) and *Time is a Squirrel* (1956).

Colum, Padraic (1881–1972). Born in Longford where his father was master of
a work house, he was educated at University College, Dublin. He wrote realistic
plays for the Abbey Theatre, among them *Broken Soil* (1903) and *Thomas Muskerry*
(1910). He spent much time in the United States from 1914; he was in Hawaii in
1924, and wrote on Hawaiian folklore. His poetry can be read in *Wild Earth*
(1907), *Collected Poems* (1932) and *The Poet's Circuits* (1960). *The Flying Swan*
(1957) is a novel; he also wrote criticism, travel books and biographies.

Columcille/Colmcille/Columba (521–597). Born in Co. Donegal, of royal
birth, he studied at Moville and Clonard, in each case directed by St Finnian. He
founded monasteries at Derry and Durrow (the Book of Durrow is reputedly
written in his hand). He established himself on the Isle of Iona in 563, where he
died, having returned to Ireland on several occasions and having made many
missionary journeys to the Picts. Reputed to have copied 300 books in his own
hand, the *Altus* and three Latin hymns are ascribed to him.

Condren, Mary. A former editor of Student Christian Movement Publications,
and author of many articles on feminist liberation theology, she has taught in the
Women in Religion Programme at Harvard Divinity School and has written *The
Serpent and the Goddess: Women, Religion and Power in Celtic Ireland* (1989).
Extract from *The Serpent and the Goddess* by Mary Condren. Copyright © 1989 by Mary
Condren. Reproduced by permission of HarperCollins Publishers Inc.

Conlon, Evelyn (*b*. 1952). Born in Monaghan, she has travelled in Asia and
Australia and now lives in Dublin. A founder member of the Dublin Rape Crisis
Centre, she has written a book on sex education for children entitled *Where Did I
Come From?*. Her first novel *Stars in the Daytime* (1989) has been followed by

Taking Scarlet as a Real Colour (1993). Her short stories have been collected in *My Head is Opening* (1987).
'I Deserve a Brandy and Port' by Evelyn Conlon from *My Head is Opening*. First published by Attic Press, Dublin, 1987. Reproduced by kind permission of the author and Attic Press.

Connolly, Susan (*b.* 1956). Born in Co. Louth, she studied music and Italian at University College, Dublin. Her poetry has appeared in *Introductions 1* (1989) and, with Catherine Phil MacCarthy, in *How High the Moon* (1991). Her first collection of poetry is *For the Stranger* (1993).
'Lily' by Susan Connolly from *For the Stranger* (Dedalus, 1993). Reproduced by kind permission of the Dedalus Press.

Cooke, Emma (*b.* 1934). Born in Co. Laois, she now lives near Limerick where she works in adult education. *Female Forms*, a collection of her short stories, was published in 1980. Her novels include *A Single Sensation* (1982) and *Eve's Apple* (1985).
Extract from the short story 'The Bridge' by Emma Cooke from *The Second Blackstaff Book of Short Stories* (Blackstaff, 1991). Reproduced by kind permission of the author.

Cowman, Roz (*b.* 1942). Born in Cork, she lived in East and West Africa for several years. She now lives in Co. Waterford where she teaches in adult education. In 1985 she won the Patrick Kavanagh Award for Poetry. Her first collection of poems was *The Goose Herd* (1989).
'Taking the Veil' by Roz Cowman from *The Goose Herd* (Salmon, 1989). Reproduced by kind permission of Salmon Publishing.

Daly, Ita (*b.* 1945). Born in Co. Leitrim and educated at University College, Dublin, she lives in Dublin. Her collection of stories *The Lady with the Red Shoes* was published in 1980. Her works include *Ellen* (1986), *A Singular Attraction* (1987) and *All Fall Down* (1992).
Extract from *Ellen* by Ita Daly © Ita Daly 1986 (Cape, 1986). Reproduced by kind permission of Random House UK Ltd.

d'Auvergne, Edmund Basil Francis. Some thirty books of his were published between 1907 and 1946; they included biographies, novels, accounts of castles and palaces, and translations.

Devlin, Bernadette Josephine (Mrs McAliskey) (*b.* 1947). Born in Co. Tyrone, where she now lives, she was educated at Queen's University, Belfast. A member of the NI Civil Rights Association and People's Democracy in 1968, she was MP for mid-Ulster from 1969 to 1974. She founded the Irish Republican Socialist Party in 1974, was shot by loyalist gunmen in 1981, and stood unsuccessfully in two Irish elections in 1982. *The Price of My Soul*, an autobiography, was published in 1969.
Extract from *The Price of My Soul* by Bernadette Devlin (André Deutsch, 1969). Reproduced by kind permission of André Deutsch and *The Observer*.

Devlin, Polly (*b.* 1944). Born in Tyrone, she is a journalist who now lives in London. She has written the *Vogue Book of Fashion: Photography* (1979; 1984) and a memoir of her childhood, *All of Us There* (1983).
Extract from *Dora* by Polly Devlin (Chatto and Windus, 1990). Reproduced by kind permission of Chatto and Windus.

Dillon, Eilis (*b.* 1920). Born in Galway and educated in Sligo she now lives in Cork, and is a member of Aosdana. An accomplished cellist, she has written many children's books, notably *The Singing Cave* (1959), in both English and Irish. Her novels include *The Bitter Glass* (1958), *The Head of the Family* (1965), *Across the Bitter Sea* (1973) and *Blood Relations* (1977). Her autobiography, *Inside Ireland*, was published in 1982.

Donaghy, Lyle (1902–47). Educated at Larne Grammar School and Trinity College, Dublin, he worked as a schoolmaster. His poetry includes *At Dawn above Aherlow* (1926), *The Blackbird: Songs of Inisfail* (1933) and *Into the Light* (1934).

Donaghue, Emma (*b.* 1969). Born in Dublin and educated at University College, Dublin, she is now undertaking research for a Ph.D. at the University of Cambridge. Her play *I Know My Own Heart: A Lesbian Regency Romance* was performed in Dublin in 1993. She has also written *Passions Between Women: British Lesbian Culture 1668–1801* (1993) and a novel, *Stir Fry* (1994).
Extract from *Stir Fry* by Emma Donoghue (Hamish Hamilton, 1994) copyright © Emma Donoghue 1994. Reproduced by kind permission of Hamish Hamilton Ltd.

Dooley, Maura (*b.* 1957). Born in Truro, of Irish parents, she grew up in Bristol and has since lived in Yorkshire, London and Swansea. She has organised writers' courses at the Arvon Foundation's Lumb Bank Centre in Yorkshire for five years, and in 1987 became Literature Officer of London's South Bank Centre. She won a Gregory Award in 1987 and has published two short collections: *Ivy Leaves and Arrows* (1986) and *Turbulence* (1988). In 1991 she published her first full-length book of poems: *Explaining Magnetism* (which was a Poetry Book Society Recommendation).
'Neighbours' by Maura Dooley from *Explaining Magnetism* (Bloodaxe Books, 1991). Reproduced by kind permission of the author and Bloodaxe Books.

Dorcey, Mary (*b.* 1950). Born in Dublin, she now lives in Co. Kerry, having lived in France, England, America and Japan. A founder member of Irishwomen United, her poetry collections include *Kindling* (1982), *Not Everyone Sees This Night* and *Moving into the Space Cleared by Our Mothers* (1991). *A Noise from the Woodshed* (1989) is her first collection of short stories.

Doyle, Roddy (*b.* 1958). He was born in Dublin where he lives and where he was until recently a secondary school teacher. He was written plays for the Dublin-based theatre company, Passion Machine, including *Brown Bread* (1987). His novels include *The Commitments* (1987), made into a successful film, as was *The*

Snapper. The Van (1991) was followed by *Paddy Clark Ha Ha Ha* which won the 1993 Booker Prize.
Extract from *The Commitments* by Roddy Doyle (William Heinemann, 1987). Reproduced by kind permission of the author and William Heinemann Ltd.

Dunlevy, Mairead. Born in Co. Donegal, she holds an MA in Archaeology, and worked in the National Museum of Ireland before becoming director of the Hurt Museum in Limerick. She has lectured widely and written many scholarly articles. She wrote the script for and presented David Shaw-Smith's documentary on Irish lace for Radio Telefís Eireann, and is the author of *Dress in Ireland* (1989).
Extract from *Dress in Ireland* by Mairead Dunlevy (Batsford, 1989). Reproduced by kind permission of B. T. Batsford Ltd.

Dunn, Joseph (1872-19??). Born in New Haven, Connecticut, he graduated from Yale University and became Professor of Celtic Languages at the Catholic University of America in Washington, DC. He wrote *The Grammar of Modern Portuguese* (1927), having earlier translated the *Táin Bó Cualnge* (1914).

Edgeworth, Maria (1767–1849). Born near Reading, the eldest child of Richard Lovell Edgeworth, she came to Ireland in 1782 and helped him to manage his estate at Edgeworthstown. She wrote for children *The Parent's Assistant* (1796); followed by *Practical Education* (1798), written with her father, and other tales. *Castle Rackrent* (1800), the first regional novel, was followed by other Irish fiction, *Ennui* (1809) and *The Absentee* (1812), both included in *Tales of Fashionable Life* (1809–12) and *Ormond* (1817). She wrote other novels, notably *Patronage* (1814) and completed her father's *Memoirs* (1820).

Egerton, George, pseudonym of Mary Chavelita Dunne (1859–1945). The daughter of an improvident Irish officer, she was born in Australia and brought up in Ireland. An Ibsenite 'new woman', she eloped to Norway (where she met Knud Hamsun) with Higginson, a married man who died in 1889. She then married George Egerton Clairmonte in 1891, and, in 1907, Golding Bright. *Keynotes* (1893), a volume of stories, established her reputation; she followed it with *Discords* (1894), *Symphonies* (1897) and *Rosa Amorosa* (1901).

Enright, Anne (*b.* 1962). Born in Dublin and educated at Trinity College, Dublin, and the University of East Anglia, she works as a Producer/Director in Radio Telefís Eireann, Dublin. Her first collection of short stories *The Portable Virgin* (1991) won the Rooney prize.
Extract from 'The Portable Virgin' by Anne Enright from *The Portable Virgin and Other Stories* (Secker and Warburg, 1991). Reproduced by kind permission of Reed Book Services.

Evason, Eileen. She now lives in Belfast where she is a social researcher and broadcaster. Her *Against the Grain: The Contemporary Women's Movement in Northern Ireland* was published in 1991.

Extract from 'Community Women's Action' by Eileen Evason from *Against the Grain: The Contemporary Women's Movement in Northern Ireland*. First published by Attic Press, Dublin, 1991. Reproduced by kind permission of the author and Attic Press.

Farquhar, George (1678–1707). Born in Londonderry, educated at Trinity College, Dublin, he had a short career as an actor, terminated by inadvertently wounding another actor in a stage duel. He wrote several comedies, *Love in a Bottle* (1698) and *The Constant Couple* (1699) being moderately successful. His experience as an officer in Lord Orrery's regiment led to the ever popular comedy *The Recruiting Officer* (1706) and his masterpiece *The Beaux Stratagem* (1707).

Ferguson, Sir Samuel (1810–86). Born in Belfast, he was called to the Irish bar in 1838. In 1867 he became first deputy keeper of Irish Records. His books include *Lays of the Western Gael* (1865), *Congal* (1872) and *Poems* (1880). His edition of the *Leabhar Breac* appeared in 1876, his *Ogham Inscriptions in Ireland, Scotland and Wales* in 1887.

Ferriter, Pierce (*c.* 1610–53). Born in Co. Kerry, he was one of the leaders in the Rising of 1641; he held Tralee Castle from 1642 to 1653. Having surrendered under a safe conduct, he was hanged without trial. A major seventeenth-century Irish poet, who wrote in syllabic verse and used assonantal metre, his poems were published in *Dánta Phiarais Feiritéir*, edited by P. O'Duinnin (1903).
Eiléan Ní Chuilleanáin's translation of 'Lay Your Arms Aside' by Pierce Ferriter reproduced by kind permission of Eiléan Ní Chuilleanáin.

Fingall, Elizabeth (Daisy) Mavis, Countess of (1860–1944). The daughter of George Burke of Danesfield, Co. Galway, she married the 11th Earl of Fingall. They lived at Killeen Castle, Co. Meath. *Seventy Years Young* (1937) chronicles her lively life.
Extract from *Seventy Years Young: Memories of Elizabeth, Countess of Fingall* by Daisy Fingall (pp.56–8, Collins, 1937, republished by Lilliput Press, 1991). Reproduced by kind permission of The Lilliput Press.

Fitzgibbon, Theodora (*née* Rosing, *b.* 1916). Born in London of Irish parents she was educated at Brussels, Paris and London. She wrote a novel *Flight of the Kingfisher* (1968) followed by autobiographies, *With Love* (1982) and *Love Lies a Loss* (1985). She is best known for her many books on Irish and international cookery, including *The Food of the Western World* (1976), *A Taste of Ireland* (1968) and *Traditional Irish Food* (1983).
'Potato Cakes' from *A Taste of Ireland in Food and Pictures* by Theodora Fitzgibbon (Dent, 1968). Reproduced by kind permission of David Higham Associates.

Friel, Brian (*b.* 1929). Born in Co. Tyrone, and educated at St. Columb's College, Derry, and St. Joseph's Training College, Belfast, he was a school teacher until 1960. He writes short stories (*The Diviner* (1983) is a selection) as well as stage drama and plays for radio. His plays include *Philadelphia, Here I Come!* (1965), *The Loves of Cass Maguire* (1966), *Faith Healer* (1979), *Translations*

(1980) and *Dancing at Lughnasa* (1990). He is the founder and director of the Field Day Theatre Company.

Extract from *Dancing at Lughnasa* by Brian Friel (Faber and Faber Ltd, 1990) © Brian Friel 1990. Reproduced by kind permission of Faber and Faber Ltd and Curtis Brown Ltd, London, on behalf of Brian Friel.

Gaffney, Maureen. She now lives in Dublin where she is Senior Clinical Psychologist with the Eastern Health Board, a Research Associate in Trinity College, Dublin, and a member of the Law Commission. She chairs the National Social and Economic Forum. A well-known broadcaster, she has written *Glass Slippers and Tough Bargains: Men, Women and Power* (1991).

Extract from *Glass Slippers and Tough Bargains: Men, Women and Power* by Maureen Gaffney. First published by Attic Press, Dublin, 1991. Reproduced by kind permission of the author and Attic Press.

Gernon, Luke. A Bencher of the King's Inns, Dublin, in the 1620s, he held a position described as Second Justice of Munster.

Gogarty, Oliver St John (1878–1957). Educated at Stonyhurst, Clongowes Wood College and Trinity College, Dublin, he became an ear, nose and throat specialist. He wrote poetry: *The Ship* (1918), *An Offering of Swans* (1924), *Others to Adorn* (1939) and *Collected Poems* (1954). His lively autobiographies include *As I Was Going Down Sackville Street* (1937) and *It Isn't This Time of Year At All* (1954). Other titles include *I Follow St Patrick* (1938), *Tumbling in the Hay* (1939) and *Mourning Became Mrs Spendlove* (1952).

'Golden Stockings' by Oliver St John Gogarty reproduced by kind permission of Oliver Duane Gogarty.

Goldsmith, Oliver (1728–74). Born in Co. Longford, he was educated at Athlone and Trinity College, Dublin. He then studied medicine at Edinburgh and Leiden and travelled in Europe from 1755–6. He settled in London, working as a hack writer but producing histories of Greece, Rome and England as well as the essays of *The Citizen of the World* (1762). His reputation rests upon two poems, *The Traveller* (1764) and *The Deserted Village* (1770) and two comedies *The Good Natured Man* (1768) and the perennial *She Stoops to Conquer* (1773) as well as his novel *The Vicar of Wakefield* (1766).

Gonne, Maud (Madame MacBride) (1866–1953). Born near Aldershot, educated by governesses in Ireland and France, she abandoned a career as an actress because of illness and became an Irish nationalist, campaigning for victims of evictions and famine and of harsh imprisonment. W. B. Yeats fell in love with her in 1889 and wrote many poems to and about her during his life. She had two children by Lucien Millevoye, a French Boulangist politician; in 1903 she married George MacBride and they had a son, Sean, in 1904. In 1905 she separated from him, continuing to live in France. After her return to Ireland she was twice imprisoned, by the British, twice by the Irish Free State. She founded Inghinidhe na hEireann in 1900; this enabled women to play a significant role in

nationalist politics. Her autobiography *A Servant of the Queen* (1937; 1994) is complemented by *The Gonne-Yeats Letters* (1992).
'Two Letters to W. B. Yeats' from *The Gonne-Yeats Letters 1893–1938: Always Your Friend*, edited by A. MacBride and A. Norman Jeffares (Hutchinson, 1992). Reproduced by kind permission of Mrs Anna White.

Gore-Booth, Eva (1870–1926). Born at Lissadell, Co. Sligo, a sister of Countess Constance Markiewicz, she was involved in the women's suffrage movement and later became a social worker in Manchester. Her published work includes *Poems of Eva Gore-Booth* (1929) and *The Buried Life of Deirdre* (130).

Gormlaith (*c*. 870–919). Daughter of the King of Ireland (879–914), she married three times and wrote laments on her husbands and her son. After her last husband was killed by the Danes in 917 she is reputed to have become a beggar and died in want. The poetry was edited by O. J. Bergin as 'Poems attributed to Gormlaith' in *Miscellany Presented to Kuno Meyer* (1912).

Greene, Angela. Born in Dublin, she now lives in Co. Louth. She won the Patrick Kavanagh Poetry Award in 1988. Her first collection of poems is *Silence and the Blue Night* (1993).
'Terrorist's Wife' by Angela Greene reproduced by kind permission of the author.

Greene, David William (1915–81). Born in Dublin, he was educated at Trinity College, Dublin, where he was Professor of Irish before becoming a Senior Professor in the Dublin Institute of Advanced Studies. He edited various Irish texts, and, with Frank O'Connor, edited and translated *A Golden Treasury of Irish Poetry AD 600–1200* (1967).

Gregory, Lady Isabella Augusta (*née* Persse, 1852–1932). Born in Co. Galway, she married Sir William Gregory (*d*. 1892) in 1880. She played a prominent part in the creation of the Abbey Theatre for which she wrote many plays, among them *Spreading the News* (1904), *The Workhouse Ward* (1908) and *The Rising of the Moon* (1907). She collected folklore and translated Irish legends in *Cuchulain of Muirthemne* (1902) and *Gods and Fighting Men* (1902). Her other work includes *Poets and Dreamers* (1903), *A Book of Saints and Wonders* (1907) and *Visions and Beliefs in the West of Ireland* (1920); her *Collected Works* are published in the Coole Edition, edited by Colin Smythe.

Grimshaw, Beatrice (*c*. 1880–1953). Born in Co. Antrim, she was educated in Caen, Belfast and London. She wrote several travel books about her adventurous journeys in Borneo and New Guinea: *In the Strange South Seas* (1907), *From Fiji to the Cannibal Islands* (1907) and *The New New Guinea* (1910). She also wrote several volumes of short stories; her novels include *When the Red Gods Call* (1910) and *South Sea Sarah* (1940).

Harding, Michael (*b*. 1953). Born in Cavan, he has lived and worked on both sides of the border. His novels include *Priest* (1986) and *The Trouble with Sarah*

Gullion (1988). His many plays include *Strawboys* (1987), *Una Pooka* and *Misogynist* (1990). He won an RTE/Bank of Ireland Award for *Una Pooka* and won the first Stewart Parker New Playwright's Bursary in 1990.
'Misogynist' by Michael Harding from *A Crack in the Emerald: New Irish Plays* (Nick Hern Books, 1990). Reproduced by kind permission of Nick Hern Books, 14 Larden Road, London W3 7ST.

Harkin, Margo (*b.* 1951). Born in Derry, she was educated at Loreto Convent Grammar School, Coleraine, and the Ulster College of Art and Design, Belfast. She worked as a teacher of art, and in community and youth development, then with the Field Day Theatre Company in 1980. She completed a Theatre Design course in London. She co-founded the Derry Film and Video Workshop with Channel Four funding. She produced *Mother Ireland*, a banned documentary, was director and co-author of *Hush-a-Bye Baby*, and made *The Bloody Sunday Murders* with Eamonn McCann. She has founded her own company, Besom Productions, and is working on schools programmes for Channel Four.
Extract from *Hush-a-Bye Baby* by Margo Harkin reproduced by kind permission of the author and Derry Film and Video.

Hartigan, Anne LeMarquand. Born in England, her mother from Ireland, her father from Jersey, she now lives in Dublin. A painter, she has written several volumes of poetry including *Return Single, Now is a Moveable Feast* (1991) and *Immortal Sins* (1993). Her plays, *Beds* and *La Corbiere*, were performed in the Dublin Theatre Festivals of 1982 and 1990 respectively.
'In That Garden of Paradise' by Anne Le Marquand Hartigan from *Wildish Things: An Anthology of New Irish Women's Writing*. First published by Attic Press, Dublin, 1989. Reproduced by kind permission of the author and Attic Press.

Haverty, Anne. Born in Co. Tipperary, she lives in Dublin. Educated at Trinity College, Dublin, she writes poetry and fiction, and is at present writing a film script. Her biography *Constance Markievicz: An Independent Life* appeared in 1988.
Extract from *Constance Markievicz: An Independent Life* by Anne Haverty (Pandora, 1988). Reproduced by HarperCollins Publishers Limited.

Hayes, Trudy (*b.* 1962). Born in Dublin, and educated at Trinity College, she lives in Dublin. Her stories have appeared in *In Dublin* and *The Irish Times* and she has written a play entitled *Out of My Head* (1992).
'Out of My Head' by Trudy Hayes reproduced by kind permission of the author.

Heaney, Seamus Justin (*b.* 1939). Born in Co. Derry, he was educated at Anahorish and Queen's University, Belfast. A school teacher until 1966, he became a lecturer at Queen's University, Belfast, from 1966–1972, subsequently holding a chair at Harvard University. His collections include *Death of a Naturalist* (1966), *Wintering Out* (1972), *North* (1975), and *Station Island* (1984). He has edited several volumes and written critical studies.
'Act of Union' by Seamus Heaney from *North* (Faber and Faber Ltd, 1990). Reproduced by kind permission of Faber and Faber Ltd and Farrar Straus & Giroux.

Herbert, Dorothea (?1768–1829). Born in Co. Tipperary, her father, a propertied rector of Muckross House, Killarney, Co. Kerry, she was educated at Miss English's School at Carrick. She lived at Carrick-on-Suir and Knockgrafton near Cashel, and wrote poetry, plays and novels, the text of which have been lost. She fell in love with a neighbour, John Roe, whose marriage to another woman brought on her mental derangement.

Extract from *Retrospections of Dorothea Herbert 1770–1806* (Gerald Howe 1929–30, Town House, 1988). Reproduced by kind permission of Town House and Country House Publishers.

Higgins, Rita Ann (*b.* 1955). Born in Galway where she now lives, her collections of poetry include: *Goddess on the Mervue Bus* (1986), *Witch in the Bushes* (1988) and *Philomena's Revenge*. Her plays include *Facelicker Come Home* (1991) and *God of the Hatchman* (1993).

Extract from 'Some People Know What It Is Like' by Rita Ann Higgins reproduced by kind permission of Salmon Poetry and Rita Ann Higgins.

Holland, Mary. She is an award-winning journalist and broadcaster, and has won widespread admiration for her coverage of events relating to Northern Ireland since 1969. She writes opinion columns for *The Irish Times* and *The Observer*. She was joint winner of the Ewart-Biggs Memorial Prize in 1989, and the International Press Corporation Award Winner in 1970. Her documentary *Greggan* won the Prix Italia in 1980.

'Unforgettable meeting of life and art' by Mary Holland (*The Irish Times*, 13.2.92). Reproduced by kind permission of *The Irish Times*.

Hooley, Ruth. Born in Belfast where she now lives, she was editor of *The Female Line* (1985), the first collection of Northern Irish women writers to be published. She has had poems published in *Poetry Ireland Review*, *Fortnight* and *The Belfast Review*.

Hyde, Douglas (1860–1949). Born in Sligo and educated at Trinity College, Dublin, he became an authority on Irish folklore; he founded the Gaelic League in 1893 and became the first President of Ireland in 1937. He translated many legends and poems and stories from Irish in *Folklore of the Irish Celts* (1873), *The Love-Songs of Connacht* (1893), *Beside the Fire* (1898) and *Legends of Saints and Sinners* (1915).

Jenkinson, Biddy. This is the pen name of an author who writes only in Irish; her collections of poetry include: *Baisteadh Gintli* (1987), *Uisci Beatha* (1988) and *San nah Uidhre* (1991). She prefers not to translate or have her work translated into English, 'a small rude gesture to those who think that everything can be harvested and stored without loss in an English-speaking Ireland'.

'Silence' by Biddy Jenkinson reproduced by kind permission of the author.

Johnson, Esther (Hester) (1681–1728). She grew up at Moor Park, Surrey, Sir William Temple's house, where Swift, who called her Stella, first met her and helped in her education. Sir William left her some property in Ireland, where she and her friend Rebecca Dingley moved, at Swift's instigation, in 1701. There –

with one visit to England — they lived for the rest of their lives. She and Swift
were close friends: she is buried in St Patrick's Cathedral, Dublin. (See Sybil Le
Brocquy's *Swift's Most Valuable Friend* (1968).)

Johnston, Jennifer Prudence (*b.* 1930). Born in Dublin, the daughter of Denis
Johnston, she was educated at Park House School and Trinity College, Dublin.
She married Ian Smyth in 1951 and David Gilleland in 1976. Her novels include
The Captains and the Kings (1972), *The Gates* (1973), *How Many Miles to Babylon*
(1874), *The Old Jest* (1979), and *The Railway Station Man* (1984). Her plays
include *Indian Summer* (1984) and *The Porch* (1986).
Extract from *The Invisible Worm* by Jennifer Johnston (Sinclair Stevenson, 1990). Repro-
duced by kind permission of Sinclair Stevenson and Felix De Wolfe.

Jones, Marie. Born in Belfast, she has been writer in residence with Charabanc
Theatre Company since its inception in 1983. Her plays include *Somewhere Over
the Balcony*, *Girls in the Big Picture*, *Gold in the Streets*, *The Hamster Wheel* and
Weddin's, Weedins, and Wakes. These plays have toured in Ireland as well as in the
USA, the UK and the USSR. She has also written *Under Napoleon's Nose* and *It's a
Waste of Time, Tracy* for The Replay Theatre Company, Belfast, as well as three
television plays for a BBC education programme called 'Life School'.
Extract from *The Hamster Wheel* by Marie Jones from *A Crack in the Emerald: New Irish Plays*
(Nick Hern Books, 1990). Reproduced by kind permission of Nick Hern Books, 14 Larden
Road, London W3 7ST.

Joyce, James (1882–1941). Born in Dublin, he was educated at Clongowes
Wood College, Belvedere College and University College, Dublin. He went to
Paris in 1902, returned in 1904, then left Ireland with Nora Barnacle. They lived
in Zurich, then Pola and Trieste, were in Zurich in the First World War, later in
Paris until the Second World War broke out. Joyce died in Zurich. His work
includes the poems of *Chamber Music* (1907) and *Pomes Penyeach* (1927), the stories
of *Dubliners* (1914) and the novels *A Portrait of the Artist as a Young Man* (1916),
Ulysses (1922) and *Finnegans Wake* (1939). *Stephen Hero* (1944) was part of a large
autobiographical novel, which led to *A Portrait of the Artist as a Young Man*.
Extract from *Ulysses* by James Joyce copyright © 1934 and renewed 1962 by Lucia and
George Joyce. Reprinted by permission of Random House Inc.

Kavanagh, Patrick (1906–67). Born in Co. Monaghan, he grew up on a small
farm, later living in Dublin. His work includes *Ploughman and Other Poems*
(1936), *The Great Hunger* (1942), *A Soul for Sale* (1947), *Come Dance with Kitty
Stobling* (1960) and *Collected Poems* (1964). He wrote novels, *The Green Fool* (1938)
and *Tarry Flynn* (1948), and his *Collected Pruse* was published in 1967.
'The Great Hunger' Section VII by Patrick Kavanagh from *Collected Poems* (Martin, Brien
and O'Keeffe, 1972). Reproduced by kind permission of the Trustees of the Estate of
Patrick Kavanagh c/o Peter Fall Literary Agent.

Keane, John Brendan (*b.* 1928). Born and educated at Listowel, Co. Kerry, he
now owns a public house there. His plays include *Sive* (1959), *Sharon's Grave*
(1960), *Hut 42* (1962), *Moll* (1972), *The Good Thing* (1975) and *The Buds of*

Ballybunion (1978). He has published poetry, stories, essays and a series of *Letters* from imaginary characters.
Extract from *Letters of an Irish Parish Priest* by John B. Keane (Mercier, 1972). Reproduced by kind permission of the Mercier Press Ltd.

Keane, Molly (Mary Nesta Skrine, *b.* 1905). Born in Co. Kildare, she married Robert Lumley Deane in 1938, and now lives in Co. Waterford. As M. J. Farrell she wrote *Spring Meeting,* one of her several very successful comedies. An early Molly Keane novel *Devoted Ladies* (1934) was followed by others and – after twenty years in which she did not write – by *Good Behaviour* (1981), which is celebrated for its black comedy. It was followed by *Time after Time* in 1983, her twelfth novel.
Extract from *Good Behaviour* by Molly Keane reproduced by kind permission of Virago Press.

Kell, Richard (*b.* 1927). Born in Co. Cork, educated in India, Belfast and Trinity College, Dublin, he has worked as a senior lecturer in English at Newcastle-upon-Tyne Polytechnic since 1970. His collections of poetry include *Control Tower* (1962), *Differences* (1969) and *Humours* (1978).
'The Gentleman Who Sneaked In' from *In Praise of Warmth* (Dedalus, 1987). Reproduced by kind permission of the Dedalus Press.

Kelleher, John V. An Irish-American scholar, he held a chair at Harvard University, his interests being in Medieval Irish history and literature and in Anglo-Irish literature.

Kelly, Maeve (*b.* 1930). Born in Co. Clare and brought up in Co. Leith, she now lives in Limerick, where she founded ADAPT, a shelter for battered women and their children. Her novels are *Necessary Treasons* (1985) and *Florrie's Girls* (1991). Her collections of short stories include *A Life of Her Own* (1976) and *Orange Horses* (1990). *Resolution* (1986) is a collection of her poems
Extract from *Orange Horses and Other Stories* by Maeve Kelly (Michael Joseph, 1991) © Maeve Kelly, 1991. Reproduced by kind permission of Michael Joseph Ltd and Sheil Land Associates.

Kenny, Mary (*b.* 1944). Born in Dublin, she now lives in London. Expelled from the Loreto Convent in Dublin at the age of sixteen, she was involved in the formation of the Irish Women's Liberation movement in the 1970s. She has spent over twenty-five years as a journalist, contributing to Dublin and London newspapers, and has published a collection of short stories *A Mood for Love* (1989).
Extract by Mary Kenny from *There's Something About a Convent Girl,* edited by Jackie Bennett and Rosemary Forgan (Virago, 1991). Reproduced by kind permission of Virago Press.

Kiernan, Kitty (*d.* 1945). Born in Co. Longford, and educated at St Ita's School, Dublin (an experimental school set up by Patrick Pearse), she joined her brother and sisters in running a hotel at Granard, Co. Longford. Harry Boland and

Michael Collins (both on the supreme Council of the IRB) fell in love with her, and she became engaged to Collins in 1922; both men, on opposite sides in the Civil War, were killed. She eventually married Felix Cronin, Quartermaster General of the Irish Free State Army, and died of Bright's Disease in 1945. Her correspondence with Collins reflects their often stormy relationship

Kitty Kiernan's 'Letter to Michael Collins, 1921' from *The Letters of Michael Collins and Kitty Kiernan*, edited by Leon O'Broin (Gill & Macmillan, 1983).

Lavin, Mary (*b.* 1912). Born in Massachusetts, she was educated at University College, Dublin, and lives in Dublin and Co. Meath. Her first collection of stories was *Tales from Bective Bridge* (1942), awarded the James Tait Black Prize: others followed including *The Becker Wives* (1946), *A Single Lady* (1956), *The Great Wave* (1961) and *Collected Stories* (1985). Her novels include *The House in Clewe Street* (1945) and *A Likely Story* (1957). She has won the Katherine Mansfield Prize and the Gregory Medal.

Extract from 'Sunday Brings Sunday' by Mary Lavin from *The Stories of Mary Lavin Vol. 2* (Constable, 1974). Reproduced by kind permission of Constable Publishers.

Lawless, the Hon., Emily (1845–1913). Born in Kildare, she wrote poetry, historical studies and novels, among them *Hurrish* (1886), *Grania* (1892) and *Maelcho* (1894). Her poetry was collected and re-published in 1965. She also wrote *The Story of Ireland* (1884) and a biography of Maria Edgeworth (1904).

Leadbeater, Mary (*née* Shackleton, 1758–1826). A Quaker, born at Ballitore, Co. Kildare, she was well educated and visited London in 1784, meeting there Edmund Burke, with whom she corresponded for many years. She married a farmer and became postmistress at Ballitore. She wrote *The Annals of Ballitore* (known as *The Leadbeater Papers*), first published in 1862. Her various moral tales include *Dialogues Among the Irish Peasantry* (1811), *The Landlord's Friend* (1813) and *Tales for Cottagers* (1814). Her *Cottage Biography, being a Collection of Lives of the Irish Peasanty* (1822) has a unique value.

Leahy, A.H. (1857–?). A fellow of Pembroke College, Cambridge, he translated *The Courtship of Ferb, a Romance of the Cuchulain Cycle* (1902) and *Ancient Heroic Romances of Ireland*, 2 volumes (1905).

Ledwidge, Francis (1887–1917). Born at Slane, Co. Meath, he worked as a road labourer, and was encouraged in his writing by Lord Dunsany. He was killed in action in France. His work includes *Songs of the Fields* (1916), *Songs of the Peace* (1917) and *Last Songs* (1918).

Lenihan, Edmund. He was born and lives in Co. Clare. Educated at University College, Galway, he is a well-known storyteller and his many books include: *Long Ago by Shannonside, Strange Irish Tales for Children* and *In Search of Biddy Early*.

Extracts from 'Alice Kyteler' and 'Aoibheall, the Banshee' from *Ferocious Irish Women* (Mercier, 1991). Reproduced by kind permission of the Mercier Press Ltd.

Lentin, Ronit (*b.* 1944). Born in Israel of Jewish Romanian parents and educated at the Hebrew University of Jerusalem, she now lives in Ireland. She is a journalist, who has written two English-language novels: *Tea With Mrs. Klein* (1985) and *Night Train to Mother* (1989). She has also written *Who is Minding the Children* (1980) with Geraldine Niland, and *Conversations with Palestinian Women* (1981). Her first two novels were written in Hebrew, published in Tel Aviv; her radio plays have been broadcast in Ireland and Israel.
Extract by Ronit Lentin from *Tea with Mrs Klein, Triad: Modern Irish Fiction*, edited by Lentin, Liddy and O'Murehadha (Wolfhound Press, 1988). Reproduced by kind permission of Wolfhound Press.

Leonard, Hugh (pseudonym of John Keyes Byrne, *b.* 1926). Born in Dalkey, Co. Dublin, he worked as a civil servant, becoming a professional playwright after fourteen years. His plays include *The Big Birthday* (1956), *A Walk on the Water* (1960), *Da* (1973) and *Kill* (1982); he has written various television plays and scripts. His books include *Leonard's Last Book* (1978) and *Home Before Night* (1979).
Extract from *Home Before Night* by Hugh Leonard. First published by André Deutsch 1979. Copyright © 1979 by Hugh Leonard. Reprinted with the permission of Penguin Books Ltd and Atheneum Publishers, an imprint of Macmillan Publishing Company.

Letts, Winifred (1882–1972). Born in Co. Wexford, she was educated in England and in Dublin; she wrote plays produced on the Abbey stage, novels including *Christina's Son* (1915) and poetry, her best-known volume being *Songs from Leinster* (1913).
'Prayer for a Little Child' from *Pillars of the House: An Anthology of Verse by Irish Women 1690 to the Present*, edited by A. A. Kelly (Wolfhound Press, 1988). Reproduced by kind permission of Wolfhound Press.

Levine, June. Born in Dublin, she is a journalist who emigrated to Canada. She edited the *Irish Women's Journal*, and has written *Sisters* (1982; 1985).
Extract from *Sisters* by June Levine (Ward River Press, 1982). Reproduced by kind permission of Poolbeg Press Ltd.

Lingard, Joan (*b.* 1932). Born in Edinburgh, brought up in Belfast, she now divides her time between Edinburgh and Canada. She wrote a quintet of novels for children, *The Kevin and Sadie Quintet* (1970-1988), arising out of the conflict in Northern Ireland in 1969. Her novels for adults include *Sisters by Rite* (1984), *Reasonable Doubts* (1986) and *The Women's House* (1989).
Extract from *Sisters by Rite* by Joan Lingard from *A Portrait of the Artist as a Young Girl*, edited by John Quinn (Methuen London, 1986). Reproduced by kind permission of Methuen London.

'Lisa' remains anonymous.
Extract from *Lisa: The Story of an Irish Drug Addict* (Poolbeg, 1982, 1988). Reproduced by kind permission of Poolbeg Press Ltd.

Longley, Edna. Born in Cork and brought up in Dublin, she was educated at Trinity College, Dublin, and is now Professor of English at Queen's University,

Belfast. Her work includes an edition of Edward Thomas, *Poems and Last Poems* (1973) and a selection of his prose (1981), *Louis MacNeice: A Study* (1988), and a book of essays, *Poetry in the Wars* (1988). She has also edited selections of work by individual Irish poets.

Extract from 'Cathleen to Anorexia' by Edna Longley from *Wildish Things: An Anthology of New Irish Women's Writing*. First published by Attic Press, Dublin, 1989. Reproduced by kind permission of the author and Attic Press.

Luddy, Maria. Educated at the Mary Immaculate College of Education in Limerick, she is a graduate of the National University of Ireland. She works as a primary school teacher in Tipperary and is currently researching the history of prostitution in nineteenth-century Ireland. With Cliona Murphy, she is editor of *Women Surviving: Studies in Irish Women's History in the 19th and 20th Centuries* (1990).

Extract from 'Prostitution and Rescue Work in 19th Century Ireland' by Maria Luddy from *Women Surviving: Studies in Irish Women's History in the 19th and 20th Centuries*, edited by Murphy and Luddy (Poolbeg, 1989).

McCafferty, Nell (*b.* 1944). Born in Derry, she is a journalist who lives in Dublin. Her work includes *The Best of Nell* (1984) and *A Woman to Blame: The Derry Baby Story* (1985).

Extract from 'In View of Circumstances' by Nell McCafferty from *In the Eyes of the Law* (Ward River Press, 1981). Reproduced by kind permission of Poolbeg Press Ltd. Extract from 'It is My Belief that Armagh is a Feminist Issue' from *The Best of Nell: A Selection of Writings over Fourteen Years*. First published by Attic Press, Dublin, 1990 (6th edition).

McCarthy, Patricia (*b.* 1944). Born in Cornwall and educated in Dublin, she has lived in Paris and Bangladesh, and is now in Sussex where she works as a secondary school English teacher. Her volumes of poetry include *Survival* (1975) and *A Second Skin* (1985).

'Abortion' by Patricia McCarthy reproduced by kind permission of the author.

McCrory, Moy. Born in Liverpool of Irish parents, she took degrees in art at the University of Liverpool and Queen's University, Belfast. Her collections of short stories include *The Water's Edge* (1985) and *Bleeding Sinners* (1985).

Extract from 'Katie-Ellen Takes on the World' from *Bleeding Sinners* by Moy McCrory © Moy McCrory (Methuen, 1985). Reproduced by kind permission of Sheil Land Associates.

Mhac an tSaoi, Marie (or Maire MacEntee, *b.* 1922). Born in Dublin, educated at University College, Dublin, and the Sorbonne, she qualified as a barrister and joined the Department of External Affairs, serving in Paris and Madrid. She is married to Conor Cruise O'Brien. Her work includes *Margadh na Saoire?* (1956), *Codladh an Ghaiscigh* (1973) and *An Galar Dubhach* (1980). *A Heart Full of Thought* (1959) contains translations from the Irish. She has won the Oireachtas prize for poetry.

'The Hero's Sleep' by Maire Mhac an tSaio reproduced by kind permission of the author.

McGahern, John (*b.* 1935). Educated at Carrick-on-Shannon, he trained as a
schoolteacher and taught at Clontarf, Dublin, from 1957 to 1964. He now lives
in Co. Leitrim. His novels include *The Barracks* (1963), *The Dark* (1965), *The
Pornographer* (1979) and *Amongst Women* (1990). Volumes of his short stories
include *Nightlines* (1971) and *High Ground* (1985).
Extract from *Amongst Women* by John McGahern (Faber and Faber Ltd, 1990). Reproduced
by kind permission of Faber and Faber Ltd.

MacGiolla Bhrighde, Niall (1861–1938). Born in Co. Donegal, a native
speaker of Irish (though he did not learn to write in Irish until he was an adult) he
won Feis prizes, and contributed poems to the *Derry People*. His poetry is
collected in *Blatha Fraoich* (1905).

McGuckian, Medbh (*b.* 1950). Born in Belfast, she is a teacher whose books
include *The Flower Master* (1982), *Venus and the Rain* (1984) and *On Ballycastle
Beach* (1988).
'Charlotte's Delivery' by Medbh McGuckian from *Marconi's Cottage* (Gallery, 1991).
Reproduced by kind permission of the author and the Gallery Press.

McGuinness, Frank. Born in Buncrana, Co. Donegal, and educated at University College, Dublin, he now lives in Dublin and lectures in English at St
Patrick's College, Maynooth. His plays include *The Factory Girls* (1982), *Observe
the Sons of Ulster Marching Towards the Somme* (1985) for which he was awarded the
Rooney Prize, *Someone Who'll Watch Over Me* (1993) and *Carthaginians* (1988). He
has written versions of plays by Ibsen and Lorca, and has also written television
drama.
Extract from *The Factory Girls* by Frank McGuinness © Frank McGuinness 1982 (Monach
Line, 1982). Reproduced by kind permission of the author and Lemon Unna & Durbridge
Ltd.

McKay, Susan (*b.* 1957). Born in Derry, she was educated at Trinity College,
Dublin. A founder member of the Belfast Rape Crisis Centre, she worked there as
Counsellor (1982–86), in Sligo as Director of a Young Unemployed Centre
(1986–87) and in Fermanagh as Community Worker (1987–89). She has been a
staff journalist with the *Sunday Tribune* since 1992.
Report of the Kilkenny Incest Case by Susan McKay (*Sunday Tribune* 9.5.93). Reproduced by
kind permission of the *Sunday Tribune*.

MacLaverty, Bernard (*b.* 1942). Born in Belfast and educated at Queen's
University, Belfast, he now lives in Scotland. His stories are included in *Secrets
and Other Stories* (1977), *Lamb* (1977), *Cal* (1983) and *The Great Profundo and other
Stories* (1987). *A Man in Search of a Pet* (1978) is a book for children.
Extract from *Cal* by Bernard MacLaverty (Cape, 1983). Reproduced by kind permission of
Jonathan Cape.

mac Liammóir, Micheál (Michael Willmore, 1899–1978). Born in Cork, he
lived in London from the age of ten to fifteen, a child actor. He studied at the
Slade, returned to Ireland in 1916, and in 1928 founded the Gate Theatre with

Hilton Edwards. He wrote plays and poetry in English and Irish, continued to paint and was known for his dramatic monologues in the 1960s, including *The Importance of Being Oscar* (1963). His autobiographical writing includes *All for Hecuba* (1946) and *Memoirs of an Irish Actor, Young and Old* (1977), and his plays *Ill Met by Moonlight* (1957) and *Where Stars Walk* (1961).
Extract from *All for Hecuba* by Micheál mac Liammóir reproduced by kind permission of the Executor of the Estate of the late Dr Hilton Edwards.

McLoughlin, Dympna. She wrote a Ph.D. at Syracuse University, New York, on *Shovelling Out Paupers: Female Emigration from Irish Workhouses 1840–70*. She is now a Junior Research Fellow at the Institute of Irish Studies in Belfast.
Extract from 'Workhouses and Irish Female Paupers 1840–70' from *Women Surviving: Studies in Irish Women's History in the 19th and 20th Centuries*, edited by Murphy and Luddy (Poolbeg, 1989). Reproduced by kind permission of Poolbeg Press Ltd.

McManus, Liz (*b.* 1947). Born in Canada, she now lives in Co. Wicklow, where she is a Democratic Left TD. She has written a novel, *Acts of Subversion* (1991) and many prize-winning short stories. She writes a weekly column in the *Sunday Tribune*.
Extract from *Acts of Subversion* by Liz McManus (Poolbeg, 1991). Reproduced by kind permission of Poolbeg Press Ltd.

Madden, Deirdre. Born at Toomebridge in Co. Antrim, educated at Trinity College, Dublin, and the University of East Anglia, she has lived in Italy but now lives in London. She has published a novella *Hidden Symptoms* (1986) and two novels, *The Birds of the Innocent Wood* (1988), which won the Somerset Maugham Award, and *Remembering Light and Stone* (1992). She won the Rooney Prize for Irish Literature in 1987.
Extract from *The Birds of the Innocent Wood* by Deirdre Madden (Faber and Faber Ltd, 1988). Reproduced by kind permission of Faber and Faber Ltd.

Mahon, Brid. Born in Dublin where she is now living, she has worked as a journalist, folklorist and author of children's books. She has written a life of Peg Woffington, entitled *A Time to Love* (1992).
Extract from *A Time to Love: The Life of Peg Woffington* by Brid Mahon (Poolbeg, 1992). Reproduced by kind permission of Poolbeg Press Ltd.

Malcolm, Elizabeth. Born in Sydney, Australia, of Irish parents, she obtained her BA from the University of New South Wales, her MA from the University of Sydney, and her Ph.D. from Trinity College, Dublin. She has taught in universities in Australia, Ireland, Norway and England. Formerly a Research Fellow at Queen's University, Belfast, since 1989 she has been Senior Research Fellow at the Institute of Irish Studies, University of Liverpool. She has published two books: *Ireland Sober, Ireland Free: Drink and Temperance in Nineteenth-Century Ireland* (1986) and *Swift's Hospital: A History of St Patrick's Hospital, Dublin, 1746–1989* (1989). She is currently editing a collection of essays on the social history of Irish medicine.

Extract from 'Women and Madness' by Elizabeth Malcolm from *Women in Early Modern Ireland*, edited by Margaret McCurtain and Mary O'Dowd (Edinburgh University Press, 1991). Reproduced by kind permission of the author and Edinburgh University Press.

Mangan, James Clarence (1803–49). Born in Dublin, he worked as a lawyer's clerk, in the Ordnance Survey and in the Library of Trinity College, Dublin. He wrote under several pseudonyms for *The Nation*; translated Germany poetry, notably in a *German Anthology* (1845), and collected the *Poets and Poetry of Munster*. He wrote many poems under his own name – an edition of them was published in 1870, another in 1897 – as well as many which appeared anonymously or pseudonymously.

Marcus, David (*b.* 1924). Educated at University College, Cork, a graduate of King's Inns, Dublin, he practised at the Irish Bar before founding and editing *Irish Writing* in 1946. He edited *Poetry Ireland*, and became Literary Editor of the *Irish Press* (1968–85). His work includes anthologies of Irish poems and stories as well as poems and short stories of his own; his novels are *Next Year in Jerusalem* (1954) and *A Land Not Theirs* (1986).
Extract from *A Land Not Theirs* by David Marcus (Transworld, 1986). Reproduced by kind permission of the author.

Medbh, Máighréad (*b.* 1959). Born in Co. Limerick, she has lived in Belfast but now lives in Dublin. She performs her poetry with music at various rock venues in Ireland. *The Making of a Pagan* (1990) is her first collection of poetry.
'Coming Out' by Máighréad Medbh from *The Making of a Pagan* (Blackstaff, 1990). Reproduced by kind permission of the Blackstaff Press.

Meehan, Paula (b. 1955). Born in Dublin, she was educated at Trinity College, Dublin, and Eastern Washington University and now teaches creative writing in schools, universities, community groups and prisons. She has published three volumes of poetry: *Return and No Blame* (1984), *Reading the Sky* (1986) and *The Man Who Was Marked By Winter* (1991).
'The Pattern' by Paula Meehan from *The Man Who Was Marked By Winter* (Gallery, 1991). Reproduced by kind permission of the author and the Gallery Press.

Merriman, Brian (*c.* 1747–1805). Born in Co. Clare, he was educated in a hedge school and by travelling poets before teaching at Feakle, Co. Clare (where he also took to farming) and later in Limerick. His reputation was gained by his long poem in Irish, *The Midnight Court*, which has been frequently translated.
Extract from *The Midnight Court* by Brian Merriman, translated by David Marcus (Poolbeg Press, 1968). Reproduced by kind permission of David Marcus.

Meyer, Kuno (1858–1919). Educated at Edinburgh and Leipzig, he lectured at University College, Liverpool, founded the School of Irish Learning in Dublin in 1903 and became Professor of Celtic at the University of Berlin in 1911. His publications on Celtic studies are numerous and include *The Voyage of Bran* (1895), *The Death Tales of Ulster Heroes* (1906) and *Selections from Ancient Irish Poetry* (1911; 1928).

Mitchell, Susan Langstaff (1866–1926). Born at Carrick-on-Shannon, a journalist, satirist and religious poet, she was assistant editor (to George Russell) on the *Irish Homestead* and the *Irish Statesman* which succeeded it. Her books include *Aids to the Immortality of Certain Persons in Ireland* (1905), *The Living Chalice and other Poems* (1908), *George Moore* (1916) and *Secret Springs of Dublin Song* (1918).

Molloy, Frances (1947–91). Born and brought up in Derry, she moved to Lancaster, returning to Ireland in 1988. She left school at fifteen and was briefly a nun. She wrote a novel *No Mate for the Magpie* (1985). The novel was largely autobiographical as were her short stories.
Extract from *No Mate for the Magpie* by Frances Molloy (Virago, 1985). Reproduced by kind permission of the author and Virago Press.

Montague, John Patrick (*b.* 1929). Born in New York, he was educated at Armagh, University College, Dublin, Yale University and Iowa University, and lives in Cork. He has taught at Berkeley, California, and University College, Cork. His poetry includes *The Rough Field* (1972), *The Great Cloak* (1978) and *Selected Poems* (1982). He edited the *Faber Book of Irish Verse* in 1974.
'Sheela-na-Gig' by John Montague reproduced by kind permission of the author and the Gallery Press.

Moore, Brian (*b.* 1921). Born in Belfast, he worked with the Ministry of Transport from 1943 to 1946, then with UNRRA in Warsaw. He emigrated to Canada and now lives in California. His work includes *The Lonely Passion of Judith Hearne* (1955), *The Luck of Ginger Coffey* (1960), *The Emperor of Ice-Cream* (1968), *Fergus* (1970), *Catholics* (1972), which won the WH Smith Award, *The Mangan Inheritance* (1979), *Cold Heaven* (1983) and *Black Robe* (1985).
Extracts from *The Lonely Passion of Judith Hearne* by Brian Moore copyright © 1955 Brian Moore (André Deutsch, 1988). Reproduced by kind permission of the author c/o Curtis Brown Ltd and André Deutsch Ltd.

Moore, Christy (*b.* 1948). Born in Co. Kildare, he now lives outside Dublin. He has worked as a bank clerk and on an oil rig before becoming a major music figure in Ireland and Britain: originally performing in Planxty and Moving Hearts he is now solo. His many albums include *Prosperous* (1972), *The Iron Behind the Velvet* (1978), as well as *The Voyage* and *Smoke and Strong Whiskey*. *King Puck* (1993) is his most recent work. His ballads reveal his commitment to various causes.
Lyrics of 'Middle of the Island' by Christy Moore and Nigel Rolfe from *The Voyage*. Reproduced by kind permission of Christy Moore, Nigel Rolfe and BAL Music.

Moore, George Augustus (1852–1933). Born in Moore Hall, Co. Mayo, he was educated at Oscott College, Birmingham, the son of a landowner who bred and raced horses and died when Moore was eighteen. He went to Paris to become a painter but turned to literature; in London, his rents having dried up, he wrote *A Modern Lover* (1883), *A Mummer's Wife* (1885) and *A Drama in Muslin* (1886). *Esther Waters* (1894) was very successful. In 1900 he moved to Dublin, the result the stories of *The Untilled Field* (1903) and *The Lake* (1905). Back permanently in

London in 1911 he produced the three volumes of *Hail and Farewell* (1911–14), a mischievous picture of the Irish literary revival and Irish Catholicism. *The Brook Kerith* (1916) and *Héloïse and Abelard* (1921) followed his *Confessions of a Young Man* (1888) and *Modern Painting* (1893).

Moore, Thomas (1779–1852). Born in Dublin, he was educated at Trinity College, Dublin, and the Middle Temple. A successful translation of *Anacreon* in 1800 was followed by *The Poetical Works of the late Thomas Little* (1801). His *Epistles, Odes and Other Poems* (1806) led to a duel with the reviewer in the *Edinburgh Review*. He began publishing his highly successful *Irish Melodies* in 1808; they were followed by *Lalla Rookh* (1817), an oriental poem influenced by Byron. Moore wrote several biographies – including one of his friend Byron – and *The Memoirs of Captain Rock* (1824). Because of financial problems he lived in France from 1819 until 1922, then in Wiltshire.

Morgan, Lady (*née* Sydney Owenson, *c.* 1775–1859). The daughter of an actor manager, she was educated at the Huguenot School, Clontarf, Dublin, and became a governess. In 1805 she published *Twelve Original Hibernian Melodies* and a novel, *The Novice of St Dominick*; these followed her first novel *St Clair, or the Heiress of Desmond* (1803). *The Wild Irish Girl* (1806) made her famous; she then wrote *O'Donnel* (1814), *Florence Macarthy* (1819) and *The O'Briens and the O'Fahertys* (1827). She also wrote accounts of her travels, *France* (1817) and *Italy* (1821). Her *Life of Salvator Rosa* appeared in 1825 and *Passages from my Autobiography* in 1859. She married Charles Morgan, a doctor, who was knighted as a wedding present by the Marquess of Abercorn; she established a lively salon in Kildare Street, Dublin.

Morrissey, Sinéad (*b.* 1972). Born in Portadown, Co. Armagh, she lived in Belfast from seven to eighteen, attending Belfast High School. She is at present an undergraduate at Trinity College, Dublin, teaching English in a secondary school in Northern Germany for a year as part of her degree course. She has won prizes for five years in the Irish Schools Creative Writing Awards and in 1990 was the winner of the Patrick Kavanagh Award for poetry.

Morrissy, Mary (*b.* 1957). Born in Dublin, she now works there as sub-editor of *The Irish Times*. She won the Hennessy Award for short stories in 1984. Her stories have appeared in various magazines and anthologies, including *Virgins and Hyacinths* (1993). Her first collection is *The Lazy Eye* (1993).
Extract from *The Lazy Eye* by Mary Morrissy © Mary Morrissy 1993 (Cape, 1993). Reproduced by kind permission of Jonathan Cape Ltd.

Morton, May (1876–1957). Born in Co. Limerick, she lived in Belfast, working as Vice-Principal of a girls' model school. Her poems were published in various magazines and broadcast on Radio Telefís Eireann and the BBC. Her volumes of poetry include *Dawn and Afterglow* (1936), *Masque in Maytime* (1948), *Spindle and Shuttle* (1951) and *Sang to the Spinning Wheel* (1952). She won the Northern Ireland Award for poetry in the Festival of Britain.

'Spindle and Shuttle' by May Morton from *Pillars of the House: An Anthology of Verse by Irish Women 1690 to the Present*, edited by A. A. Kelly (Wolfhound Press, 1988). Reproduced by kind permission of Wolfhound Press.

Mulkerns, Val (*b.* 1925). Born in Dublin and educated at the Dominican College there, she worked as a civil servant from 1945 to 1949. Her stories appeared in *The Bell* of which she became Associate Editor. Her novels include *A Time Outworn* (1951), *The Summerhouse* (1984) and *Very Like a Whale* (1986). Her short stories are collected in several volumes, among them *Antiquities* (1978) and *An Idle Woman* (1981). These two volumes, with her novel *The Summerhouse*, were awarded the Allied Banks' Prize for Literature in 1984.
Extract from *Very Like a Whale* by Val Mulkerns (John Murray (Publishers) Ltd). Reproduced by permission of John Murray (Publishers) Ltd and the Peters Fraser and Dunlop Group Ltd.

Murdoch, Iris (*b.* 1920). Born in Dublin and educated at Somerville College, Oxford, she worked in the Treasury and UNRRA before becoming a Fellow of St Anne's College, Oxford. Her works include *Under the Net* (1954), *A Severed Head* (1961), *An Unofficial Rose* (1962), *The Italian Girl* (1964), *The Red and the Green* (1963), a novel about Ireland, and *Bruno's Dream* (1961). There followed *The Sea, The Sea* (1978) which won the Booker Prize, and *Nuns and Soldiers* (1980). She has written plays, essays and a book on metaphysics.
Extract from *The Red and the Green* by Iris Murdoch © Iris Murdoch 1963, 1984 (Chatto and Windus, 1984). Reproduced by kind permission of Random House UK Ltd.

Murphy, Dervla (*b.* 1931). Born in Co. Waterford, she spends most of her time travelling – and writing travel books. These include *Full Tilt – Ireland to India with a Bicycle*, *In Ethiopia with a Mule*, *Tibetan Foothold*, *Eight Feet in the Andes*, and *Transylvania and Beyond* (1992). She has written an autobiography *Wheels Within Wheels* (1979).
Extract from *Wheels Within Wheels* by Dervla Murphy (John Murray (Publishers) Ltd, 1979). Reproduced by kind permission of John Murray (Publishers) Ltd.

Nicholls, K.W. (b. 1934). Born in England of Irish parentage, he was educated at Trinity College, Dublin, and is now a Statutory Lecturer at University College, Cork. He is the author of *Land Law and Society in Sixteenth-Century Ireland* (1978).
Extract from 'Irish Women and Property in the Sixteenth Century' by K. W. Nicholls from *Women in Early Modern Ireland*, edited by Margaret McCurtain and Mary O'Dowd (Edinburgh University Press, 1991). Reproduced by kind permission of the author and Edinburgh University Press.

Ni Chonaill, Eibhlin Dubh (*c.* 1748–*c.* 1800). She married an O'Connor, who died six months later, then eloped with Colonel Art O'Leary who formerly served with the Irish Brigade in Austria and settled near Macroom. He was ambushed and shot by soldiers in May 1773 after he had been outlawed, having challenged a Protestant neighbour, Morris, who had offered him five pounds – in the terms of the Penal Laws, for O'Connor was a Catholic – for his famous mare. His widow had the soldiers responsible transported; Morris was shot dead by O'Leary's brother. There are various editions of the widow's lament for her husband.

Ní Chuilleanáin, Eiléan (*b.* 1942). Born in Cork and educated at University College, Cork, and the University of Oxford she now lectures at Trinity College, Dublin. Her poetry is collected in *Acts and Monuments* (1973), *Site of Ambush* (1975), *Cork* (1977), *The Second Voyage* (1977; 1986), *The Rose Geranium* (1981) and *The Magdalene Sermon* (1989). She edited *Irish Women: Image and Achievement* (1985).
'Those People' and 'Pygmalion's Image' by Eiléan Ní Chuilleanáin from *The Magdalene Sermon* (Gallery, 1989). Reproduced by kind permission of the author and the Gallery Press.

Ní Dhomhnaill, Nuala (*b.* 1952). Born in England, she grew up in Nenagh, Co. Tipperary, speaking Irish. Previously resident in Turkey she now lives in Ireland. Her work includes *An Sealg Droighin* (1981) and *Fear Suithinseach* (1984).
'Blodewedd' by Nuala Ní Dhomhnaill, translated by John Montague, from *The Pharaoh's Daughter* (Gallery, 1990). Reproduced by kind permission of the Gallery Press.

Ni Dhuibhne, Eilis (*b.* 1954). Born in Dublin, and educated at University College, Dublin, she is an assistant keeper at the National Library of Ireland. Her work includes a novel, *The Bray House* (1990), two collections of short stories, *Blood and Water* (1988) and *Eating Women is Not Recommended* (1991). She has also written three books for children.
Extract from 'The Flowering' by Eilis Ni Dhuibhne from *Eating Women is Not Recommended*. First published by Attic Press, Dublin, 1990. Reproduced by kind permission of the author and Attic Press.

Ní Ghlinn, Áine (*b.* 1955). Born in Co. Tipperary and educated at University College, Dublin, she now lives in Dublin where she works as a presenter/reporter with Radio Telefis Eireann and Radio Na Gaeltachta. Her first collection of poetry *An Cheim Bhriste (The Broken Step)* was published in 1984. *Gairdin Phartais agus Danta Eile (The Garden of Paradise and Other Poems)* was awarded the Bhord na Gaeilge Award at Listowel writers week in 1987. *Mna as an nGath* (1990), non-fiction stories based upon the lives of well-known women, won an Oireachtas Award. *Deithne is Daoine* (1992) is a collection of myths.
'Curves' and 'The Broken Step' by Áine Ní Ghlinn reproduced by kind permission of the author.

O'Brien, Charlotte Grace (1845–1909). The daughter of William Smith O'Brien, with whom she spent much of her childhood abroad, she fought for better conditions for emigrants, and was prominent in the Gaelic League. Her work includes a novel, *Light and Shade* (1878); a play, *A Tale of Venice* (1881); and poetry, *Lyrics* (1887).

O'Brien, Edna (*b.* 1932). Born in Co. Clare, she was educated at Loughrea and Dublin where she studied pharmacy. Her novels include *The Country Girls* (1960), *Girls in their Married Bliss* (1964), *August is a Wicked Month* (1965),

Johnny I Hardly Knew You (1977) and *Returning* (1982). Her volumes of short stories include *The Love Object* (1968) and *A Fanatic Heart* (1985).
Extract from *Night* by Edna O'Brien (Weidenfeld and Nicolson, 1972) © Edna O'Brien 1972. Reproduced by kind permission of Weidenfeld and Nicolson.

O'Brien, Jean (*b.* 1952). Born in Dublin, where she is a member of the Dublin Writers' Workshop. Her poetry has appeared in various anthologies including *Between the Circus and the Sewer* and *Trinity Workshop Poets 1*. She has also written a pamphlet *Working the Flow* (1992).
'Celebrating the Light of the Moon' by Jean O'Brien reproduced by kind permission of the author.

O'Brien, Kate (1897–1974). Born in Limerick, she was educated there and at University College, Dublin. She worked as a journalist and translator with a particular interest in Spanish history and literature. Her novels include *Without My Cloak* (1931), *Mary Lavelle* (1936), *The Land of Spices* (1941), *That Lady* (1946), *As Music and Splendour* (1958) and *Presentation Parlour* (1963). She wrote plays, travel books and a biography, *Teresa of Avila* (1951).
Extract from *Mary Lavelle* by Kate O'Brien (Virago, 1984). Reproduced by kind permission of Virago Press.

O'Brien, Kate Cruise (*b.* 1948). Born in Dublin, she was educated there. A journalist and short story writer, she has published *A Gift Horse and Other Stories* (1978) and *The Homesick Garden* (1991). She has won the Hennessy Award and the Rooney Prize.
Extract from *The Homesick Garden* by Kate Cruise O'Brien (Poolbeg, 1991). Reproduced by kind permission of Poolbeg Press Ltd.

O'Callaghan, Julie (*b.* 1954). Born in Chicago, she now works in the library of Trinity College, Dublin. She has published two collections of poetry: *Edible Anecdotes* (1983) and *What's What?* (1991), a Poetry Book Society Choice. She has also written poetry for children.
'Pep Talk to Poets from their Sales Manager', 'Yuppie Considering Life in Her Loft Apartment', 'Content and Tasteful' and 'Change' by Julie O'Callaghan from *What's What* (Bloodaxe Books, 1991). Reproduced by kind permission of the author and Bloodaxe Books.

O'Casey, Sean (John Casey, 1884–1964). Born in Dublin, self-educated, he worked as a labourer and was secretary of the Irish Citizen Army. His plays include *The Shadow of a Gunman* (1923), *Juno and the Paycock* (1924) and *The Plough and the Stars* (1926). The Abbey Theatre rejected *The Silver Tassie* (1928) and O'Casey subsequently stayed in England, writing many other plays including *Red Roses for Me* (1946) and *The Bishop's Bonfire* (1955). His autobiography ran to several volumes: *I Knock at the Door* (1939), *Pictures in the Hallway* (1942), *Drums under the Windows* (1945), *Inishfallen, Fare Thee Well* (1949), *Rose and Crown* (1952) and *Sunset and Evening Star* (1954).
Extracts from 'The Plough and the Stars' and 'Juno and the Paycock' by Sean O'Casey from *Three Plays* (Macmillan, 1957). Reproduced by kind permission of Pan Macmillan Publishers Ltd.

O'Connor, Clairr (*b.* 1951). Born in Limerick, and educated at University College, Cork, she now lives in Maynooth. A secondary school English teacher, she has published a novel, *Belonging* (1991), and a collection of poetry, *When You Need Them* (1989). Her play, *Getting Ahead*, was broadcast on BBC Radio 4.
Extract from 'For the Time Being' by Clairr O'Connor from *Wildish Things: An Anthology of New Irish Women's Writing*. First published by Attic Press, Dublin, 1989. Reproduced by kind permission of the author and Attic Press.

O'Connor, Frank (pseudonym of Michael O'Donovan, 1903–66). Born in Cork, he left school at twelve and was imprisoned during the Irish Civil War. He wrote short stories, his first volume being *Guests of the Nation* (1931). *The Stories of Frank O'Connor* were published in 1952. He translated Irish poetry in *Kings Lords and Commons: An Anthology from the Irish (1959)*. *The Backward Look: A Survey of Irish Literature* (1967) reveals his critical gifts; his autobiographies are *An Only Child* (1962) and *My Father's Son* (1968).
'Men and Women', 'A Learned Mistress' and 'Grania' translated by Frank O'Connor reproduced by kind permission of Peters Fraser and Dunlop Group Ltd.

O'Connor, Sinéad (*b.* 1966). Born in Dublin, she has lived in London and Los Angeles before returning to Dublin. A singer and songwriter, her albums include *I Do Not Want What I Haven't Got*, which has been top of the charts, and includes a hit single *Nothing Compares 2U*. Her first album *The Lion and the Cobra* was also very successful. She starred in Margo Harkin's film *Hush-a-Bye Baby* (1990) and has recently begun publishing her poetry.
Lyrics from 'The Last Day of Our Acquaintance' from the album *I Do Not Want What I Haven't Got*. Words and music by Sinead O'Connor © 1990 EMI Music Pub Holland BV, UK. Reproduced by kind permission of EMI Music Publishing Ltd, London WC2H 0EA.

O'Donnell, Mary (*b.* 1954). Born in Monaghan, she lives in Co. Kildare and, having been a teacher and librarian, is a drama critic and broadcaster. *Reading the Sunflowers in September* (1990) is her first volume of poetry. She has also written short stories, *Strong Pagans* (1990), and a novel, *The Lightmakers* (1992). In 1988 she won the William Allingham award for poetry.
'Cot Death' by Mary O'Donnell from *Reading the Sunflowers in September* (Salmon). Reproduced by kind permission of Salmon Publishing.

O'Faolain, Julia (*b.* 1932). Born in London, a daughter of Sean O'Faolain, she was educated at University College, Dublin, Rome and the Sorbonne. Her novels include *Godded and Codded* (1970), *No Country for Young Men* (1980) and *The Irish Signorina* (1984). Her short stories include *Man in the Cellar* (1974) and *Melancholy Baby and other Stories* (1978). She and her husband Lauro Martines have edited *Not in God's Image: Women in History from the Greeks to the Victorians* (1973). Her translations are written under the name of Julia Martines.
Extract from *No Country for Young Men* by Julia O'Faolain © Julia O'Faolain 1980 (Allen Lane, 1980). Reproduced by kind permission of Rogers, Coleridge and White Ltd and Penguin Books Ltd.

O Faolain, Nuala. One of nine children, she grew up in rural Co. Dublin, and was educated at University College, Dublin; after taking her BA and MA there,

she took a B.Phil. at the University of Oxford before returning to become a lecturer at University College, Dublin. She then became a BBC radio and television producer, making programmes for the Open University. She worked in Europe, America, Iran and Northern Ireland before returning to Ireland to work as a television producer with Radio Telefis Eireann. She joined *The Irish Times* as columnist and features writer; she has won awards for her broadcasting and journalism.
'Bishop Casey and the Conflict of Public and Private Lives' by Nuala O Faolain (*The Irish Times*, 11.5.92). Reproduced by kind permission of the author and *The Irish Times*.

O'Faolain, Sean (John Whelan, *b.* 1900). Born in Cork, he was educated at Presentation College, University College, Cork, and Harvard University. He fought on the Republican side in the Civil War. He taught at Boston College and Strawberry Hill Teachers' Training College from 1929 to 1933, and then returned to Ireland. His novels include *A Nest of Simple Folk* (1934), *Bird Alone* (1936) and *And Again?* (1979). His short stories can be read in *Selected Stories* (1978) and *Collected Stories* (1980; 1981; 1982). He has written biographies, an autobiography (*Vive Moi!* (1964)), travel books, and literary criticism including *The Short Story* (1948) and *The Vanishing Hero* (1956).
Extract from the short story 'The Faithless Wife' by Sean O'Faolain reproduced by kind permission of Rogers, Coleridge and White Ltd.

O'Grady, Standish (1846–1928). Born in Castletown Bere, Co. Cork, he was educated at Trinity College, Dublin, was called to the Bar but became a journalist. He wrote many novels with a historical basis which stressed the heroic. Among them are *Red Hugh's Captivity* (1889), *The Coming of Cuchullain* (1894), *Ulrick the Ready* (1896) and *The Flight of the Eagle* (1897). He also wrote the *History of Ireland's Heroic Period* (1878–80) and *The Story of Ireland* (1894).

O'Hagan, Sheila (*b.* 1933). Born in and now living in Dublin, having spent many years in England, she won the Patrick Kavanagh Award in 1991 and the *Sunday Tribune* Hennessy Award for Poetry in 1992. Her first collection of poetry is *The Peacock's Eye* (1992).
'Going to the Gaiety' by Sheila O'Hagan from *The Peacock's Eye* (Salmon, 1992). Reproduced by kind permission of Salmon Publishing.

O'Hegarty, Willhelmina Rebecca (*née* Smith, 1890–1962). Born in Co. Derry, she was educated at Bedford College, University of London, and taught at a secondary school before marrying P. S. O'Hegarty. On her return to Ireland she joined Cumann na mBán, was chairwoman of Saor an Leanbh, and was Treasurer for twenty years of the first Irish College in Donegal. With Mary Kettle she founded the Joint Committee of Women's Societies and Social Workers, which lobbied for women's rights and on behalf of children living in poverty.

O'Huiginn, Tadhg Dall (*c.* 1550–1617). Born in Ulster, he and his wife and child were murdered in Sligo after he had written a satire on six men of the O'Haras who had emptied his house of food and drink. In 1922 Eleanor Knott edited and translated his work in *A bhuil Aganin dai chui Tadhg Dall Ó h Uiginn (1550–91)*.

O'Malley, Mary. She was born in and lives in Galway after spending eight years in Portugal where she taught at the New University of Lisbon. *A Consideration of Silk* (1990) is her first collection of poems; it has been followed by *Where the Rocks Float* (1993). She won the *Sunday Tribune* Hennessy Award for Poetry in 1990. Verses from 'The Cloven Rock' by Mary O'Malley reproduced by kind permission of the author.

O'Meara, Aileen (*b*. 1960). Born in Co. Offaly, she now lives in Dublin. Formerly a journalist with the *Sunday Tribune* she now works with Radio Telefís Eireann. She has twice won the A. T. Cross Woman Journalist of the Year Award (News Category, 1987; Social Affairs Category, 1989).
Extract from 'Women and Poverty' by Aileen O'Meara from *Letters from the New Island*, edited by Dermot Bolger (Raven Arts Press). Reproduced by kind permission of the author and Raven Arts Press.

O'Neill, Joan. Born in Dublin, she now lives in Co. Wicklow. She has written a novel for teenagers, *Daisy Chain War* (1990) and a sequel *Bread and Sugar* (1993). *Promised*, a novel for adults, was published in 1991.
Extract from *Daisy Chain War* by Joan O'Neill. First published by Attic Press, Dublin, 1990. Reproduced by kind permission of the author and Attic Press.

O'Neill, Mary Devenport (1879–1967). Born at Loughrea, Co. Galway, she was educated at Eccles Street College and the National College of Art, Dublin. Her two one-act plays, *Bluebeard* and *Sain*, were performed in 1933 and 1945 by Austin Clarke's lyric theatre company. *Prometheus and Other Poems* was published in 1929.

O'Neill, Moira (pseudonym of Agnes Nesta Shakespeare Higginson, 1863–1955). She married W. C. Skrine (their daughter writes as M.J. Farrell/ Molly Keane). Born in Co. Antrim, she lived in Co. Kildare and in Co. Wexford. She collected *Songs of the Glens of Antrim* (1907). Her poetry included *An Easter Vacation* (1893) and *Collected Poems* (1933).

O'Reilly, John Boyle (1844–90). Born at Dowth, Co. Louth, he was apprenticed to a printer. He joined the IRB, enlisted in the British Army, was sentenced to death for IRB activity, but instead was transported. He escaped from Australia to the United States and settled in Boston, editing the *Pilot*. He wrote a novel, *Moondyne* (1880).

O Siadhail, Micheál (*b*. 1947). Born in Dublin, educated at Clongowes Wood College and Trinity College, Dublin, and the University of Oslo, he lectured in Linguistics at Trinity College, Dublin, and is now working in the Institute for Advanced Studies, Dublin. A member of Aosdana, he writes poetry in Irish, *An*

Bhliain Bhisigh (1978), and in English, *Springnight* (1983) and *The Image Wheel* (1985). *Hail! Madam Jazz* (1992) is a volume of new and selected poems. 'While You Are Talking' from *Hail! Madam Jazz: New Selected Poems* by Micheál O Siadhail (Bloodaxe Books, 1992). Reproduced by kind permission of the author and Bloodaxe Books.

Parnell, Frances (Fanny) (1845–82). The favourite sister of Charles Stewart Parnell, she was born in Avondale, Co. Wicklow, her mother the daughter of an American Admiral. A romantic nationalist, who emigrated to America in 1874, she wrote patriotic verse as 'Aleria' for the *Irish People*, the *Boston Pilot* and *The Nation*, and launched the Ladies' Land League in 1880. Her best-known poem is 'Hold the Harvest'.

Pilkington, Letitia (1712–50). Born in Dublin, she married The Revd Matthew Pilkington from whom she soon separated, going to London where she was imprisoned for debt. Rescued by Colley Cibber, she set up a printshop. She wrote plays; her *Memoirs* (1748) were followed by *The Celebrated Mrs Pilkington's Jests* (1751).

Power, Patrick C. (*b.* 1928). Educated at University College, Galway, he was awarded a Ph.D. in 1971. He worked as a national school teacher for over forty years, four of them in Tipperary and much of the remainder in Ballyneale near Carrick-on-Suir. He has published many books including histories of Waterford and of South Tipperary, a *Literary History of Ireland* and *The Story of Anglo-Irish Poetry*. He has also edited a dual language version of Brian Merriman's *The Midnight Court* and translated Myles na Gopaleen's *An Beal Bocht* as *The Poor Mouth*.
Extract from *The Book of Irish Curses* by Patrick C. Power (Mercier, 1974). Reproduced by kind permission of the Mercier Press Ltd. Extract from *Encounter*, translated by Patrick C. Power, reproduced by kind permission of Patrick C. Power.

Reid, Christina. Born and educated in Belfast, she now lives in London. Her prize winning plays include *Tea in a China Cup* (1980), *Joyriders*, *My Name, Shall I Tell You My Name?*, *The Belle of Belfast City* and *Lords, Dukes and Earls*. For television she wrote *Did You Hear the One About the Irishman?* and for radio *The Last of a Dyin' Race*.

Riddick, Ruth (*b.* 1954). Born in Dublin, where she now works with the Irish Family Planning Association as an Education Officer, she is the founder Director of Open Door Counselling, the non-directive pregnancy counselling service which successfully appealed to the European Court of Human Rights against the Irish Government's ban on information about abortion in counselling.
'Towards a Feminist Morality of Choice' by Ruth Riddick from *The Abortion Papers Ireland*. First published by Attic Press, Dublin, 1992. Reproduced by kind permission of the author and Attic Press.

Rivers, Elizabeth (1903–64). Born in England, she was educated at the Royal Academy, London, and the Ecole de Fresque, Paris. A well-known painter, wood-engraver and illustrator, she lived on Inishmore in the Aran Islands from 1935 to 1941 and then moved to Dalkey, Co. Dublin. She wrote and illustrated *A Stranger in Aran* (1946) and *Out of Bondage* (1951), based on her travels in Palestine. In later life she worked in stained glass with Evie Hone.

Robinson, Mary (*b*. 1944). Elected President of Ireland in 1991, she was born in Mayo and educated at Trinity College, Dublin, where she was Reid Professor of Constitutional and Criminal Law from 1969 to 1975. She was lecturer in European Community Law from 1975 to 1990. She was a member of the Senate (1969–89), Senior Counsel 1980–90 and a member of the International Committee of Jurists, Geneva, from 1987 to 1990.
Extract from Mary Robinson's Inaugural Speech reproduced by kind permission of President Mary Robinson.

Roddy, Moya. Born in Dublin, she lived in London where she studied media at the Central London Polytechnic, and now lives in Galway. She has worked on *Diverse Reports*, a Channel Four current events programme. In 1987 she was commissioned to write a screenplay for the British Film Institute. *The Long Way Home* (1992) is her first novel.
Extract from *The Long Way Home* by Moya Roddy. First published by Attic Press, Dublin, 1992. Reproduced by kind permission of the author and Attic Press.

Rodgers, William Robert (1909–69). Born in Belfast, educated at Queen's University, Belfast and the Presbyterian Theological College, he became a Minister in County Antrim until he joined the BBC in London as a producer and scriptwriter in 1946. His volumes of poetry include *Awake! And Other Poems* (1941), *Europa and the Bull* (1952) and *Collected Poems* (1971). His *Irish Literary Portraits* appeared in 1972.
'Lent' by W. R. Rodgers from *Poems: W. R. Rodgers* (Gallery, 1993). Reproduced by kind permission of the author and the Gallery Press.

Ross, Martin. *See* Somerville and Ross.

Ros, Amanda McKittrick (1860–1939). Born in Co. Down, Anna Margaret McKittrick married Andrew Ros, the stationmaster at Larne. Trained as a teacher, she published *Irene Iddesleigh* (1897) at her own expense; *Delina Delaney* and *Donald Dudley* followed. Her poems appeared under the titles *Poems of Puncture* (1936) and *Fumes of Formation* (1933); she also wrote music and songs. She married a farmer after her first husband died. Her incomplete novel *Helen Huddlestone* (1969) included a final chapter by James Loudan.

Salkeld, Blanaid (1880–1959). Born in Pakistan of Irish parents, she spent most of her childhood in Ireland, then, married to an Englishman in the Indian Civil Service, lived in India before returning to Ireland where she acted (as Nell Byrne) in the Abbey Theatre's second company. Her work included *Hello Eternity*

(1933), *The Engine is Left Running* (1937), *A Dubliner* (1942) and *Experiment in Error* (1955).

Sayers, Peig (1873–1958). Born at Dunquin, Co. Kerry, she spent many years on the Great Blasket where she was known as the Queen of Storytellers. Her autobiography *Peig* (1936) is now an Irish classic, as is *Machtramh Sean Mhra* (1939). S. Ennis has translated her *An Old Woman's Reflections* (1962).
Thanks for The Educational Company of Ireland for 'Farewell to Youth' from *Peig*, translated into English by Bryan MacMahon. First published by the Talbot Press, 1974.

Scannell, Honora Josephine Yvonne. Born in Co. Kerry, she was educated at Trinity College, Dublin, the University of Cambridge, the University of Paris, the Hague and the King's Inns, Dublin. A fellow of Trinity College, Dublin, and a Senior Lecturer in Law there, she is a former Chairwoman of the Women's Political Association and chaired the Environmental Awareness Bureau from 1985 to 1988. She has written on Environmental Law and women's rights, her books including *The Law and Practice Relating to Pollution Control in Ireland* (1974; 1982) and *Environmental Law in Ireland* (1991).
Extract from 'The Constitution and the Role of Women' by Dr Yvonne Scannell from *De Valera's Constitution and Ours*, edited by Brian Farrell (Gill & Macmillan, 1989). Reproduced by kind permission of Gill & Macmillan Publishers.

Shaw, George Bernard (1856–1950). Born in Dublin, he was educated at Wesley College, Dublin. In 1876 he went to London and wrote five unsuccessful novels (including *Cashel Byron's Profession* (1886)). He achieved distinction as a musical critic, then as a drama critic. His first play was *Widowers's Houses* (1893), but he was not successful as a dramatist until after the turn of the century, though he had by then written *The Philanderer*, *Mrs Warren's Profession*, *Arms and the Man*, *Candida* and *Caesar and Cleopatra*. After the First World War his plays became popular, were regularly produced and read: they included *Man and Superman* (1903), *Major Barbara* (1907), *The Doctor's Dilemma* (1911), *Androcles and the Lion* (1916), *Pygmalion* (1916) and *St. Joan* (1928). He was awarded the Nobel Prize for Literature in 1925.
Extract from *The Adventures of the Black Girl in Her Search for God* (Constable, 1932) and 'Aphorism' by George Bernard Shaw reproduced by kind permission of the Society of Authors.

Sheridan, Frances (*née* Chamberlaine, 1724–66). Born in Dublin, she learned to read and write in secret – her posthumous novel *Eugenia and Adelaide* was written when she was fifteen; she published her *Memoirs of Miss Sidney Biddulph* (1761) after she and her husband Thomas Sheridan (their second son was Richard Brinsley Sheridan) came to London. She wrote several comedies, *The Discovery* (1763) being the best known. In 1764 the couple went to France to escape their creditors: she died at Blois.

Sheridan, Richard Brinsley (1751–1816). Educated at Dr White's School in Dublin and afterwards at Harrow, he moved to Bath with his family in 1771 where he fell in love with Elizabeth Linley, eloped with her to France and married her in 1773. *The Rivals* was staged successfully at Covent Garden in 1775; the same year there followed *St Patrick's Day* and *The Duenna*. He bought half the patent of Drury Lane Theatre from David Garrick in 1776, and the remaining half in 1778. *The School for Scandal* was staged there in 1777; he followed it with *The Critic* in 1779. He became a politician in 1780, holding ministerial positions for thirty years. Drury Lane, renovated in 1794, burnt down in 1809 and Sheridan was ruined; he died in poverty.

Simms, Katharine (*b.* 1946). Educated at Trinity College, Dublin, where she graduated in History and Political Science and then took a Ph.D. in Medieval History, she worked for some years in the Dublin Institute for Advanced Studies as a Senior Research Fellow. Married, with two children, she now lives in Maynooth, Co. Kildare, and is a Senior Lecturer in the History Department, Trinity College, Dublin. Her published work includes a book entitled *From Kings to Warlords, the Changing Structure of Gaelic Ireland in the later Middle Ages*.
Extract from 'Women in Gaelic Society' by Katharine Simms from *Women in Early Modern Ireland*, edited by Margaret McCurtain and Mary O'Dowd (Edinburgh University Press, 1991). Reproduced by kind permission of the author and Edinburgh University Press.

Slade, Jo (*b.* 1952). Born in Hertfordshire, she was educated in Dublin at the National College of Art and now lives in Limerick. She is a painter whose first collection of poems, *In Fields I Hear Them Sing*, was published in 1989.
'In Fields I Hear Them Sing' by Jo Slade from *In Fields I Hear Them Sing* (Salmon, 1990). Reproduced by kind permission of Salmon Publishing.

Smyth, Ailbhe. She lives in Dublin and is Director of Women's Studies at University College, Dublin. A former editor at Attic Press, she has written *Women's Rights in Ireland* (1884), *Irish Women Academics* (1985) and *Feminism in Ireland* (1988). She is editor of *The Abortion Papers, Ireland* (1992).
Extract from 'A Great Day for the Women of Ireland: The Meaning of Mary Robinson's Presidency' by Ailbhe Smyth from *The Canadian Journal of Irish Studies* (Vol. XVIII no. 1, July 1992). Reproduced by kind permission of Ailbhe Smyth. Extract from 'A Sadistic Farce: Women and Abortion in the Republic of Ireland' from *The Abortion Papers, Ireland*. First published by Attic Press, Dublin, 1992. Reproduced by kind permission of the author and Attic Press.

Somerville and Ross: Somerville, Edith Oenone (1858–1949). Born in Corfu, she was educated privately at home and studied art in London and Paris. She lived at Drishane, the family house at Castletownshend, Co. Cork, and was Master of the West Carbery Hunt. The 'Ross' of this literary partnership was Edith's cousin, Violet Florence Martin (1861–1915), born at Ross, Co. Galway, and educated at Alexandra College, Dublin. Their books include *An Irish Cousin* (1889), *The Real Charlotte* (1894), *Some Experiences of an Irish RM* (1899), *Further Experiences of an Irish RM* (1908) and *In Mr Knox's Country* (1915). After Violet Martin's death Edith continued to write under the name Somerville and Ross, this work including *Irish Memories* (1917), *The Big House at Inver* (1952), *An*

Incorruptible Irishman (1932), a biography of her great grandfather Charles Kendal Burke, and *Notions of Garrison* (1942).

Starkie, Enid (1898–1970). Born in Dublin, she was educated at Alexandra College, Dublin, the Sorbonne and Somerville College, Oxford, where she was a Research Fellow from 1946 to 1955, a Professional Fellow from 1955 to 1965, and an Honorary Fellow 1966 to 1970. Her books included: *Baudelaine* (1933; a 2nd version 1957), *Arthur Rimbaud* (1938; 1947), *The Rimbaud Contribution* (1951), *Andre Gide* (1954), *English Literature and France 1851–1939* (1959) and *From Gautier to Eliot* (1960).
Extract from *A Lady's Child* by Enid Starkie (Faber and Faber Ltd, 1941). Reproduced by kind permission of David Higham Associates.

Stephens, James (1882–1950). Brought up in an orphanage, he was a solicitor's clerk, then Registrar of the National Gallery of Ireland (1915–24). He subsequently lived in Paris and London. His principal book is *The Crock of Gold* (1912). Others include *The Charwoman's Daughter* (1912), *Deirdre* (1923), and *Etched in Moonlight* (1928). His books of poetry include *Insurrections* (1909), *The Hill of Visions* (1912) and *Collected Poems* (1954). He was an excellent radio broadcaster. His radio talks are contained in *James Seamus and Jacques* (1964), his short stories, selected by Augustine Martin, in *Desire and Other Stories* (1981).
'The Red-Haired Man's Wife', 'A Woman is a Branchy Tree', *The Crock of Gold* and 'Miss Makebelieve of Dublin' by James Stephens reproduced by kind permission of The Society of Authors on behalf of the copyright owner, Mrs Iris Wise.

Sterne, Laurence (1713–68). Born in Clonmel, educated at Halifax Grammar School and Jesus College, Cambridge, he was appointed to a living at Sutton-on-the-Forest and made a prebendary of York; he later moved to Coxwold, in the East Riding of Yorkshire. *The Life and Opinions of Tristram Shandy* appeared between 1759 and 1767, *The Sermons of Mr Yorick* (1760) caused some scandal. His health deteriorated; he and his wife and daughter lived at Toulouse and Montpellier (1762–64); they remained in France, while he returned to England. *A Sentimental Journey Through France and Italy* followed in 1768. His posthumous *Journal to Eliza* (1775) was written to Mrs Draper, with whom he fell in love in 1767, who had subsequently to accompany her husband to India.

Strong, Eithne (*née* Glensharrold O'Connell, *b.* 1923). Born in Co. Limerick and educated at Scoil Mhuire, Ennis, she was a civil servant before her marriage to Rupert Strong. She went to Trinity College, Dublin, and teaches as well as writes. Collections of her poems are *Songs of Living* (1961), *Flesh – The Greatest Sin* (1980), *My Darling Neighbour* (1985) and short stories, *Patterns* (1981), in English; her Irish writing includes *Cirt Óibre* and *Fuil agus Fallai* (1983).
'Juxtaposition' and 'Statement to Offspring' by Eithne Strong. Reproduced by kind permission of the author.

Sweetman, Rosita (*b.* 1948). Born in Dublin, her first book, *On Our Knees*, was a collection of profiles of a cross-section of Irish people from North and South. *On*

Our Backs (1979) is written in a similar format, focusing on the subject of sex. She has written a novel, *Fathers Come First*.

Swift, Jonathan (1667–1745). Born in Dublin, he was educated at Kilkenny College and Trinity College, Dublin. Secretary to Sir William Temple in 1689, he left for a parish in Northern Ireland in 1694, returning to Temple in 1696. In 1699 he became Vicar of Laracor, Co. Meath. He negotiated on behalf of the Church of Ireland in London, becoming intimate with the Tory Ministry, on whose behalf he edited *The Examiner* and wrote powerful political pamphlets. In 1713 he was appointed Dean of St Patrick's Cathedral in Dublin. His works include *A Tale of a Tub* (1704) and, appended to it, *The Battle of the Books*, and *Gulliver's Travels* (1726). His *Journal to Stella*, written to Esther Johnson, covers his years in London from 1710 to 1713. His intervention in Irish affairs produced the devastating satire of *The Drapier's Letters* (1724) and *A Modest Proposal* (1729).

Synge, John Millington (1871–1909). Born at Rathfarnham near Dublin and educated at Trinity College, Dublin, and the Royal Irish Academy of Music, he studied abroad and lived briefly in Paris. He wrote about the Aran Islands and Co. Wicklow where he set his plays, which included *The Shadow of the Glen* (1903), *Riders to the Sea* (1904), *The Well of the Saints* (1905) and *The Playboy of the Western World* (1907). The last caused riots at the Abbey Theatre when first staged there. *The Tinker's Wedding* (1907) and *Deirdre* (1910) were both produced in the Abbey; his *Works*, containing poems and essays as well as plays, appeared in 1910.

Taylor, Alice (*b*. 1938). Born in Co. Cork, where she now lives, she has written three memoirs of Irish country life: *To School Through the Fields* (1988), *Quench the Lamp* (1990) and *The Village* (1992). She has also published *An Irish Country Diary* (1988), *Close to the Earth: Poems of Country Life* (1989) and a children's book, *The Secrets of the Oak*.
Extract from 'The Chapel Woman' by Alice Taylor from *The Village* (Brandon Press). Reproduced by kind permission of Brandon Press.

Thomson, David (1914–92). Born in India of Scottish parents, he was educated in Britain. He lived in Ireland for ten years, which furnished him with the material for his memoir, *Woodbrook* (1974). He wrote two novels and three children's books. He worked in the BBC for many years and won the McVitie Prize for *Nairn* in 1987.
Extract from *Woodbrook* by David Thomson © David Thomson 1977 (Barry & Jenkins, 1977). Reproduced by kind permission of Random House UK Ltd.

Trevor, William (pseudonym of Trevor Cox, *b*. 1928). Born in Co. Cork and educated at St Columba's College and Trinity College, Dublin, he worked as a sculptor before becoming a writer. His novels include *The Old Boys* (1964), *Mrs Eckdorf in O'Neill's Hotel* (1968), *The Children of Dynmouth* (1976), *Fools of Fortune* (1983). His short stories include *The Ballroom of Romance* (1972) and *Beyond the Pale* (1981); he has written plays and *A Writer's Ireland. Landscape in Literature* (1984).

Extract from *Attracta* by William Trevor reproduced by kind permission of the author.

Tynan, Katharine (1861–1931). Born in Dublin, she was educated at Drogheda, and lived at the family farm at Clondalkin, Co. Dublin. She married Henry Linkson (*d*. 1919), who became a Resident Magistrate in Mayo. She wrote prolifically (105 novels; twelve collections of short stories). *Collected Poems* (1930) include several poems which assured her a place in the history of the Irish literary revival. She wrote four volumes of memoirs.

Waddell, Helen Jane (1889–1965). Born in Tokyo and educated at Queen's University, Belfast, she was a distinguished Latinist whose work included *The Wandering Scholars* (1927) and *Medieval Latin Lyrics* (1929); her translations include *Beasts and Saints* (1934) and *The Desert Fathers* (1936). Her novel *Peter Abelard* (1933) has proved very popular.
'I Shall Not Go To Heaven' by Helen Waddell from *Helen Waddell: A Biography* by Dame Felicitas Corrigan OSB. Reproduced by kind permission of Dame Felicitas Corrigan.

Wall, Mervyn Eugene Welpy (*b*. 1908). Educated at Belvedere College, University College, Dublin, and Bonn, he entered the Irish Civil Service, worked on Radio Eireann from 1948 to 1957 and then became Secretary of the Irish Arts Council. His novel *The Unfortunate Fursey* (1946) was followed by *The Return of Fursey* (1948), *Leaves for the Burning* (1952) and *Hermitage* (1982). He has written short stories – *A Flutter of Wings* (1974) – and three plays.
Extract from *Leaves for the Burning* by Mervyn Wall (1952). Reproduced by kind permission of the author.

Waller, John Francis (1809–94). Born in Limerick and educated at Trinity College, Dublin, a barrister and man of letters, he succeeded Charles Lever as editor of the *Dublin University Magazine*. His work includes *Ravenscroft Hall* (1852), and, under the name 'Freke Slingsby', poems collectively titled *The Slingsby Papers* (1852). *Peter Brown* (1872) was another volume of his poems.

White, Victoria (*b*. 1962). Born in Dublin where she now lives and works as a journalist and drama critic, having spent a year teaching in Italy at the University of Pavia. Her first collection of short stories, *Raving Autumn*, was published in 1990.
Extract from 'Mr Brennan's Heaven' by Victoria White from *Raving Autumn* (Poolbeg, 1990). Reproduced by kind permission of Poolbeg Press Ltd.

Wilde, Lady Jane Francesca (*née* Elgee, 1826–96). Born in Wexford, she wrote as 'Speranza' in *The Nation* and published *Poems* (1864); as Lady Wilde (she married Sir William Wilde in 1851), she edited various volumes of Irish folklore, including *Ancient Legends of Ireland* (1887).

Wilde, Oscar Fingal O'Flahertie Wills (1856–1900). Born in Dublin, he was educated at Portora Royal School, Trinity College, Dublin and Magdalen College, Oxford. His prize poem 'Ravenna' appeared in 1878, his *Poems* in 1881, his novel *The Picture of Dorian Gray* in 1891. In 1892 he wrote *Salome* in French and his play *Lady Windermere's Fan*. It was followed by *A Woman of No Importance* (1894), *An Ideal Husband* (1895) and *The Importance of Being Ernest* (1895). After serving two years' imprisonment for homosexual practices he wrote *The Ballad of Reading Gaol*. *De Profundis* appeared posthumously in 1905.

Yeats, William Butler (1865–1939). Born in Dublin, he spent much of his childhood in Sligo, attended schools in London and Dublin and the School of Art in Dublin. His first major poem, *The Wanderings of Oisin* (1889), was followed by a series of volumes, his early pre-Raphaelite, mythological, symbolist, Celtic twilight poetry culminating in *The Wind Among the Reeds* (1899). He was involved in creating the Abbey Theatre, Dublin, with Lady Gregory and others, and wrote verse plays for it. He lived in London, spending summers at Coole Park, Co. Galway; in 1917 he bought a medieval tower at Ballylee, Co. Galway. Hopelessly in love with Maud Gonne from 1889, he married Georgie Hyde Lees in 1917, returned to Dublin in 1922, becoming a Senator of the Irish Free State and winning the Nobel Prize in 1923, his poetry having gained modernity and strength in *The Tower* and *The Winding Stair* which continued up to *Last Poems* (1938). He also wrote much prose, essays, autobiographies and *A Vision*.

'Crazy Jane Talks with the Bishop' and 'Crazy Jane Grown Old Looks at the Dancers' from *The Poems of W. B. Yeats: A New Edition*, edited by Richard J. Finneran. Copyright 1933 by Macmillan Publishing Company, renewed 1961 by Bertha Georgie Yeats. Reprinted with permission of Macmillan Publishing Company. 'He Wishes for the Cloths of Heaven' and 'The Song of Wandering Aengus' from *The Poems of W. B. Yeats: A New Edition*, edited by Richard J. Finneran, New York, Macmillan 1983. Reprinted with permission of Macmillan Publishing Company. Extracts from 'Deirdre' and 'Cathleen Ni Houlihan' from *Collected Plays of W. B. Yeats*. Copyright 1934, 1952 by Macmillan Publishing Company. Copyright renewed 1962 by Bertha Georgie Yeats, and 1980 by Anne Yeats. Reproduced with permission of Macmillan Publishing Company.

Thanks also to the Irish Sisters of Charity for permission to reproduce the extract from *The Irish Sisters of Charity Centenary Brochure*. The extract from 'Mother Mary Martin' by Art Byrne and Sean McMahon from *Lives of 113 Great Irish Women and Irish Men* (Poolbeg, 1990) reproduced by kind permission of Poolbeg Press Ltd.

INDEX